THE LIBRARY
OF NUMISMATICS

GENERAL EDITOR: PHILIP GRIERSON

COINAGE AND MONEY UNDER THE ROMAN REPUBLIC

COINAGE AND MONEY UNDER THE ROMAN REPUBLIC

ITALY AND THE MEDITERRANEAN ECONOMY

MICHAEL H. CRAWFORD

METHUEN & CO LTD
LONDON

First published in 1985 by
Methuen & Co. Ltd, 11 New Fetter Lane, London EC4P 4EE

© *1985 Michael H. Crawford*

Printed in Great Britain by the
University Press, Cambridge

All rights reserved. No part of this book may be reprinted or reproduced or utilized in any form or by any electronic, mechanical or other means, now known or hereafter invented, including photocopying and recording, or in any information storage or retrieval system, without permission in writing from the publishers.

British Library Cataloguing in Publication Data

Crawford, Michael, 1939–
Coinage and money under the Roman Republic.
(*The Library of numismatics*)
1. Coinage—Rome—History
II. Title   II. Series
332.4′042′0937   HG1026

ISBN 0-416-12300-7

CONTENTS

Preface vii
List of figures ix
List of maps xiii
List of tables xv
List of appendices: finds xvi
List of appendices: coinage and money xviii
List of abbreviations xix

1 THE PEOPLES OF ITALY 1

2 THE EARLY REPUBLIC 17

3 THE APPEARANCE OF ROMAN COINAGE 25

4 THE SECOND PUNIC WAR 52

5 THE PO VALLEY 75

6 THE ROMANS IN SPAIN 84

7 THE ROMANS IN SICILY 103

8 FROM THE FREEDOM OF THE GREEKS TO THE SACK OF CORINTH 116

CONTENTS

9   AFRICA UNDER CARTHAGE AND ROME   133

10   THE IMPERIAL REPUBLIC   143

11   THE LEGACY OF ATTALUS   152

12   FROM NANNUS TO CAESAR   161

13   THE YEARS OF CRISIS: ITALY   173

14   THE YEARS OF CRISIS: THE EMPIRE   195

15   THE BALKAN QUESTION   219

16   THE END OF THE FREE STATE   240

17   THE EMPEROR AUGUSTUS   256

Appendices: FINDS   281
Appendices: COINAGE AND MONEY   334

Index of places and peoples 349
Index of persons 352
Index of subjects 353

PREFACE

Debate about the economy of the Hellenistic world and about the consequences of the Roman conquest of that world has tended to revolve inconclusively around problems of growth and decline. Yet one complex of facts is clear: at the beginning of the Hellenistic period, there was no coinage at Rome and a wide variety of coinages was in use elsewhere; by the time of Augustus, not only was the whole of the Mediterranean world under Roman rule, most of it was taxed by Rome and used the Roman monetary system and Roman coinage.

The aim of this book is to trace the history of Roman coinage and the spread in its use, within the context of the economy and society of the different areas involved, and to assess the impact of the revolution in the monetary history of the Mediterranean world brought about by Rome.

Much of the argument is based on patterns of coin finds, and in order not to present a completely unreadable text, I have secluded the bulk of this kind of evidence in a series of Appendices, where I have assumed familiarity with the conventions used among intending readers. I have also at times drawn without explicit citation on the material in the Italy fascicle of the third edition of *Historia Numorum*, now in the press. I have also systematically avoided the terms *aes signatum* and *aes grave*, since it is clear that the ancient sources meant by such terms something quite different from what they have come to mean in modern times; their use has been the source of endless, but avoidable, confusion. All dates are BC unless otherwise indicated.

It would not have been possible to write this book without a great deal of help and advice and I should like to thank, for information or discussion, the late D. F. Allen, D. C. Braund, P. A. Brunt, T. V. Buttrey, R. A. G. Carson, R. G. G. Coleman, T. J. Cornell, J. C. Edmondson, A. S. Hall, M. K. Hopkins, G. K. Jenkins, L. Keppie, P. Kinns, the late C. M. Kraay, H. B. Mattingly, F. G. B. Millar, A. D. Momigliano, D. Nash, J. A. North, J. R. Patterson, K. St. Pavlowitch, M. J. Price, R. Reece, J. M.

Reynolds, J. S. Richardson, A. L. F. Rivet, the late E. S. G. Robinson, N. K. Rutter, C. H. V. Sutherland, M. Thomas, D. J. Thompson, M. Vercnocke, T. R. Volk, D. R. Walker, H. Whitehouse, T. P. Wiseman, L. Bonfante, C. A. Hersh, R. C. Knapp, W. Metcalf, R. Ross Holloway, R. J. Rowland, M. Amandry, J. Andreau, Cl. Brenot, J.-L. Ferrary, J.-M. Flambard, J.-B. Giard, G. Le Rider, J.-P. Morel, Cl. Nicolet, H. Nicolet-Pierre, C. Peyre, O. Picard, J.-C. M. Richard, J.-P. Vallat, H. Zehnacker, H.-R. Baldus, C. Boehringer, Th. Fischer, P. R. Franke, H. Galsterer, D. Kienast, M. Koch, H. Küthmann, C. Marek, H. W. Ritter, H.-D. Schultz, A. U. Stylow, W. Trillmich, H. Bloesch, A. Giovannini, S. Hurter, H.-M. von Kaenel, A. Walker, G. Dembski, the late O. Mørkholm, Ch. A. Moushegian, A. Kunisz, L. Morawiecki, J. Pecírkă, E. Chirila, the late M. Chiţescu, V. Mihailescu Bîrliba, B. Mitrea, G. Poenaru Bordea, C. Preda, A. Şaşeanu, I. Mirnik, H. Ceka, Y. Youroukova, M. Oeconomidou, the late I. Varoucha, N. Olçay, E. Arslan, X. Asdrubale Pentiti, M. Caccamo Caltabiano, L. Camilli, G. Clemente, F. Coarelli, E. Corradini, S. De Caro Balbi, E. De Juliis, G. D'Henry, E. Fabbricotti, C. Franciosi, A. Gabucci, A. Giardina, G. Gorini, A. Greco, U. Laffi, E. Lo Cascio, G. Manganaro, L. Michelini Tocci, F. Panvini Rosati, N. Parise, M. Pasquinucci, A. Pautasso, P. Petrillo Serafin, E. Pozzi, L. and S. Quilici, A. Siciliano, S. Sorda, A. Stazio, M. Tizzoni, M. Torelli, A. Travaglini, A. Tusa Cutroni, B. Virgilio, P. Visonà, L. Avellá, M. Campo, F. Chavés Tristan, R. M. S. Centeno, E. Collantes Vidal, G. Fatas, M. P. Garcia Bellido, P. Pau Ripollés, E. Ripoll, M. Ruiz Trapero, N. Tarradell-Font, L. Villaronga, M. de Castro Hipolito.

I should also like to thank Christ's College, Cambridge, the University of Cambridge, the British School at Rome and the British Academy for generous financial support; Sylvia Sylvester and Rozalyn Todd for secretarial assistance; Philip Grierson for asking me to write this book and Anna Fedden and her colleagues for the patience with which they have waited for it and the skill with which they have handled it; Andrew Burnett for the generosity with which he has given of his time and knowledge and for the pleasure that our friendship has brought.

That this book has been completed at all is the result of a term spent as a Visiting Professor at the University of Pavia, where at the invitation of its Rector, Professor Marco Fraccaro, I lived in the Collegio Cairoli, and where I worked in the Istituto di Archeologia, in the company of Professor C. Saletti, Professor C. Maccabruni and Dr M. Harari, and in the Istituto di Storia Antica, in the company of Professor A. Bernardi, Professor P. Tozzi, Professor D. Magnino, Dr D. Ambaglio, Dr L. Boffo, Dr E. Noé and Dr R. Scuderi, at the invitation of Emilio Gabba; in gratitude for that invitation and for what I have learnt from him and in recognition of all that I owe to the country of his birth and formation, I dedicate this book to him.

Michael H. Crawford

LIST OF FIGURES

1	Early Etruscan silver coinage	3
2	'Ramo secco' bar	4
3	The coinage of Magna Graecia	26
4	The coinage of Campania in the fourth century	28
5	The Mars/Horse's head ROMANO issue	28
6	Early Roman bronze coinage	30
7	The Apollo/Horse ROMANO and Hercules/Wolf and twins ROMANO issues	31
8	The coinage of Locri	33
9	The third-century coinage of Neapolis	35
10	The Goddess/Lion ROMANO and Minerva/Horse's head ROMANO issues	39
11	The Roma/Victory ROMANO issue and contemporary cast bronze coinage	42
12	Italian cast bronze coinage	44–5
13	The coinage of Campania in the third century	47
14	Etruscan bronze coinage	48
15	The ROMA issues	50
16	The quadrigatus and contemporary cast bronze coinage	53
17	The denarius system	54–5
18	The coinage of Capua	63
19	The coinage of Arpi and Salapia	64
20	The coinage of Luceria	65
21	The coinage of Brundisium	66

22	The Italian coinage of Carthage	67
23	The coinage of the Brettii and Lucani	68
24	Late Etruscan silver coinage	70
25	Roman silver and bronze coinage of the early second century	73
26	The drachm coinage of the Po valley	77
27	The fractional coinage of the Po valley	78
28	The coinage of Emporiae and the Barcids	88
29	The Iberian bronze and silver coinages of the north	92
30	The coinage of Saguntum	96
31	The coinages of Ikalesken and the Guadalquivir valley	99
32	The coinages of Carteia and Andalusia	100
33	The Sicilian coinage of Carthage during the First Punic War	106
34	The coinage of Syracuse	107
35	The Sicilian coinage of Carthage during the Second Punic War	108
36	The Sicilian issues of Rome during the Second Punic War	112
37	The coinages of the Sicilian allies of Rome of the Second Punic War	113
38	The coinage of Sicily under Roman rule	114
39	The coinage of Athens	119
40	The coinage of Euboea	120
41	The coinages of the Sitochoro hoard	121
42	The coinages in circulation in the Peloponnese	122
43	The new-style coinage of Athens	126
44	The coinages of the 'leagues'	127
45	The coinage of Macedon	130
46	The coinage of Thasos and Maronea	131
47	The coinage of Carthage during the First Punic War	135
48	The coinage of the Libyans	136
49	The coinage of Carthage before and during the Second Punic War	139
50	The issues of the Cani hoard	139
51	The coinage of Numidia	141
52	Roman bronze coinage of the middle of the second century	144
53	Roman silver coinage of the middle of the second century	145
54	The Alexander issues of Asia Minor	154
55	The issues of Alabanda and Side	155
56	The wreathed issues of Asia Minor	156
57	The coinages of Rhodes, Cappadocia, Pontus and Bithynia	157
58	The cistophoric coinage of Pergamum	158

LIST OF FIGURES

59	The cistophoric coinage of Aristonicus and Rome	159
60	The coinage of Massalia	164
61	The issue of Flaccus at Massalia	166
62	Quinarii of southern Gaul	167
63	Monnaies-à-la-croix	168
64	The coinage of central Gaul before Caesar	172
65	The growth in the Roman money supply	176
66	Roman silver coinage of the late second century	179
67	Roman bronze coinage of the late second century	180
68	Denarii of the insurgents in the Social War	181
69	The revival of the quinarius	182
70	The semuncial bronze coinage and the sestertius	184
71	The issues of L. Piso and his colleagues	186
72	The issues of Sulla and his associates	188
73	The restored issues of Sulla	189
74	The pattern of hoarding in Roman Italy	192
75	The issue of Q. Oppius	197
76	The Sullan imitations of the tetradrachms of Athens and the post-Sullan issues of Athens	198
77	The last silver coinages of Macedon	199
78	The bronze coinage of Cyrenaica	200
79	The issues of the Limani hoard	201
80	The issues of Mithridates VI	202
81	The issues of the last Seleucid kings	204
82	The coinages of the Syrian cities	204
83	The Roman coinage of Syria	205
84	The debasement of the coinage of Egypt	207
85	The proconsular cistophori	209
86	The bronze coinage of Thessalonica	210
87	The issues of C. Annius	211
88	The Iberian coinage in the Sertorian period	212
89	The issue of Cn. Lentulus	213
90	The issues of the Spanish cities in the Sertorian period	213
91	The coinage of Ketouibon	215
92	The gold and silver coinages of Gaul in the age of Caesar	216
93	The coinages of Gaul after Caesar	217–18
94	The coinage of Apollonia and Dyrrachium	224

95	The barbarous coinages of the Balkans	228
96	The coinage of Koson	237
97	The Roman coinage of Thrace	238
98	The issues of Caesar during the First Civil War	242
99	The gold issue of A. Hirtius	242
100	The bronze issue of C. Clovius	243
101	The issues of Pompey	244
102	The issues of Caesar as dictator	245
103	The coinage of the First Civil War in Greece	246
104	The coinage of Lycia	247
105	The issues of Juba I and the Pompeians	248
106	The issues of 42	249
107	The coinage of the dynasts	250–1
108	The issues of Crete and Cyrenaica	254
109	The issues of Antony and Cleopatra	255
110	The early issues of Augustus	257
111	The revival of mainstream coinage under Augustus	258
112	The reformed bronze coinage of Augustus	259
113	The cistophori of Augustus	262
114	The coinage of Syria	263
115	The coinage of Egypt	263
116	The mainstream Augustan coinage of Spain	264
117	The mainstream Augustan coinage of Gaul	265
118	The eastern bronze coinages of Augustus	267
119	The coinages of the kings	268
120	The coinage of Roman Cappadocia	269
121	The coinage of the Nabataeans	269
122	The Augustan city coinages of Spain	272
123	The portrait issues of Augustus and Tiberius in the cities	274
124	The coinage of Noricum	278

LIST OF MAPS

1	The regions of Italy	2
2	The distribution of 'ramo secco' and associated bars	5
3	Etruria	6
4	Umbria and Picenum	8
5	Central Italy	10
6	Southern Italy	13
7	The early Hellenistic coinage of Magna Graecia and Campania	27
8	The circulation of Etruscan bronze coins	49
9	Early hoards of victoriati	57
10	The Po valley	76
11	Hoards of the drachm coinage of the Po valley	77
12	Finds of specimens of the drachm coinage of the Po valley with legends	78
13	The situla people	80
14	Roman and Latin colonies in the Po valley	82
15	The Iberian peninsula	85
16	Second Punic War hoards in the Iberian peninsula	89
17	Second-century Roman and Iberian denarius hoards	98
18	The pattern of Iberian silver coinage production	101
19	The pattern of Iberian bronze coinage production	101
20	Sicily	104
21	Macedonia and Greece	117
22	The Macedonian regions	129
23	Africa	134
24	The kingdom of Attalus	153

LIST OF MAPS

25	Gaul	163
26	Early hoards with Roman coins in southern Gaul	167
27	Hoards in Italy between 146 and 91	178
28	Syria	203
29	Illyria	220
30	The Mazin and related finds	222
31	Hoards of Republican denarii in Dalmatia	226
32	Hoards of Augustan denarii in Illyria	237
33	Spain under Augustus	273

LIST OF TABLES

1	Early Roman silver coinage	34
2	Italian cast bronze coinage	46
3	Growth in the volume of production of the as	61
4	Sicilian hoards of the Second Punic War	110–11
5	The coinage of the Libyans	137–8
6	Asses and sestertii	148
7	As and sestertius	149–50
8	Mints of the proconsular cistophori	208

LIST OF APPENDICES: FINDS

1	Finds of Greek coins in Etruria in the classical period	281
2	Finds of 'ramo secco' bars	282
3	Hoards in Magna Graecia around 300	282
4	Hoards in Campania around 300	282
5	Hoards including Campanian coins in Magna Graecia	282
6	Hoards including *pegasi* and Sicilian coins in Italy	283
7	Penetration of coinage into the Appennines	283
8	Finds from Valle d'Ansanto	284
9	Finds of Minerva/Horse's head and Goddess/Lion bronzes	285
10	Hoards including Italian cast bronze coinage	285
11	Finds of Etruscan struck bronze	286
12	Hoards from south Italy between 241 and 218	286
13	Finds of Mars/Eagle gold pieces	286
14	Finds of Minerva/Bull asses	287
15	Second Punic War hoards of Italian coins	287
16	Second Punic War finds in Bruttium	287
17	Finds of Carthaginian coins from Italy	290
18	Movement of coinage in the Second Punic War	291
19	Second Punic War hoards of Roman silver coins	292
20	Second-century hoards	293
21	Finds of Greek silver with coins of the denarius system in Italy	293
22	Finds of the drachm coinage of the Po valley	294
23	Hoards of Roman silver coins in the Po valley	296
24	Association of silver of Cisalpine Gaul and Roman bronze	297

LIST OF APPENDICES: FINDS

25	Finds of cast bronze coinage in the Po valley	297
26	Finds of Greek coins in the Po and Adige valleys	298
27	Second Punic War hoards in Spain	299
28	Finds of cast bronze coinage in Spain	301
29	Hoards of Iberian denarii	301
30	Hoards including Roman denarii in Spain between 125 and 91	303
31	Hoards including Roman bronze in Spain	304
32	Hoards of Iberian bronze coinage	304
33	Finds of early Roman coins in Sardinia	305
34	Finds of coins in Corsica	305
35	Finds of cast bronze coinage in Sicily	306
36	Second Punic War hoards in Sicily	306
37	Second- and first-century bronze hoards in Sicily	307
38	Finds of Italian and Sicilian bronze coinage in Greece	308
39	Hoards in Greece	309
40	Hoards of overstruck Boeotian bronze coinage	316
41	Hoards of small silver and bronze coinage in Greece	316
42	Hoards of denarii in Africa	316
43	Finds of Greek coins in southern Gaul	317
44	Early hoards with Roman coins in southern Gaul	318
45	Hoards in peninsular Italy after 146	318
46	Finds of eastern bronze coinage in Italy and Sicily	319
47	Hoards in Greece of the period of Mithridates	320
48	Hoards in Macedonia	320
49	Hoards of cast bronze coinage in Jugoslavia	321
50	The movement of coinage across the Adriatic	322
51	Hoards of coins of Apollonia and Dyrrachium	325
52	Hoards of Republican denarii in Dalmatia	325
53	Hoards of Republican denarii in Russia, Poland, Czechoslovakia and Hungary	325
54	Hoards of Republican denarii in Romania and Bulgaria	326
55	Hoards of the period of Actium	330
56	Hoards of bronze coinage in Gaul after Caesar	330
57	Hoards of precious metal coinage in Gaul after Caesar	331
58	Finds on the Great Saint Bernard	332
59	The coinage of the upper Rhone valley	332
60	Hoards in Noricum	332

LIST OF APPENDICES:
COINAGE AND MONEY

A	Non-Roman measures of capacity in Lucania	334
B	The mint of Fistelia	334
C	The silver content of coins of Magna Graecia	335
D	Overstrikes	336
E	The mint of Petelia	338
F	The metal content of the drachm coinage of the Po valley	338
G	The Roman conquest and the ownership of land in the Po valley	339
H	The Iberian coinage	340
I	The coinage of Emporiae	342
J	The coinage of Saguntum (Arse)	343
K	The coinage of Saetabi (Saeti)	344
L	Sicilian units of reckoning	344
M	The coinage of Histiaea	345
N	Sestertii in Cato	346
O	The coinage of Corduba	346
P	The coinage of Valentia	347
Q	Overstrikes of Spanish bronze coins	347
R	The evidence for slaves from Dacia	348

LIST OF ABBREVIATIONS

I BOOKS

Ailly	P.-P. Bourlier, Baron d'Ailly, *Recherches sur la monnaie romaine* (Lyon, 1864–9)
ANRW	*Aufstieg und Niedergang der römischen Welt. Geschichte und Kultur Roms im Spiegel der neueren Forschung* (Berlin, 1972 onwards)
E. Babelon, *Traité*	E. Babelon, *Traité des monnaies grecques et romaines* (Paris, 1901–32)
Bf.	M. Bahrfeldt, *Nachträge und Berichtigungen zur Münzkunde der römischen Republik* (i–iii, Vienna, 1897–1918)
BMCCaria	*A catalogue of the Greek coins in the British Museum, Caria* (London, 1897)
BMCCyrenaica	*A catalogue of the Greek coins in the British Museum, Cyrenaica* (London, 1927)
BMCItaly	*A catalogue of the Greek coins in the British Museum, Italy* (London, 1873)
BMCRE	*Coins of the Roman Empire in the British Museum* (London, 1923 onwards)
BMCRR	*Coins of the Roman Republic in the British Museum* (London, 1910)
BMCSicily	*A catalogue of the Greek Coins in the British Museum, Sicily* (London, 1876)
CAH	*The Cambridge Ancient History* (Cambridge, 1923–39)
CIL	*Corpus Inscriptionum Latinarum* (Berlin, 1893 onwards)

J. B. Colbert de Beaulieu	J. B. Colbert de Beaulieu, *Traité de numismatique celtique* I (Paris, 1973)
8 Cong.Num.	*Actes du 8ᵉ Congrès International de Numismatique* (Paris and Basle, 1976)
9 Cong.Num.	*Actes du 9ᵉ Congrès International de Numismatique* (Louvain-la-Neuve and Luxembourg, 1982)
11 Cong.Frontier Studies	*Akten des XI Internationalen Limeskongresses* (Budapest, 1977)
Corpus	*Corpus des trésors monétaires antiques de France*
ESAR	T. Frank, *An Economic Survey of Ancient Rome* (Baltimore, 1933–40)
FGH	F. Jacoby, *Fragmente der griechischen Historiker* (Berlin, 1923 onwards)
FIRA	S. Riccobono, *Fontes Iuris Romani Antejustiniani* (Florence, 1941)
M. Grant, *FITA*	M. Grant, *From Imperium to Auctoritas* (Cambridge, 1946)
Haeberlin	E. J. Haeberlin, *Aes grave* (Frankfurt-am-Main, 1910)
HN³	*Historia Numorum* (Oxford, 3rd. edn, forthcoming)
Hübner	E. Hübner, *Monumenta Linguae Ibericae* (Berlin, 1893)
I.Delos	*Inscriptions de Delos*
IG	*Inscriptiones Graecae*
IGCH	M. Thompson, et al., *An Inventory of Greek Coin Hoards* (New York, 1973)
IGRR	R. Cagnat, *Inscriptiones Graecae ad Res Romanas Pertinentes* (Paris, 1906–27)
ILLRP	A. Degrassi, *Inscriptiones Latinae Liberae Rei Publicae* (Florence, 1957–63)
ILS	H. Dessau, *Inscriptiones Latinae Selectae* (Berlin, 1892–1916)
INC Jerusalem	*International Numismatic Convention, Jerusalem, 27–31 December 1963* (Tel Aviv and Jerusalem, 1967)
Inscr.Ital.	*Inscriptiones Italiae*
IRT	J. M. Reynolds and J. B. Ward-Perkins, *The Inscriptions of Roman Tripolitania* (London, 1952)
Jenkins and Lewis	G. K. Jenkins and R. B. Lewis, *Carthaginian Gold and Electrum Coins* (London, 1963)
P. Marchetti	P. Marchetti, *Histoire économique et monétaire de la deuxième guerre punique* (Brussels, 1978)
Mirnik	I. A. Mirnik, *Coin Hoards in Jugoslavia* (Oxford, 1981)

LIST OF ABBREVIATIONS

Th. Mommsen, *RMw*	Th. Mommsen, *Geschichte des römischen Münzwesens* (Berlin, 1860)
Th. Mommsen, *RSt*	Th. Mommsen, *Römisches Staatsrecht* (Leipzig, 1887)
Mon.Etr.	*Contributi introduttivi allo studio della monetazione etrusca* (Rome, 1976)
MSR	F. Hultsch, *Metrologicorum Scriptorum Reliquiae* (Leipzig, 1864–6)
Müller	L. Müller, et al., *Numismatique de l'ancienne Afrique* (Copenhagen, 1860–2)
OGIS	W. Dittenberger, *Orientis Graeci Inscriptiones Selectae* (Leipzig, 1903–5)
ORF	E. Malcovati, *Oratorum Romanorum Fragmenta* (Turin, 1955)
PCIA	*Popoli e civiltà dell'Italia antica* (Rome, 1974–8)
Poccetti	P. Poccetti, *Nuovi documenti italici* (Pisa, 1979)
K. Raddatz	K. Raddatz, *Die Schatzfunde der iberischen Halbinsel* (Berlin, 1969)
RE	A. Pauly, G. Wissowa and W. Kroll, *Real-Encyclopädie der klassischen Altertumswissenschaft* (Stuttgart, 1893 onwards)
Rerum Rom.Fontes	M. R. Torelli, *Rerum romanarum fontes* (Pisa, 1978)
RRC	M. H. Crawford, *Roman Republican Coinage* (Cambridge, 1976)
RRCH	M. H. Crawford, *Roman Republican Coin Hoards* (London, 1969)
RIC	*Roman Imperial Coinage* (London, 1923 onwards)
P. Salama	P. Salama, 'Circulation monétaire de Maurétanie' in *II Simposi Numismatic*, 109
A. Sambon	A. Sambon, *Les monnaies antiques de l'Italie* (Paris, 1903)
Sannio	*Sannio* (Rome, 1980)
S. Scheers	S. Scheers, *Traité de numismatique celtique* II (Paris, 1977)
Schürer[2]	E. Schürer, *The History of the Jewish People in the Age of Jesus Christ*, revised by G. Vermes and F. Millar (Edinburgh, 1973 onwards)
Sherk	R. K. Sherk, *Roman Documents from the Greek East* (Baltimore, 1969)
SIG	W. Dittenberger, *Sylloge Inscriptionum Graecarum* (Leipzig, 1915–24)
II Simposi Numismatic	*II Simposi Numismatic de Barcelona* (Barcelona, 1980)
SNG	*Sylloge Nummorum Graecorum*

SNR	*Sylloge Nummorum Romanorum*
Società Romana	A. Giardina and A. Schiavone, *Società romana e produzione schiavistica* (Bari, 1981)
Vetter	E. Vetter, *Handbuch der italischen Dialekte* (Heidelberg, 1953)
Vives	A. Vives y Escudero, *La moneda hispanica* (Madrid, 1926)

2 JOURNALS

ABSA	*Annual of the British School at Athens*
Acta Mus.Nap.	*Acta Musei Napocensis*
Acta Num.	*Acta Numismatica*
AD	Ἀρχαιολογικὸν Δελτίον
AE	Ἀρχαιολογικὴ Ἐφημερίς
AEA	*Archivo Español de Arqueologia*
AIIN	*Annali dell'Istituto Italiano di Numismatica*
AJA	*American Journal of Archaeology*
AJAH	*American Journal of Ancient History*
AJP	*American Journal of Philology*
Annali	*Annali dell'Istituto di Corrispondenza Archeologica*
Ant.Class.	*L'antiquité classique*
Arch.Anz.	*Archäologischer Anzeiger*
Arch.Class.	*Archaeologica Classica*
Arch.Jug.	*Archaeologia Iugoslavica*
Arch.Laziale	*Archaeologia Laziale*
Arch.Rep.	*Archaeological Reports*
Arh.Vestnik	*Arheološki Vestnik*
ASNP	*Annali della Scuola Normale di Pisa*
Ath.	*Athenaeum*
AttiCESDIR	*Atti del Centro Studi e Documentazione sull'Italia Romana*
Atti e Memorie	*Atti e Memorie dell'Istituto Italiano di Numismatica*
BCAR	*Bulletino della Commissione Archeologica Comunale di Roma*
BCH	*Bulletin de Correspondance Hellénique*
BIAB	*Bulletin de l'Institut Archéologique Bulgare*
BIArch	*Bulletin of the Institute of Archaeology of the University of London*

LIST OF ABBREVIATIONS

BMzB	*Berliner Münzblätter*
BNJ	*British Numismatic Journal*
Boll.It.di Num.	*Bollettino Italiano di Numismatica*
BPI	*Bollettino di Paletnologia Italiana*
BSFN	*Bulletin de la Société Française de Numismatique*
BSNR	*Buletinul Societatii Numismatice Române*
Bull.Arch.Sard.	*Bullettino Archeologico Sardo*
Bullettino	*Bullettino dell'Istituto di Corrispondenza Archeologica*
Calif.St.Class.Ant.	*California Studies in Classical Antiquity*
CE	*Chronique d'Egypte*
CQ	*Classical Quarterly*
CR	*Classical Review*
Dd'A	*Dialoghi di archeologia*
DHA	*Dialogues d'histoire ancienne*
Ec.Hist.Rev.	*Economic History Review*
Eph.Dac.	*Ephemeris Dacoromana*
GGA	*Göttingsche Gelehrte Anzeigen*
Hell.	*Hellenica*
Hesp.	*Hesperia*
Hist.	*Historia*
INJ	*Israel Numismatic Journal*
J.Chem.Soc.	*Journal of the Chemical Society*
JIAN	*Journal international d'archéologie numismatique*
JMP	*Jaarboek voor Munt – en Penningkunde*
JNG	*Jahrbuch für Numismatik und Geldgeschichte*
JOAI	*Jahreshefte des Osterreichischen Archäologischen Instituts*
JRS	*Journal of Roman Studies*
MAAR	*Memoirs of the American Academy in Rome*
MAL	*Memorie della Classe di scienze morali e storiche dell'Academia dei Lincei*
Mat.Arch.	*Materiale și Cercetări Arheologice*
MDAI(M)	*Mitteilungen des Deutschen Archäologischen Instituts, Abt. Madrid*
MDAI(R)	*Mitteilungen des Deutschen Archäologischen Instituts, Röm. Abt.*
MEFR	*Mélanges d'archéologie et d'histoire de l'Ecole Française de Rome*
MEFRA	*Mélanges d'archéologie et d'histoire de l'Ecole Française de Rome. Antiquité*

Mem.R.Ac.Sc.Torino	*Memorie della Reale Accademia delle Scienze di Torino*
MH	*Museum Helveticum*
Mitt.Ost.Num.Ges.	*Mitteilungen der Osterreichischen Numismatischen Gesellschaft*
Mon.Ant.	*Monumenti antichi pubblicati dall'Academia dei Lincei*
MusN	*Museum Notes*
NC	*Numismatic Chronicle*
NCirc	*Numismatic Circular*
NH	*Numario Hispanico*
NK	*Numizmatikai Közlöny*
NSc	*Notizie degli scavi*
NZ	*Numismatische Zeitschrift*
PAE	*Praktika tês archaiologikês etaireias*
PBSR	*Papers of the British School at Rome*
PCPhS	*Proceedings of the Cambridge Philological Society*
PdelP	*Parola del Passato*
Per.di Num.e Sfrag.	*Periodico di numismatica e sfragistica*
QTic	*Quaderni Ticinesi*
RA	*Revue archéologique*
RAL	*Rendiconti della Classe di Scienze morali, storiche e filologiche dell' Accademia dei Lincei*
RAN	*Revue archéologique de Narbonnaise*
Rass.Num.	*Rassegna numismatica*
RBN	*Revue belge de numismatique et de sigillographie*
REA	*Revue des études anciennes*
REL	*Revue des études latines*
Rev.Et.Lig.	*Revue d'études ligures*
Rev.Et.Roum.	*Revue d'études roumaines*
RFIC	*Rivista di filologia e di istruzione classica*
RhM	*Rheinisches Museum*
RIL	*Rendiconti dell'Istituto Lombardo, Classe di lettere, scienze morali e storiche*
RIN	*Rivista italiana di numismatica e scienze affini*
Riv.Stud.Lig.	*Rivista di studi liguri*
RN	*Revue numismatique*
RSA	*Rivista storica dell'antichità*
SCIV	*Studii şi Cercetări de Istorie Veche*

LIST OF ABBREVIATIONS

SCN	*Studii şi Cercetări de Numismatică*
SDHI	*Studia et Documenta Historiae Iuris*
SE	*Studi Etruschi*
SM	*Schweizer Münzblätter*
SNR	*Schweizerische Numismatische Rundschau*
Stud.Clas.	*Studii Clasice*
TAPA	*Transactions and Proceedings of the American Philological Association*
Trans.Roy.Hist.Soc.	*Transactions of the Royal Historical Society*
Wiss.Mitt.aus Bosn.	*Wissenschaftliche Mitteilungen aus Bosnien*
ZfN	*Zeitschrift für Numismatik*

I

THE PEOPLES OF ITALY

The Greeks who settled the coast of Italy from Tarentum to Pithecusae (Ischia) from the eighth century onwards naturally brought with them from their *poleis* of origin the notion of a certain weight of precious metal designated by the community as a monetary unit.[1] And, in the course of the sixth century, the *poleis* of Magna Graecia adopted the institution of coinage, along with the rest of the Greek world. In Italy, as elsewhere, the production and use of coinage long remained largely Greek phenomena, limited to the *poleis* and their *chorai*, whether these were created by expulsion, subjection or assimilation of and intermarriage with the existing native populations. The peoples of Italy themselves for the most part retained systems which involved the accumulation, and eventually no doubt the transfer by weight, of lumps of copper or various copper alloys.

Towards the end of the fourth century, the Romans and other Italian peoples began to produce their own coinages and to use imported coinages, a step which often involved the assimilation of local reckoning in bronze to imported systems of reckoning in silver. We shall see that the pattern varied, partly as a consequence of the diverse forms taken by contact between native and Greek. Two facts stand out: while the actual production of coinage outside Magna Graecia and Campania was still a relatively restricted phenomenon before the beginning of the third century, the use of coinage, like that of the alphabet, was widespread in Italy by the end of the third century, although the evidence is not very informative about *how* it was used; and the Roman conquest of Italy soon meant that few mints avoided Roman influence. Many communities indeed struck for the first time as a direct result of the Roman presence, existing Italian mints came to strike under Roman auspices, and even Greek mints lost their independence.

Apart from Magna Graecia, the areas that require consideration are Etruria, Latium

1 *La moneta in Grecia e a Roma* (Bari, 1982), 5.

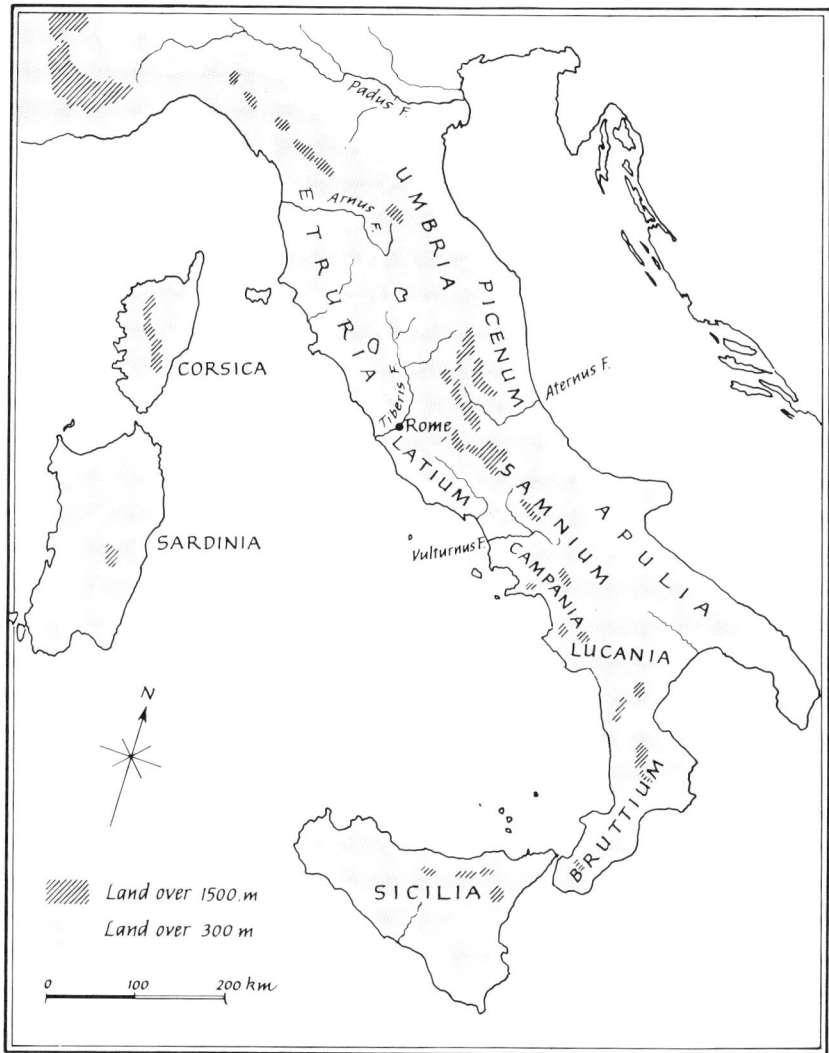

1 The regions of Italy

and her neighbours, Picenum, Umbria, Campania, the Oscan areas of the centre and the south, Apulia and Bruttium (Map 1). The culture of archaic and classical Etruria is too familiar to require characterisation here; the process of urbanisation had begun at the latest in the ninth century, the area was in close contact with the Greek world from the eighth century, deriving therefrom, *inter alia*, its alphabet. It is in this context striking that the institution of coinage was, for all practical purposes, not adopted in Etruria for three centuries after its adoption by the Greek *poleis* in the west. There is one issue of silver which may be attributed to Vulci and to the fifth century, three

1 Early Etruscan silver coinage

Silver piece of Vulci:
  Gorgon running l./Wheel; around, *thezi*   BM *PCG* II C 1
Uncertain silver piece:
  Chimera l./Blank   BM 1956–5–2–2
Uncertain silver piece:
  Boar r. on rocky ground/Blank   BM 1958–5–6–1
Didrachm of Populonia:
  Facing head of Gorgon; below, X/Blank   BM 1946–1–1–1

issues of silver which are perhaps of the fourth century (Fig. 1). There is also some evidence that Greek coinage circulated in Etruria in the classical period, in the form of a couple of hoards and a number of isolated finds; but the bulk of the coinage of Etruria probably belongs in the third century (App. 1 and p.69).

On the other hand, uncoined copper as a form of mobile wealth (in what was by now a highly differentiated society) acquired a distinctive guise in late archaic and classical Etruria; this is the place and period to which belong the bars with 'ramo secco' pattern (Fig. 2) and the bars associated therewith by form and fabric; both types were made of highly ferruginous copper and would have been useless as metal without further refining.[2] The characteristic provenance is Etruscan, both in Etruria proper and in the Etruscan area of the Po valley (Map 2 with App. 2); there is one

---

2 A. Burnett and P. Craddock, in J. Swaddling (ed.), *Italian Iron Age Artefacts in the British Museum* (London, 1984), 'Italian currency bars'.

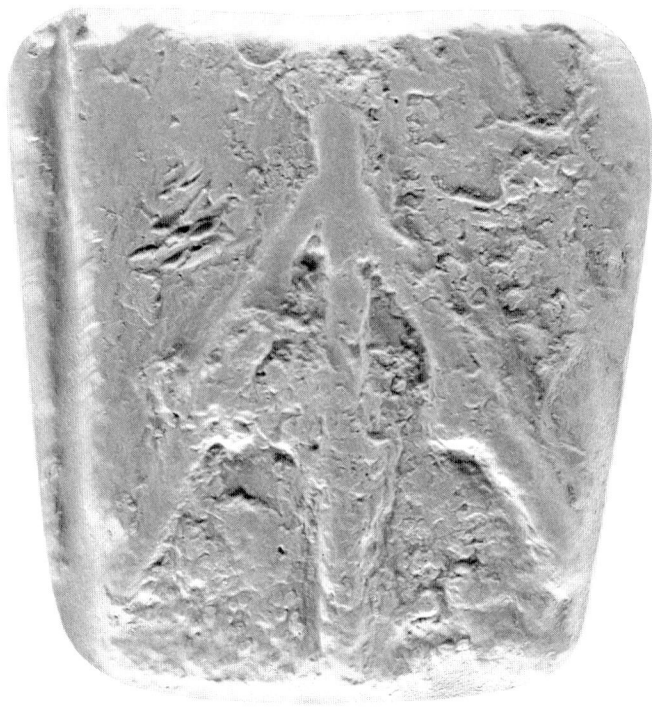

2 'Ramo secco' bar

Reverse similar

BM 74.14.102

outlying find in the north, from Este – with this exception, the lumps of bronze from Este and its surroundings seem to me to be something quite different – rather more finds in the south, the Via Tiberina and Ardea in Latium, the Fucine Lake in the territory of the Marsi, Pontecagnano and perhaps Stabiae in Campania, and above all the recent find at Bitalemi in Sicily; a bar with a staff on both sides, probably cognate, comes from near Teramo, one with a herring-bone pattern on both sides from Todi. It is the Bitalemi find which shows that the bars were first produced in the sixth century;[3] and some pieces were apparently still in existence when the third-century hoards of Vulci (*RRCH* 10), Ariccia in Latium (*RRCH* 13, bar with Herring-bone pattern/Dolphins) and La Bruna (*RRCH* 16) were deposited. Yet despite the spread

3 Compare a bar without types from a sixth-century context at Grammichele in Sicily (App. 2). The finds of these bars in Illyria are another matter, see p.222.

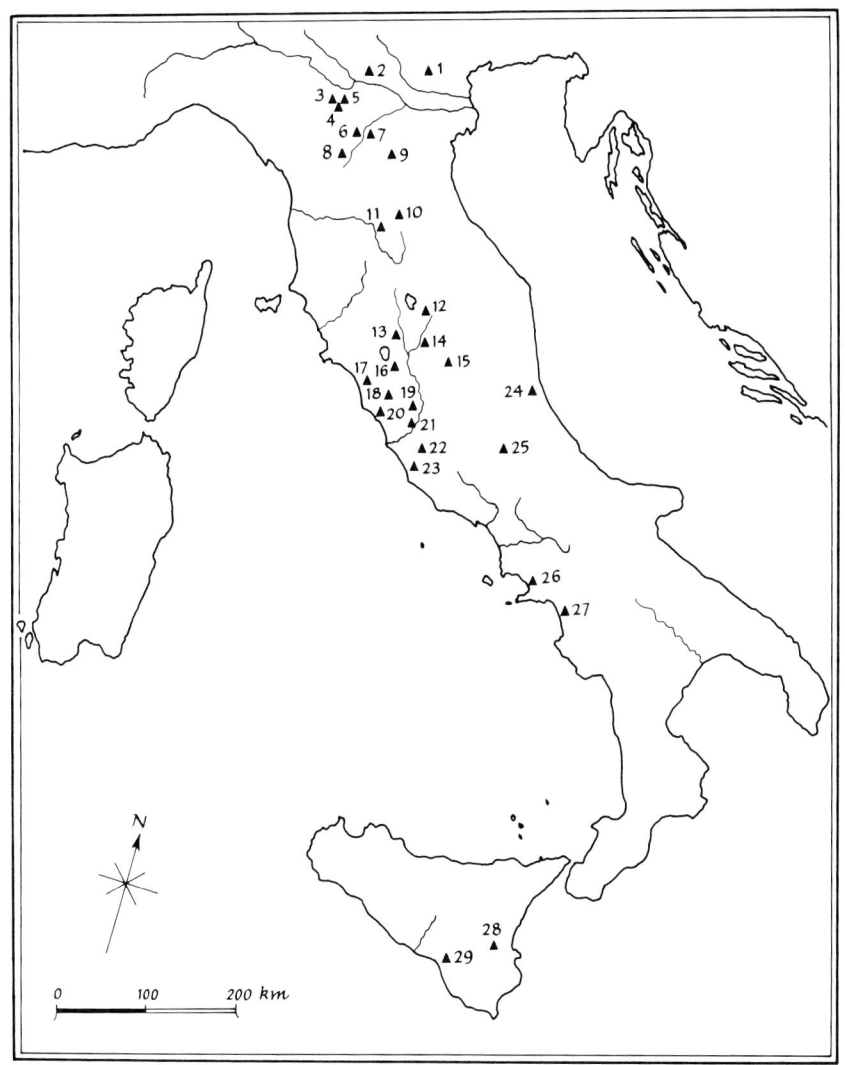

2   The distribution of 'ramo secco' and associated bars

1 Este; 2 Mantova; 3 Quingento near Parma; 4 San Polo d'Enza;
5 Campègine; 6 Modena; 7 Castelfranco Emilia;
8 Levizzano; 9 Marzabotto; 10 Monte Falterona; 11 Fiesole; 12 Perugia;
13 Fabbro near Orvieto; 14 Todi; 15 La Bruna near Spoleto; 16 Vitorchiano;
7 Vulci; 18 Vicarello; 19 Castelnuovo di Porto; 20 Cerveteri; 21 Via Tiberina;
22 Ariccia; 23 Ardea; 24 Teramo; 25 Lago Fucino; 26 Stabiae;
27 Pontecagnano; 28 Grammichele; 29 Bitalemi

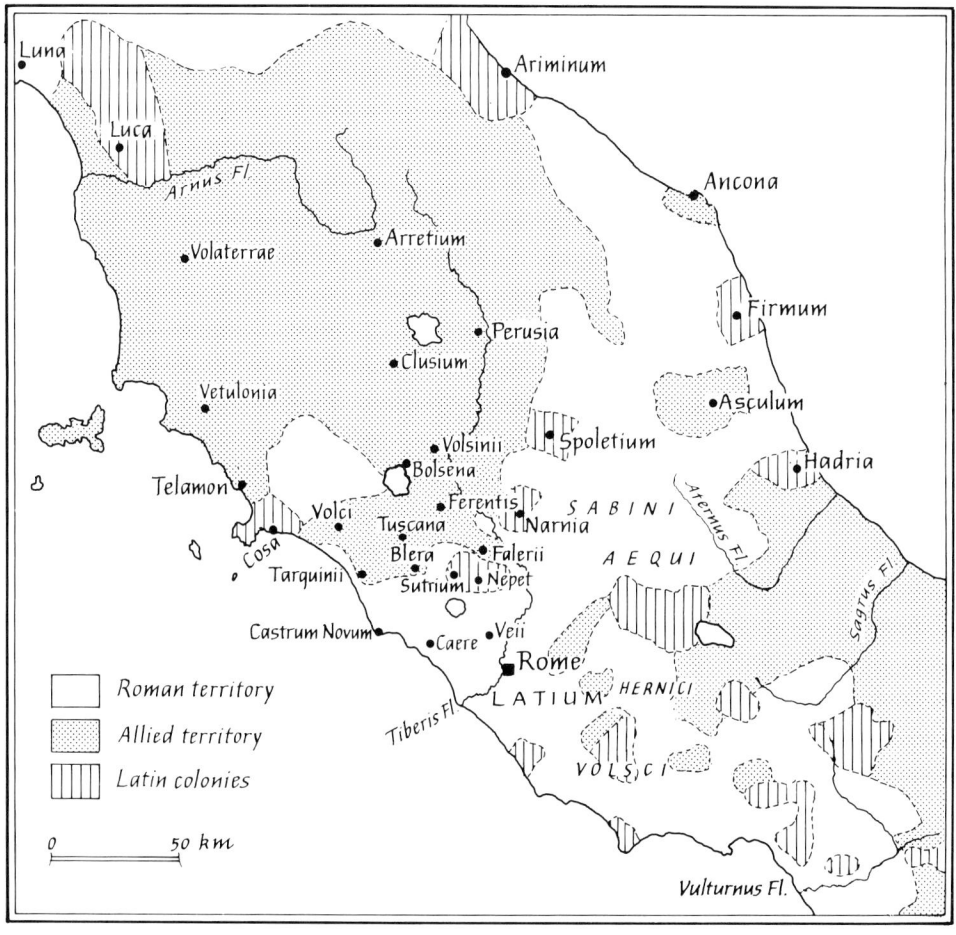

3 Etruria

Based on L.R. Taylor, *Voting Districts of the Roman Republic* (Rome, 1960), 'Italia tributim discripta', correcting the status of Telamon

and the duration of the fashion, these bars were never more than bullion passing by weight.[4]

More generally, it is important to observe that the process of conquest by Rome had by the third century generated a very marked division within Etruria between north and south (Map 3). There is no call here to consider the status of Caere; but

[4] It is wearisome to the soul to have to go on saying that Pliny, *NH* xxxiii, 43, 'Servius rex primus signavit aes', refers to the striking of coinage and that the Bitalemi find has nothing whatever to do with this particular fantasy of Pliny; see A. Burnett and P. Craddock (n.2), and p.18 n.3.

it is clear that by the early third century Etruria south of a line from Tarquinii to Sutrium and Nepet was not only *ager Romanus*, but also in practice part of the Roman sphere. Sutrium and Nepet were Latin colonies of the early fourth century; to their north lay a thin swathe of land belonging to Vulci, Tarquinii, Tuscana, Blera and Ferentis; beyond lay the Latin colony of Cosa (of 273) and another stretch of *ager Romanus*, acquired from Vulci (along with what became the territory of Cosa) after the final defeat of Vulci in 280. The measure of Roman control up to this point is clear enough: when the governing class of Volsinii (Orvieto) was faced with internal dissent in 265–264, it was to Rome that it turned; and the community of Volsinii was simply moved from Orvieto to Bolsena. Only to the north did Etruscan social structures remain largely intact down to the second century. Whereas in the inscriptions of Tarquinii, Vulci and Volsinii it is usual for men to record their magistracies, clearly under Roman influence, this is rare in Clusium, Arretium, Perusia, Vetulonia and Volaterrae. It is only in these northern areas that the term *lautni* for freed slaves of foreign origin appears and that freed native 'serfs' are identified by family names derived from forenames. It is a matter of guesswork how far Roman institutions influenced the freeing of slaves or 'serfs' in northern Etruria.[5] Within southern Etruria, there were differences: by the second century, the votive and architectural terracottas of Veii, Punta della Vipera (in the territory of Castrum Novum) and Caere were Roman in character, while the artistic production of Vulci, Tarquinii, Tuscana and Ferentis remained Etruscan in character, but was in the last stages of decline.[6]

Archaeologically distinct in some respects from the area to the north from about 1000, and in some respects related to the inhuming 'Fossakultur' area to the south (p.10), Latium nonetheless remained closely linked to Etruria throughout the period of urban development and on into the archaic period. The nature of the source material for Rome makes it worthwhile to attempt a separate account of the early stages of her monetary history (Ch.2). The Falisci to the north were close to the Latins in material culture and in language, forming an alien enclave in Etruscan territory; they became part of the Roman sphere in the fourth century and their attempted rebellion in 241 was entirely forlorn; the community of Falerii was moved from Civita Castellana to S. Maria di Falleri. To the south, much Latin territory was overrun by the Volsci in the fifth century; but Roman control over Latium, the Volsci and the Hernici was asserted in the course of the fourth century. As far as the Volsci and the Hernici are concerned, there is no evidence that either people was literate before the Roman conquest;[7] the entire area may be treated for our purposes as part of Latium.

5 H. Rix, in *Caratteri dell'ellenismo* (*Prospettiva* Supp.1) (Florence, 1977), 64, 'L'apporto dell'onomastica personale alla conoscenza della storia sociale'.
6 M. Torelli, in *Hellenismus in Mittelitalien* (Göttingen, 1976), 97, 'La situazione in Etruria'.
7 The Antinum inscription is Marsian; the Velitrae inscription, whatever else it may be, is probably not Volscian, see M.H. Crawford, *Ath.* 1981, 542.

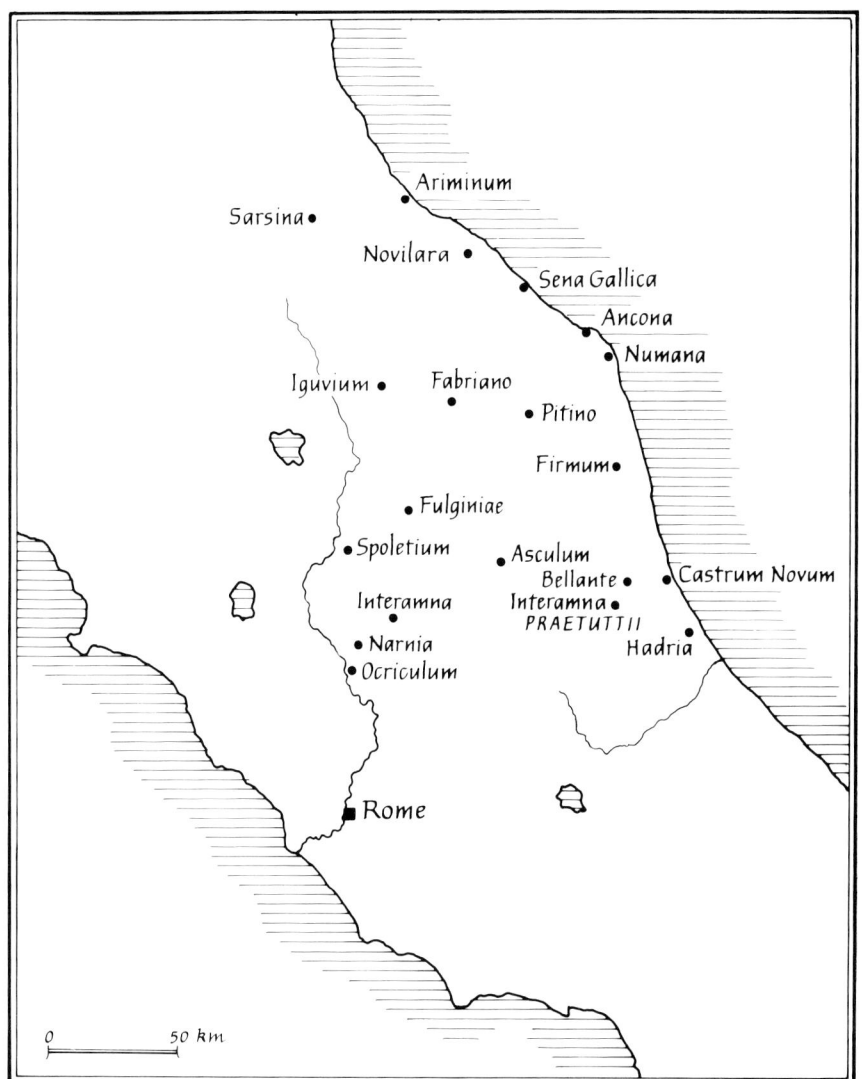

4 Umbria and Picenum

The same is true of the Sabini and the Aequi to the north and north-east. There are faint traces of the Sabine language in the archaic and classical periods,[8] but there is no good evidence that they or the Aequi ever used their own languages for public monuments.[9]

8 D. Briquel, *MEFRA* 1972, 789, 'Sur des faits d'écriture en Sabine et dans l'ager Capenas'.

9 The Collemaggiore inscription is too uncertainly reported to provide reliable testimony.

Umbria consisted essentially of the area between the upper course of the Tiber and the Appennines, together with some territory to their east, although less than was eventually designated as part of Umbria by Augustus (Map 4). In the fourth century Umbria formed, along with Picenum and Samnium, one of the most isolated areas of Italy. The early material culture of Umbria is inadequately known, but it is clear that the area was literate and urbanised before the Roman conquest.[10] Fighting in Umbria is recorded intermittently from 310, with Ocriculum just over the frontier coming to terms with Rome in 308;[11] the process of conquest was concluded with the defeat of the Sarsinates in 266. The Latin colony of Narnia, just north of Ocriculum, was founded in 299 and the Latin colony of Spoletium in 241; with Interamna Nahars probably a community of Roman citizens and Fulginiae certainly a *praefectura*, almost all of south-east Umbria was now effectively Roman.[12]

The cultural affinities of Picenum appear to have been in part with the opposite coast of the Adriatic, as well as with the rest of early Iron Age Italy; there are tombs at Fabriano and Pitino which show traces of Etruscan influence and Greek imports occur sporadically throughout the area; an enclave of Villanovan culture has been identified in the area of the later Latin colony of Firmum.[13] Monumental inscriptions occur in the north at Novilara and at a number of sites in the south in the sixth and fifth centuries; the alphabets are of Greek origin, the language in the southern area certainly Italic.[14] There are also examples of monumental sculpture from Numana and Novilara as well as from Ariminum.[15] But there is little trace of social change as a result of contact with the Greek world; there are very few Picene inscriptions and the habit of erecting them seems to have died out; there is little evidence for urbanisation before the Roman conquest.

The coastal strip to the north of the Greek *polis* of Ancona had been overrun by the Gauls in the fourth century and Roman military activity and colonisation in the area was largely concerned with these enemies. There was perhaps a Roman colony at Castrum Novum in 289; the Roman colony of Sena Gallica was certainly founded in 283, the Latin colonies of Ariminum and Firmum in 268 and 264. Elsewhere, the territory of the Piceni apart from that of Asculum became *ager Romanus* and in due course an area of substantial Roman settlement. It is striking that the third- or second-century bronze coinage of Ancona does not appear to have penetrated into the hinterland.

The fortunes of the Praetuttii were in many respects similar to those of the Piceni.

---

10 M. Verzar, in *Hellenismus in Mittelitalien* (n.6), 116, 'Archäologische Zeugnisse aus Umbrien'.

11 I have no views on when the treaty with Camerinum (allegedly of 310) was actually concluded.

12 W.V. Harris, *Rome in Etruria and Umbria* (Oxford, 1971), 98–101.

13 D. Lollini, in *PCIA* V, 120–1, 160–1, 162–5; M. Zuffa, ibid., 323.

14 A. Morandi, *Le iscrizioni medio-adriatiche* (Florence, 1974); A. Marinetti, *SE* 1981, 113, 'Il sudpiceno come italico', with further material.

15 F. Magi, in *Problemi dell' Umbria* (Gubbio and Perugia, 1964), 175, 'Le stele arcaiche dal Tirreno all'Adriatico', at 184.

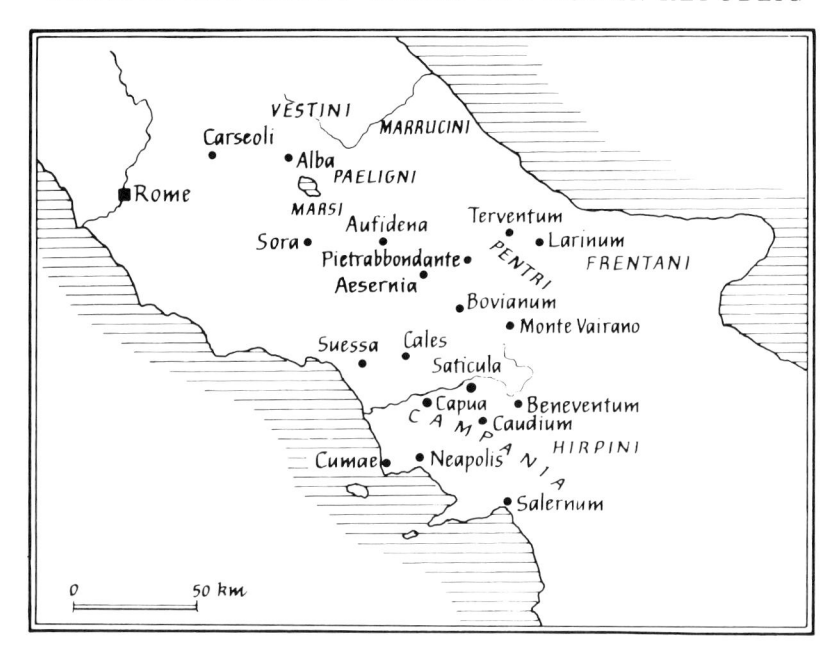

5 Central Italy

There are some early traces of contact with Etruria;[16] there is also a sculptured *stela* from Bellante; but here, as in south Picenum, such inscriptions as there are, in a similar alphabet and language, die out after the fifth century.[17] There are no traces of urbanisation before the Roman conquest. The area came under Roman control in or after 290 and the Latin colony of Hadria was founded between 289 and 283. The Latin name of the chief town of the Praetuttii, Interamna Praetuttiorum, implies heavy Roman settlement.

With Campania, we move back into the world of the inhuming 'Fossakultur', the Iron Age culture of western Italy from the River Tiber to the toe after 900 (Map 5); there are a number of cremating Villanovan enclaves in Campania and south of Salernum in the ninth century, but at any rate in Campania it appears that by 750 there remained only a mosaic of native cultures.[18] Greek colonies at Cumae and Neapolis and Etruscan dependencies at Capua and elsewhere (from 650) were both overlaid by the Samnite invasion of the second half of the fifth century. The Roman absorption of this extraordinarily mixed area, with Greek, Etruscan and Samnite elements, was certainly her most crucial imperial experience in the Italian peninsula.

16 For the imported material from Campovalano, see V. Cianfarani, in *PCIA* V, 41–54.

17 See n.14, also A.L. Prosdocimi, in *Le iscrizioni prelatine in Italia* (Rome, 1979), 137, for the Penna Sant'Andrea inscriptions.

18 M.W. Frederiksen, in D. and F.R. Ridgway (eds), *Italy before the Romans* (London, 1979), 277, 'The Etruscans in Campania'.

The process of conquest formed part of the long struggle against the Samnites; it involved the foundation of a sequence of Latin colonies, Cales (334), Suessa (313), Saticula (313) and Beneventum (268), the incorporation of the northern Campani as *cives sine suffragio* and a treaty with the one surviving Greek *polis* of Neapolis (326). The southern area remained independent, with a treaty whose provisions are unknown.

The Oscan areas of the centre and the south of Italy were in the fourth century politically fragmented and at various stages of development.[19] The historical record knows of a variety of small peoples in central Italy, along with the Samnite peoples, the Samnite conquerors of Campania, the Lucani and the Bruttii. Within this area the diversity is enormous; thus the archaeological record reveals both the isolation of a community such as Aufidena and the open and urban society of Samnite Campania. In the north, Marsi, Vestini, Paeligni and Marrucini occupied a series of relatively isolated lake or river basins. The Samnites and the Frentani to the south occupied respectively the upper and lower reaches of the Sagrus, Trinus and Bifernus valleys. Here, on the whole, the Romans left well alone. Latin colonies at Alba Fucens (303) and Carseoli (298), at Sora (303) and at Aesernia (263) closed the three routes out of the mountains to the west (the southern route down the Calor was closed by Beneventum). Some of the territory of the Vestini was incorporated and the Romans seized a swathe of territory, the *ager Taurasinus*, to cut off the Pentri from the Hirpini;[20] but otherwise the peoples concerned probably saw little in the way of a Roman presence even after the conquest.

The area as a whole is an interesting one. Although there is little trace of urbanisation before the end of the second century and settlements were no doubt small and dispersed, the level of civilisation and organisation of the area is not to be underestimated. All the peoples in question were capable of building very substantial hill-forts as places of refuge from Roman invasions;[21] some of these, such as Monte Vairano, eventually began to develop as urban centres, and the Samnite economy was predominantly agricultural, not pastoral.[22]

In the northern part of the area, later the territory of the Marsi, Vestini and Marrucini, a group of curious statues and *stelae*, apparently classical rather than Hellenistic, seems to reflect contact with the Greek world, no doubt via Greeks on their way to Adria and other sites in the Po valley. The Capestrano, Casteldieri and Crecchio inscriptions from the territory of the Vestini, Paeligni and Marrucini show an attempt akin to those further north to adopt a classical Greek alphabet in the sixth or fifth centuries. It seems likely that a people (or group of peoples) related to the

---

19 Some areas show affinities with the east coast of the Adriatic.
20 Note Dion. Hal. xx, 17 (20, 9) for the harshness of the Roman treatment of at least part of Samnium.
21 See G. Conta Haller, *Ricerche su alcuni centri fortificati* (Naples, 1978), with the review by E. Gabba, *Ath.* 1979, 171.
22 For Monte Vairano see *Sannio*, 321; for the Samnite economy see G.W. Barker, *Antiquity* 1977, 20, 'The archaeology of Samnite settlement in Molise'.

Praetuttii and the Piceni was here absorbed by or developed into the peoples who inhabited the area in the Hellenistic period; all of these have left some inscriptions of this period in their own languages, though in the Latin alphabet. There are parallels for this pattern of Roman influence, since it is in my view likely that the Greek cults of the Dioscuri, of Apollo and of Victory were, like the alphabet, mediated to the Marsi by Rome.

As far as Samnites and Frentani are concerned, an alphabet was acquired from the Etruscans and Greeks in Campania, without Roman mediation, as early as 400.[23] It is clear in general, however, that much of Samnium remained a great deal less developed than the territory of the Frentani; here, there is not only the piece of perhaps classical sculpture from Atessa, analogous to those from further north, but also evidence of urbanisation and of substantial imports from the Greek world at Larinum in the fourth and third centuries. It is true that there is some sculpture which *may* be early Hellenistic rather than second century from Samnium, from Bovianum and Terventum;[24] but some bronze helmet cheek pieces from Pietrabbondante are probably to be seen simply as booty. Only in the area of Caudium, on the way to Beneventum, geographically part of Campania, are there many Greek imports in the classical period (compare App. 8).[25]

The Vallo di Diano and the long river valleys flowing south into the Ionian Sea were in the historical period the land of the Lucani (Map 6); cousins of the Samnites, they had in the course of the fifth and fourth centuries absorbed the earlier population of the area, which had already been partly Hellenised by contact with the Greek *poleis* on the coast. The Lucani adopted an alphabet based on the Greek alphabet (with some Samnite features) in the course of the fourth century;[26] and in some cases they developed forms of communal organisation analogous to those of a Greek *polis*: an eponymous *archon* (rather than the normal Oscan magistrate, the *meddix*) seems to appear at Monte Serra near Vaglio in the fourth century.[27] The archaeological evidence reveals a considerable degree of urbanisation in the area as a whole; Greek goods were imported and imitated on a large scale. A votive deposit at Garaguso near Potentia includes early silver of Magna Graecia, which has also been found at Matera. Volceii, which we shall see producing coins during its revolt from Rome during the Second Punic War (p.46), had an urban nucleus in the sixth century and a walled circuit in the fourth century; it imported black-figure ware in the fifth century, Paestan and Gnathia ware later.[28]

23 M. Lejeune, *REL* 1957, 88, 'Sur les adaptations de l'alphabet étrusque aux langues indo-européennes d'Italie'; *REA* 1970, 271; 1972, 1, 'Phonologie osque et graphie grecque'.
24 *Sannio*, 231; the group from Agnone is surely late.
25 B. d'Agostino, in *PCIA* II, 194–5, 205–9.
26 M. Lejeune (n.23).
27 D. Adamasteanu, *In memoriam C. Daicoviciu* (Cluj, 1974), 9, 'Nummelos: archon o basileus lucano'.
28 *NSc* 1971, 424 (Garaguso); *Mon.Ant.* 1973, 226 (Matera); *Forma Italiae* III, 2, p.18 (Volceii).

The area as a whole came under Roman control at the turn of the fourth and third centuries; much of the Vallo di Diano was confiscated along with some land to the south and south-east and became *ager Romanus*, and the land earlier taken by the Lucani from the Dauni was now used for the Latin colony of Venusia, founded in 291; a Latin colony was also sent to Paestum in 273. The worst sufferings of the area came during the Hannibalic War, with the abandonment of many urbanised or partly urbanised

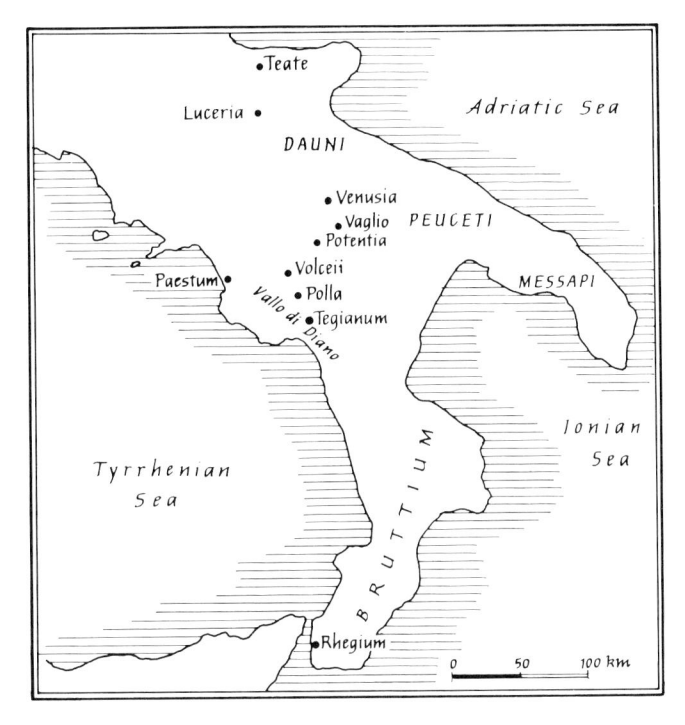

6 Southern Italy

centres. Yet, at any rate in northern Lucania, functioning urban communities continued to flourish down to the Social War and beyond.[29] The southern part of the area was, however, substantially depopulated.

The similarities and contrasts between Bruttium and Lucania are instructive. In Bruttium also, Oscan invaders absorbed an earlier population, which had begun to make use of the art of writing.[30] Like the Lucani, the Bruttii are first attested in the fifth century, but did not develop to the same extent a civilisation of their own; on the other hand, there is simply less territory in Bruttium which is neither coastal plain nor uninhabitable mountain and the Greek *poleis* initially controlled the bulk of the

29 See *JRS* 1981, 156.

30 M. Lejeune, *REA* 1973, 1, 'Les épigraphies indigènes du Bruttium'.

area; the *chora* of Rhegium in particular remained largely intact. Although Hellenisation no doubt did not extend very far down the social scale, in terms of area it extended its influence over most of Bruttium. The Bruttii and the Greek *poleis* alike suffered severely in the Hannibalic War and its aftermath.

Apulia was the only area of the south where a population remained largely undisturbed from the first moment of contact with the Greeks. The Dauni in the north certainly and the Peuceti in the centre probably lost some territory to the Lucani; and contact with the Lucani gave the Messapi (otherwise known as Iapyges) in the south the gentile name system common to the whole of central Italy.[31] But in general the Hellenisation and urbanisation of the area progressed uninterrupted down to the Roman conquest in the third century. Apulia is indeed the only area of Italy where the institution of coinage was adopted by native communities on any scale before the arrival of the Romans, and the third-century coinages of the area are particularly prolific.

Such evidence as there is makes it clear that within Italy there existed considerable diversity not only of monetary systems, but also of actual units of weight, as well as of linear measures and measures of capacity. As we shall see, the process of conquest by Rome did not at once eliminate this diversity.

The only clear literary testimony relates to linear measures: Varro (*RR* i, 10, 1) and Frontinus (30 L = 13 Th) record that whereas the Roman unit for land measurement was one of 120 by 120 feet, in Umbria, in Oscan territory and in Campania, with its Oscan population, the *vorsus* (mentioned also by Hyginus 122 L = 85 Th) was a unit of 100 by 100 (Oscan) feet. In addition, the Oscan foot was not the same length as the Roman foot. Epigraphical evidence also reveals the perpetuation in Lucania of a system of measures of capacity which is not Roman: a group of numbered *dolia* from a villa near Volceii and a site near Polla bear inscriptions which give their capacity in (Roman) *urnae* or in another unit which is not named or in both. It is, however, clear that the non-Roman unit divides into twelve, not ten, smaller units (App. A).

If one turns to monetary systems, it is apparent that the unit of reckoning in both Umbrian and Oscan areas was not the as, but the nummus. The term is attested both in inscriptions and on coins and the balance of probability is that, like the as, the nummus was always a quantity of bronze:

> Iguvium (in Umbria), Vetter 239
>   In the second period of the engraving of the tablets (Va + Vb 1–7)
>   *numer* and *nurpener* (*nummus* and (?) *novus dupondius*) appear.
>   In the third period (Vb 8–18 and VIIb) *a*(*sses*) appear.

---

[31] H. Rix, *ANRW* I. 2, 700, 'Zum Ursprung des romisch-mittelitalischen Gentilnamensystems'; for the Dauni see M.L. Nava, *Stele Daunie* 1 (Florence, 1980), with M.H. Crawford, *JRS* 1982, 221.

Tegianum, *ILLRP* 674
   Building costs in *nummi*.
Rossano di Vaglio, Poccetti 175
   Building cost in *nummi*.
Teate, *HN*³ (forthcoming)
   Coins tariffed in *nummi*.
Luceria, *ILLRP* 504 (with J. Heurgon, *BSFN* 1963, 278)
   Fine in *nummi*.
Venusia, *HN*³ (forthcoming)
   Coins tariffed in *nummi*.

Nummus is of course a loan word, from the *coin* terminology of Magna Graecia or Sicily, which presumably reached Umbria via Etruria, but the Oscan world without intermediary; it is interesting that, whereas the Romans, who also borrowed the word, seem to have taken it over with its original meaning of 'standard coin' and initially to have specified 'nummus denarius', 'nummus sestertius' and so on, Umbrian and Oscan usage appears to have been more restricted.

It is also apparent that a number of Italian communities divided their monetary units by ten and not by twelve, as the Romans and Etruscans did. The evidence is entirely numismatic and poses a number of problems. The communities involved are Ariminum, Hadria, the Vestini, Luceria, Venusia, Capua in revolt from Rome, finally a number of mints in Apulia (p.64); it does not seem likely that the practice is Umbrian or Oscan in origin, despite the Umbrian and Oscan use of a decimal system for linear measures and despite the issues of Capua. The decimal division of monetary units seems rather to reflect a uniformity of approach along the Adriatic coast,[32] and one thinks of the possibility of an earlier population, whether 'Italic' or not, partly overlaid by the Oscan invasion.

It will, finally, become apparent that the Etruscan and Italian communities which produced a cast bronze coinage did so with a variety of weight standards for their units. It would theoretically be possible to suppose that units lighter than the Roman pound were produced in parallel with the various stages of reduction of the Roman unit from its original level (p.55); but the Etruscan evidence makes this view impossible (p.46) and it is easier to suppose that a community or group of communities could adopt a weight standard for its bronze unit quite freely, just as the Oscan foot was different from the Roman. The evidence for actual weight standards in the different parts of Italy, apart from that of the coinage, is sparse. For

---

[32] Th. Mommsen, *RMw* 204–5, asserted that units divided by ten did not have an autonomous existence, but emerged only as 10/12 of asses divided by twelve; this view seems unreasonable and does not follow from the fact that S was never used as the equivalent of °°°°°; I do not understand Mommsen's second argument (for the use of the term 'nummus' and for coins with S°°°° see p.65).

the Frentani, there is one weight of 366 gm.;[33] taken in conjunction with the evidence of the coinage (p.43), it suggests a measure of uniformity along the Adriatic coast. For Etruria the following weights for the unit are attested:[34]

Chianciano	250 gm.
Chiusi	214–212 gm. (inferred from construction of balance)
Chianciano	212 gm.

Small in bulk, the evidence is enough to suggest that one should be open-minded about the possibility of differing weights for the pound in Italy and of different ways of subdividing it.[35]

The overall impression of Italy before the Roman conquest is of great diversity, in monetary practices and in almost every other way; the effect of this diversity on the monetary history of the Roman Republic is one of the central themes of this book.

33 *Sannio*, 318.
34 G.F. Gamurrini, *Mon.Ant.* 1, 1889, 159, 'Della libbra etrusca'. The weight from Cortona, marked II and weighing 560 gm., seems to relate to a weight from Pannonia, of Imperial date. I do not know what to make of the weight of 990 gm. with fifteen dots from Grosseto, L. Donati and M. Michelucci, *La Collezione Ciacci* (Rome, 1981), 313.
35 The casual and *a priori* rejection of both possibilities by P. Marchetti, 296 n.24 and 433 n.6, carries no weight.

2

THE EARLY REPUBLIC[1]

Not only is Rome down to the late fourth century a state without a coinage, there is in addition no evidence that any use was made of the coinage of other states.[2] The archaeological record of the city of Rome is devoid of coin finds earlier than the third century; in this respect Rome can be seen to diverge from Etruria, whose own coinage is also for the most part of relatively late date, but where coinage of other states appears at any rate in some places from the fifth century onwards (App. 1). The absence of coinage from Rome before the late fourth century is of course only one aspect of the general isolation of Rome, attested by the rest of the archaeological record and to a lesser extent by the literary record. The late appearance of coinage at Rome is no doubt also to be related to the fact that she did not demand tribute from her Italian allies, but men.

Absence of coinage, however, does not mean absence of money and much of what I have to say here relates to the role of money in the early Republic. But any attempt to discuss this subject must face the problem of the sources. Relentlessly modernising, they persistently discuss the early Republic in terms of the monetary conventions of their own times, including, of course, the use of coinage, and in terms of the economic thought, if that is not too grand a term, of the late Republic and early Empire, heavily influenced by Greek experience.

It is not simply that an obsession with etymology on the one hand and a desire to make Rome as advanced as possible as early as possible on the other hand combined to attribute coinage to the kings. As appears in a number of ways, the whole apparatus of writing about the early Republic presupposed the use of coinage in the same way as in the lifetime of the writers.

To consider first the invention of coinage, Pliny (claiming to follow Timaeus)

---

1 This chapter is a revised version of 'The early Roman economy, 753–280 BC', in *Mélanges J. Heurgon* (Rome, 1976), 197.

2 Livy ix, 40, 15–16, obviously refers to silver-smiths' establishments and not to banks.

attributed bronze coinage to Servius Tullius,[3] while Varro thought that Servius Tullius produced silver coinage.[4] An alternative tradition, starting from the similarity between Numa and *nummus*, attributed coinage to Numa Pompilius, the second king of Rome.[5] A third tradition took the invention of coinage back to Saturn.[6]

None of this need detain us very long. More serious is the effect on our sources of the assumption that coined money circulated in early Rome. In 502, according to Livy, captives were auctioned; Livy apparently assumes the monetary conventions of the late Republic.[7] In 476, according to the tradition, T. Menenius was fined 2000 asses, with Dionysius of Halicarnassus carefully and erroneously explaining that an as was at that date a bronze coin weighing a pound.[8] For 456, a corn distribution is recorded by Pliny, at a price per modius of one as, clearly from the context a coin of little value (Pliny, *NH* xviii, 15). Our sources also present us for the early and middle Republic with a picture of an elaborate machinery of state loans to cope with indebtedness; in doing so they are surely guilty of anachronism.[9]

If the rewriting of Roman history to make it follow later patterns may be suspected in the case of measures to deal with indebtedness, it is virtually certain in the case of an extraordinary procedure attributed to Servius by Dionysius of Halicarnassus. In order to count his population, Servius allegedly compelled men, women and children to dedicate at a festival a different kind of coin (Dion. Hal. iv, 15, 4). An alternative version was taken over by Dionysius from L. Piso Frugi, according to which births, deaths and comings of age of male members of the population had to be registered by the dedication of a coin at a different temple in each case (Dion. Hal. iv, 15, 5 = L. Piso Frugi, fr. 14 Peter). The latter version is redolent of the concern with Roman military manpower of the Gracchan age,[10] the former, with its unparalleled attribution of an interest in women and children to an early census, is perhaps the product of the Augustan age, when the basis of the Roman census was changed to count the entire population, not just adult males.

After this cautionary introduction, what I should like to do is to try to trace the history of money in early Rome, then look very briefly at what can be said of the

3 Pliny, *NH* xxxiii, 42–4 (see p.6 n.4); cf. xviii, 12; also Cassiodorus, *Variae* vii, 32, 4. See also below, p.19.
4 *Annales*, fr. 1 Peter; so also Volusius Maecianus (*MSR* ii, 66).
5 Isidore xvi, 18, 10; Epiphanius (*MSR* ii, 105); John Lydus, *de mens.* i, 17; Suidas, s.v. *assaria*.
6 Tertullian, *Apol.* x, 8; Isidore xvi, 18, 3; Plutarch, *QR* 274e; Macrobius, *Sat.* i, 7, 21.
7 Livy ii, 17, 6; for a collection of the evidence for booty in the early Republic see T. Frank, *ESAR* I, 24 and 43.
8 Livy ii, 52, 5; Dion. Hal. ix, 27, 3; for other evidence of anachronism see R.M. Ogilvie *ad loc.*

9 State loans are suggested at Dion. Hal. v, 69, put into effect at Livy vii, 21, 4–8; note also the speeches at Livy xxii, 60, 4; Appian, *BC* iii, 17, 64 and 20, 73. State loans occur sporadically under the Empire, see my article in *Annales* 1971, 1230, n.5 (p.240, n.1) and discussion in text.
10 In view of the registration of deaths and births by the dedication of, *inter alia*, a coin, attributed to Hippias by [Aristotle], *Oec.* ii, 1347a 14–17, it is perhaps legitimate to suppose that Piso was filling out his narrative with activities imported from Greek sources.

early economy of Rome and finally consider the developing use of money by the Roman state.

It is as true for the Roman world as for the Greek that the most important stage in the early history of money is the designation by the state of a fixed metallic unit, not the invention of coinage; the expression of the unit in the form of coinage is relatively unimportant.[11] When did Rome reach the stage of designating a fixed metallic monetary unit?

I mentioned earlier that Pliny reported Timaeus as attributing bronze coinage to Servius; the passage is much discussed, without agreement being reached. But it seems to me that Timaeus, a contemporary of the first Roman coinage and an acute and diligent student of Roman affairs, cannot have attributed bronze coinage to Servius. I believe on balance that Timaeus attributed the designation at Rome of a metallic unit, the as of bronze, to Servius.[12] For what it is worth, that is what the author of the *de viris illustribus* attributes to Servius. Certainly the 'Servian' census, which appears to be Timaeus' main concern, is perfectly comprehensible in terms of metallic units, weighed out without being produced in coined form.

The problem is to decide whether Timaeus as thus understood (also the author of the *de viris illustribus*) was right. I shall argue later that the 'Servian' census, at any rate in the form described by Timaeus and later writers, is an institution dating from the fourth century, though the possible existence of a structured organisation of the population in some form under Servius makes the attribution of the developed form to him an intelligible mistake.

As far as the designation of a fixed metallic monetary unit is concerned, there is an alternative tradition, at first sight of considerable plausibility. Romans of the late Republic and after believed that wealth in Rome in early times consisted largely of cattle, whence the word *pecunia*. (The fact that they went on falsely to assert that the earliest coinage commemorated this fact by using a cow as its type is neither here nor there.) As a corollary, it was believed that fines in early times were in cattle and sheep and that two laws in the course of the fifth century provided for their conversion into fines in quantities of bronze.

But the tradition is in some respects incoherent and self-contradictory. There is no agreement about the content of the *suprema multa* – two cows and thirty sheep according to Dionysius of Halicarnassus x, 50, 2, two sheep and thirty cows according to Gellius xi, 1, 2; Festus 129 L and 268–70 L, thirty cows only according to Festus 220 L. Furthermore, according to Dionysius x, 50, 2 and (by implication) Cicero, *de re pub.* ii, 60, the Lex Aternia Tarpeia of 454 simply laid down what the *suprema multa* was to be in cattle and sheep, while Gellius xi, 1, 2 and Festus 268–270 L regard the Lex Aternia Tarpeia as laying down equivalents in bronze for cattle and sheep.[13] When

---

11 See *La moneta in Grecia e a Roma* (Bari, 1982), 5.
12 See the discussion in *RRC* I, pp.35–7.
13 There is nothing of economic significance to be gleaned from the equivalences of 1 cow = 100 asses, 1 sheep = 10 asses (associated with the year 509 by Plutarch, *Pob.* 11).

we move on from the Lex Aternia Tarpeia, the situation gets no better. Festus 268–270 L attributes the establishment of the *suprema multa* to the year 452. The step from fines in kind to fines in bronze seems to be attributed by some sources to the Lex Iulia Papiria of 430.[14]

Quite apart from all the incoherences, I find it incredible that fines were ever levied in Rome in cattle and sheep. Just as in the Homeric world the fact that wealth was thought of as consisting in part of cattle and evaluated in terms of cattle does not mean that cattle were ever *used* as money for purposes of payment, so for Rome it does not follow from the existence of wealth in the form of cattle that cattle were levied as fines. I regard the whole apparatus of fines in kind recorded by the sources as so much learned speculation, starting from the etymology of the word *pecunia* and cognate words.[15] A metallic unit is clearly implied by the Twelve Tables of 450, with a penalty of 25 units of bronze for *iniuria*;[16] there is also the fact mentioned earlier, that fines in asses (thought of by the sources as coins, to be taken by us as weights of bronze) are mentioned by Livy and Dionysius of Halicarnassus for 476.[17]

To return to Servius Tullius, was he the creator of a metallic unit designated as a certain weight of bronze? I hope to have eliminated the evidence that points in the opposite direction and find it difficult to imagine Rome still without such a unit at the end of the sixth century. There is one specific indication that the adoption of such a unit occurred relatively early, the etymology of the word *scrupulus*, in classical Latin 1/288 of a pound and of a *jugerum*; the word derives from *scrupus* and means 'small stone', and therefore designated a weight before it designated (surely at an early date) an area.

The metallic unit of early Rome was of course a pound of bronze, an as; the as remained the Roman monetary unit, despite successive reductions in weight after its appearance in the form of coin, down to c.141; in practice, it was made up, before its appearance in the form of coin, of pieces of bronze, a practice vestigially perpetuated in the practice of manumission and testamentary disposition *per aes et libram* throughout the Republic: the placing of a piece of bronze – any piece of bronze – in a pair of scales marked a notional act of sale of the slave being manumitted and of the estate being transmitted. The Roman contract of sale and the extension of a purely symbolic version of the act of sale to the procedures of manumission and testamentary disposition

---

14 Cicero, *de re pub.* ii, 60; Festus 220 L; Livy iv, 30, 3 (the notes of R.M. Ogilvie there and on iii, 31, 5 are confused).
15 Gellius xi, 1, 4 has mistaken a theoretical reconstruction by Varro for an actual fact. E. Benveniste, *Le vocabulaire des institutions indo-européennes* I (Paris, 1969), 47, regards the derivation of *pecunia* from *pecus* as mistaken; but compare the word *adgregare*, and see F. Gnoli, *SDHI* 1978, 204, 'Di una recente ipotesi sui rapporti tra pecus, pecunia, peculium'. By the time of the Twelve Tables *pecunia* simply meant property.
16 Gellius xvi, 10, 8 and xx, 1, 12 with Festus 508 L and Gaius iii, 223 = *XII Tab.* 8, 3–4; compare Festus 498 L for gold by weight in 380.
17 See also the list of passages in the note of R.M. Ogilvie on Livy ii, 52, 5.

presumably post-dated the designation by the state of a fixed metallic monetary unit and hence fall between Servius Tullius and the Twelve Tables. By way of contrast, an interesting consequence follows from acceptance of the view that Servius Tullius designated the as as the Roman monetary unit: for since money was a *res nec mancipi*, the list of objects which were *res mancipi* (objects which could be alienated by the procedure known as *mancipatio*) was presumably closed before Servius Tullius. Sale of *res nec mancipi* by *traditio* had come into existence by the time of the Twelve Tables.

If then we can accept that a state-designated metallic monetary unit existed at Rome from the middle of the sixth century,[18] what of the development of the early Roman economy? The spectacular evidence of tomb finds suggests a very striking concentration of wealth in mobile form already from the beginning of Period III in Latium onwards, say from about 750;[19] this concentration of wealth seems much more striking than that attested by hoards of bronze in earlier periods.[20] I take it that what was happening was that certain dominant groups, whose dominance was expressed in terms of control over extensive land-holdings, were stimulated by the availability of status-defining and status-enhancing luxury imports to demand from the lower orders an agricultural surplus which could be exchanged for these imports; in other words the origin of the wealth of the upper orders in early Latium – *locupletes* – was derived from the land.[21]

It is also clear, however, that a surplus was available to what was becoming an urban community, as well as to individuals, and that this surplus could be deployed for communal purposes in quite complex ways. I accept the substantial accuracy of literary records of temple building in Rome, confirmed by archaeological finds, and it seems likely that more was involved than mere distraining on goods or services. In other words, both materials and skills had to be bought for the community and in some cases bought from abroad. I am also inclined to accept as authentic at any rate some of the early records of purchases of corn from abroad. I shall argue later that taxation in Rome belongs with the introduction of pay for the army and suspect that for an earlier period some form of liturgy system existed for raising money, when

18 Note that in Etruria the practice of marking objects of value with the name of the donor and sometimes also of the recipient disappears about 550, see M. Cristofani, *PdelP* 1975, 132, 'Il "dono" nell'Etruria arcaica'. It is attractive to link the development of 'la moneta' and the end of 'il dono'.

19 See C. Ampolo, *Dd'A* 1970–71, 37, 'Su alcuni mutamenti sociali nel Lazio tra l'VIII e il V secolo', esp. 46–9 for the tomb-finds, also the discussion after the paper; D.R. Ridgway, *JRS* 1976, 211, for the date.

20 R. Peroni, *PdelP* 1969, 134 = *Italy before the Romans* (p.10, n.18), 7, 'From Bronze Age to Iron Age'; M.A. Fugazzola Delpino, in *PCIA* IV, 43.

21 I am not persuaded by F. Tamborini, *Ath.* 1930, 299 and 452, 'La vita economica nella Roma degli ultimi re', that Etruscan influence made Rome a mercantile and manufacturing centre in the sixth century, in which trade guilds played their part; nor by A. Alföldi, *Entretiens Hardt* 13 (Geneva, 1967), 223, 'Zur Struktur des Römerstaates', at 266, that the early Roman economy was pastoral not agricultural. A. Watson, *Rome of the Twelve Tables* (Princeton, 1975), 4, n.3, notes that 'the importance of farming is to be observed in many of the provisions of the XII Tables'.

booty did not suffice. But it seems likely that any liturgy system functioned in terms of a designated monetary unit from Servius Tullius onwards.

At all events, the record of temple building and the archaeological evidence of imports to Rome show that both individuals and the community became poorer between the early fifth century and the fourth century, no doubt largely as a result of the not conspicuously successful warfare of the period. The indebtedness of some of the plebs, presumably as a result of loans in kind, and the political ambitions of others combined to produce confrontation between plebeians and patricians. The ultimately peaceful resolution of the conflict clearly owed much to the availability of land to all elements of Roman society as a result of the increasingly successful wars of the fourth century and the consequent enrichment of everyone relative to what each had possessed before.[22] Meanwhile, over the fifth and fourth centuries, in the interests of deploying the whole community to aid the process of conquest, there gradually evolved the complex articulation of the entire citizen body which characterised Rome of the middle and late Republic.

As mentioned above, ancient authors from Timaeus onwards believed that a complex division of the people into property classes defined in monetary terms formed the basis of army recruitment and political organisation from the time of Servius Tullius.[23] I find this implausible, but the question is in the present context unimportant. We need to know, however, by what date property classes within the citizen body had emerged at Rome.

The question is bound up with the problem of the introduction of money taxation; for the institution of *tributum* presumably presupposes a knowledge of the property held by the citizens of Rome. *Tributum* presumably in turn came into existence to fund pay for the army.

According to Roman tradition, the introduction of pay for the army took place in connection with the siege of Veii in 406. The fact that the information is preserved by Diodorus xiv, 16, 5, as well as by Livy, iv, 59, 11–60, 8, is perhaps encouraging, since he perhaps used sources writing earlier than the large-scale invention of Roman history between 500 and 300 that took place from the late second century onwards.[24]

It is in any case certain that the adoption of pay antedates the adoption of coinage and also that the levels of pay were a great deal lower than the three asses a day probably attested for the second century.[25] The first point emerges from the word

22 The centrality of the land problem in the political struggles of the early Republic emerges clearly from the sequence of *leges agrariae*, culminating in the Lex Licinia Sextia of 367 (on the authenticity of which see my remarks in *CR* 1971, 253).
23 The classic texts are Livy i, 42–3; Dion. Hal. iv, 15–17.
24 For the sources of Diodorus see A. Klotz, *RhM* 1937, 206, 'Diodors römische Annalen'; *stipendium triplex* for the cavalry appears in Livy vii, 41, 8 (342 BC).
25 There is no way of telling whether the system of deductions from pay to cover food and so on provided by the state goes back to the beginning or evolved later. For three asses a day in the second century, see p.149.

stipendium, implying, as Roman antiquarians saw, that pay was originally weighed out, not counted out.[26] The second point emerges from a consideration of the early history of the Roman coinage. As we shall see, Roman bronze coinage from 214 onwards had as by far its commonest denomination the as, in which soldiers were by then paid. This was not true before 214, when the as was relatively uncommon and fractions of the as far commoner. The change in pattern of issue no doubt reflects the fact that before 214 soldiers were paid, daily, less than an as and therefore paid in fractions of the as, which formed as a result the dominant element of the circulating medium (p.60).

Other evidence supports the date of 406 as that at which pay was instituted for the Roman army, evidence deriving from the existence of the institutions of *tributum* and indemnities levied on foreign peoples. For the Livian traditions on *tributum* and on indemnities levied on foreign peoples, presumably to help fund army pay, are remarkably consistent with the date of 406 for the adoption of pay; and it is hardly likely that invented traditions would have bothered to be so consistent.[27] Army pay, to be financed from revenue from public land, is proposed in 424 (Livy iv, 36, 2), shortly before its actual institution. The repercussions of that act then echo through the succeeding pages of Livy, with *stipendium* (army pay) regularly linked with *tributum*.[28] Actual levies of *tributum* are mentioned, clearly anachronistically, in 508 and 495,[29] then in 378, 377 and 347.[30] Indemnities levied on foreign peoples are mentioned, again clearly anachronistically, in 475 (Livy ii, 54, 1), then regularly from 394 onwards.[31]

It remains extraordinarily difficult to assess the economic consequences of the introduction at Rome of regular taxation and state payments. One may assume that the developed Roman census system with five separate property classes evolved gradually after 406, in order to graduate the burden of contributing *tributum* according to the different levels of wealth in Roman society.[32] There is no way of telling just how the different levels came to be fixed, but it is worth at least asking how the

---

26 Pliny, *NH* xxxiii, 42–3; Isidore xvi, 18, 8; see also Varro, in Nonius 853 L, *stipendium appellabatur quod aes militi semestre aut annuum dabatur*; a fragmentary definition of Festus, s.v. [*Pondo*], may be restored to convey the information that bronze passed by weight before the adoption of coinage; for *aes* in military pay see also Festus 2 L, 61 L, 358–9 L and the word *aerarius*.

27 Livy casually assumes pay for Etruscan soldiers in 508 (ii, 12, 7), as he does for Hernican in 362 (vii, 7, 5) and for Samnite in 296 (x, 16, 8).

28 iv, 60, 4–5; v, 4, 5–7; 5, 4; 10, 3–10; 11, 5; 12, 3–13; 20, 5–8; cf. x, 46, 6; Festus 508 L; Pliny, *NH* xxxiv, 23.

29 ii, 9, 6 (see R.M. Ogilvie *ad loc.*); 23, 5.

30 vi, 31, 4; 32, 1 (for building the city wall, for which see *Roma Medio-Repubblicana* (Rome, 1973), 7); vii, 27, 4.

31 v, 27, 15 (Falisci); 32, 5 (Volsinii); viii, 2, 4 (Samnites); 36, 11 (Samnites); ix, 41, 7 (Etruscans); 43, 6 (Hernici); 43, 21 (Samnites); x, 5, 12 (Etruscans); 46, 12 (Falisci). The levying of indemnities never displaced the mulcting of foreign peoples of some of their land (on which see E. Gabba on Appian, *BC* i, 7, 26).

32 Note also the tax on orphans attributed to Camillus and 403 (Plutarch, *Cam.* 2) and the *vicesima libertatis*, first attested for 357 (Livy vii, 16, 7), both presumably evoked by the need to raise money for army pay.

qualifying level for the lowest class came to be fixed. This involves the problem of the *heredium*.

Two *iugera* were regarded by Varro, *RR* i, 10, 2, as forming the standard *heredium* of early Rome (for the word note *XII Tab.* 7, 3); the possibility that the figure is not wholly imagined is suggested by the fact that colonial allotments were sometimes of two *iugera* in relatively recent times.[33] Since two *iugera* are inadequate to support a family, one must suppose that if a Roman peasant possessed two *iugera* he also had access to other land. In the late Republic there was a category of common land and it is reasonable to suppose that a peasant might supplement an income from his freehold by grazing on such common land; it is also possible that a peasantry dependent on rich members of the elite was dependent precisely because it paid (in kind) for the right to use some of their land, in addition to its own.[34]

If, however, recruitment of peasants to the legions was to be based, as it was, on the possession of the property qualification of the lowest class, it was necessary for this to be set at a level which included the holders of two *iugera* allotments in colonies and elsewhere. I suspect that at this level the designation of a figure in asses and the assessment of property were largely arbitrary processes and sometimes wonder how much the property qualification for serving in the legions ever really meant.

As for the *heredium* itself, this seems to me also an arbitrary entity. I suspect that at some date before the adoption of a system of five classes and perhaps during the reign of Servius Tullius, freehold tenure of land, *some* land, was accepted as a necessary qualification for service in the legions and the figure was arbitrarily fixed at two *iugera*, the amount of land a man and an ox could plough in a day.

When Rome introduced coined money, she moved with relative rapidity to a use of it that was for the ancient world not unsophisticated. Although we can only see very dimly what is happening in the period before the introduction of coinage, we can see enough, I think, to be aware of its importance. Building on the experiences gained in the state enterprises of the period of the monarchy and the early Republic, Rome created a complex taxation system based on assessments of property which at the top levels must have borne some relationship to reality and went on to use that system to fund an army which eventually conquered the Mediterranean.

---

33 E. Gabba, *RIL* 1978, 250, 'Per la tradizione dell'heredium romuleo', argues that the *heredium* is a learned construct of the second century BC; I agree that many features of the relevant tradition are such a construct, but I am not sure that all are.

34 I note in passing that the relative emancipation of the Roman peasantry during the fifth and fourth centuries presumably led to the need for alternative dependent labour and suspect that slavery is already more important in early Rome than is normally suspected. The prominence of slavery as an institution in the fifth century is reflected in the Twelve Tables, which allude both to testamentary manumission and to succession to freedmen. For the fourth century see M.I. Finley, *Ancient Slavery and Modern Ideology* (London, 1980), 83. See W.V. Harris, *War and Imperialism* (Oxford, 1979), 59, for the enslavement of some 60,000 war captives by Rome between 297 and 293.

3

THE APPEARANCE OF ROMAN COINAGE

In the late fourth century the production and use of coinage in south Italy were largely limited to the *poleis* of Magna Graecia (Fig. 3). Large silver and silver fractions of Tarentum, Metapontum, Heraclea, Thurium (occasionally still of Sybaris), Croton, Caulonia, Locri, Terina and Velia circulated together in the area; a few hoards contain a small number of *pegasi*, a few other hoards contain gold of Tarentum, Metapontum or Locri, two hoards consist of gold of Tarentum and Macedon or of Macedon and Ptolemy I (App. 3); two hoards, of bronze of Metapontum from Metapontum (*IGCH* 1935; compare *Mon.Ant.* 1973, 180 (Pisticci) and 226 (Matera)), of silver fractions of Croton from Croton (*IGCH* 1939), perhaps reflect a tendency attested elsewhere for small change to circulate locally (Map 7).

In the *chora* of Rhegium the circulating medium seems as usual to have been Sicilian (*IGCH* 1944, 1945); while in Campania the coinage of Neapolis and related mints was apparently dominant (see below).

Exceptions to the pattern of localised circulation are few: a hoard from Sala Consilina in the Vallo di Diano contained, not surprisingly, a few pieces of Neapolis and Poseidonia as well as the issues characteristic of hoards from Tarentum and the south; and a few pieces of Poseidonia found their way into one hoard from Metapontum; one hoard from Cariati on the coast between Thurium and Croton contained, perhaps surprisingly, material of Tarentum and the south, Sicilian material and Campanian material.

The Sala Consilina hoard is interesting as evidence of the penetration of Greek coinage into Lucanian territory; in addition, Greek coinage penetrated into the interior of Bruttium and into Messapian and Peucetian territory, appearing as far north as Altamura and Ruvo. As far as Lucania and Bruttium are concerned, it is worth recalling the continuation of bronze coinage at Poseidonia after the Lucanian takeover and the production of essentially similar coinages at Greek Croton or Locri, Oscanised Medma, Hipponium or Laus, Bruttian Consentia.

As far as Apulia is concerned, bronze coinage was produced at Messapian Uzentum, probably early in the third century, while a large number of Apulian mints struck silver obols and occasionally diobols or hemiobols, Naretum, Caelia, Rubi, Canusium, Arpi, Teate. The issues of Arpi are varied and prolific and clearly cover a substantial period; there is in addition an issue of didrachms from Arpi. A somewhat worn obol of Arpi occurred in the Torchiarolo hoard, which places the issue some time before 265 (App. 5); the didrachms appear to be of the same weight standard as that of Tarentum before its reduction around 280 (p.34). All these coinages probably belong to the period before the effective involvement of Rome in the area with the Pyrrhic War, along with the bronzes of Naretum and the earliest bronzes of Arpi.

The most remarkable area is Campania, where coinage on the Greek model was produced on a large scale by Oscan communities, whether Oscanised Greek *poleis* such as Cumae or communities which had never been Greek. The monetary history of Campania is indeed crucial to an understanding of that of Rome (Fig. 4). For the

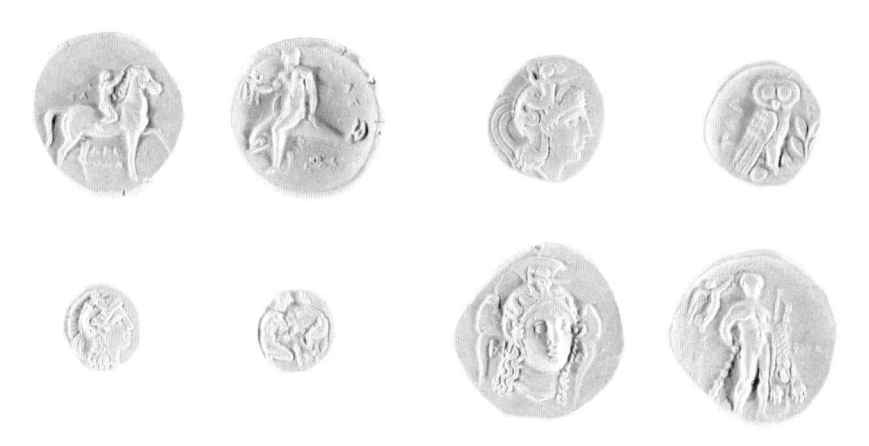

3 The coinage of Magna Graecia

Didrachm of Tarentum, Period VI:
  Horseman r., crowning horse; above, ΣΑ; below, ΑΓΑΘΩΝ/Dolphin-rider l., holding
    tripod; above, ΤΑΡΑΣ; below, ΓΑΣ   BM 1918–2–4–37
Drachm of Tarentum:
  Helmeted head of Athena r./Owl r. with olive-branch; on l., ΤΑΡ   *BMCItaly* 310
Diobol of Tarentum:
  Helmeted head of Athena r./Heracles strangling lion; above, owl   BM 1946–1–1–245
Didrachm of Heraclea:
  Facing head of Athena; on l., monogram; on r., Ε/Facing Heracles crowned by Victory;
    on l., [ΗΡΑΚΛΕΙ]ΩΝ; on r., ΦΙΛΩΝ   BM 1918–2–4–7

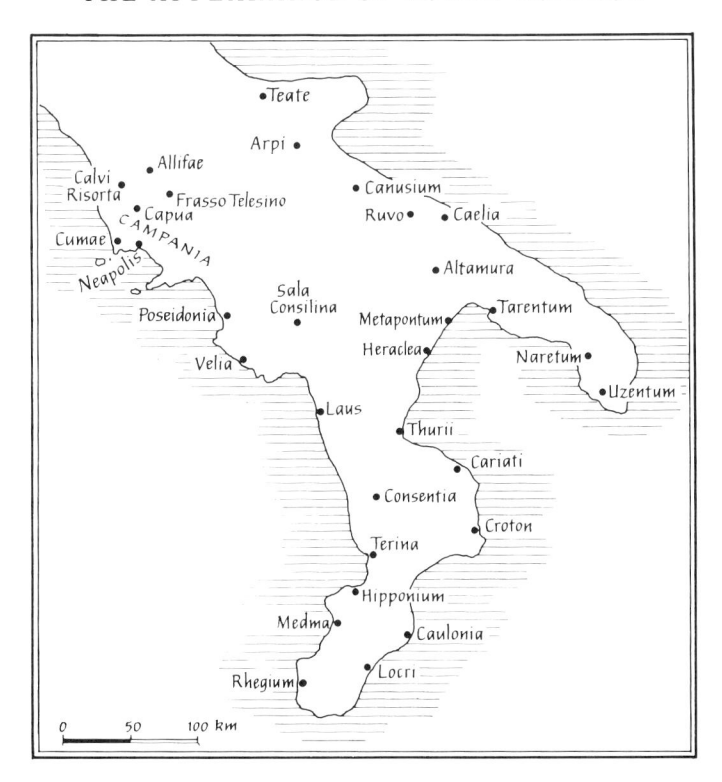

7   The early Hellenistic coinage of Magna Graecia and Campania

coinage of Cumae continued after the Samnite takeover in 421/0 (p.10) and coinages were also produced for 'Hyrina' (the commonest form of the legend), Nola, the Campani (= Capua), the Fenserni, 'Fistelia' (the commonest form of the legend) and Allifae. In my view, not only was coinage produced at Neapolis throughout the fourth century, but at least Cumae and Hyrina also continued to strike didrachms down to and perhaps beyond the middle of the fourth century.[1] Fistelia and Allifae struck prolific issues of obols and smaller pieces for much of the century. There was even a revival of coinage at Cumae later in the century (surely before 338); and the earlier fourth-century coinages of Campania were very much in circulation at the end of the century.

Much of the Campanian material in question appears in a third-century hoard from Calvi Risorta (Cales, App. 4): didrachms, a hemidrachm and obols from the Greek *polis* of Neapolis, didrachms from the Oscanised *polis* of Cumae, didrachms of Hyrina

---

1 M.H. Crawford, *CR* 1983, 108; for the hoards see App. 4. For the mint of Fistelia see App. B.

4 The coinage of Campania in the fourth century

Didrachm of Neapolis:
   Head of Parthenope r.; behind, Artemis with two torches; below, APT[EMI](doros)/
   Man-faced bull r. crowned by Victory; below, monogram; in exergue,
   [N]ΕΟΠΟΛΙΤΩ[Ν]   BM 1946–1–1–68

Obol of Fistelia:
   Facing head/Dolphin, barley-corn, mussel; around, *fistlus*   BM 1946–1–1–87

and Nola, obols of Allifae, didrachms and obols of Fistelia and anonymous obols normally attributed to Fistelia (compare the Frasso Telesino, Campania and Capua hoards); the Calvi Risorta hoard also contains one obol of the Peripoloi Pitanatai, clearly a group of mercenaries similar to the Mamertini, but functioning as an autonomous unit somewhere in the south of Italy.

The earliest issues of Roman coinage are to be seen not simply as a response to the exigencies generated by the need to operate in an area accustomed to the use of coinage, but also as a stage in the coinage of Greek and Oscan Campania. Taken as a whole, the earliest stage of the Roman Republican coinage consists of silver and token bronze fractions on the Greek model and cast bronze coins based on an as or unit weighing a Roman pound or thereabouts. There is no doubt that by the time we get to the First Punic War, the issues in the two sequences were produced in parallel (see below). But it is no longer possible to hold that (with the insignificant exception of two tiny bronze issues) the two sequences began together in 280 and hence that the issues in

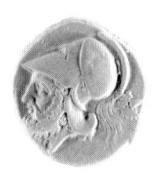

5 The Mars/Horse's head ROMANO issue

Didrachm of Rome, *RRC*, no. 13/1:
   Helmeted head of bearded Mars l.; behind, oak-spray/Horse's head r. on base; behind,
   corn-ear; on base, ROMANO   BM 1949–4–11–967 (obv.), 1946–1–1–33 (rev.)

the two sequences were produced in parallel from the beginning. It is now clear that the earliest Roman issue of silver coinage is of about 310–300, and the early stages of the two sequences must therefore be considered separately.

The earliest Roman didrachm is that which bears the types Helmeted head of bearded Mars/Horse's head ROMANO, accompanied by a silver fraction (Fig. 5).[2] The latter is a minor puzzle, since it is known from two citations, which may be of the same specimen; it is not (or they are not) now available for study and the paucity of the material makes it hard to say whether the denomination is a twelfth of a didrachm (an obol) or a tenth of a didrachm (a litra); the former view is clearly right on other grounds.[3]

The didrachm poses problems of a more serious nature. The hoard evidence now available makes it clear that the issue belongs in the late fourth century.[4] Given this, Metapontum, never more than a tentative suggestion, is clearly impossible as a mint; the weight standard, about 7.3 gm., is that of Neapolis, but there are difficulties in the way of regarding Neapolis as the mint, as Andrew Burnett points out; to assign the issue to Rome is to assign it to a vacuum, for no other silver issues can be assigned to Rome for a generation or more and this issue never circulated there.

Perhaps one should try a different tack and consider the purpose of the issue, bearing in mind the fact that the weight standard is that of Neapolis, not that of Tarentum, rather higher at 7.9 gm., and the fact that the issue had no successor anywhere for a generation. An isolated issue suggests an isolated cause and the most obvious candidate is the building of the Via Appia from Rome to Capua, perhaps between 312 and 308; if this is right, the issue can be regarded as a Campanian issue (though we shall see that it circulated elsewhere) and it does not matter very much precisely where it was actually struck. The issue was perhaps produced in improvised surroundings; only four obverse dies were used, but fifteen reverse dies,[5] an abnormally high ratio of obverse to reverse dies.

Two bronze issues reinforce the view that the early Roman use of struck coinage consisted in producing it as an isolated act, without impact on practice in Rome (Fig. 6); they are the small issue with the purely Neapolitan types Head of Apollo/Forepart of man-headed bull ΡΩΜΑΙΩΝ, struck at Neapolis on some unknown occasion soon

---

2 *RRC*, no. 13; A. Burnett, *QTic* 1978, 121, 'The first Roman silver coins'; *Romano* may represent the genitive plural *Romano(rum)* or the archaic *Romano(s)*, with *nummus* understood; compare the two alternative legends on the coinage of Neapolis (p.34).

3 In Sicily and in Magna Graecia the didrachm was known as a *nomos*; it contained ten *litrai* in Sicily and sometimes in Magna Graecia, where the subdivision into twelve *oboloi* was also used. The numismatic evidence (see above) makes it clear that the obol, and not the litra, was the norm in Campania.

4 A. Burnett, *SNR* 1977, 91, 'The coinages of Rome and Magna Graecia in the late fourth and third centuries BC'. P. Lévêque, in *Les Dévaluations à Rome* 2 (Rome, 1980), 3, 'La genèse et les premières réductions du monnayage romain', says nothing of interest.

5 For the types see *RRC* II, p.713; A. Burnett (n.2), 131.

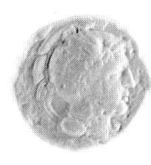

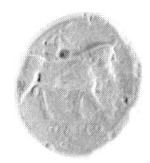

6   Early Roman bronze coinage

Bronze of Neapolis:
  Laureate head of Apollo r./Forepart of man-faced bull r. above waves, star on flank;
  above, ΝΕΟΠΟΛΙΤΩΝ; behind, lyre   *BMCItaly* 148
Bronze of Rome, *RRC*, no. 1/1:
  Laureate head of Apollo r./ Forepart of man-faced bull r., star on flank; above,
  ΡΩΜΑΙΩΝ   Vienna
Bronze of Rome, *RRC*, no. 2/1:
  Helmeted head of Minerva r./Man-faced bull r.; above, star; in exergue, [R]OMANO
                                                                           Naples, F113828

after the treaty between Rome and Neapolis of 326 and virtually forming part of the coinage of Neapolis,[6] and an issue known from a single specimen with the types Helmeted head of Minerva/Man-headed bull [R]OMANO. This is a heavier piece, weighing 6.14 gm., and is probably also an issue at Neapolis (*RRC*, no. 2). Our knowledge of the history of the period does not allow us to say *why* either issue was produced, but it is worth emphasising that both must because of their unparalleled nature reflect events of some importance. It is also worth emphasising that their production will have ensured the continuation of at least some Roman involvement in the production of coinage.

It is only in or after the Pyrrhic War that a relatively unbroken sequence of Roman struck coinage begins, with the didrachm Head of Apollo/Horse galloping ROMANO (Fig. 7).[7] Struck from ten obverse and nine reverse dies, the issue was produced around 270; given that the fourth Roman didrachm issue is essentially a coinage of the First Punic War (see below) and that the third issue was quite substantial, it seems best to assign the second issue to the period of the Pyrrhic War. I see no particular reason to assign it to Rome and the mint is best left uncertain. The obverse type can and

6 *RRC*, no.1; A. Burnett (n.2), 126 (300–280, but probably somewhat earlier), at n.4 refuting V. Picozzi, *QTic* 1979, 159, 'Q. Ogulnio, C. Fabio coss'. The date in the 330s advanced by M. Caccamo Caltabiano, *RSA* 1981, 33, 'La serie ΡΩΜΑΙΩΝ', is impossible.

7 *RRC*, no. 15; A. Burnett, *QTic* 1980, 169, 'The second issue of Roman didrachms'. The revised chronology for the early coinage of the Republic involves abandoning the hypothesis advanced in *RRC* I, pp.42–3, that it was under the control of the censors; we do not know what administrative arrangements were made.

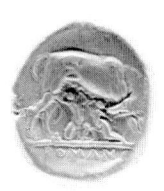

7   The Apollo/Horse ROMANO and Hercules/Wolf and twins ROMANO issues

Didrachm of Rome, *RRC*, no. 15/1b:
   Laureate head of Apollo l.; before, ROMANO/Horse galloping r.; above, star
                                                                                               Paris, de Luynes

Didrachm of Rome, *RRC*, no. 20/1:
   Head of Hercules r., hair bound with ribbon/She-wolf r., suckling twins; in exergue,
   ROMANO   BM cast

should be seen as precisely evoked by the situation in which Rome found herself during the Pyrrhic War, with a pressing need to represent herself as a friend and defender of the Greek *poleis* of Magna Graecia (I see the reverse type as a variant of the Horse's head type of the previous issue). For to the Greek world after 279/8, Apollo symbolised chiefly his role as a defender of civilisation against barbarism, arising out of the salvation of Delphi from the Gauls in that year; but successful resistance to the Gauls was a Roman achievement as well as a Greek one; it is likely that, in placing Apollo on her independent silver coinage, Rome was aware of Apollo as the symbol of the victory of 279/8 and concerned to adopt him as the symbol of her own recent victories over the Gauls of 295 and 284–282.[8]

One further issue of didrachms preceded the First Punic War, that with Head of Hercules/She-wolf and twins ROMANO, substantially larger than either of the first two issues (*RRC*, no. 20, Fig. 7). It cannot be assigned with any certainty to a particular mint and it is perhaps best to be agnostic rather than assign it to Rome; for that assignation is based on the supposed significance for Rome of the types – Hercules is perhaps Hercules Victor, the she-wolf suckles Romulus and Remus – and on the fact that in the literary tradition 269/8, close to if not in fact the date of the issue, was remembered as a crucial date in the history of the Roman coinage. The sources are contradictory and in part clearly wrong:[9] the *Periocha* of Livy and Zonaras record

---

8 See, at greater length, *Rome and the Greek East. Conquest and Culture* (forthcoming), Ch.1.

9 Conveniently available in *Rerum Rom. Fontes*, 238–9; I do not propose to analyse the obvious errors in Pliny (H. Zehnacker, *Ktema* 1979, 169, 'Pline l'Ancien et l'histoire de la monnaie romaine', discusses the consequences of Pliny's moralising approach). We should actually be much better off if this wretched text did not exist, despite the further attempt to rescue its credit by E. Lo Cascio, *AIIN* 1980–81, 335, 'Il primo *denarius*', at 354–7.

that the Roman people now used silver for the first time, Pliny that silver was now struck for the first time (by Rome), Jerome and Syncellus that silver was now struck in Rome for the first time. Andrew Burnett first suggested that what lies behind all this is the distribution of the proceeds of the sale of booty described in Dionysius xx, 17, and this inference may be strengthened by the observation that Zonaras' account of the victory in question immediately precedes his notice of the use of silver at Rome.[10] If this is right, no inference may be drawn about the production of coinage at Rome; the problem also arises of how far the distribution took place in Roman coin (wherever struck), foreign coin or silver bullion by weight. I have no certainty as to what the answers are; but it is worth observing that the distribution precedes by a few years the production of the fourth issue of Roman didrachms (see below); coinage *had* arrived in Rome and its production stretches in an almost unbroken line from this moment to the fall of the Roman Empire in the west.

The long history of the use of money at Rome (Ch.2) makes it unlikely that the arrival of coinage had in the first instance any very dramatic effect, whether on public finance or on private economic activity, quite apart from the small scale of the early Roman issues. The period of the Pyrrhic War, however, was a period of change in the monetary history of Magna Graecia: the needs of war provoked among both friends and enemies of Rome a number of very substantial coinages, the strains of war led in some cases to reductions in weight or to resort to debasement, for some mints the events of these years put an end to all production of coinage, established patterns of circulation were altered.

If one rejects as fictional the notices of Roman involvement in Iapygia in 307 and 302, Roman military activity south or east of Samnium before the Pyrrhic War can be seen to be limited to occasional forays for short distances into Lucania or Apulia. But the foundation of Venusia in 291 was followed by Roman intervention in Thurium perhaps in 285 and certainly in 282. In the latter year garrisons were also placed in Croton, Locri and Rhegium. Thurium was recovered by Tarentum already in 282; in 280, the year after the outbreak of war, Croton and Locri rebelled against Rome, while control of Rhegium was only retained by its garrison by means of a massacre of the inhabitants. It was only from 277 onwards that Rome gradually succeeded in regaining control; Croton and Locri were probably recovered in that year, and Pyrrhus was finally defeated at Malventum, renamed Beneventum, in 275. The surrender of Tarentum followed in 272.

When war broke out between Rome and Tarentum in 281, Tarentum, Metapontum, Heraclea, Thurium, Croton, Locri, Velia and Neapolis were all major producers of silver coinage (Caulonia, Terina and Poseidonia had ceased striking silver by 300). Tarentum, Metapontum, Heraclea, Thurium and Croton were all forced to reduce

---

10 A. Burnett (n.4), 116; he would not now necessarily hold that no silver coinage was struck at Rome until after 269.

8 The coinage of Locri

Didrachm of Locri:
 Laureate head of Zeus l.; below, monogram/Roma seated r. crowned by Pistis l.; on l.,
 ΡΩΜΑ; on r., ΠΙΣΤΙΣ; in exergue, ΛΟΚΡΩΝ   BM *PCG* V C 14

Tetradrachm of Pyrrhus:
 Head of Zeus l., wearing oak-wreath; below, A/Dione seated l., holding sceptre; on l.,
 ΠΥΡΡΟΥ; on r., ΒΑΣΙΛΕΩΣ   BM 1946-1-1-656

the weight standard of their didrachms in the face of the burden imposed by the war, from 7.9 gm. to 6.6 gm. It is also striking that such analyses as are available of silver of Magna Graecia show almost without exception a silver content of about 90 per cent or a little more (App. C). The range is about the same as that covered by the analyses of D.R. Walker of Roman didrachms down to and including the issue produced during the First Punic War.[11] In the present state of the evidence, since none of the Greek issues analysed can be closely dated, it is not possible to say whether the Pyrrhic War had any effect other than to bring about a reduction in weight at Tarentum and the other mints. It would be worth undertaking a proper series of analyses. As Metapontum, Heraclea, Thurium and Croton were knocked out of the war, they ceased to strike silver, mostly for ever.[12]

During the war, Locri struck tetradrachms of Attic weight for Pyrrhus; after this alien issue, she produced the last of her own silver issues, didrachms of reduced weight standard (7.25–7.10 gm., close to that of the Hercules/Wolf and twins ROMANO issue) with Pistis crowning Roma as the reverse type (Fig. 8). The great city of Tarentum alone survived the effect of the war to go on producing silver coinage as an ally of Rome during the First Punic War and again, in the course of her revolt from Rome, during the Second Punic War.

11 D.R. Walker, in *Metallurgy in Numismatics* I (London, 1980), 56. For the next group of issues see p.42.

12 Metapontum struck a small issue for the Lucanian allies of the Brettii during the Second Punic War, see p.69. For later bronze of Heraclea, and of Thurium as Copia, see p.71.

It is reasonable to hypothesise that it was the Pyrrhic War which evoked the substantial issues in silver of Rome's allies Velia and Neapolis in these years (see Table 1). Velia struck no silver thereafter, though we shall see (p.71) that she produced a substantial bronze coinage as late as the first century. Neapolis, however, continued to strike silver and bronze; she produced an enormous issue of didrachms and bronzes, both distinguished by the presence of the letters IΣ on the reverse, which belong to the period of the First Punic War (Fig. 9). There followed a group of issues, of bronze only, but of considerable complexity, with six different types in simultaneous production:

> Head of Apollo/Man-headed bull with Victory above
> Head of Apollo/Lyre and omphalos, Head of Dioscurus/Horseman

TABLE 1. Early Roman silver coinage

TARENTUM	VELIA	NEAPOLIS	Date	ROME
V	VI[1]	Head r./ΝΕΟΠΟΛΙΤΗΣ[2]		
VI	VII			
				Mars/Horse's head
			305/300	
	VIII	Head r./ΝΕΟΠΟΛΙΤΩΝ[2]		
Reduction[3]			280	
VII	IX	Head l./No letter, E, IB, BI		
				Apollo/Horse
			270	
VIII[4]		Head l./IΣ		Hercules/Wolf and twins Roma/Victory

The periods are those of A.J. Evans for Tarentum, C.M. Kraay (in *SNG* (Oxford)) for Velia. The construction of the table owes much to A. Burnett.

1. The *pegasi* of Acarnania, 55 of which formed the only non-Italian element in the Mesagne hoard (*IGCH* 1971), belong to this period.
2. There are also two anomalous pieces, A. Burnett, *SNR* 1977, 96, n.20.
3. The weight reduction, to 6.6 gm., occurs also at Metapontum, Heraclea, Thurium and Croton.
4. The production of the so-called Campano-Tarentine issues belongs in this period (A. Burnett, in *Coin Hoards* 4, 42); their legends are Tarentine, their typology part Tarentine and part Campanian, their weight standard Campanian. The series remains mysterious; it only seems to turn up, rather worn, in much later hoards, and then with predominantly Campanian material (*IGCH* 1992, Gioia del Colle; *IGCH* 1994, Lucania 1860; *IGCH* 2019 = *Coin Hoards* 3, 46, Catanzaro; *Coin Hoards* 1, 70, Montegiordano; *IGCH* 2009 = *Coin Hoards* 4, 42, South Italy; *IGCH* 2011, Sessa; *IGCH* 2210, Vulcano; other hoards are even less revealing). The issue of didrachms at Teate also belongs in this period (A. Burnett, loc.cit.).

Head of Artemis/Cornucopiae, Head of Apollo/Tripod
Head of Apollo/Forepart of man-headed bull.

It is not easy to offer a convincing reason for the cessation of silver coinage at Velia before 264 and of all coinage at Neapolis before 218; Roman intervention is clearly not in question and one is left to hypothesise exhaustion of resources; but why?

The years between 300 and the surrender of Tarentum saw a number of changes in the patterns of circulation hitherto characteristic of Magna Graecia and Campania, the most obvious being of course the appearance of Mars/Horse's head ROMANO didrachms on the scene. Eight hoards are now known with this as their only Roman issue, three Campanian, four Apulian, two Lucanian. The penetration of the first issue of Roman didrachms into south-eastern Italy is indeed part of a larger phenomenon, the penetration of Campanian material in general. This is a quite new feature of the monetary history of Magna Graecia at the beginning of the third century and is clearly to be related to Roman activity in the area in general and to the Pyrrhic War in particular. The other side of the coin is represented by the Capua (Santa Maria Capua

9   The third-century coinage of Neapolis

Didrachm of Neapolis:
  Head of Parthenope l.; behind, facing head of Helios/Man-faced bull r., crowned by
  Victory; below, I; in exergue, ΑΟΠΟΛΙΤΩΝ   *BMCItaly* 122
Bronze of Neapolis:
  Laureate head of Apollo l.; before, ΝΕΟΠΟΛΙΤΩΝ; behind, M/Man-faced bull r.,
  crowned by Victory; below, IΣ; in exergue, KE   *BMCItaly* 211
Bronze of Neapolis:
  Laureate head of Apollo l.; behind, monogram/Lyre and omphalos; in exergue,
  ΝΕΟΠΟΛΙΤΩΝ and laurel-branch tied with fillet   *BMCItaly* 236
Bronze of Neapolis:
  Laureate head of Apollo l.; behind, cornucopiae/Tripod; around, ΝΕΟΠΟΛΙΤΩΝ
                                                                    BMCItaly 204

Vetere) hoard (?), where Campanian material, the Roman issues with Mars/Horse's head and Roma/Victory, two pieces of Roman cast bronze coinage and material from Tarentum, Metapontum, Croton and Velia are associated (App. 5).

The pattern of the hoards of Magna Graecia in this period also reflects activity of Pyrrhus with which the Romans were not directly connected, the Sicilian adventure. For it is with Pyrrhus' return from Sicily that the presence of *pegasi* in Bruttium is to be connected;[13] some of the hoards contain in addition Sicilian material proper and issues of Pyrrhus himself (App. 6).

Perhaps the most decisive consequence of the Pyrrhic War, however, and even more of the First Punic War was the spread of the use of coined money on the Greek model to the Appennine areas of Italy. We have already had occasion to notice in different contexts a number of hoards from Lucania, from the east close to Apulia, insofar as localised (App. 5). The phenomenon is in fact far more widespread (App. 7).

Within a single overall picture, one difference is immediately apparent, namely the earlier arrival of coinage in Lucania, Samnium, the territory of the Frentani and the territory of the Marsi than among the peoples of the northern Appennines. This is partly the result of the earlier history of the areas concerned, partly the result of geographical factors.

We have seen (p.12) that Lucania and the territory of the Frentani were both areas characterised by contact with and imports from Magna Graecia in the classical period. The same is true for parts of Samnium, notably the area near Beneventum (p.12). And it must also be likely that existing links between Samnite Campania, areas of Samnium close to Campania and more distant areas facilitated the penetration of coined money in the third century. The case of Beneventum is interesting, since it is probable that the foundation of the Latin colony in 268 is to be seen as in part explaining the presence of the material in the Benevento hoard. But the area had always occupied an intermediate position between Samnite Campania and central Samnium. And Roman colonisation can hardly provide a general explanation, since the only other colonies in southern Appennine Italy are Aesernia (263) and Alba Fucens (303). The explanation is rather to be sought in the service of men from Appennine Italy, under Roman control by 281, as we have seen, with Roman armies in the Pyrrhic War and thereafter. There is from the time of the Pyrrhic War onwards an uninterrupted sequence of issues of Roman coinage and there is no doubt that these were produced to a very large extent in order to pay Roman troops. We are told (Polybius vi, 21, 5) that the maintenance of the allied troops serving under Roman command was the responsibility of the communities which supplied them, and it looks as if these communities began to feel themselves obliged from the time of the Pyrrhic War onwards to acquire coined money with which to pay their men. The *ad hoc* nature

---

13 For *pegasi* in Sicily see *La moneta in Grecia e a Roma* (Bari, 1982), 58.

of this approach emerges very clearly from the mixed assemblages of coinage which found their way back to the communities concerned. Some coinage, no doubt, also found its way back as booty; but this had been a possibility much earlier and I do not doubt that the use of coinage by the Italian contingents with the Roman armies was a major factor in the monetisation of the areas from which they came.

It is significant that the first coinage to arrive is normally Roman, alone or in association with other coinages. A point of method is involved. The fact that a coin found at Pietrabbondante belongs to the fourth century need not imply that the coin arrived there in that period. A late third-century hoard may well contain coins of the fourth century, so that one may always regard an isolated fourth-century coin in Samnium as the survivor of a group of coins which only penetrated in the third century. It is in this context important that the period of the Second Punic War (p.71) sees a major change in the pattern of circulation in Italy. Down to this period Greek or Hellenised issues circulated along with Roman issues or issues produced on a Roman model; thereafter the circulating medium of Italy is almost exclusively Roman. Given the pattern of finds in Samnium, it is clear that the Second Punic War provides a *terminus ante quem* for the arrival of coinage in the area. But it is possible to be more precise.

As far as central Samnium is concerned, the passage from a world without coinage to a world with coinage can be documented at Campochiaro (App. 7), where recent excavations have revealed two dumps of material which are significantly different. The first dump, probably of material of the late fourth and early third century, contained bones, bricks, black-glazed pottery and coarse ware. The second dump, substantially later, contained not only black-glazed pottery and coarse ware, but also bronze and terracotta votive offerings, wall plaster, architectural terracottas, iron and bronze tools, and finally a small group of coins. The date of the coins is not in every case certain, but one may well accept a date around 300 for some of the pieces without supposing that they arrived at Campochiaro at that time. Nor is the absence of coins from the first dump the only reason for rejecting such a supposition.

One of the coins of the second dump is a bronze of the Syracusan democracy and the most economical hypothesis is to suppose that it arrived at Campochiaro in the context of the military operations of the Second Punic War; it is also reasonable to suppose that the other bronzes arrived at the same time, since they are, along with the Syracusan bronze, characteristic components of hoards of the period of the Second Punic War.

The other material from Campochiaro is also significant, a group of bronzes recognised by the excavators as a scattered hoard, again characteristic of the period of the Second Punic War; and a group of didrachms of the years between the two wars, which also seems to me to be a scattered hoard, even if the archaeological evidence does not demonstrate this. If it is a hoard, it carries the arrival of coinage at Campochiaro back to the period after the First Punic War. From the sanctuary of Pietrabbondante, two hoards of the period of the First Punic War have long been known. Recent excavations have produced a group of coins from the dump of earth used in the course of the construction of Temple B; the arrival of this group belongs in the years after 240 (a worn didrachm of Tarentum is associated with other material of later date, mostly Roman, and must have arrived at Pietrabbondante with this material).

Similarly, in the sanctuary of San Giovanni in Galdo and in the settlement of Monte Vairano, the coins found in the excavations belong in the same context, namely a penetration of coinage during the third century, certainly brought about by the involvement of troops from these zones in the First and Second Punic Wars. It was precisely these wars which created the monetary unity of Italy. And as Emilio Gabba points out to me, the unitary vision of Polybius (vi, 19–26) of the functioning of the Roman and allied army is dramatically confirmed.

Obviously, the process was much slower in northern Appennine Italy, without previous contacts with the usages of the Greek world. The fact that the pattern in the territory of the Marsi is apparently similar to that in the south is to be seen as the result of the fact that the area was very early an area of Roman penetration. The colony of Alba Fucens was founded already in 303 and must have played a major role in the penetration of Roman usages (see p.11). By way of contrast the mountainous areas of northern Appennine Italy were not only difficult of access, but had never been in significant contact with the Greek world and received in the third century no colonies founded by Rome. We shall see that when a number of Italian communities came to emulate Rome not only in the use of coinage, but also in its production, differences between north and south are again apparent.

Major and perplexing elements of the early Roman coinage system remain to be considered. I have already mentioned two rare issues of struck bronze, probably produced virtually as part of the coinage of Neapolis. But there are two very large issues, whose function must be elucidated, the Goddess/Lion ROMANO issue and the Minerva/Horse's head ROMANO issue (Fig. 10). The latter used to be associated with the first Roman didrachm, but it is now clear that it is much later (see below). Although it is clearly right to argue that the two issues were struck in different mints and circulated for the most part in different areas,[14] their zones of circulation are not mutually exclusive; it is reasonable to accept the natural inference from the Ardea and Pietrabbondante hoards, where the Goddess/Lion issue appears as the only Roman struck issue, that it was the earlier of the two issues, produced before the end of the Pyrrhic War (see App. 9). Speculation on exactly when, where and why the issue was produced is not in the present state of knowledge profitable.

The enormous Minerva/Horse's head issue, on the other hand, was certainly struck at Cosa during the First Punic War, along with a small number of pieces which bear

---

14 A. Burnett (n.2), 130.

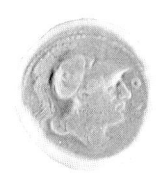

10   The Goddess/Lion ROMANO and Minerva/Horse's head ROMANO issues

Bronze of Rome, *RRC*, no. 16/1a:
  Female head r., hair bound with ribbon, usually with necklace/Lion walking r., usually holding spear in mouth; in exergue, ROMANO   *BMCRR* Romano-Campanian 26
Bronze of Rome, *RRC*, no. 17/1g:
  Helmeted head of Minerva r.; around, R[OMA]NO/Horse's head l., usually on base; around, ROMA[NO]   Vatican 23
Bronze of Cosa
  Helmeted head of bearded Mars r./Horse's head r., on dolphin; around, COSANO   BM

the ethnic of Cosa itself.[15] I should like to suggest that Cosa, with its excellent harbour and the enclosed lagoons of Orbetello to the north, was where the Romans built and trained their first fleet and that the Minerva/Horse's head bronzes were struck on that occasion and to meet the expenses connected with that venture.

The remaining element of the early Roman coinage system is the cast bronze coinage and associated currency bars. There is no doubt that by the time we get to the ROMA issues of didrachms, these, struck bronze and cast bronze formed together a single issue (see below). But although the relative sequence of cast bronze issues is, like the relative sequence of silver issues, reasonably secure, the absolute dates are less sure. In the case of the silver issues we have one isolated late fourth-century issue and a Pyrrhic War issue, then an issue which follows the war and a First Punic War issue; the cast bronze issues need not be in any way in phase. I think that the idea of producing a cast bronze coinage is dependent on having already produced a silver coinage; for I doubt if the notion of producing a coinage based on a unit, an as, of about a pound of bronze, with fractions and (occasionally) multiples would have occurred to anyone who had not already produced coinage of some sort.[16] I place the beginning of Roman cast bronze coinage after that of Roman silver coinage and that of Italian cast bronze coinage later still. The cast bronze coinage of Rome and central Italy can be seen

15 T.V. Buttrey, *MAAR* 34, 1980, 5, 'Cosa. The coins'.
16 The words *libra* and *uncia* were perhaps borrowed at this point, *libra* from an uncertain source, *uncia* perhaps from Sicel via Greek, K.M.D. Rosen, *Language* 40, 1964, 21, 'Latin uncia'.

as in one respect rather advanced, with its explicit marks of value. But it remained a form of coinage without close parallels in the ancient world.

Even if one does attempt to arrange silver and cast bronze in phase, two arrangements are possible:

SILVER	CAST BRONZE
Mars/Horse's head	
	Dioscuri/Mercury
Apollo/Horse 8–point star ⎫	⎧ Apollo/Apollo
16–point star ⎭	⎩ Dioscurus/Apollo[17]
Hercules/Wolf and twins	Roma/Roma
Roma/Victory	Wheel

or:

SILVER	CAST BRONZE
Mars/Horse's head	
	Dioscuri/Mercury
Apollo/Horse 8–point star	
16–point star	
Hercules/Wolf and twins	Apollo/Apollo
	Dioscurus/Apollo
Roma/Victory ROMANO	Roma/Roma (10 ounces)
(6 scruples)	
	Wheel[18]

I do not feel strongly about the respective merits of these two schemes, but perhaps now prefer the second, since under it the silver stabilises at a weight standard of six scruples and the as at a weight standard of ten ounces at the same time; if the Hercules/Wolf and twins didrachm and the Apollo/Apollo cast bronze go together, the same silver:bronze ratio already applies there also. Andrew Burnett acutely points out that the weight standard of the semunciae of the first issue of cast bronze makes it clear that they represent a point of transition to the second, which is heavier than the first (the reasons are mysterious). This would suggest that there is little or no gap between the two issues. In addition the fact that none of the datable material from Nemi is much earlier than the period of the Pyrrhic War suggests that the cast bronze coinage found with it, beginning with the Dioscuri/Mercury issue, is also no

---

17 On the assumption that the two parts of the silver issue correspond to one complete and one incomplete series of denominations of cast bronze.

18 On the assumption that the tressis is the equivalent of and the replacement for the didrachm, see n.21.

earlier than about 280.[19] One may speculate that the need to administer the *agri quaestorii* acquired in 290 (*Lib. Col.* 253, 17 L; 349, 17 L) played a part in the decision to produce the first issue of cast bronze coinage.

Associated with the first three issues of cast bronze coinage, Dioscuri/Mercury, Apollo/Apollo, Dioscurus/Apollo, those where the as weighs fully or over a pound, is a curious group of currency bars, weighing about five pounds each. Like the cast bronze coinage they are made of highly leaded bronze. Precisely when and why they were produced is mysterious, but they presumably belong to the period of the Pyrrhic War and the years which followed.[20] The bars may have served for the distribution of booty.

The substantial puzzle, however, is how the cast bronze coinage and the struck bronze coinage were related to each other. For in the case of the former face value and metal value presumably approximated and it is indeed possible using a plausible silver:bronze ratio of 1:120 to calculate that a didrachm of six scruples was worth three asses of ten ounces; the struck bronze coinage was clearly a token coinage, however.[21] The two are found together in hoards and were produced as complementary parts of single issues from 240 and one cannot therefore evade the problem by arguing that the two coinages had nothing to do with each other.[22] On the other hand, one may argue that token bronze coinage came into the Roman world by the back door, as it were. The two issues produced at Neapolis may be seen as belonging to the monetary history of Campania; and if I am right about the Minerva/Horse's head ROMANO issue, it may be seen as a deliberately token issue produced for a specific occasion. The intervening Goddess/Lion ROMANO issue may well be similar in character. After the First Punic War regular issues of struck bronze were produced at Rome; but they did not last to the end of the didrachm coinage and can be seen as essentially alien. It is remarkable that those to whom cast bronze issues were paid did not, so far as we know, use them to forge token bronze issues; that they did not is remarkable evidence of the moral cohesion of Roman Italy in the third century.

The First Punic War faced the Romans for the first time with the need to finance an overseas campaign; it also saw an enormous upsurge in the production in Italy of issues evoked by the demands of Rome. I shall argue later (p.106) that the coinage

---

19 M. H. Crawford, in *Mysteries of Diana* (Nottingham, 1983), 71.
20 See *RRC*, nos. 3–12; A. Burnett and P. Craddock (p.3, n.2). The bars with naval types are, I think, acceptable during the Pyrrhic War. I now incline to accept the authenticity of the Amphora/Spearhead bars and wonder if one should also accept the Trident/Thunderbolt bars reported from Tarquinia by R. Garrucci, *Le monete dell'Italia antica* (Rome, 1885), 6 (actually three specimens). The Pegasus/Thunderbolt bars bear the legend ROMANOM, the Branch/Incuse tendril bars probably also.
21 See A. Burnett (n.2), 139, for the view that the issues of the Roman token bronze coinage should be regarded as obols (with occasional multiples or fractions). I decline to follow the more detailed speculations of E. Lo Cascio, *AIIN* 1980–81, 335, 'Il primo *denarius*', at 341–5.
22 As H. Zehnacker, 'Libella', in *Varron. Grammaire antique et stylistique latine* (Paris, 1978), 75–82.

11 The Roma/Victory ROMANO issue and contemporary cast bronze coinage

Didrachm of Rome, *RRC*, no. 22/1:
   Helmeted head of Roma r.; behind, control-symbol, cornucopiae/ Victory r. attaching wreath to palm-branch; behind, ROMANO; before, control-letters, HH

   BM 1935–6–19–61

As of Rome, *RRC*, no. 21/1:
   Helmeted head of Roma r.; behind, I   Reverse same type l.   BM 1919–11–20–138
Sextans of Rome, *RRC*, no. 24/7:
   Tortoise; below, two dots/Wheel   *BMCItaly* 18

principally used by the Romans in Sicily was the coinage of their ally Hieron II and should like here to concentrate on the pattern of coinage in Italy.

The Romans themselves certainly produced the Roma/Victory ROMANO issue of didrachms during the war and probably the Roma/Roma and Wheel series of cast bronze coinage, adopting for both silver and bronze a weight standard lower than that which had obtained hitherto (p.40). We have seen that the Minerva/Horse's head ROMANO issue of struck bronze coinage was probably produced at Cosa to pay for the building of a Roman fleet and the didrachms and the cast bronze coinage should both be regarded as produced for circulation in Italy (Fig. 11).

The pattern of Italian coinage in this period is complex, moulded in part by Roman

THE APPEARANCE OF ROMAN COINAGE

demands and in part by local traditions. The most remarkable element in the pattern is the cast bronze coinage of Italy, which I propose to consider here as a whole (Fig. 12). We have already seen (p.14) that a system of reckoning in pounds of bronze was native to central Italy, as well as to Rome. For a brief period in the third century, a remarkably large number of mints produced a cast bronze coinage similar to that of Rome;[23] many of these Italian issues can reasonably be regarded as derivative from the Roman issues; though there is no absolute certainty, I believe that this is true of all.[24] Numerous issues are based on an as of about 300 gm.,[25] sometimes followed by pieces of reduced weight, comparable to the Roman issues of reduced weight produced during the Second Punic War. Other issues are based on an as of about 350–400 gm.

One homogeneous group of mints, which operated with an as of about 300 gm., includes Tarquinii,[26] Tuder,[27] Reate, perhaps Praeneste, Carseoli and Firmum in central Italy; further one unassigned series with as to semuncia, two unassigned asses and three unassigned semisses. There is almost no evidence which might allow us to establish the dates when these mints functioned; but since none of them apart from Tuder produced pieces of reduced weight there is no objection to supposing that apart from Tuder they functioned during the First Punic War; Tuder presumably functioned during the Second Punic War.

The mints producing coins on the heavier weight standard of 350–400 gm. were Ariminum, Hadria, the mint of the Vestini and a mint presumably in the same region, which it is tempting to identify with Asculum Picenum, the only other unincorporated community in the area. It is in any case interesting to observe that both the weight standard and the division of the as into ten unciae instead of twelve are the same from Ariminum in the north to the territory of the Vestini in the south; it is reasonable to infer that both weight standard and as division derived from the original population of the area and survived both the Gallic conquest of the north and the arrival of the Vestini in the south (the Umbrian presence at Ariminum also appears to have made

---

23 The standard work is E.J. Haeberlin, *Aes Grave* (Frankfurt-am-Main, 1910); E.A. Sydenham, *Aes Grave* (London, 1926) adds little, later works even less. There is much valuable discussion of cast bronze coinage in R. Thomsen, *Early Roman Coinage* (Copenhagen, 1957–61). There are a number of grotesque objects sometimes regarded as cast bronze coinage: a lump with a cross on each side, found at Tarquinii, weighing 367.35 gm. (Haeberlin, p.277); another with Janiform heads of Maenad and Silenus/Head of antelope, weighing 906.05 gm. (Haeberlin, p.280); another with Head of Gorgon/(other side blank), weighing 313.80 gm. (Haeberlin, p.24); another with Triquetra/Trident, found at Todi, weighing 484.18 gm. (Haeberlin, p.24).

24 See p.39; compare R. Thomsen (n.23), 244–56.

25 Compare the weight standards of the earliest Roman issues, *RRC*, nos. 14, 18–19, 21, 24, 25/4–9, 26/5–8, 27/5–10, 35–8.

26 Tarquinii also produced currency bars apparently intended as dupondii. The Roman weight standard used at Tarquinii is an interesting measure of the Romanisation of southern Etruria (see p.6).

27 Tuder also produced cast bronze coinage on a local weight standard, see below, and struck bronze coinage, see p.48.

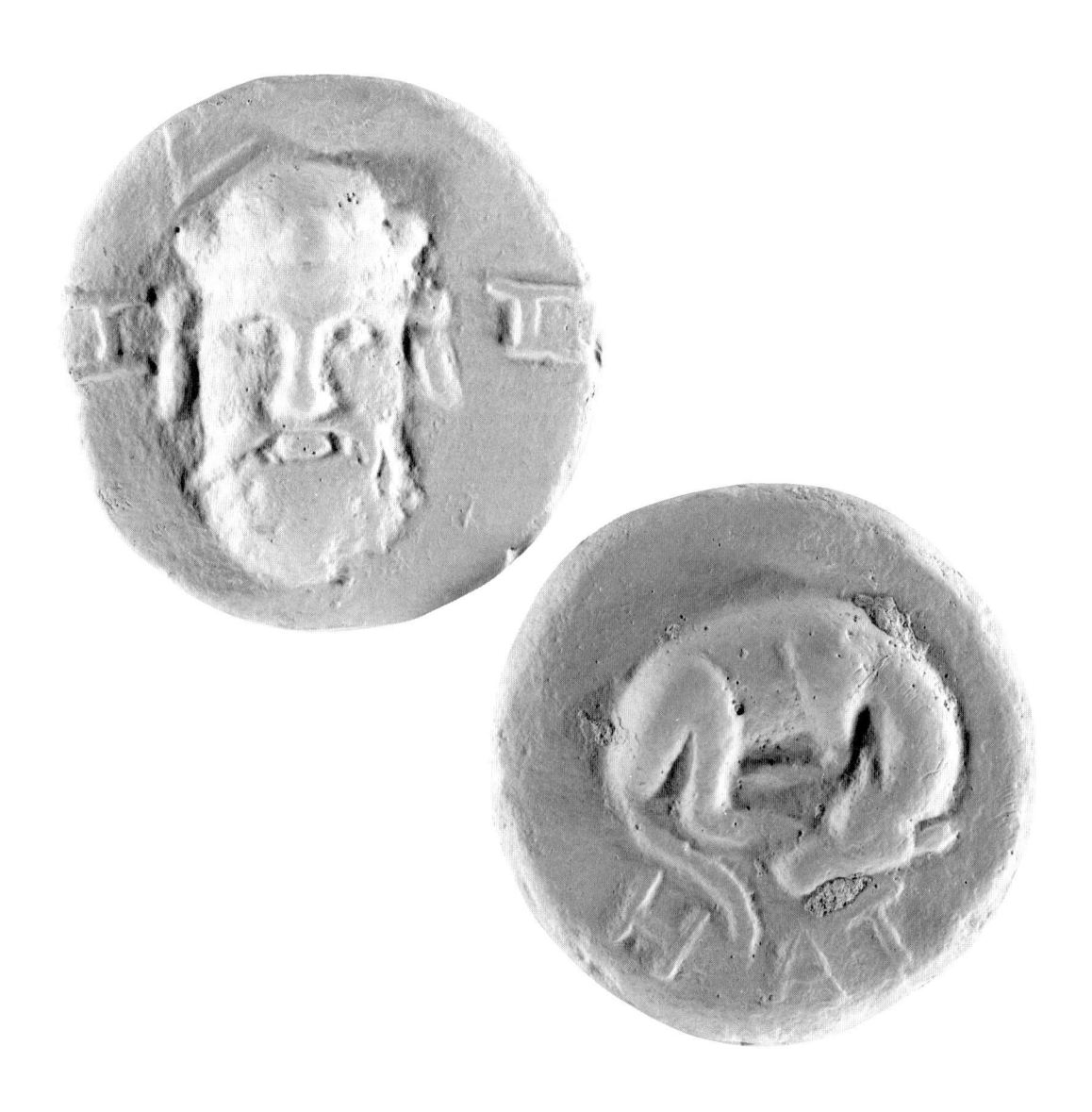

12   Italian cast bronze coinage

As of Hatria:
  Facing Silenus head; above, L(ibra); on either side, H/Dog; below, HAT   BM cast

12   Italian cast bronze coinage (*cont.*)

As of Volaterrae:
Janiform head wearing *petasus*/Club; around, *velathri*; on l., I   BM cast

no difference). In this context the Roman weight standard of Firmum requires explanation and one may see the colony as involving the injection of a completely alien population into the territory of the Piceni; it is relevant that Firmum and Asculum Picenum remained bitter enemies at least until the time of the Social War. By way of contrast, other evidence makes it clear that at any rate at Ariminum there was substantial continuity of population into the period of the Latin colony.[28] It may also be relevant that the area later occupied by the colony of Firmum was an enclave of Villanovan culture in Picene territory (see p.9).

   A further homogeneous group of mints, which operated with an as of about 300 gm., includes Luceria and Venusia in Apulia; there are also two unassigned asses. At Luceria and Venusia issues of reduced weight were produced and this suggests that the entire product of these two mints belongs to the period of the Second Punic War. In addition, although it displays the division of the as into ten unciae characteristic of the Adriatic coast, cast bronze coinage is a wholly alien import in terms of the monetary traditions of the area and it is very hard to envisage this occurring except in response to Roman needs during the Second Punic War.

28 M. Zuffa, in *La città italica e etrusca preromana* (Bologna, 1970), 299, 'Abitati e santuari suburbani di Rimini dalla protostoria alla romanità.'

The Second Punic War also evoked the production of five series of cast bronze coinage on a reduced weight standard where none had been produced before. One was perhaps produced at Ausculum in Apulia in parallel to the reduced series of Luceria and Venusia; at least two were produced by rebel communities in Lucania and Samnium, Volceii and Meles.

A wholly separate group is formed by the issues of Etruria and Umbria, which were produced on a weight standard based on an as of about 200 gm. (p. 16). The only link between these issues and the rest occurs at Tuder, which apparently produced cast bronze coinage first on the local Umbrian weight standard and then on a full and a reduced Roman weight standard. All the issues based on the local Etruscan or Umbrian weight standard are to be assigned to the period of the First Punic War.

The only issues of cast bronze coinage of any size are the issue of Hadria, the reduced issues of Luceria and Tuder and some of the Etruscan issues. These last share the principal characteristic of Etruscan coinage in general, namely that of functioning in complete isolation. As for the others, one is left with the very powerful impression that they are in monetary terms a marginal phenomenon. Only five central Italian hoards are known where Italian and Roman cast bronze coinage are hoarded together, from Vulci, Ariccia, Pietrabbondante, Termoli and Rimini; there are only two hoards known consisting of Italian cast bronze coinage only, from Castelnuovo della Daunia and Venosa (App. 10). The pattern of these hoards is confirmed by the pattern of isolated finds and shows that circulation was extremely localised (Table 2). It seems likely to me that most of the issues are either issues which are in part symbolic and

TABLE 2. Italian cast bronze coinage

Tarquinii	Reate	Praeneste (?)	Carsioli	Firmum
Libral	Libral	Libral	Libral	Libral
Local	Regional	Local[1]	Regional	Local
Vestini	Hatria	Ariminum		
Heavy libral	Heavy libral	Heavy libral		
Regional	Regional	Local		
Luceria	Venusia			
Libral	Libral			
Local	Local			
Post-semilibral				
General				
Uncial				
Regional				

1 Except for an isolated specimen from Perugia.

connected with the foundation of a colony or issues produced in order to provide for the distribution of booty. Some of the issues may of course have been produced to pay troops returned from campaign, but I doubt whether in general they are of any great importance in fiscal terms.

As far as silver and struck bronze are concerned, we have already had occasion to observe, not only the production of Roman coinage at Cosa, but also the production of a small quantity of coinage in the name of Cosa itself during the First Punic War; and we have also looked at the coinages of Rome's principal allies and enemies among the Greek *poleis* during the Pyrrhic War and the First Punic War. It is necessary in addition to consider a number of other coinages evoked by the military exigencies of these years, some of them very large indeed.

There is in the first place a small and curious group of issues produced by the Latin communities of Alba Fucens, Norba and Signia; they consist of obols (also diobols and hemiobols at Alba) and should probably be seen as struck to pay troops during the Pyrrhic War. They are interesting not only as examples of issues produced for military purposes by communities operating under the Roman aegis; they are also remarkable in that they appear to be copied from Greek coinage systems largely independently of Roman borrowings and in that the coinage of Alba Fucens comes from a community deep in the Appennines.

A much more substantial group of issues comes from Campania (Fig. 13). Cales, Suessa, Teanum, Aesernia and Compulteria all produced large or very large issues of bronzes whose types, Head of Apollo/Man-headed bull with Victory above, are borrowed from the coinage of Neapolis. (The mints of Suessa, Teanum, Aesernia and Nuceria also produced bronzes with distinctive local types, the last in addition fractional pieces.) Apart from these major mints, two minor mints whose location is unknown, Irnum and Malies, produced coinages with similar types, as well as

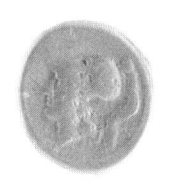

13   The coinage of Campania in the third century

Bronze of Cales:
   Laureate head of Apollo l.; before, CALENO; behind, corn-ear/Man-faced bull r.;
   above, lyre; below, B; in exergue, CALENO   *BMCItaly* 17
Bronze of Cales:
   Helmeted head of Minerva l./Cock r.; on l., star; on r., CALENO   *BMCItaly* 28

fractional pieces. Of the major mints, Cales, Suessa and Teanum produced another group of very large issues with the types, Head of Minerva/Cock; Aquinum, Caiatia and perhaps Telesia also struck with these types.

There is no doubt that all these issues are contemporary with the First Punic War issues of Neapolis, produced in order to aid the Roman military effort (p.34), and they should be regarded as fulfilling a similar function. It is conspicuous that all the mints involved lie in Campania, which we have already seen to be an area with a long tradition of coinage (p.26). The only apparent exceptions are Aquinum and Aesernia; but the former lies very close to Campania to the north and should be regarded as culturally part of Campania; Aesernia, although technically in Samnium, lies on the border between Samnium and Campania and was in any case a Latin colony. Similarly the small issue produced with distinctive local types at Beneventum was produced in an area of Samnium long under heavy Greek influence and again by a Latin colony.

At Paestum, to the south, a substantial issue of bronze coinage covers the period of the First Punic War (it cannot possibly be earlier than the time of the Pyrrhic War).

The other two areas where coinage was probably produced during the First Punic War are Etruria and Umbria on the one hand, Apulia on the other. In northern Umbria, the mint of Ariminum, apart from cast bronze coinage, produced a substantial issue of struck bronzes, with the types Head of Vulcan/Gallic warrior, which circulated fairly widely. Tuder produced struck bronzes in this general period, as did an area, not precisely defined, in eastern Etruria and the city of Vetulonia; the latter issues are tiny, the former enormous (Fig. 14). Given that, like the rest of the coinage of Etruria and Umbria, they did not circulate elsewhere (App. 11 with Map 8), one must assume that if they were evoked by Roman needs during the Pyrrhic War or the First Punic War, soldiers to whom they were paid were only paid at the end of the campaign; this is indeed in any case not unlikely. (There is also a small gold issue which may belong to this period.)

14   Etruscan bronze coinage

Bronze of Etruria, Sambon 146:
    Male head r. wearing animal-skin head-dress/Dog running l.; below, ς BM Cl.I.15
Bronze of Etruria, Sambon 145:
    Head of Negro r./Elephant r.; below, v BM 1946-1-1-31

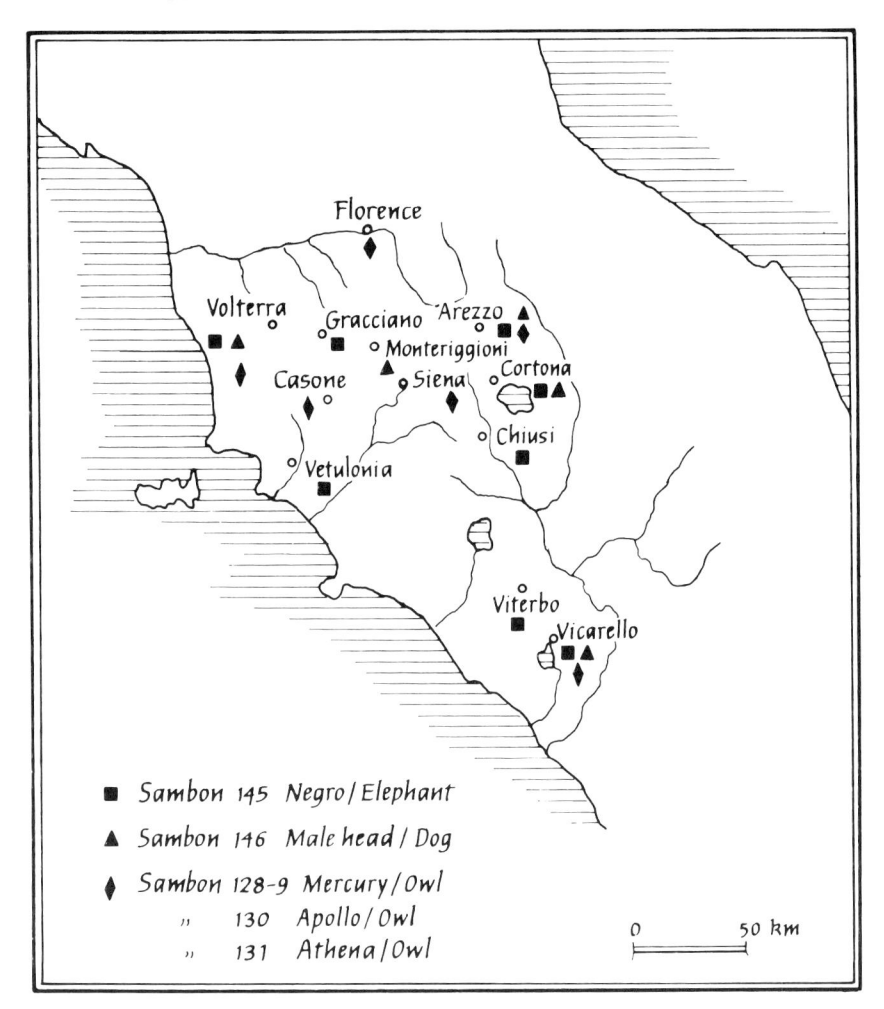

8 The circulation of Etruscan bronze coins
See App. 11

In Apulia the large issues of Arpi with Horse/Bull probably belong during the First Punic War; the early issues of the nearby town of Salapia should probably also be assigned to this period. Further to the north, the one issue of the Frentani cannot be closely dated. It shares a form of legend with the first issue of the chief town of the Frentani, Larinum; both perhaps belong to the period of the First Punic War.

After the ordeal of the First Punic War was over, the coinage produced by Rome consisted simply of a sequence of associated issues of didrachms, struck bronze and cast bronze (Fig. 15). The didrachms and struck bronze now bore the legend ROMA, which represents a move away from the normal Greek pattern of the ethnic in the

15   The ROMA issues

Didrachm of Rome, *RRC*, no. 25/1:
   Helmeted head of Mars r./Horse's head r.; behind, sickle; below, ROMA
   BMCRR Romano-Campanian 59
Didrachm of Rome, *RRC*, no. 26/1:
   Laureate head of Apollo r./Horse l.; above, ROMA
   BMCRR Romano-Campanian 68
Didrachm of Rome, *RRC*, no. 27/1:
   Helmeted head of Mars r.; behind, club/Horse r.; above, club; below, ROMA
   Naples hoard
Bronze unit of Rome, *RRC*, no. 27/2:
   Helmeted head of Mars r.; behind, club/Horse r.; above, club; below, ROMA
   BMCRR Romano-Campanian 53
Bronze double-unit of Rome, *RRC*, no. 27/3:
   Head of Hercules r./Pegasus r.; above, club; below, ROMA   Oxford (obv.), Bari (rev.)
Bronze unit of Rome, *RRC*, no. 27/4:
   Head of Hercules r.; before, L/Pegasus r.; above, bow; below, ROMA
   Paris, A3389 (obv.), A3388 (rev.)

genitive case.[29] At the same time, the end of the war enabled the mint to bring about an improvement in the fineness of the silver didrachms.[30]

Contemporary with the Roman didrachms of the period immediately after the First Punic War is a group of silver issues, again largely from Campania. They were produced by the mints of Cales, Suessa and Teanum, as well as by Cora to the north and Nuceria to the south. It is probably best to regard these isolated issues of silver as struck in order to distribute booty in an appropriately ostentatious manner after the victory over Carthage.

In 240, a contemporary observer would have regarded the traditional coinage systems of Italy as largely intact; although the mints of the south apart from Tarentum had largely ceased operation, the pattern of circulation was superficially similar to what it had long been. A group of hoards contains recent issues of Tarentum in substantial quantities, together with a scattering of earlier issues of other mints of Magna Graecia (App. 12). The Second Punic War was to be far more devastating in its effect.

---

29 For the date of the transition, see A. Burnett (n.4), 114; there is no point in discussing H. W. Ritter, *Zur römischen Münzprägung im 3.Jh.v.Chr.* (Marburg, 1982), since he does not discuss any of the numismatic evidence for chronology.

30 D.R. Walker (n.11), 56.

4

THE SECOND PUNIC WAR

The Roman coinage system from 225 onwards consisted of the last issue of didrachms,[1] with the legend ROMA and the types Janiform heads of Dioscuri/Jupiter in quadriga, and of an associated issue of cast bronze coinage, with the following types (Fig. 16):

As	Head of Janus/Prow
Semis	Head of Saturn/Prow
Triens	Head of Minerva/Prow
Quadrans	Head of Hercules/Prow
Sextans	Head of Mercury/Prow
Uncia	Head of Roma/Prow

The didrachms, or quadrigati, fall into three main groups and four minor groups, distinguished on stylistic grounds. Of the latter, *RRC*, nos. 31–4, little can be said. Of the former, the first, *RRC*, no. 28, accounts for the vast bulk of the quadrigatus coinage; it comprised in its first phase quadrigati, drachms, and gold staters and half-staters with the types Janiform heads of Dioscuri/Oath-taking scene; the purity of the quadrigati and drachms is very high.[2] In its second phase the group comprised quadrigati and a fraction which may be a tenth or a sixth (p.59). The second group, *RRC*, no. 29, likewise comprised quadrigati, drachms, and staters and half-staters; the purity of the quadrigati is again high. The third group, *RRC*, no. 30, comprised only quadrigati and drachms.

A problem arises at this point. It is clear from the analyses already cited that in its second phase the main group was fairly heavily debased; and the two quadrigati

---

[1] For the date see *RRC*, pp.40–2; p.51, n.29, for confirmation of the view that the change in legend from ROMANO to ROMA falls after the First Punic War. The suggestion of E. Lo Cascio (p.41, n.21), 345–8, that the Prow series of cast bronze coinage belongs to the First Punic War, disregards the evidence.

[2] D.R. Walker (p.33, n.11), 56–8.

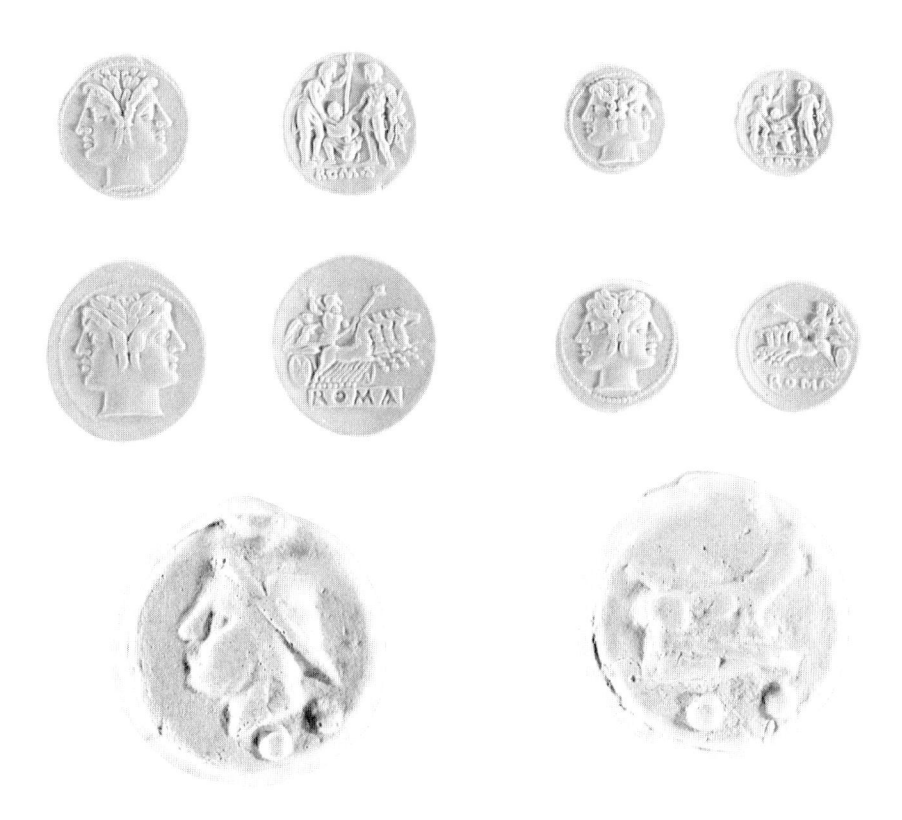

16   The quadrigatus and contemporary cast bronze coinage

Gold stater of Rome, *RRC*, no. 28/1:
  Janiform head of Dioscuri/Oath-taking scene; in exergue, ROMA
  BMCRR Romano-Campanian 75

Gold half-stater of Rome, *RRC*, no. 28/2:
  Janiform head of Dioscuri/Oath-taking scene; in exergue, ROMA
  BMCRR Romano-Campanian 77

Quadrigatus, *RRC*, no. 28/3:
  Janiform head of Dioscuri/Jupiter with thunderbolt and sceptre in quadriga r., driven by
  Victory; on tablet, ROMA   BM Naples hoard 42

Half-quadrigatus, *RRC*, no. 28/4:
  Janiform head of Dioscuri/Jupiter with thunderbolt and sceptre in quadriga l., driven by
  Victory; in exergue, ROMA   *BMCRR* Romano-Campanian 111

Sextans of Rome, *RRC*, no. 35/5:
  Head of Mercury l.; below, two dots/Prow r.; below, two dots   BM cast

17   The denarius system

60–as gold piece, *RRC*, no. 44/2:
   Helmeted head of bearded Mars r.; below, LX/Eagle on thunderbolt; below, ROMA
   BMCRR Rome 185

40–as gold piece, *RRC*, no. 44/3:
   Helmeted head of bearded Mars r.; below, XXXX/Eagle on thunderbolt; below, ROMA
   BMCRR Rome 188

20–as gold piece, *RRC*, no. 44/4:
   Helmeted head of bearded Mars r.; below, XX/Eagle on thunderbolt; below, ROMA
   BM, Clark

Anonymous denarius, *RRC*, no. 44/5:
   Helmeted head of Roma r.; behind, X/Dioscuri r.; on tablet, ROMA   *BMCRR* Italy 90

Anonymous quinarius, *RRC*, no. 44/6:
   Helmeted head of Roma r.; behind, V/Dioscuri r.; on tablet, ROMA
   BMCRR Rome 207

Anonymous sestertius, *RRC*, no. 44/7:
   Helmeted head of Roma r.; behind, IIS/Dioscuri r.; on tablet, ROMA   *BMCRR* Rome 13

so far analysed which can be certainly attributed to the third group were also debased. I suspect that the group comprised also a phase of high purity, to which the drachms and some quadrigati belong; and I am sure that the main group comprised a phase of even greater debasement than emerges from D.R. Walker's analyses, and that at the same time the weight of the quadrigatus was reduced.[3] At this point the didrachm coinage of Rome was at an end.

3 *RRC*, p.570 with n.2; pl.IV, 9; Ailly, pl.XLVI, 3; *BMCRR* Romano-Campanian 150 (in second edition).

17 The denarius system (*cont.*)

Anonymous victoriatus, *RRC*, no. 44/1:
   Laureate head of Jupiter r./Victory r. crowning trophy; in exergue, ROMA
   NC 1970, pl.iv, 1
Anonymous as, *RRC*, no. 56/2:
   Laureate head of Janus; above, I/Prow r.; above, I; below, ROMA   Paris
Anonymous triens, *RRC*, no. 56/4:
   Helmeted head of Minerva r.; above, four dots/Prow r.; above, ROMA; below, four dots
   BMCRR Rome 253

Meanwhile, the weight standard of the cast bronze coinage had also undergone a sequence of changes; the as no doubt still in theory weighed ten ounces at the outbreak of the war, but in practice it weighed rather less (*RRC*, no. 37); the weight standard was reduced first to a semilibral level, with an as in theory of six ounces, then to a triental and finally to a quadrantal level.[4] The year 217 still seems to me the most plausible occasion for the semilibral reduction,[5] given the overall chronology of the Roman coinage of this period.

In or just before 211, an entirely new coinage system was created, based on a

4 The argument of E. Lo Cascio (p.41, n.21), 347–8, that the triental standard did not exist, since if it had existed, semilibral sextantes would have been overstruck into triental quadrantes, is of no weight, since triental quadrantes were cast, not struck.
5 The argument of P. Marchetti, 297–9, that the triental standard belongs to this year, depends on a false chronology for the coinage of Etruria, see *HN*³, s.v.; I accept that it is not possible to use the sum voted for the votive games of 217 as an argument, see P. Marchetti, in *Les dévaluations à Rome* 1 (Rome, 1978), 28–9, though I continue to suspect that there is a relationship between the semilibral reduction and the sum voted.

sextantal standard, on an as of two ounces.[6] The system consisted on the one hand of gold pieces, with the types Head of Mars/Eagle, of 60, 40 and 20 asses (App. 13), of the denarius, quinarius and sestertius, with the types Head of Roma/Dioscuri, of 10, 5 and 2½ asses, and of the as and its fractions, the semis, the triens, the quadrans, the sextans, the uncia, the semuncia; on the other hand, of the victoriatus, with the types Head of Jupiter/Victory crowning trophy, and occasionally its double or its half (Fig. 17).[7] The victoriatus weighed three-quarters of a denarius, but unlike the other elements of the system it bore no mark of value to relate it to that system. I know of no new arguments which might bear on the relative chronology of the victoriatus and the rest of the system; it is clear from the evidence from Morgantina that there can be only the tiniest interval, if any, between victoriatus and denarius, and it seems best to regard them as contemporary.[8] What has become clear as a result of recent analyses is that the victoriatus was struck from the outset with a silver content which fluctuated between less than 95 per cent and less than 75 per cent,[9] while the denarius and its fractions were of a very high degree of purity. If it is true that the victoriatus and the rest of the denarius system were contemporary, it follows that Rome quite deliberately set out to meet a part of its obligations in debased currency. A distribution map of early hoards of victoriati from Italy reveals that they come exclusively from the Greek or Hellenised areas of Apulia, Campania or northern Lucania (for Cisalpine Gaul, see p.75; and for the later pattern in Italy, see p.74) (Map 9).

The rest of the denarius system apart from the victoriatus also reveals the strains which the reform of the coinage had imposed; it is clear that from the outset the

---

6 For the date see T.V. Buttrey, *QTic* 1979, 149, 'Morgantina and the denarius', implicitly refuting the arguments of P. Marchetti, 343, for 214; I am currently preparing a corpus of coin finds from archaeological contexts in Italy, which will establish the date with even greater certainty. It is probable that the new elective office of moneyer was created to oversee the production of the new coinage, *RRC*, pp.601–3; H.B. Mattingly, *AIIN* 29, 1982, 9, 'The management of the Roman Republican mint'; the elective nature of the office emerges with absolute clarity from Cicero, *de leg.* ii, 6.

7 *RRC*, no.95/2; 98A/3 (with anomalous types); p. 89 below. There is no reason whatever to suppose with E. Lo Cascio (p.41, n.21), 351–2, that the presence of the mark of value S on the half carries with it the implication that the victoriatus was thought of as consisting of ten smaller units.

8 *RRC*, p.7. The argument of E. Lo Cascio (p.41, n.21), 348–51, for the priority of the victoriatus depends on the fantastic view that the bronze coinage of the Roman Republic passed from the quadrantal standard to the half and then the quarter thereof, before the sextantal standard was adopted. It suffices to inspect the sequence of issues in Sicily and at Luceria to be convinced of the folly of this notion.

9 D.R. Walker (p.33, n.11), 58–61; a victoriatus (*RRC*, no. 44/1) analysed by A.A. Gordus and J.P. Gordus in C. Beck (ed.), *Archaeological Chemistry* (Washington, 1974), 124, has the following content:
Ar 85.7/83.4
Cu 13.8/16.1
Au 0.45/0.43.
The figure of 65 per cent silver for the victoriati analysed by P. Petrillo Serafin, *Arch.Class.* 1976, 99, 'Ripostigli monetali romano-repubblicani sottoposti ad analisi', seems very dubious.

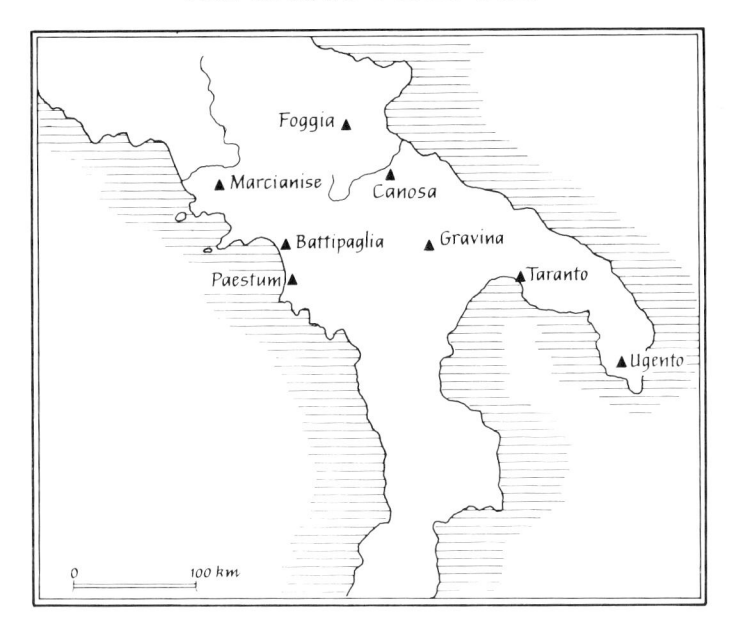

9 Early hoards of victoriati

sextantal standard for the bronze coinage was widely disregarded; and there are even some issues of the denarius or its fractions which are underweight.[10]

When Hannibal invaded Italy in 218, he not only succeeded in inflicting in the course of three years a sequence of devastating defeats on the Romans, but also changed the pattern of coinage in Italy out of all recognition and for ever. The immediate consequence of the Roman loss of control over large areas of Italy was a progressive dispersal of the production of coinage; only with the end of the war was production concentrated once again at the mint of Rome. In addition, it was the strain of the war which led to the rapid reduction in the weight of the Roman bronze unit and the debasement of the Roman silver didrachm. The complete collapse of the Roman monetary system was followed by the creation *ex novo* of the denarius system, which

10 *RRC*, p.596, nn.2–3 for the bronze coinage; it is clear that the issue of dupondii overstruck on sextantal asses is close in time to the date of the asses, since one can see that these were hardly worn when overstruck, *contra* C.A. Hersh, *NC* 1977, 19, 'Notes on the chronology and interpretation of the Roman Republican coinage', at 24; H.B. Mattingly (n.6), at 19, n.46; sextantal asses continued to be produced long after this ephemeral and fiduciary issue of uncial dupondii.

RRC, p.595, n.5 for the silver coinage; a hoard from Cuenca, to be published by L. Villaronga, shows that an even larger number of light denarii belongs in the period of the heavy denarius.

The reconstruction of the monetary history of the Second Punic War by P. Marchetti, 277–353, is built on sand, since it assumes that the existence of an issue on an uncial standard by a certain date implies *the* adoption of *the* uncial standard for bronze.

For the views of P. Marchetti on the retariffing of the denarius, see p.146.

lasted with minor modifications until the third century AD. Meanwhile, a wide variety of mints struck both on behalf of Rome and on behalf of Hannibal; many had never struck before and few struck again after the war was over. The chaotic conditions in which many of the mints striking during the Second Punic War operated emerges very clearly from the prevalence of the practice of overstriking, instead of preparing blanks from scratch; this is as true of Roman coinage as it is of Italian (App. D). One interesting group of overstrikes, on bronzes of Acarnania and Oeniadae, results from the use of booty acquired by Rome in the course of the First Macedonian War (compare App. 26 for a bronze of Acarnania travelling to Cisalpine Gaul with a Roman settler there). Finally, the scale of military activity led to the dispersal of coins far from their mints of origin to an extent not previously witnessed.

One issue of cast bronze coinage was perhaps produced in Cisalpine Gaul before 218 (App. 14), but the crucial step towards the dispersal of the production of coinage by Rome was taken in 217 when the Senate wrote to Mammula, praetor in Sardinia, to say that they were unable to provide for his army and to instruct him to take what steps he could. This did not lead immediately to the production of coinage in Sardinia, but in the course of the next year a Roman mint was established in Sicily, producing *inter alia* cast bronze coinage, which was wholly alien to the monetary traditions of the area. This mint progressively increased production and within the period of the didrachm coinage a mint had been opened at Luceria in Apulia. It may well be that there were already other Roman mints operating in Italy, but the rest of the Roman coinage of this period bears no mint marks and stylistic criteria have proved so far inadequate to distinguish the products of different mints. With the institution of the denarius coinage, the existing Sicilian mint was joined by a second; coinage now began to be produced in Sardinia and two major mints and a number of minor mints began operation in Italy.[11]

Probably the most important consequence of the introduction of the denarius system was the welding of all the different forms of coinage at Rome into a single whole. As we have seen, the earliest Roman coinage consisted of cast bronze asses weighing about a pound and their fractions, together with silver didrachms and token bronze pieces. Once it is admitted that Mommsen's equation between an as and a scruple of silver is wrong,[12] we are left without any specific information on how the two component parts of the earliest Roman coinage were related to each other.[13] Clearly *ad hoc*

---

11 See *RRC*, pp.3–28; also pp.65–6 below.
12 See *RRC*, p.622. I here repeat with modifications the argument of *RRC*, pp.625–8.
13 Gold presumably stood in a fixed relationship to silver, though we have little reliable information on what this was: early evidence from Rome (Livy i, 53, 3; 55, 8; etc.) is clearly fictional (so rightly Th. Mommsen, *RMw*, 197, n.80); a ratio of 1:10 was prescribed apropos of the Aetolian indemnity in 189; thereafter we are in the dark again until the age of Augustus; the equation between gold and silver in Livy xxxviii, 55, 6–12 occurs in a speech and is worthless as evidence (*contra* Th. Mommsen, *RMw*, 402, n.115); for the equation in Suetonius, *Caes.* 54, see p.243, n.6.

equations were made;[14] and I have argued that the first major (semilibral) weight reduction was only possible because the new asses were placed in the same official relationship with silver as the old.[15]

But the earliest evidence of an official equation built into the monetary system is provided by the decussis apparently of the last (quadrantal) weight reduction before the institution of the denarius system (*RRC*, no. 41/1); since for the denarius system the Romans decided to make the silver unit worth ten asses, it is difficult to avoid the conclusion that when the decussis was produced it was worth the same as the then existing silver unit.[16] If this is right, the silver:bronze ratio is 1:120, the same as that displayed by the denarius system.[17] When this was created, gold, silver and bronze were all given marks of value to make their relationship explicit; one scruple of gold was worth 20 asses, four scruples of silver were worth 10 asses; gold:silver is here 1:8, silver:bronze 1:120.[18]

A substantial problem remains. The earliest asses were simply coins weighing a pound of bronze and presumably worth more or less just that (p. 39); on the other hand the face value of both quadrantal and sextantal asses was also probably not far distant from that of their metal content.[19] Yet the purpose of the semilibral reduction was presumably to produce coins of the same face value as before but of lower metal content.[20] At some stage, presumably with the quadrantal standard, this policy was apparently abandoned; an adjustment of state payments must be postulated as a necessary consequence. The occurrence of such an adjustment is attested by the structure of the coinage; for in all issues of cast bronze coinage down to and including the Prow series of semilibral standard the lowest denominations were normally the commonest; with the Prow series of post-semilibral standard the pattern changed

14 See p.40; I no longer believe that totalling is involved in the *elogium* of C. Duillius (*Inscr.Ital.* xiii, 3, no. 69), where 3700 nummi of gold, 200,000–300,000 nummi of silver and 2,900,000–3,400,000 pounds of bronze appear.
15 *JRS* 1964, 29, 'War and finance', at 31.
16 The nomos of 10 litrae common in Sicily provided an obvious precedent; see also p.29 n.3.

Note also the unique fraction of the quadrigatus (*RRC*, no. 28/5); if this was a tenth it was presumably worth an as; but for A. Burnett (p.29, n.2), 139, the coin was a sixth; Varro, *LL* v, 174, *nummi denarii* (in error for *quadrigati*) *decuma libella ... et erat ex argento parva*, is in any case most likely to be only the result of learned speculation.
17 6 scruples of silver = in bronze 10 by 72 scruples (the theoretical weight of a quadrantal as); note that the weight standard of the decussis is not absolutely certain (R. Thomsen (p.43, n.23), 42).
18 For an earlier discussion of the contrast between the two systems see *JRS* 1964, 30–1; I remain convinced that the Oath-scene gold piece with the mark of value XXX is false (see *RRC*, p.548), despite its casual acceptance by P. Marchetti, 318.
19 A ratio of silver:bronze of 1:120 was normal for the Hellenistic world, M.J. Price, *Essays in Greek Coinage presented to Stanley Robinson* (Oxford, 1968), 90, 'Early Greek bronze coinage', at 103; see also E.S.G. Robinson (n.25 below), 41.

As the Roman Republic coined and put into circulation ever greater quantities of silver (on a scale unparalleled in the Greek world), bronze perhaps became relatively more valuable; silver:copper under Augustus is perhaps notionally 1:55, see p.260.
20 See n.15 above.

markedly and the as became (as it was for the whole of the first half of the second century) the commonest denomination; clearly at this point and this point only were soldiers paid enough for asses to be needed in large quantities and for the as to become the characteristic component of legionary pay (Table 3). By contrast, the levels of census assessments were apparently not changed.[21]

I should therefore wish to reconstruct the monetary history of the period from 218 to 211 thus:

	PRECIOUS METAL	BRONZE
218	Didrachms of 6 scruples	Libral, tariffed at intrinsic value
217	Unchanged	Semilibral, thus becoming fiduciary
216	(Gold issue)	Unchanged
215–214	Unchanged	Post-semilibral (triental to quadrantal); when quadrantal, tariffed at intrinsic value again, with consequential adjustment of state payments
214	(Tenth of didrachm)	(Decussis)
213–212	Silver debased	Unchanged
211	Denarius	Sextantal

The creation of the denarius system thus falls in two stages: a rash attempt to restore the bronze coinage as a coinage of intrinsic value led to pressure on the silver coinage, which was debased; Rome then took special measures to acquire bullion, as we shall see in a moment, and was able to restore the silver coinage and relate it to a bronze coinage of sextantal as opposed to quadrantal standard.

The account here given of the history of the monetary system of Rome during the Second Punic War fits well with what is known of the financial vicissitudes of the same period. In the early years of the war, metal (for coinage) seems to have been available. Apart from *tributum* and other normal sources of revenue, not to mention reserves, there was a loan from Hieron in 216 (Livy xxiii, 21, 5). In 215 a *tributum duplex* was decided on, presumably in contrast to *tributum simplex* hitherto (Livy xxiii, 31, 1–2). But at this point sources of revenue dried up. The loan from Hieron could not be repaid (Livy xxiii, 38, 12) and at the end of the year there was no money available with which to supply the Spanish army (Livy xxiii, 48, 4–8).

A novel method of financing Roman operations was adopted, the use of credit.[22] The contract for supplies to the Spanish army was let on the condition that payment would be made later (Livy xxiii, 48, 9–49, 4). The following year sailors were paid directly by wealthy individuals, not by the state (Livy xxiv, 11, 7–9), and credit was

---

21 Livy xxiv, 11, 7–8 (see p.150).
22 The use of credit included in 215 the reduction of the weight standard of the bronze coinage to a triental level, the coinage thereby becoming even more fiduciary than it was already.

TABLE 3. Growth in the volume of production of the as

RRC	14	18	21	24	25	26	27	35	36	38	39	41	57-8
Decussis	.	.	.	.	.	.	.	.	.	.	.	3	.
Quincussis	.	.	.	.	.	.	.	.	.	.	.	1[1]	.
Tressis	.	.	.	1	.	.	.	.	.	.	.	17	.
Dupondius	.	.	.	14	.	.	.	.	.	.	.	19	.
As	95	104	18	44	18	7	22	1168[2]	80	40	.	365	19[3]
Semis	108	100	30	70	55	3	54	312	32	46	.	200	7
Triens	160	111	39	76	52	.	47	395	28	18	54	96	6
Quadrans	136	128	36	83	69	2	62	266	21	26	59	45	2
Sextans	203	163	85	130	67	1	63	208	45	219	96	106[4]	2
Uncia	102	105	135	.	35	.	74	184	.	271	73	172[4]	3
Semuncia	76	.	64	.	.	.	.	.	.	346	79	24[4]	.
Quartuncia	.	.	.	.	.	.	.	.	.	92	.	.	.

The figure for each issue and denomination represents the number of coins listed by Haeberlin, unless otherwise stated.

1   Unique piece, not known to Haeberlin.
2   This enormous total must be discounted; it is almost entirely accounted for by the existence of a single hoard, the Cerveteri hoard, which contained 1569 asses of this issue and most of which passed into the collections studied by Haeberlin.
3   The figures in this column are those provided by the Paris collection.
4   This figure includes one piece with corn-ear (for the uncia with corn-ear, Haeberlin's no.151, see Haeberlin's illustration).

again used, to finance the building operations of the censors (Livy xxiv, 18, 10-11, cf. 2 for *inopia aerari*). The owners of slaves manumitted to fight refused payment for the time being (Livy xxiv, 18, 12). After contributing their possessions, orphans and widows were to be supported by state purchases on credit on their behalf (Livy xxiv, 18, 13-14). Equites and centurions offered to do without their pay (Livy xxiv, 18, 15).

But from 212 onwards metal again began to become available and the state in addition took active steps to make it available. Booty was coming in almost every year from 212 (Syracuse) onwards, down to 206 (Spain).[23] In addition, the state used the triumviri mensarii to levy metal from private individuals in Rome when faced with an empty treasury in 210 (Livy xxvi, 35-6; Festus, s.v. *Tributorum conlationem*) – one

23 See T. Frank, *ESAR* I, 80-1 and 83; after Syracuse (Livy xxv, 31, 8-11) there was Capua (xxvi, 14, 8), Nova Carthago (xxvi, 47, 7; Polybius x, 19), Tarentum (xxvii, 16, 7; Plutarch, *Fab*. 22) and the battle of the Metaurus (xxvii, 49, 6; Polybius xi, 3); for booty from Spain in 206 see xxviii, 38, 5. The produce of the Spanish mines will also have become available from 209 onwards. It is not clear how it was intended to finance the building programme of 212 (xxv, 7, 5).

of the very rare occasions on which an ancient state effectively mobilised the resources of its wealthy members; the gold in the *aerarium sanctius* was also used in 209 (Livy xxvii, 10, 11–13); and money was raised by renting out the *ager Campanus* (Livy xxvii, 11, 8.) It is significant that 2,400,000 denarii could be provided in 210 for Scipio to take to Spain (Polybius x, 19, 1–2), though the fact that pay was in arrears by 206 (Polybius xi, 25–30 with commentary of F.W. Walbank) provides eloquent testimony of the narrowness of the margin on which the Romans operated.

Credit financing, by contrast, disappears from the record, until Scipio was forced to use it in 205, perhaps partly for political reasons, as well as financial ones (though the state was forced soon after to sell land to raise cash, Livy xxviii, 46, 4). The year 211 stands out as the beginning of a period in which the production of the new denarius coinage was eminently possible.[24]

It is time to turn to the other coinages of Italy of the period of the Second Punic War, whether struck for Rome or for Hannibal (App. 15). The finances of the Carthaginian invasion of Italy are not easy to unravel. There is no evidence that Hannibal brought with him any of the coinage produced by the Carthaginians in Spain (p.87) and no trace of issues of any size produced by him before the last years of the war, when he was hemmed in in Bruttium;[25] at this point he may be regarded as running what almost amounted to a separate state with the production of coinage as a corollary,[26] but it looks as if in the initial stages he expected to keep his troops happy with booty and the expectation of rewards at the end, while living off the country and the allies of Carthage.

These, on the other hand, tended to produce substantial coinages from the moment of their revolt from Rome. Obviously, the wish to symbolise independence will have played a part; but this cannot explain the size of some of the issues and it appears that the communities in question possessed fiscal structures in which the production of coinage had a substantial role to play. There is in this context now no significant difference between the practice of long-established Greek mints and that in areas only recently introduced to the use of coined money (p.36).

Hannibal's greatest prize was perhaps Capua, which joined him after the battle of Cannae, along with its allies Atella and Calatia. All produced coinage, Capua in

---

24 I should perhaps say in passing that there is not a shred of evidence for linked monetary fluctuations in Egypt and Rome, *contra* L.H. Neatby, *TAPA* 1950, 89, 'Roman-Egyptian relations during the third century BC', at 94; Cl. Nicolet, *Annales* 1963, 417, 'A Rome pendant la seconde guerre punique'.

    The attempt of P. Marchetti to construct a balance sheet for the Roman Republic during the Second Punic War, 274–5, is wholly forlorn; quite apart from uncertainties over the pay of the Roman soldier (p.145), Livy xxxix, 7, 5, can only by the reckless cumulation of hypotheses be regarded as providing evidence for the *tributum* levied by Rome during the war.

25 The classic account is that of E.S.G. Robinson, *NC* 1964, 37, 'Carthaginian and other south Italian coinages of the Second Punic War'.

26 There is no evidence for the view that the Carthaginian issues in Italy adopted a Roman or Italian weight standard, *contra* P. Marchetti, 432–6.

18 The coinage of Capua

Gold piece of Capua:
   Head of Tanit l./Victory in biga r.; in exergue, *k*   BM 1919–11–20–19
Silver piece of Capua:
   Head of Jupiter r./Eagle r. on thunderbolt; on r., *kapu*   BM 1937–6–6–19
Sextans of Capua:
   Head of Hercules r./ Lion r. holding spear; above, two dots; in exergue, *kapu*
                                                                                                          BMCItaly 2
Sextans of Capua:
   Laureate head of Jupiter r.; on l., two stars/Oath-taking scene; on l., two stars; in
   exergue, *kapu*   *BMCItaly* 6
Uncia of Capua:
   Head of Diana r./Boar r.; above, dot; in exergue, *kapu*   *BMCItaly* 4

gold, silver and bronze, the latter on a very large scale, Atella and Calatia in bronze, on a small scale (Fig. 18). The gold of Capua consisted of drachms of Attic weight, the silver of reduced didrachms (compare the coinage of the Brettii, p.67). All three mints overstruck Roman pieces in order to produce their own bronze issues; one has the impression that almost the entire coinage of Atella was produced by this means (App. D). The weight standard adopted by Capua was the Roman quadrantal standard; issues on a sextantal standard followed; financial difficulties forced Capua to abandon even this standard for its last issues before its recapture in 211.

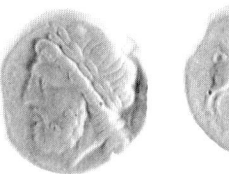

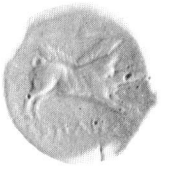

19 The coinage of Arpi and Salapia

Bronze of Arpi:
  Laureate head of Zeus l.; before, ΔAZOY; behind, thunderbolt/Boar r.; above, spearhead; in exergue, ΑΡΠΑΝΩΝ   McClean 406
Bronze of Salapia:
  Laureate head of Zeus r.; before, ΣΑΛΑΠΙΝΩΝ; behind, thunderbolt/ Boar r.; above, wreath; in exergue, [Π]ΛΩΠΙΟ[Υ]   McClean 472

Two problems arise. It is striking that the bronze unit of the rebel cities was divided into ten not twelve, denominations from the quincunx downwards being produced. I know of no evidence that this division existed at Capua earlier and suppose that its use resulted from a wish to differentiate the new coinage from the Roman coinage as sharply as possible, despite the basic similarity of weight standard. There is also a curious group of silver issues marked oo, oΠ, and o; Π clearly stands for *pente*, five, and we have here a double, a one-and-a-half piece and a unit. The pieces bear no legend; but the ratio of bronze to silver is acceptable if we equate the unit with the bronze unit of Capua of quadrantal standard and the system of reckoning links the pieces with Capua.

The other major cities to fall to Hannibal after Cannae were Arpi and Tarentum. The city of Salapia, close to and often associated with Arpi, was not taken by Hannibal until 214; Arpi was recaptured in 213, Salapia in 210. The Second Punic War coinages of the two cities are nonetheless homogeneous and clearly belong together (Fig. 19).

They also provide a key to the understanding of the coinages of Apulia as a whole in this period. Both are purely Greek in character, without marks of value, and stand in marked contrast to the Apulian coinages which consist of issues without marks of value as well as issues with marks of value, on the Roman model. Since most of these coinages were small and do not turn up in hoards, the problem of dating them is substantial; but a plausible pattern emerges if one places the two categories either side of the Roman shift to the denarius system, with its careful use of marks of value

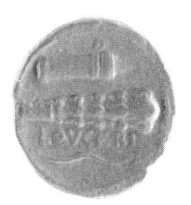

20 The coinage of Luceria

Quincunx of Luceria:
   Helmeted head of Minerva r.; above, five dots/Wheel; between spokes, LOVCERI   BM
Triens of Luceria:
   Head of Hercules r./Quiver, club, LOVCERI, bow   BM

everywhere except on the victoriatus and the double victoriatus. It remains true, of course, that the issues without marks of value *may* be somewhat earlier.

In the north of Apulia, the Roman effort clearly depended heavily not only on the purely Roman coinage produced at Luceria, but also on the native products of that mint and on the mints of Venusia, Teate and, to a lesser extent, Larinum (Fig. 20). The native products of the mint of Luceria consisted, as we have seen, of cast bronze coinage, on a heavy and a reduced standard (p.45). These issues were followed by a purely struck series; at various times the nummus, its half, the quincunx, and denominations down to the semuncia were produced. At Venusia, there were again heavy and reduced issues of cast bronze coinage, followed by two issues of struck bronze coinage; in the last phase, the double nummus and the nummus, of twenty and ten unciae, were struck, marked N.II and N.I.

Further north, at Teate and Larinum, there were no issues of cast bronze coinage, but two issues and one issue respectively of bronze on the Greek model, without marks of value. At Teate in the next phase, the nummus and denominations from quincunx to uncia were struck, at Larinum, denominations from quincunx to semuncia. It is remarkable that a substantial element of the coinage of Venusia was produced by overstriking the coinage of friend and foe alike; there is one overstrike on a coin of the Brettii, one on a coin of Brundisium, one on a coin of Campania, two on coins of Rome (App. D).

The Romans seem to have found the decimal division of the unit at Luceria confusing. After their own initial perfectly normal issue there (*RRC*, no. 43), they avoided striking the as (*RRC*, no. 97), but struck instead the dextans, with the mark of value S°°°°; this was clearly regarded as ten twelfths of the Roman as, but was, I suggest, regarded as the equivalent of the Lucerian unit and deliberately left as the

21 The coinage of Brundisium

Semis of Brundisium:
  Laureate head of Neptune r.; on l., Victory; on r., M. BIT/Dolphin-rider l. holding
  Victory and lyre; above, S; below, BRVN *BMCItaly* 14

Quadrans of Brundisium:
  Laureate head of Neptune r.; on l., Victory; below, three dots/ Dolphin-rider r. holding
  lyre; on l., Victory and monogram; below, BRVN and three dots BM

largest Roman denomination produced. Only at the very end was the dextans replaced by the as.[27]

The other coinage which stands out is the coinage of the harbour town and Latin colony of Brundisium, produced on an enormous scale (Fig. 21). Purely Roman in character, it was produced first on a post-semilibral standard, then on a sextantal standard and finally, perhaps still during the Second Punic War, on a range of much lighter standards, no doubt as a result of financial stress. It is reasonable to suppose that the entire coinage is to be related to Roman naval activity in Greece in connection with the First Macedonian War and, perhaps, with the Second Macedonian War and the war against Antiochus III.

When Tarentum joined Carthage after the battle of Cannae, the acropolis remained in Roman hands. The Hannibalic coinage of Tarentum should be regarded as covering the entire period of the revolt; at the same time, the mint of Metapontum began production again. Both mints struck half and quarter shekels,[28] Tarentum perhaps gold,[29] both mints bronze.[30]

But the most impressive numismatic products of the Carthaginian invasion of Italy were the coinages of Hannibal himself in Bruttium, and of his Bruttian and Lucanian allies. These coinages are particularly well known because the final recapture of the area by the Romans led to the burial and loss of an enormous number of hoards; these indeed reveal only too well the scale of the disaster which befell this part of Italy (App. 16).

27 I should now regard *RRC*, no. 97/23 as merely a light specimen of no. 97/16; note the style.
28 Not victoriati, *contra* P. Marchetti, 440–1; by randomly designating a coinage as overvalued or not, it is possible to make almost any issue the same denomination as any other.
29 P. Marchetti, 437–8.
30 P. Marchetti, 455–7.

22 The Italian coinage of Carthage

Half-shekel of Carthage struck in Bruttium:
   Head of Tanit l./ Horse r.; above, *uraeus*   BM cast
Bronze unit of Carthage struck in Bruttium:
   Head of Tanit l./Horse's head r.   BM cast

It remains unclear how far Hannibal struck coins before he came to base himself in Bruttium (Fig. 22). There are two issues of electrum fractions of the shekel, of the same fineness, one with types adopted from the Roman quadrigatus, the other with normal Punic types, Head of Tanit/Horse. The vertical die-axis may be cited in both cases as an argument for Carthage as a mint, but since one issue of purely Italian provenance has this die-axis it seems better to regard the rule as allowing of exceptions than to suppose that coins were minted at Carthage solely for use in Italy.

As far as the electrum is concerned, the first issue seems Italian because of its typology and because of its provenance;[31] the second has some African provenances and a multiple of the shekel which goes with it is in the museum at Cagliari.

The rest of the Hannibalic coinage of Italy is straightforward and belongs entirely to Bruttium. There is an issue of silver quarter-shekels, with vertical die-axis, but exclusively Bruttian provenance; an issue of silver half-shekels and quarter-shekels, with an associated issue of bronze, with Head of Apollo/Horse, all with irregular die-axis; and an issue of silver half-shekels and quarter-shekels, which shares with issues of the Brettii a tiny Γ as engraver's mark; finally, a large group of bronzes, units and halves. It should be noted that the weight standard of the Punic issues of Bruttium does not seem to have anything to do with that of the issues of the Brettii.

The coinage of the Brettii is particularly impressive in its complexity (Fig. 23). After an initial issue of bronze, of the same weight as the large bronzes of Hieron II and the Mamertini, there followed an issue in silver associated with an issue in bronze consisting of unit, half, quarter and sixth. The piece of silver weighed about 5.80 gm. and may be regarded like the comparable piece from Capua (p.63) as a reduced

---

31 There are eight pieces in the Museo Nazionale di Napoli, one in the Museo Civico di Lucera and perhaps two from Manduria (A. Travaglini, *Inventario dei rinvenimenti monetali del Salento* (Rome, 1982), 156).

23 The coinage of the Brettii and Lucani

Gold piece of Brettii:
  Diademed head of Poseidon l.; below, dolphin and Γ/Amphitrite with Eros on sea-horse r.; on r., shell; below, ΒΡΕΤΤΙΩΝ   BM *PCG* V C II

Silver piece of Brettii:
  Head of Nike r.; on l., shell/Standing nude figure wearing horned head-dress and holding staff in l. hand; on l., ΒΡΕΤΤΙΩΝ; on r., candelabrum; above, dolphin   BM 1938–6–15–15

Bronze of Brettii:
  Helmeted, bearded head of Ares l.; olive-wreath around/Enyo r. holding shield and spear; on l., ΒΡΕΤΤΙΩΝ; on r., M and lyre   BM, Lloyd 555

Silver piece of Lucani:
  Helmeted head of Athena r./Corn-ear; on l., monogram; on r., club; owl countermark   BM, Lloyd 262

Bronze of Lucani:
  Laureate head of Zeus r./Eagle l.; around, ΛΟΥΚΑΝΟΜ   BM, Skinner 1

Bronze of Brettii:
  Laureate head of Zeus r./Eagle l.; on l., thunderbolt; around, ΒΡΕΤΤΙΩΝ   *BMCItaly* 79

didrachm. Given the inter-relationship of the pieces in bronze I find it tempting to regard them as (fiduciary) drachm, triobol, trihemiobol and obol.

The next group of issues consisted of gold drachms and hemidrachms on the Attic standard and pieces in silver weighing 4.80 gm. and 2.40 gm. It seems to me perverse to suppose that the latter have anything to do with the denarius and I should suppose that they represent a radically reduced didrachm and drachm.

All the issues so far mentioned usually bear the Γ which we have seen as an engraver's mark on Punic issues and its absence from the great block of issues in bronze which remain provides a prima facie reason for supposing that none of these are contemporary with the gold and silver just described. There is a further reason. There are four groups of bronze of the Brettii which are in question, with the first three of which bronze of the Lucani is associated. These issues have precisely the same weights and structures, but come from a people whose silver issue was a Punic half-shekel. Since the bronze cannot fit naturally with both Brettian and Lucanian silver it may be best to suppose that it fits with neither. It consists of doubles, units, halves, quarters and sixths and I should suppose that we are dealing with (fiduciary) didrachms, drachms, triobols, trihemiobols and obols.

Apart from the coinages of Hannibal and of the Brettii and the Lucani, the emergence of what I have characterised as a Carthaginian state in Bruttium evoked substantial coinages in bronze at Locri and Croton.[32] It may also be that the mint of Terina was revived in this period. A mint which had never struck before, that of Petelia, was certainly pressed into service to produce within a very brief period a substantial coinage (App. E). In the area between Bruttium and Tarentum lay Thurium and Heraclea,[33] both for a time unwilling allies of Hannibal; they too were forced to contribute to the war effort.

On the west coast of Italy, there are two major coinages whose production should be related to the Roman effort in the Second Punic War, that of Paestum and the last issues of Etruria.[34] At Paestum two series of issues were produced, the first anonymous, ranging from sextans to quartuncia of sextantal standard; the second distinguished by various symbols, ranging from triens to uncia, of light sextantal standard.

The issues of Etruria, mostly of Populonia, are even more extensive (Fig. 24). The silver coinage of Populonia as a whole consisted of three phases, with pieces marked X (= 10 units) weighing first 8.30 8.00 gm., then a half of this, then a quarter. Other denominations in silver were also struck. Associated with the second phase is a coinage in gold and issues in bronze, as well as issues in bronze of Vetulonia; associated with the third phase are issues in bronze, as well as issues in bronze of Vetulonia. The

---

32 See P. Marchetti, 446–51, for Locri.
33 See P. Marchetti, 451–4, for Thurium.

34 There are a couple of bronze and a couple of silver issues of Etruria which cannot be precisely assigned.

24 Late Etruscan silver coinage

Didrachm of Populonia:
   Facing head of Gorgon; below, XX/Crosses BM, Lloyd 5
Didrachm of Populonia:
   Facing head of Hercules/Club *BMCItaly* 1
Didrachm of Populonia:
   Facing head of Minerva/Star and crescent; around, *pupluna* BM, Lloyd 8
Drachm of Populonia:
   Laureate head of Apollo r.; behind, X/Blank BM, Lloyd 24

coinage of the first phase seems quite detached from and much earlier than the coinage of the second phase (p.2).

The vast bulk of the coinage consists of silver pieces marked XX (= 20 units) of the second phase, which displays all the marks of being an emergency coinage; some dies are now represented by as many as 110 specimens, others by a single specimen. In addition, a proportion of the issue is heavily debased. Perhaps contemporary, but produced elsewhere, is a second group of silver issues, where the piece marked Λ (= 5 units) is initially 11.00 gm.; a reduction of the standard to a half followed.

Given the coastal situation of Paestum, Populonia and Vetulonia, I should be tempted to regard the coinages under discussion here as evoked by the naval preparations of the Second Punic War.

We have already seen that a large part of the coinage produced by and for Hannibal in Bruttium went underground and stayed there with the recovery of the area by the Romans. But I suspect that the bronze issues of the allies and enemies of Rome during the Second Punic War functioned as part of the circulating medium at any rate for a time to a greater extent than the evidence suggests at first sight. There are two reasons for this supposition. In the first place a number of hoards basically of Roman bronze contain isolated Italian or even Ptolemaic pieces and it is reasonable to suppose that these were treated as the Roman denomination to which they most closely corresponded in size (App. 20); it is clear that there was no ideological barrier to the circulation of 'rebel' issues. In the second place, one of the consequences of the Hannibalic War was the dispersal far to the north of Sicilian and south Italian coins; many are very worn, presumably as a result of prolonged circulation, and it would be unreasonable to suppose that no part of the process occurred after the coins had left their places of origin (Apps. 17–18). It is also worth drawing attention to the Larino hoard, which would not be available for study were it not for recent scientific excavations, consisting of bronzes of Larinum, Luceria and Salapia, with Roman silver and bronze (App. 20). But by the middle of the second century, Roman bronze coinage was clearly dominant throughout Italy, except perhaps in the territories of those few Italian communities which continued to produce coinage in the second century. As far as silver is concerned, even before 211, the sheer scale on which Roman coinage was being produced to finance the war against Hannibal had resulted in the simple submergence of the other coinages of the Italian peninsula (App. 19).

The Italian mints which functioned in the early second century are those of Paestum, perhaps Velia, Vibo, Rhegium, Copia, perhaps Heraclea, Brundisium and Ancona. The thing which unites the mints under consideration is that they were all harbours, in a period when Rome required fleets for use against Philip V, Antiochus III and Perseus. It is also clear (Livy xxxv, 16, 3; Polybius xii, 5, 1–3, on Locri in the 150s) that the contribution of ships at the demand of Rome involved a community in expense and it seems reasonable to suppose that this fact lies behind the issues of Paestum and the other cities.[35]

The only issues in Italy which are certainly later than the first generation of the second century are those of Paestum, Velia and Heraclea. The last two, allied communities to the Social War, then *municipia*, struck bronze coinage down to the end of the second century and in the case of Velia down to the age of Caesar; Paestum, a Latin colony to the Social War, then briefly a *municipium*, then a Roman colony, struck down to the age of Tiberius.[36] I should be inclined to regard the continuation of coinage at Velia and Heraclea as the consequence of the preservation relatively intact of the structures of a Greek *polis*. I was clearly once much too cavalier in arguing that the continuation of coinage at Paestum at this date required no special

---

[35] The provision of ships (and presumably crews) by an Italian community has nothing to do with the manning of *Roman* ships, the crews of which consisted by the time of the Second Punic War of Romans, slaves and foreigners indiscriminately (Th. Mommsen, *St.* 659, n.3), who were paid by Rome (Livy xxiii, 21, 2).

[36] There is no call to discuss the traditional view that such matters were regulated by Rome.

explanation.[37] I should now be inclined to explain the perpetuation of coinage at Paestum in terms of the proximity of Velia; the coinage of Velia certainly circulated at Paestum.[38] This view is compatible with the near certainty that issues of coinage at Paestum were sometimes, perhaps increasingly, struck in order to be distributed to the citizens by members of the elite, and not to serve any real fiscal need. The fact that no other mints followed the examples of Heraclea, Velia and Paestum may be explained in terms of an absence of resources, an absence of occasion and above all an absence of will, in the face of the sheer volume of coinage issued by Rome.

With the end of the Second Punic War, the production of coinage was concentrated at the mint of Rome (Fig. 25). The production of issues of gold had ceased in 209, that of the sestertius had probably ceased by the same time; the quinarius perhaps lasted a little longer and two isolated issues were produced during the early second century, each attested by a single surviving specimen.[39] But the silver coinage of Rome in the first generation of the second century consisted essentially of denarius and victoriatus, the latter produced only intermittently. I assume that the mint saw no reason to avoid the occasional production of a fiduciary denomination (p.56). Since the denarius was now struck at 84, not at 72, to the pound, the weight of the victoriatus was correspondingly lower.

But the vast bulk of the coinage produced by Rome was in bronze; for nearly a decade, indeed, in the 160s and the 150s, the production of silver was virtually suspended. The armies of the Republic in this period must have been paid largely or entirely in bronze.[40] The dominance of bronze during the first generation of the second century emerges not only from the pattern of the coin hoards of the period (App. 20), but also from the role which early second-century issues played in circulation for three whole centuries after they were produced. Hoards which are certainly of the late Republic, because they contain one or two pieces of that period, may otherwise consist almost entirely of asses of the late third or early second century. Early Republican asses were halved in enormous quantities in the Augustan age (p.261). And as late as the reign of Nerva, 13 per cent of the Bolsena hoard still consisted of asses of this period.

The pattern of production of the Republican bronze coinage, indeed, makes it difficult to date some hoards with precision. As we shall see, the as was not struck between the issue of C. Antestius (p.183) and that of C. Fonteius and then only in relatively restricted quantities; as a result, hoards of asses only may always and must sometimes belong to the second half of the second or indeed to the first century. For

---

37 *La monetazione di bronzo di Poseidonia-Paestum* (*AIIN* 18–19 Supp.) (Rome, 1973), 47, 'Paestum and Rome. The form and function of a subsidiary coinage'.

38 P. Ebner, *RIN* 1970, 10, 'Rinvenimenti monetari a Paestum'. There is no likelihood whatever that the group of coins from c.300 to Tiberius, reported at 21, either comes from Croton or is a hoard (= *Coin Hoards* 2, 132).

39 As *RRC*, no. 139/1 (University of Pavia); *RRC*, no. 156/2.

40 I doubt whether the mention of a *nummus argenteus* in the military oath located by L. Cincius in 190 (Gellius xvi, 4, 2) is authentic.

25 Roman silver and bronze coinage of the early second century

Denarius of Cn. Domitius, *RRC*, no. 147/1:
　Helmeted head of Roma r.; behind, X/Dioscuri r.; below, CN.DO; in frame, ROMA
　　　　　　　　　　　　　　　　　　　　　　　　　　　　　　　　Paris, A9127
As of Cn. Domitius, *RRC*, no. 147/2:
　Laureate head of Janus; above, I/Prow r.; above, CN.DOM; before, I; below, ROMA
　　　　　　　　　　　　　　　　　　　　　　　　　　　　　　　　Berlin
Quadrans of C. Saxula, *RRC*, no. 176/4:
　Head of Hercules r.; behind, three dots/Prow r.; above, C.SAX; before, three dots;
　below, ROMA　　　　　　　　　　　　　　　　　　　　　　　　Munich
Sextans of Maenius, *RRC*, no. 143/5:
　Head of Mercury r.; above, two dots/Prow r.; above, shield and MAE; before, two dots;
　below, ROMA　　　　　　　　　　　　　　　　　　　　　　　BM 1938–4–8–13
Semis of Q. Marius, *RRC*, no. 148/2:
　Laureate head of Saturn r.; behind, S/Prow r.; above, Q.MARI; before, S; below,
　ROMA　　　　　　　　　　　　　　　　　　　　　　　　Rochetta à Volturno hoard

instance, the Fontanarosa hoard contains no fractions of the as, but many halved asses; this fact and the degree of wear which the hoard displays allow us to attribute it to the Augustan age.

Nonetheless, there are some hoards of asses and fractions, showing where preserved no signs of long circulation, which may with some reason be regarded as buried soon after the date of the latest coin in the hoard; they stand in striking contrast to the absence of hoards of denarii between the Second Punic War and the Rome hoard of the 150s (*RRCH* 131). These bronze hoards also come from almost all areas of peninsular Italy, Etruria, Latium, Appennine Italy (App. 20). In this respect they stand in contrast to a different phenomenon, namely the later pattern of circulation of the victoriatus. We have seen (p.56) that in the beginning this coin circulated in the Greek areas of Italy; it penetrated early to Cisalpine Gaul, where it became the unit of reckoning (p.81). But in peninsular Italy, late hoards of victoriati, either with denarii which date them or so worn that they must belong to the same period, occur without exception in Appennine Italy (App. 20); I have no explanation to offer of this pattern, which does not seem random (compare App. N). The presence of silver in some form is in any case a prelude to the later presence of denarii in enormous quantities.

5

THE PO VALLEY[1]

The material culture of the Po and Adige valleys was distinct from that of peninsular Italy from the beginning of the Bronze Age in the early second millennium onwards; by the time the Romans appeared on the scene, diversity within the area had been substantially reduced by the Celtic invasion (Map 10). In the zone in the south-east now known as Emilia, a distinctive local culture overlaid by the Etruscan domination of about 525–400 was overwhelmed by the Boii and the Lingones. In the north-west, the peoples characterised by the culture known as the Golasecca culture, which centred on the valleys of the Lago Maggiore and the Lago di Como and penetrated into those of the Lago d'Orta and the Lago d'Iseo, saw at least the lower parts of their valleys settled by the Libici and the Insubres; to their east lay the Cenomani. Only in the north-east beyond the Adige did the Veneti, despite some Celtic settlement, remain independent. Continuity in this last area down to the Roman period means that the archaeological and inscriptional record of the area is relatively good, revealing a partly urbanised and partly literate society at least from the fifth century.

The archaeological record of the Celts themselves is poor,[2] partly no doubt because they occupied the Po valley for less than two centuries before the Roman conquest began, partly because they settled for the most part in the centre of the valley, an area subject to erosion and silting by the river and also to the systematic structuring of the land which accompanied the eventual process of Roman settlement. There is little trace of anything that can be called urbanisation in pre-Roman Cisalpine Gaul, except in the territory of the Veneti, though there is some evidence for social differentiation. In any case, the accumulation of wealth by individuals in a society which expected wealth to be redistributed is not necessarily very significant; and we should not follow our Roman sources in minimising the degree of organisation achieved by that society.

1 See the important recent account of the Po valley during the Republic in P.A. Brunt, *Italian Manpower* (Oxford, 1971), Ch.13.

2 See the fine analysis by M. Zuffa, in *I Galli e l'Italia* (Rome, 1978), 138.

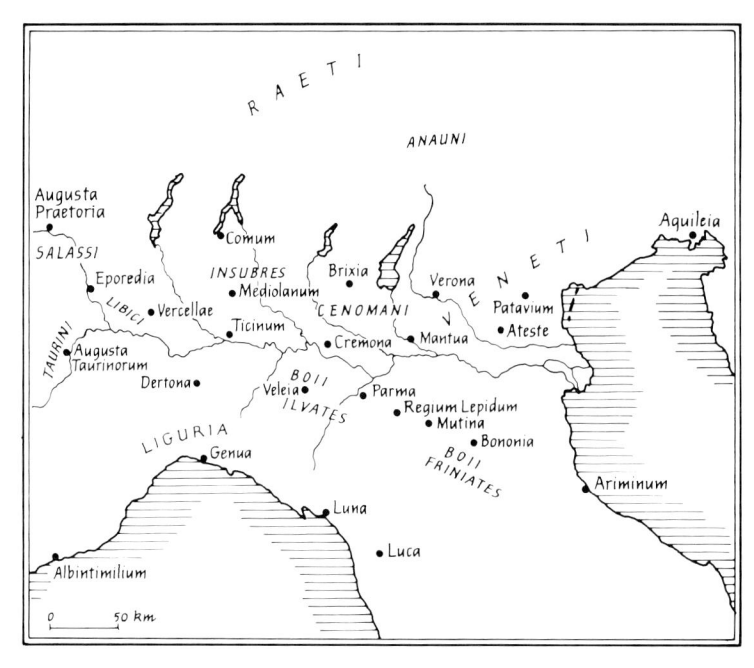

10   The Po valley

In many ways a knowledge of the coinage of Cisalpine Gaul helps us to an assessment of the communities which lived there, rather than vice versa.

This coinage consisted essentially of silver units copied probably from the first issue of the light drachms of Massalia, produced from about 225 onwards (p.161). Much is unclear about this coinage, despite the impressive work of A. Pautasso. He has identified twelve main groups of 'drachms' with weights ranging from 2.90 gm. to 2.00 gm. and a variable silver content;[3] four of the groups bear the names TOVTIOPOVOS, PIRAKOS, ANAREKARTOS (all retrograde) and RIKOI (Fig. 26); in addition there are coins which are conventionally called 'obols', attested by one hoard from Serra Ricco and a few other specimens (Pautasso 22–37, compare 19–21, Fig. 27).[4] (For a quite separate group produced in the area of Martigny see p.277.)

The general pattern of distribution is clear. The Burwein hoard may be excluded

---

3 *Le monete preromane dell'Italia settentrionale* (Varese, 1966). There are also two preliminary issues, α and β, and a few isolated pieces, Pautasso 13–14 (compare nos. 509–10) and 17–18, which are probably light drachms rather than half-drachms. No profit is to be derived from R. Chevallier, *La romanisation de la Celtique du Po* (Rome, 1983), 274–82.

4 Genova 1953–4, *Archeologia in Liguria* (Genoa, 1975), 87; Garlasco, information from A. Pautasso; for Pignone see App. 24; it is not clear whether any of these specimens possesses an intelligible legend. Pautasso 15–16 are pieces weighing rather less than 2 gm. which seem by their style to be associated with 22–37.

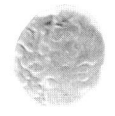

26   The drachm coinage of the Po valley

Drachm, Pautasso Group 4:
   Laureate head of Artemis r./Lion r.; above, blundered legend   Lockett 25
Drachm, Pautasso Group 10:
   Laureate head of Artemis r./Lion r.; above, RIKOI   Oxford

from consideration, partly because it stands alone in the area north of the mountain range which closes the valley of the Lago di Como, partly because it looks like a contaminated hoard. Isolated pieces left by travellers crossing the Great Saint Bernard and around the Lac de Genève and Lac de Joux are similarly uninformative. Nor do the pieces from Penzance and Civita Castellana tell us very much; the Civita

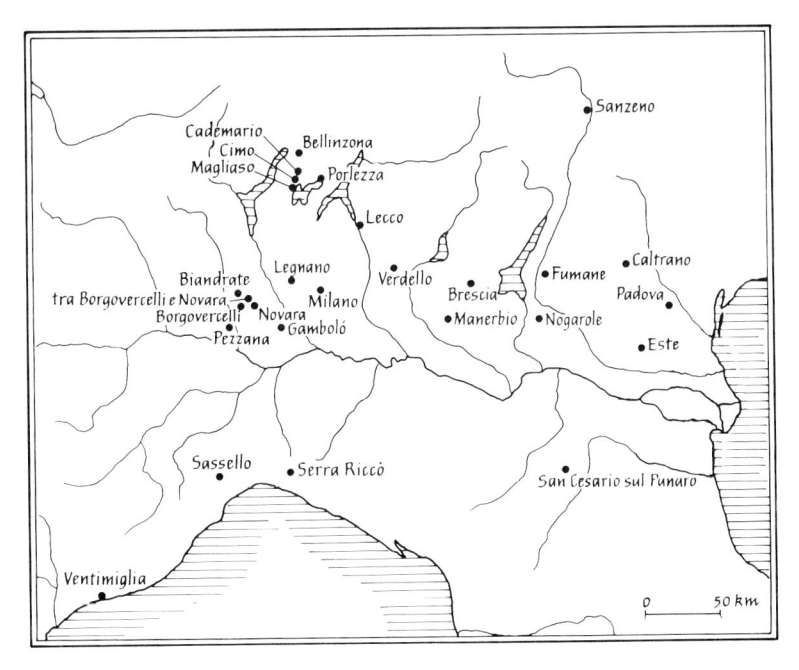

11   Hoards of the drachm coinage of the Po valley
See A. Pautasso (p.76, n.3)

27   The fractional coinage of the Po valley

Fraction, Pautasso Group 24:
   Laureate head of Artemis r./Animal r.; above, star; below, uncertain symbol   BM
Fraction, Pautasso Group 31:
   Female head r./Animal l.; above, star; before, branch   BM

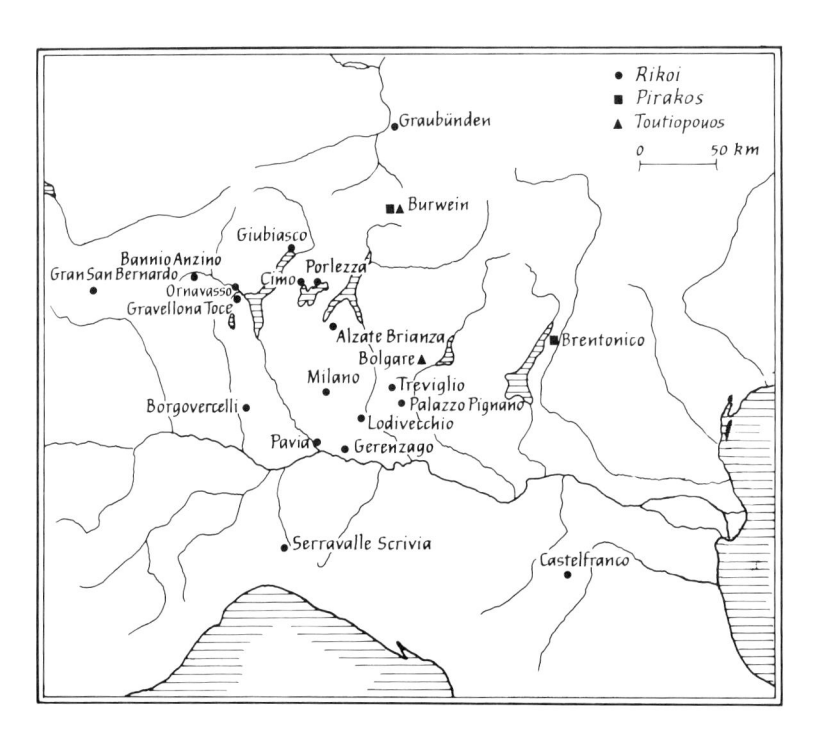

12   Finds of specimens of the drachm coinage of the Po valley with legends
See A. Pautasso (p.76, n.3); for Bannio Anzino, also *AIIN* 2, 1955, 184; for
Castelfranco Emilia, *QTic* 1975, 48; for Graubünden,
L. Coltellini, *Pro-memoria ossia congetture sopra una medaglia
etrusca di argento trovata nel Paese de' Grigioni* (1790)

Castellana hoard is presumably booty. There are five areas where the coinage occurs in substantial quantities, Liguria, the territory of the Insubres and the valleys to the north, the territory of the Cenomani, the territory of the Veneti and finally the area north of the Lago di Garda and along the upper Adige valley (App. 22 with Maps 11–12).

Only the Celtic presence in the Po valley holds these areas together; the Veneti were not Celtic, as we have seen, and Liguria appears to have shared a common culture with the area of the Golasecca culture before they were separated by the Celtic invasion, naturally with some Celtic settlement in both areas; and the area north of the Lago di Garda and along the upper Adige valley seems to have been inhabited by people who were, like the people north of the Alps, Raeti. Given that the bulk of the finds comes from the centre of the Po valley, one might in fact be tempted to regard the coinage as being of the Insubres or the Cenomani and as spreading out from there, but for the fact that one group is found only in the territory of the Veneti, the obols in effect only in Liguria. There is also the problem that the alphabet used on the issues with names is that of a group of inscriptions from the very small area, characterised by the Golasecca culture, normally regarded as that of the Lepontii, though the Gordian knot may be cut by arguing that the language of the Lepontii was Celtic.

It seems then that the coinage is best regarded as originating with and produced largely by the Insubres and the Cenomani, with one group, Pautasso 8, produced by the Veneti, and one group, Pautasso 22–37 and associated pieces, produced in Liguria. One may compare the diversity in other respects of the area characterised by the phenomenon of 'situla art', an area which overlaps with the area with which we are concerned.[5] The presence of the coins in the area north of the Lago di Garda and along the upper Adige valley should not in my view be regarded as reflecting production; some of the pieces found bear inscriptions in the Lepontic alphabet and cannot have been produced in an area which used the Raetic alphabet; there is no group which is exclusive to this area and the finds are for the most part of single pieces; they should be regarded as strays lost by men on their way to the great iron-producing centre of Sanzeno.[6] The absence of a coinage which may be attributed to the Boii is perhaps to be related to the diffuse pattern of settlement in the territory which they occupied.[7]

The evidence for chronology is not as good as one would wish; but pieces (apart from singletons) found in the territory of the Veneti are always found with Roman coins and the tabulation of the material in App. 22 (compare App. F) makes it clear

---

5 L. Bonfante, *Out of Etruria* (Oxford, 1981), 33, 'The world of the situla people'; 66, 'Situla people and Etruscan art'; see Map 13.

6 For which see J. Nothdurfter, *Die Eisenfunde von Sanzeno im Nonsberg* (Mainz, 1979).

7 C. Peyre, *La Cisalpine gauloise* (Paris, 1979), 32–3; in matters of economic history, Peyre perhaps modernises unduly.

13 The situla people
Based on L. Bonfante (p.79, n.5)

that the coinage begins on a small scale in the last quarter of the third century. The coinage was surely in the first instance struck in the course of the various wars of the Gallic tribes against Rome from 225 onwards and evoked directly by the needs of those wars, whether the tribes were on the whole hostile to Rome, like the Insubres and Ligures, or on the whole friendly, like the Cenomani and Veneti.

As in other cases, the coinage of the Celtic tribes of the Po valley may be taken as evidence of the process of state formation, a process perhaps also attested by the enigmatic inscription of a 'Kuitos lekatos' from Briona. It is in the highest degree unlikely that any of the Celtic tribes of the Po valley possessed much in the way of fiscal organisation before the beginning of their wars with Rome from 225 onwards (for a possible Roman issue of this period in the Po valley, of cast bronze coinage, see

App. 14). The actual process of state formation, begun under Roman influence, was of course aborted by the Roman conquest. But some of the structures created clearly remained. The coinages of the Cenomani and the Insubres, for which the evidence is reasonably good, probably continued at any rate for a couple of decades after they made peace, in 197 and 194 respectively; but what is most remarkable is that a Romanised version of the monetary system of Cisalpine Gaul and Liguria before the Roman conquest was perpetuated under Roman rule.

Despite the brutality of the Roman conquest, despite the extent of Roman settlement in Cisalpine Gaul, despite the penetration of Roman coinage, the quinarius, roughly equivalent in value to the drachm of the Celtic tribes, served as the unit of reckoning of the Po valley and Liguria down to the late Republic (Livy xli, 13, 7 (177); *ILLRP* 517; the references to *bigati* at Livy xxxiii, 23, 7 and 9; 37, 11, cannot be authentic); hoards in the area often contain a high proportion of victoriati revalued as quinarii or of quinarii (App. 23), the Romans actually on a number of occasions struck quinarii for circulation in the area;[8] most important of all, the last issue of Cisalpine drachms, that with the legend RIKOI, was produced in the last quarter of the second century, in the same general period as the first Roman issues of quinarii in Cisalpine Gaul (App. 22).

The monetary history of Cisalpine Gaul, however, is not principally the result of government initiative. Cisalpine Gaul was not part of the Roman empire overseas, it was part of Italy and was indeed in the third and second centuries an area of intensive Roman colonisation (Map 14). It was therefore not necessary in the course of the process of Roman conquest to take specific administrative measures such as those taken in relation to the monetary systems of Spain, Sicily and the east. But Cisalpine Gaul was more than an area of colonisation, organised as colonisation had been in the earlier stages of the conquest of peninsular Italy. Polybius' view of the Po valley as a promised land (ii, 15) was no doubt typical and the area was certainly the goal of individual immigration.[9] Furthermore, the ownership of land in the Po valley by Italian cities in the late Republic was probably the result of investment in those lands by individuals in the second century (see App. G). Even independent Mediolanum and Verona were clearly both heavily Romanised by the turn of the second and first centuries, in order to produce the philosopher Catius and the poet Catullus in the next generation. The two Celtic building inscriptions from Como, a type of inscription characteristic of organised communities in peninsular Italy, and the bilingual boundary stone from Vercelli should be regarded as products of the process of Romanisation.

At least one reason for the attractiveness of the Po valley for colonisation,

---

8 *RRC*, pp.628–30 = pp.181–3 below.
9 See U. Ewins, *PBSR* 1952, 54, 'The early colonisation of Cisalpine Gaul'; *PBSR* 1955, 73, 'The enfranchisement of Cisalpine Gaul'; for the relative scarcity of coinage in a developing area, its consequential over-valuation and the resulting appearance of cheapness, see F. Braudel, *The Mediterranean* (London: Fontana, 1975), 384.

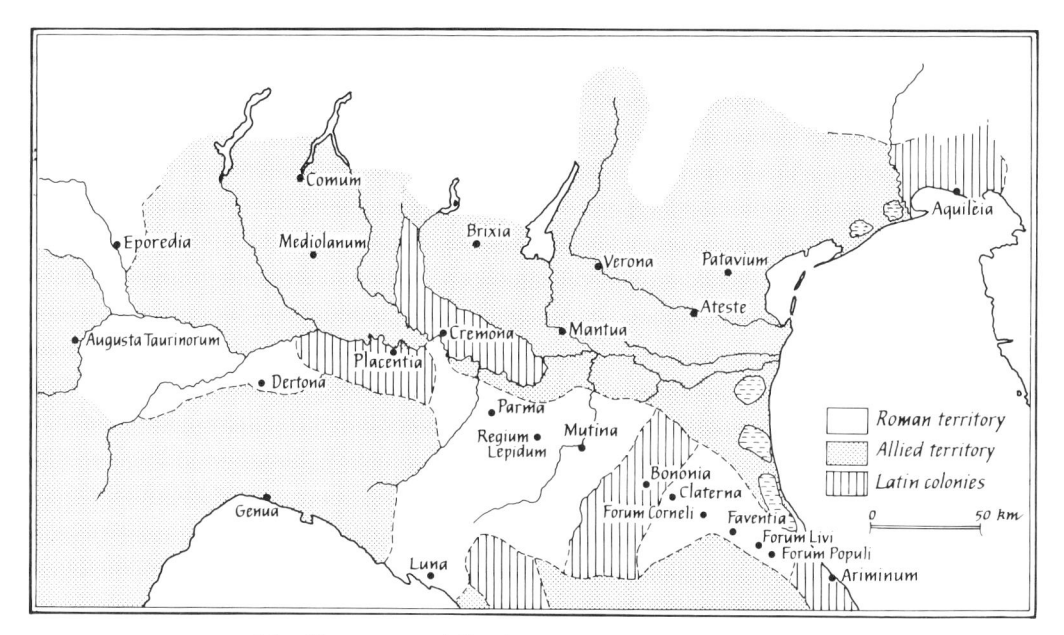

14 Roman and Latin colonies in the Po valley
Based on L.R. Taylor, op. cit., and U. Ewins (p.81, n.9)

immigration and also investment in land has been identified by Emilio Gabba, namely the availability of a dependent labour force, between slave and free. There is little doubt that the humbler elements of the Celtic population were used by Romans and Italians as forced labour; an indication of their status may be inferred from the fact that the Insubres, Cenomani and perhaps other tribes (though presumably not the Veneti) were debarred by their treaties with Rome from access to Roman citizenship. In certain areas, colonial elites (at Bononia and Aquileia even ordinary colonists received large allotments), wealthy immigrants and those investing in land simply replaced the upper classes of Celtic society; the exploitation of the native labour force on the part of these outsiders was no doubt more intensive.

This form of symbiosis between Romans and natives surely helps to explain the survival in Roman dress of indigenous monetary structures. At the end, of course, the normally clear Roman distinction between slave and free was extended also to Cisalpine Gaul,[10] and the local system of reckoning disappeared along with the last survivors of the Celtic issues of the Po valley. The process of transition may perhaps be seen in the Lex Rubria de Gallia Cisalpina (*FIRA* i, no.19), where one procedure is laid down for cases involving *pecunia certa credita, signata forma publica populei Romanei* below 15,000 HS, a different procedure for cases involving other entities or claims

10 For a freedman with a Celtic name in an inscription from the territory of Dertona, see M.V.A. Gallina, *RIL* 1978, 241. See Strabo iii, 4, 17 (165) for the *hire* of labour in Liguria.

below 15,000 HS or cases where judgment may be given *omnei pecunia*.[11] But the survival for a century and a half of the local system of reckoning is to be seen as the result of the survival of a Celtic system of social relations. It is necessary to suppose that the need to produce coinage in the course of the wars of the third and second centuries led at least the Insubres and the Cenomani to create some kind of fiscal structure. Levies of taxation were presumably organised in such a way as to make use of the existing relations of dependence between the lower and upper classes; the monetary usages which emerged in consequence became sufficiently embedded in the strata which survived the Roman conquest to impose themselves in part on the conquerors.

It is in this context important to observe that there is now a significant amount of evidence for the circulation together from the early second century onwards of drachms of the Celtic tribes and Roman Republican bronzes of the denarius system (App. 24). (I incline to regard hoards of cast bronze coinage north of the Appennines as representing booty, App. 25.) Given the equivalence of drachm and quinarius, a drachm was of course worth five asses before the retariffing of the denarius; it is also interesting that Polybius uses the semis to record prices in Cisalpine Gaul (ii, 15, 1–2). Independent evidence for the use in the Po valley of Roman units of reckoning in a native context comes from the inscription on a second-century silver bowl now in Pavia, inscribed with the name of its native owner and its weight in fractions of the Roman pound.[12]

11 See *Archeologia in Liguria* (Genoa, 1975), 68 = *AE* 1976, 229, for an inscription from a villa at Varignano recording rents in sestertii.
12 A. Stenico, *Ath.* 1964, 157, 'Coppa d'argento al Museo Civico di Pavia'; M.G. Tibiletti Bruno, ibid., 168, 'Note leponzie-ligure', at 183. The Roman balance from Ceraino, near Verona, F. Gamurrini, *Annali* 1869, 266, cannot be closely dated.

6

THE ROMANS IN SPAIN

The Roman victory in the Second Punic War (218–200) brought with it the definitive acquisition of the territory ruled by Carthage in Spain and of the former kingdom of Hieron II in Sicily; immediately after the war, Rome provoked the first of her great wars in the east and found herself within ten years for all practical purposes in control of most of the Hellenistic world. The scale of acquisition of territory and influence was only paralleled by the eastern conquests of Pompey.

The monetary histories of the three areas seem at first sight very different. In Greece and Asia Minor, the Roman presence had no obvious effect whatsoever; Roman coinage is not found in Greece before Sulla, with a few readily comprehensible exceptions; and traditional systems of reckoning remained in use down to the age of Augustus and, with some modifications, down to the third century AD. The penetration of Sicily by Roman coinage, which began during the Second Punic War, continued after the war; but in the age of Cicero, issues of Syracuse and other Greek communities also circulated, along with coins issued by the Roman authorities in Panormus and elsewhere. Finally, in Spain, the Romans at a certain point created an Iberian coinage modelled on the denarius coinage.

A remarkable diversity of monetary expedients, to all appearances. Yet there perhaps lies behind this diversity a coherent approach to the problems posed in monetary terms by Roman involvement in activity outside peninsular Italy. I have argued briefly elsewhere that Roman awareness of her acquisition of an overseas empire led Rome already around 200 to rethink her approach to the control of her dependents;[1] and I should like now to argue that the attention of Rome was, on a number of occasions in the second century, turned specifically to the monetary systems of the areas under her control.

Eastern Spain in the Hellenistic period may be regarded as comprising three zones

---

1 *The Roman Republic* (London, 1978), 73.

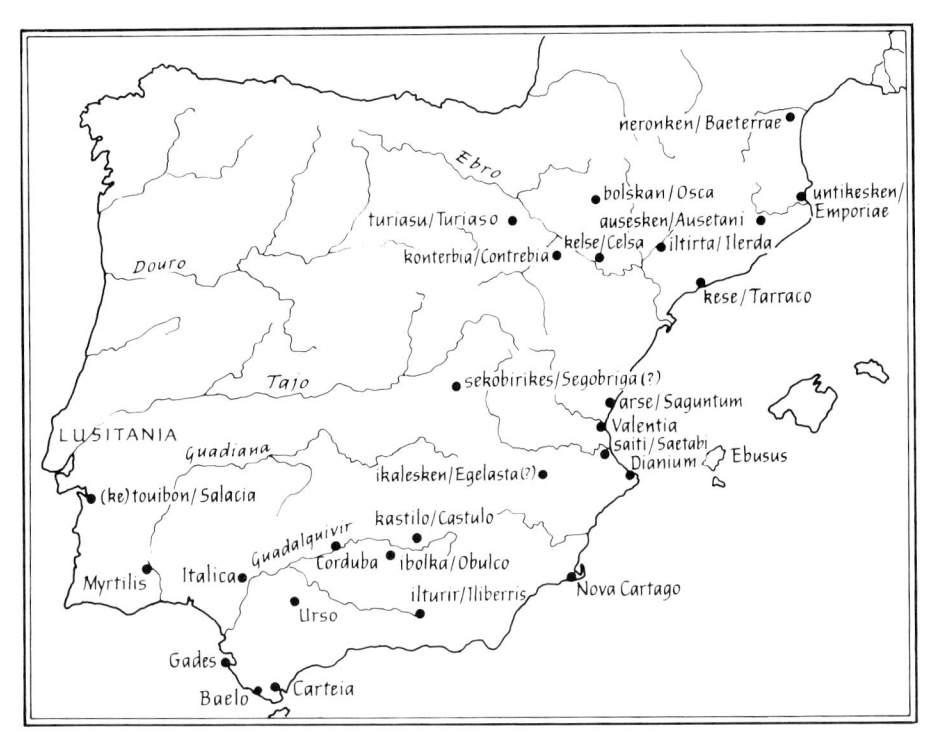

15 The Iberian peninsula

(Map 15): the east coast and the lower Ebro valley, characterised by a language and a script which were both Iberian; the upper Ebro valley and the head of the Duero valley, characterised by a Celtic language and a cognate Iberian script; and a zone in the south characterised by an Iberian language and a different Iberian script, conventionally known as Turdetanian. The Mediterranean coast north of the Pyrenees as far as Ensérune belongs with the first zone. The second zone has been characterised since antiquity as Celtiberian and does in fact seem to have been an area of Celtic penetration, despite the fact that the La Tène phase of Celtic material culture is barely attested archaeologically in Spain.[2]

In none of the three areas does there seem to have been much progress towards state formation and the creation of fiscal institutions. The acquisition of the technique of writing in both Iberian and Celtic areas is obviously of some significance. The import

2 J. Untermann, *Die Inschriften in iberischer Schrift aus Südfrankreich* (Wiesbaden, 1980), for south-western France (the finds from Aubagnan and Lattes are insignificant outliers); J.-P. Mohen, in P.-M. Duval and V. Kruta (eds), *Les mouvements celtiques* (Paris, 1979), 46, and W. Schule, M. Koch and M. Faust, in *Actas del II coloquio sobre lenguas y culturas prerromanas de la península ibérica* (Salamanca, 1979), 197, 387 and 435, for early Iron Age Celtic penetration into the Iberian peninsula; P.F. Stary, *MDAI(M)* 1982, 114, 'Keltische Waffen auf der iberischen Halbinsel'.

of Greek and Phoenician goods was limited down to 625 to the south coast, whence it stimulated the creation of the Orientalising culture of the Guadalquivir valley;[3] imported goods began thereafter to appear also on the south-east coast and in Catalonia, penetrating occasionally into the interior. The import of foreign goods does not seem on the whole to have functioned in Spain, as it did elsewhere, as a stimulus to marked social differentiation and the development of urban centres. In southern Spain, in the classical period, Greek goods seem to have arrived through Carthaginian intermediaries and to have generated no native response.[4] A native tradition of monumental sculpture did emerge on and near the south-east coast, an area where Attic pottery was imported in substantial quantities in the fifth century. As we shall see, this is one area where coinage begins relatively early. In Catalonia and south-western France, Greek pottery and bronzes were imitated from the sixth century onwards and the area saw both continuing imports in the classical period and the beginnings of social differentiation and urbanisation.[5]

A certain familiarity with money among the different native peoples is obviously perfectly possible. One of the few known inscriptions in the Iberian language and the Greek alphabet is perhaps a record of monetary transactions;[6] and Iberian mercenaries were probably sometimes paid in cash, although there are few hoards of Greek or Punic coins from outside the area of Emporiae and the coast down to Hemeroskopeion (Dianium).[7]

The only Spanish silver issues which are certainly earlier than the arrival of Hamilcar in 237 are those of Emporiae, Rhode and Gades, all based on a drachm of about 4.80 gm., a standard whose origin is unknown (for the reduction at Emporiae during the Second Punic War see App. I); there are also bronze issues of Rhode and Gades. The possibility that some of the Iberian imitations of the drachms of Emporiae are earlier than 237 is a real one (Fig. 28) (for 'monnaies à la croix' in France, imitations of Rhode, see p.166); and it is interesting to observe the presence in the hinterland of Emporiae of a large number of small 'tribes', attested by the literary sources for the Roman period. The existence of a substantial number of different

---

3 B.B. Shefton, in H.G. Niemeyer (ed.), *Phönizier im Westen* (Mainz, 1982), 337, 'Greeks and Greek imports in the south of the Iberian peninsula'.

4 J. Boardman, *The Greeks Overseas* (London, 1980), 215.

5 Ibid., 218; J.J. Jully, *Les importations de céramique attique en Languedoc méditerranéen, Roussillon et Catalogne* (Besançon and Paris, 1981).

6 A. Schulten, *Arch.Anz.* 1933, 517; J. Caro Baroja, in *Historia de España*, dir. por R. Menendez Pidal, I, 3 (Madrid, 1954), 749. The third-century (?) Iberian weights from the provinces of Valencia and Alicante, discussed by L. Villaronga, *Ampurias* 1970–71, 297, may relate to the reduced drachms of Emporiae; they are based on a unit of 8.48 gm.

7 *IGCH* 2310; 2319–20; *IGCH* 2316 is of no use. For Spanish mercenaries expecting and getting pay and *dona* presumably in cash by the late third century see Livy xxiv, 49, 7; xxx, 21, 3–5; Plutarch, *Cato* 10; Livy xxxiv, 19, 1–6, cf. 17, 4. Compare Appian, *Iber.* 37, 148, for the penalty imposed on Indibilis for his revolt.

groups of imitations of drachms of Emporiae reflects this pattern[8]; the archaeological evidence for the beginning of urbanisation in the area forms part of the same picture. We shall see in due course (p. 97) that the monetary history of the area of Emporiae under Roman rule is rather different from that of most of the rest of Spain.

The Carthaginians do not seem to have created a real fiscal structure in the area under their control, a fact which is perhaps not surprising if one considers that Hamilcar started with no more than the city of Gades and that the Barcids had less than twenty years before the outbreak of war with Rome. It is in any case clear from Polybius (iii, 13,7) that the Carthaginian exploitation of the interior was quite unsystematic. The striking of a coinage in Spain by the Carthaginians was in fact an initiative which had no outcome, despite the fact that the coinage was produced on a considerable scale.[9] There was one tiny issue, whose weight standard cannot be identified with absolute certainty; it may be Attic or it may be that of Emporiae. The other silver issues of the Barcids were based on the Carthaginian shekel of 7.20 gm. and thus formed part of the Carthaginian monetary system as a whole, but did not fit naturally into existing patterns of monetary circulation in the peninsula (Fig. 28). We may presume that the structure of the Barcid coinage reflects the financial policy of Hamilcar and his successors, but the details of this policy are lost beyond recall. Two points may be made: as L. Villaronga has shown, the weight standard of the gold issues of the Barcids, 7.50 gm., reflects the fact that twelve silver shekels were equivalent to one gold piece in a world where the gold:silver ratio was one to eleven and a third; similarly, the weight standard of the various bronze issues, with the unit rising from over 8.00 gm. to over 10.00 gm., must reflect the number of bronzes to the shekel and the silver:bronze ratio. (For finds of small bronzes see App. 27.) Secondly, the financial difficulties of the Barcids during the Second Punic War are reflected in the decline in the weight of the silver shekel from 7.20 gm. to about 7.00 gm.

It is also interesting to note that, although one can observe in hoards with Hispano-Punic coins the transition from quadrigatus to victoriatus or denarius, the coins with which Roman coins are most often hoarded in Spain in the early period are coins of Emporiae and their Iberian imitations (see App. 27 and Map 16). Much of the drachm coinage of Emporiae was indeed produced to serve Roman ends during the Second Punic War (App. I). The Carthaginians probably ceased to produce coinage in Spain even before the departure of Hasdrubal in 207, after the loss of

---

8 L. Villaronga, *Numismatica Antigua de Hispania* (Barcelona, 1979), 113, for the legends; also *RN* 1979, 43, 'La drachme ibérique ILTIRKESALIR' (discounting the hypothesis of Brettian influence on the weight standard and the view that the Romans described this coinage as *argentum Oscense*).

9 First identified by E.S.G. Robinson, 'Punic coins of Spain and their bearing on the Roman Republican series', in *Essays H. Mattingly* (Oxford, 1956), 34; corpus in L. Villaronga Garriga, *Las Monedas Hispano-Cartaginesas* (Barcelona, 1973). See also J. Pellicer, *Acta Num.* 1982, 57, 'Vuit pesals púnics'.

28 The coinage of Emporiae and the Barcids

Drachm of Emporiae:
   Head of Persephone r.; around, dolphins/Pegasus r.; below, ΕΜΠΟΡΙΤΩΝ   BM
Imitation of drachm of Emporiae:
   Head of Persephone r.; around, dolphins/Pegasus r.; below, blundered legend   BM
Shekel of Barcids:
   Head of Melqart l./Horse r. with palm behind   BM cast
Shekel of Barcids:
   Head of Melqart l./Horse r. with palm behind   BM cast

Carthago Nova in 209, and their coinage rapidly disappeared, a point to which I shall return.

Iberian hoards of the period of the Second Punic War also contain a number of other issues whose production was clearly provoked by the war: of Ebusus, an old Punic settlement, now certainly involved in the war as an ally of Carthage and producing silver and bronze coinage;[10] and of Arse (= Saguntum) and Saeti (= Saetabi), the former striking in the course of her unsuccessful attempt to resist the imposition of Carthaginian rule and also for Carthage, both striking after the liberation of their cities (see Apps. J and K).

The presence of the Romans in Spain from 218 was accompanied by the arrival of a certain number of Roman silver pieces, quadrigati, in due course victoriati and denarii, along with some Greek coins from areas where Roman armies were operating

---

10 M. Campo, *Las monedes de Ebusus* (Barcelona, 1976).

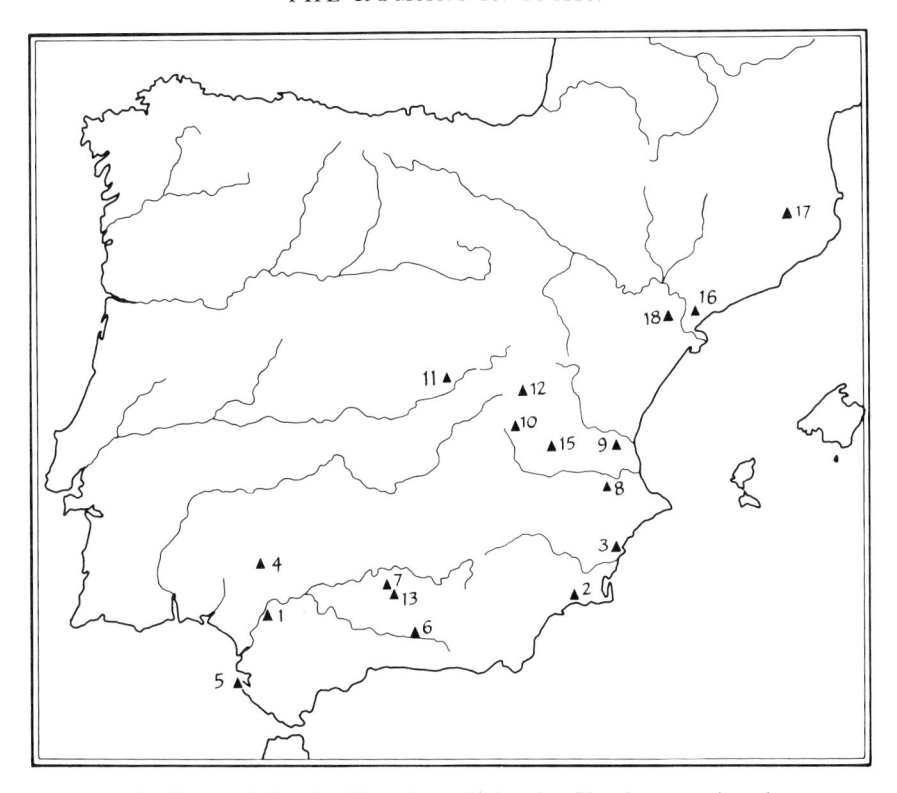

16 Second Punic War hoards in the Iberian peninsula

1 Sevilla; 2 Mazarron; 3 La Escuera; 4 Montemolin; 5 Cadiz;
6 Granada; 7 Martos; 8 Mogente; 9 Cheste; 10 Valera; 11 Drieves;
12 Cuenca; 13 Los Villares; 14 Ebro valley (not marked);
15 La Plana di Utiel; 16 Tivisa; 17 Las Ansies; 18 Coll del Moro

(App. 27).[11] It seems, however, that only two issues were actually produced by the Romans in Spain between 218 and the governorship of C. Annius in the early first century, both tiny issues of victoriati or its associated denominations.[12] The hypothesis of E.S.G. Robinson, that Scipio Africanus struck coins with his portrait on the obverse and the reverse of the last series of Hispano-Punic shekels, is frankly incredible, as L. Villaronga has shown (n.9). One cannot suppose that Scipio, who went to great lengths to refuse the title of king when it was offered by his Spanish troops, put his portrait on an issue of coinage and, what is more, an issue with a distinctively Punic

11 See L. Villaronga, *Ampurias* 1973, 247, for a small hoard of bronzes of Rhodes from Rosas, also no doubt the result of troop movements. Most of the isolated finds of Greek coins from Spain belong to this period.

12 Maria Paz Garcia Bellido (forthcoming); *RRC*, no. 96/1, with a further fragment in the Martos hoard (App. 27). The supposed die for this latter issue is in fact a later forger's hub.

reverse. To this argument formal ones may be added; the coins held by Robinson to be portrait coins of Scipio bear little resemblance to each other; they cannot all be of Scipio and there is no reason to suppose that any are; it also appears from hoard evidence and the evidence of weight standards that the Hispano-Punic issues in question are not the latest of the series; they display certain stylistic affinities with Iberian denarii and are best regarded merely as barbarously executed Punic pieces.

The problem is not simply, however, that the Roman administration of Spain generated in effect no Roman coinage in Spain for over a century. That in itself is not remarkable. The problem is that after the end of the Second Punic War Roman silver coinage appears for all practical purposes not to have travelled to or circulated in Spain until the end of the second century, although the behaviour of Roman bronze coinage was, as we shall see, quite different.[13]

In the first place, a careful look at the Cordova hoard, one of the few sizeable hoards of Roman and Iberian silver coins of the second century preserved for study, reveals that the latest and finest Republican denarii are markedly more worn than the finest Iberian denarii (*NC* 1969, pl.vi). This suggests that there was a time-lag of some years between the striking of the Republican denarii in question and their arrival in Spain and that, although the latest Republican denarius in the hoard is of about 110, the hoard was not actually buried till the last years of the century. Other evidence supports the view that at times in the second century and even in the first century Republican coins were slow in arriving in Spain and were not being brought in on a regular basis in the context of the administration of the two Spanish provinces.

The condition of the Republican and Iberian coins (all but one of bronze) from the camps at Numantia is significant.[14] Of the Republican coins from the camp of 153 and 137, none is described as being in excellent condition (the denarius of Sex. Pompeius, published with the coins from the camp of 153 and 137, was not found in the excavations, but bought in the neighbourhood); of the Iberian coins, six are so described. Similarly, the Scipionic camps of 134/3 provided no Republican, but two Iberian coins in excellent condition; the camp of 75/4 provided one Republican, against two Iberian coins in excellent condition.

Furthermore, the latest Roman coins from the camps at Numantia are mostly earlier than the dates of the camps. The latest Republican pieces from the camp of 153 and 137 (excluding the denarius of Sex. Pompeius) and from the camps of 134/3 are of about 160 or earlier (hence their worn state). The latest Republican piece from the camp of

---

13 I here reproduce with major revisions the essential arguments of *NC* 1969, 79, 'The financial organisation of Republican Spain'.

14 A. Schulten, *Numantia* IV (Munich, 1929), 235–56. The piece of Bolskan is apparently the core of a plated piece and is best excluded from the argument at this point (compare p.93 below). The discussion of H.J. Hildebrandt, *MDAI(M)* 1979, 238, 'Die Römerlager von Numantia', treats asses as semisses and vice versa, treats as one population the coins from different camps and operates in any case with a tiny sample.

75/4 is an uncia with Head of Roma/Double cornucopiae ROMA (*RRC*, no. 308/4b) of the late second century. (For the finds from Castra Caecilia see App. O.)

If then it is true that between 137 and the war against Sertorius there was no swift and steady flow of Republican coins into Spain, it seems improbable that the Roman troops serving in Spain were paid entirely or even predominantly with Roman coinage.

In the second place, between the hoards of the Second Punic War and the hoard from Pozoblanco closing in about 120, there are precisely two hoards which may reflect the movement of Roman silver coinage to Spain and they are singularly unrevealing. The hoards in question are two hoards of victoriati, one of worn pieces from Numantia, which perhaps travelled thither as a group with a Roman soldier in 153 or 137, another of worn pieces from near Murcia, which should also be regarded as having arrived as a group in the middle of the second century.[15] One may suppose that the owners of both hoards were soldiers recruited in Gallia Cisalpina (see p.81); one may also observe that the hoards do not include any coins struck in Spain and in consequence doubt whether they can be taken as evidence of the coinage actually in circulation there. Given the scale of Roman military activity in Spain in the second century, it cannot be argued that Roman silver coinage was in circulation in large quantities but was not hoarded and lost.[16]

Let us turn to the Iberian and Celtiberian denarius coinage. This consists of a silver piece and a bronze unit – the usual types are Male head/Horseman – of the weight of a denarius, with silver and bronze fractional pieces; the model for the whole system was clearly the denarius coinage (App. H, Fig. 29). Equally clearly, the system was not created until after the period to which belong the Second Punic War hoards discussed above. But the problems involved in dating the creation of the system are substantial. Style and letter-forms seem to me fallible guides; and the faint possibility that the reverse type of the denarius is borrowed from the bronze coinage of Hieron of Syracuse does not get us very far. Nor are metrological arguments to be trusted; for at Rome between 211 and the 90s, where the history of the bronze coinage is relatively well known, not only did the weight standard of the as twice fall and rise again, but what is more, issues linked by shared dies were sometimes produced on different weight standards. Thus I view, for instance, L. Villaronga's chronology for the beginning of the bronze coinage with incredulity.[17] Nor are hoards as much help as they might be, since it is rarely clear whether an issue is missing from a hoard because it is later than the closing date of the hoard or because it belongs to a different area. The finds from Numantia provide one fixed point and the hoards which include Roman denarii of the late second century provide another. But much remains uncertain. The finds from Numantia make it clear that the Iberian denarius coinage began before

---

15 *RRCH* 118; C. Balda Navarro, *El Proceso de Romanización de la Provincia de Murcia* (Murcia, 1975), 179.

16 See M.H. Crawford, *PBSR* 1969, 76, 'Coin hoards and the pattern of violence', for the link between military activity and the non-recovery of coin hoards, also p.193.

17 L. Villaronga (n.8), 119–22.

29 The Iberian bronze and silver coinages of the north

Denarius of Tarraco:
   Male head r./Horseman r. holding branch and with second horse; below, *kese*   BM
As of Emporiae:
   Helmeted head of Minerva r.; around, CNCGRLCF Q/Pegasus r.; above, star; below, EMPORI   Paris, de Luynes
As of Tarraco:
   Male head r.; behind, club/Horseman r. holding branch; below, *kese*   BM
Semis of Tarraco:
   Male head r./Horse galloping r.; below, *kese*   BM
Triens of Tarraco:
   Male head r.; behind, four dots/Horse walking r.; above, four dots; below, *kese*   BM
Quadrans of Tarraco:
   Male head r.; behind, caduceus/Forepart of Pegasus r.; above, three dots; below, *kese*   BM
Sextans of Tarraco:
   Male head r.; behind, caduceus/Dolphin r.; above, two dots, below, *kese*   BM

137, the date of the reoccupation of Camp III by C. Hostilius Mancinus.[18] Since some of the Iberian coins from this camp show some wear, the date of the institution of the Iberian denarius coinage may be placed in the first half of the second century. Attempts to estimate how far back it is to be placed by arguments from the volume of Iberian coinage are obviously prospectless. The evidence as a whole shows at any rate that by the time the Scipionic camps were occupied in 134–133 the mints of Untikesken, Iltirta, Kese, Arsaos, Baskunes, Bolskan, Sekia, Sesars, Belikiom and Sekaisa had begun to produce bronze. In addition, the core of a plated denarius of Bolskan carries with it the implication that the production of silver had also begun.

The Cordova hoard itself once seemed to be of some chronological significance. As observed by G. K. Jenkins,[19] the amount of wear shown by the most worn, and therefore presumably earliest, of the Iberian denarii is comparable with that shown by the earliest Roman denarii. These are of the first third of the second century, which suggests that the Iberian denarii should perhaps not be of *widely* different date.

Another argument once appeared to place the institution of the Iberian coinage in the first third of the second century. Of the two large groups of Iberian denarii in the Cordova hoard, those of Bolskan are more worn than those of Ikalesken and are generally held, surely rightly, to have begun earlier.[20] It is remarkable that despite this greater wear their average weight is 4.01 gm. (plated and halved coins are excluded from the average), approaching the weight of Republican denarii of the earliest period. It is these denarii which are represented in Spanish hoards of the Second Punic War (App. 27), and it is tempting to hold that the Iberian denarius coinage began when these denarii still dominated the circulating medium. By way of contrast, the denarii of Ikalesken in the Cordova hoard have an average weight of only 3.84 gm., close to the average weight of the Republican denarii in a typical hoard of the middle of the second century, the West Sicily hoard, 3.87 gm.[21] But given that Roman denarii did not travel to Spain during the two generations after the end of the Second Punic War, the denarii produced during that war may still have served as models for the early Iberian denarius coinage, at a point when lighter denarii had long been in circulation elsewhere. There is no objection to supposing that the weight of the Iberian denarius in due course drifted down of its own accord.

18 O. Gil Farres, followed without discussion by R. Martin Valls, *Boletin del Seminario de Estudios de Arte y Arqueologia* 1966, 207, has argued that the Iberian denarius coinage dates from after 133. Since he does not discuss the evidence of the finds from Numantia, his arguments are not convincing.
19 *MusN* 1958, 57, 'Notes on Iberian denarii from the Cordova hoard'.
20 Ibid., 66. The date suggested there for the close of the first period of activity of the mint of Bolskan is modified in *Numario Hispanico* 1958, 135, 'A Celtiberian hoard from Granada', at 136.
21 *RRCH* 135. For the weight-standards of the denarii of Bolskan and Ikalesken, see also G.K. Jenkins (n.19), 142–4. The argument used there that Bolskan could not have copied the heavy Roman denarius standard because she did not also copy the light standard is fallacious. A mint, having once adopted a Roman standard, could obviously keep to it even if the Roman standard changed slightly.

A third argument now seems to me to weigh very strongly. Not only are there no hoards of Roman denarii from Spain between the Second Punic War and the last quarter of the second century, there are almost no hoards of Iberian denarii which may be assigned to this period either (App. 29). The 'Hostalrich' hoard certainly and one or two others perhaps belong here, but that is all. There is certainly no long sequence of hoards of Iberian denarii earlier than those with Iberian and Roman denarii. It is very hard to push the institution of the Iberian denarius far away from the date of these hoards.

If on balance the institution of the Iberian coinage belongs on numismatic grounds at some point towards the end of the first half of the second century, it remains to see if the historical evidence suggests a precise date. At this point, however, it is no longer possible to evade a consideration of the function of the Iberian denarius coinage. It is in my view most plausible to suppose that it was initially struck at the behest of the Romans in order to convert some of the revenue of the two provinces into a coinage which could be used without more ado for the payment of Roman troops. If they then used the coinage to purchase supplies in the areas where it had been struck and issued, the strong tendency of the Iberian denarius coinage to circulate locally finds a ready explanation. As we shall see, the view that the Iberian denarius coinage initially served Roman ends is perfectly compatible with the acceptance of an independent element in its later history.

There are several relevant considerations, apart from the general one that the Romans are likely to have used coinage in order to meet their financial obligations in Spain, that the Iberian denarius coinage is for at any rate part of the second century the only available candidate and that the Romans are unlikely to have left its availability to chance. It seems to me probable that already in the second century soldiers serving abroad were credited with part of their *stipendium* and paid this part on their return. But they surely needed some money while on service.

The principal argument starts from the fact that the major mints of Iberian denarii on the whole produced their coinages in sequence (see App. 29); and while it is rather hard to see why this should have occurred in the ordinary way of things, it is possible to imagine how it could have been the result of the exigencies of the Roman strategy for the conquest of Spain. A second argument lies in the astonishing typological and denominational uniformity of the Iberian denarius coinage. It is also relevant that Iberian coinage does not seem to have circulated outside the Iberian peninsula, with insignificant exceptions.[22] It is very odd that those for whom it was designed almost

---

22 There was obviously interchange of coinage between the Iberian areas on either side of the Pyrenees, see J.-C.M. Richard, *Mél. Casa Velasquez* 1972, 51, 'Monnaies gauloises du cabinet numismatique de Catalogne'; *Numisma* 1973–74, 195, 'Monnaies antiques de la péninsule Ibérique dans le sud de la France'; L. Villaronga, 'Les monedes iberiques en el Llenguadoc', in *Els pobles pre-romans del Pirineu* (Puigcerda, 1978), 257; D. Nash, *Settlement and Coinage in Central Gaul* (Oxford, 1978), 336; Y. Roman, *De Narbonne à Bordeaux* (Lyon, 1983), 150–69.

never exported it, if the coinage was a response to local needs, whether economic or social,[23] despite the fact that it was perfectly compatible with mainstream Roman coinage. It is also surely significant that the production and use of Iberian denarii are not characteristic either of the developed areas of the north-east coast or of the Baetis valley.

The most probable date for the creation of the Iberian denarius coinage once seemed to me to be 197. For this year, according to Livy, six praetors were elected for the first time (xxxii, 27, 6) and one was assigned to each of the Spanish provinces, M. Helvius receiving Hispania Ulterior, C. Sempronius Tuditanus Hispania Citerior (xxxii, 28, 2–11). They were instructed to establish the boundaries of the two provinces and the institution of the Iberian coinage as a medium for paying taxation could also have formed part of their duties. But it is not clear that the provinces actually were established in 197;[24] and the arguments of J.S. Richardson, that down to 180–178 the Roman organisation of Spain was far too unsystematic to have generated a local coinage under Roman control, seem to me compelling.[25] Those years might themselves have been the occasion for the creation of the coinage; but if they are treated as furnishing a *terminus post quem*, 155–154 are equally plausible. For the Romans were then faced for the first time for nearly a generation with the need to fight a major war. The balance of the numismatic evidence seems to me to favour this late date. (I decline to speculate on what Livy or his source meant by *argentum Oscense*, xxxiv, 10, 4–7 (195); 46, 2 (194); xl, 43, 6 (180).)

I regard 155–154, then, as virtually certain for the introduction of the Iberian silver coinage; it remains theoretically possible that the bronze coinage begins earlier, but I do not believe it.[26]

If we hold that the Iberian denarius coinage is a product of the 150s, it is perfectly possible to write an intelligible monetary history of Republican Spain. For we have seen (p.72) that down to the early 150s, Roman troops were paid in bronze, presumably the bronze which turns up in the Roman camps at Numantia and which therefore did travel to Spain in the first half of the second century;[27] Livy xl, 35, 4 (180) makes it clear that in this period pay for the army was normally sent from Rome to Spain. Since bronze hoards are rare compared with silver, it is not a matter for

---

23 As argued by M. Koch, *Gnomon* 1978, 554, reviewing J. Untermann, *Monumenta Linguarum Hispanicarum* (Wiesbaden, 1975); R.C. Knapp, *NC* 1977, 1, 'The date and purpose of the Iberian denarii'; in *Actas del II Coloquio* (n. 2), 465, 'Celtiberian conflict with Rome: policy and coinage.'

24 G.V. Sumner, *Arethusa* 1970, 85, 'Proconsuls and *provinciae* in Spain'.

25 *JRS* 66, 1976, 139, 'The Spanish mines and the development of provincial taxation', at 147–51.

26 H.J. Hildebrandt, *Acta Num.* 1981, 57, 'Los hallazgos de monedas de bronce', though starting from unwarranted metrological assumptions, arrives at much the same conclusions as mine on the dating of the Iberian bronze coinage.

27 Compare P.R. Arriols and L. Villaronga, 'Troballa esporadica de bronzes romans republicans' (forthcoming) for a sequence of 151 Republican bronzes down to C. Serveilius M.f. found recently around Numantia.

30 The coinage of Saguntum

Drachm of Saguntum:
  Laureate head of Hercules r.; before, dolphin/Butting bull r.; above, shell; in exergue,
  arsgidar BM
As of Saguntum:
  Male head l.; behind, caduceus/Helmeted horseman r.; above, star; below, *arse* BM

surprise that no hoards are known; we are lucky to have the camps at Numantia to document both the arrival of Republican bronzes in Spain and their supersession by Iberian bronzes after the 150s. Since Roman troops in Italy were paid in silver as well as bronze from 157 onwards (p.143) it is intelligible that a coinage created for Spain in 155–154 consisted of both metals. The silver and the bronze for the new coinage doubtless came from the taxes of the two Spanish provinces. These, along with extra levies, I suspect, had hitherto been paid in a mixture of Roman coinage and bullion; the Romans of course computed its value in their own terms (Livy xl, 47, 10; Appian, *Iber.* 44, 182–3; 50, 214); similarly the commutation of the 5 per cent levy of corn for cash must have been arranged in Roman monetary terms.

The relatively late date proposed for the creation of the Iberian denarius coinage perhaps helps to explain why the area of Emporiae continued for a long time in possession of its own monetary system. Segaro, San Llop, La Barrocca and Gerona (*IGCH* 2342, 2347–48, 2350), of the late second and early first century, still consist of substantial numbers of drachms of Emporiae, with Roman denarii and in two cases a few Iberian denarii from Kese. Further south, the hoard of La Vall' d'Almonesir, of the first half of the second century, consists solely of silver of Saguntum (Fig. 30). (It may indeed be that the second-century silver coinage of Saguntum is to be regarded as evoked by the needs of the mining area near Nova Carthago.) The coinage of Ebusus, similarly, seems to have continued to dominate the circulating medium of the island (*IGCH* 2345–46, the latter with one piece of Iol, 2351).[28]

---

[28] There is one hoard from the mainland, *IGCH* 2344; for the broadly similar pattern revealed by finds of single pieces see M. Campo, in *Atti I Cong.Int.Stud.Fen.Pun.* (Rome, 1983), 145, 'Las relaciones de Ebusus con el exterior'; for the coins of Ebusus from Campania see App. 46.

Two further points. First, if the Iberian denarius coinage was a Roman creation, it was a creation which up to a certain point reflected the Iberian situation. In one respect the Romans were fortunate: under the pressure of the Second Punic War the weight standard of the silver of Emporiae had been reduced towards that of the Roman denarius; and in creating the Iberian denarius coinage on more or less the standard of the Roman denarius, the Romans were adopting a standard close to an already existing native one. It is also important to remember that the legends of the Iberian denarius coinage were in the native scripts and languages of Catalonia, Andalusia and Aragon, which looks like an attempt at conciliation on the part of the Romans, in the first instance of the Iberian element in Emporiae and of the Iberian population in its hinterland. The association of Roman and Emporitan coinage during the Second Punic War clearly underlay the form in which the Iberian denarius coinage was created.

Second, the monetary history of Iberia throws into sharp relief the problem of the fiscal status of Italy. We shall see (p.187) that it is likely that the communities of Italy continued to pay their own local taxes down to the Social War. Now it is obviously possible that they levied these taxes in whatever Roman coinage was in circulation and thus paid the contingents they supplied to the Roman army. But if almost no Roman coinage travelled to Spain during the last two generations of the second century, either Rome simply used Iberian coinage when it became available to pay the Italian troops serving in Spain or she recouped by some means from the Italian communities the cost of their pay in Spain. *If* it was the case that some of the money used ultimately for the pay of Italian troops abroad was actually collected on their behalf by Rome, that would give added point to the grievances of the Italians reported by Appian (*BC* i, 7, 30).

I argue then that Rome paid for her presence in Spain down to the 150s largely with her own bronze coinage and that in 155–154, when she might have used her massive new silver issues, she instituted instead the Iberian denarius coinage. There were no fiscal reasons for Roman silver coinage to travel to Spain and for a period after 155–154 almost none did.

The problem arises of why Roman silver coinage did travel to Spain in the last generation of the second century. We have already seen that the coinage in question seems to have been somewhat worn by the time it arrived in Spain and this suggests very strongly that it arrived in a private context. A glance at the distribution of the hoards closing with Roman denarii of 125–92 confirms the view that we should look at economic rather than fiscal considerations in our search for an explanation (App. 30 with Map 17).

The hoards come almost exclusively from the hinterland of Emporiae, the most developed area of pre-Roman Spain (p.86), the east coast and the Baetis valley with the coast to the west; these are precisely the chief areas of Roman and Italian influence and settlement, conspicuously the territory of Emporiae and the rich mining zones

17 Second-century Roman and Iberian denarius hoards
See Apps 30 and 29

around Nova Carthago, Castulo and Italica;[29] it is in the Ebro valley that road building is attested in the Republican period (*ILLRP* 461–2: two milestones from Ilerda and one from near Barcino; see also Strabo iii, 4, 9; Polybius iii, 39 with commentary of F.W. Walbank); and it is from this area that Rome drew the auxiliary troops who served before Asculum in the Social War.[30] The picture of incipient Romanisation which emerges from the recently discovered bronze inscription from Contrebia fits well with everything else that is known of this area under the Republic.[31] As far as the east coast and the south are concerned, four towns of Roman origin are attested in the late third or the second century, Valentia on the east coast (138 BC), Italica and

29 A.J.N. Wilson, *Emigration from Italy* (Manchester, 1966), 22–7; note that Caesar recruited legionaries in Spain in 61; A. Garcia y Bellido, *Hispania* 26, 1966, 497, 'Los "mercatores", "negotiatores" y "publicani" como vehículos de romanización en la España preimperial'.

30 See P. Sillières, *Mél. Casa Velasquez* 1977, 31, 'La Camino de Anibal', for the Republican route from Saetabi to Castulo; J.M. Roldan Hervas, *Hispania y el Ejército Romano* (Salamanca, 1974), 31. Nothing is to be learnt from P. Bosch Gimpera, *Mélanges J. Carcopino* (Paris, 1966), 141, 'Les soldats ibériques agents d'hellénisation et de romanisation'.

31 J.S. Richardson, *JRS* 1983, 33, 'The Tabula Contrebiensis'.

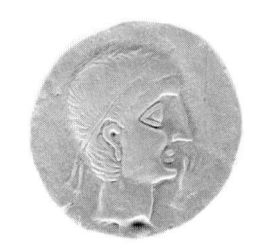

31   The coinages of Ikalesken and the Guadalquivir valley

Denarius of Ikalesken:
  Male head r./Horseman l. holding shield and with second horse; in exergue, *ikalesken*
  BM

As of Castulo:
  Diademed male head r.; before, hand/Sphinx r.; before, star; in exergue, *kastilo*   Paris

Corduba in the Guadalquivir valley (206 and 169 or 152/1 BC), Carteia on the south coast (171 BC).[32] It is to such areas that Italian wine and pottery were imported during the Republic and in such areas that monumental sculptures of the Republican period and pavements of *opus signinum* are attested; there developed in Baetica in the age of Augustus and in Tarraconensis in the age of Tiberius the production of wine for export.[33]

I should argue therefore that the pattern of Roman silver coinage in Spain in the late second century reflects the presence of Roman and Italian settlers and the introduction of Roman monetary usages. This view may be confirmed in a number of ways. Both Emporiae and the area around Italica are characterised by mixed hoards of Roman and local bronzes (App. 31). The hinterland of Emporiae is characterised in addition by the presence of three substantial hoards of local bronze only (App. 32), and it seems likely that even if coinage on a Roman model was originally imposed from outside, the production of bronze coinage spread rapidly, in Baetica as well as in the north-east, to serve local ends (Fig. 31). It is also worth drawing attention,

32 See in general H. Galsterer, *Untersuchungen zum römischen Städtewesen auf der iberischen Halbinsel* (Madrider Forschungen 8) (Berlin, 1971), 7–16. Since the foundation of Corduba is not mentioned by Livy, the second date is the more likely. I remain agnostic about whether Ti. Sempronius Gracchus had anything to do with Iliturgi.

33 A. Tchernia, in P. Garnsey, K. Hopkins, C. R. Whittaker (eds), *Trade in the Ancient Economy* (London, 1983), 87, 'Italian wine in Gaul', at 91 (for imports to the region of Emporiae and the Sierra Morena mines); A. Garcia y Bellido, in *Mélanges J. Carcopino* (Paris, 1966), 419, 'Esculturas hispano-romanas de época republicana' (the coast from Emporiae to Tarraco, the area of Nova Carthago, the Guadalquivir valley); R. Etienne, in *Neue Forschungen in Pompeji* (Recklinghausen, 1975), 309, 'A propos du vin pompeien'.

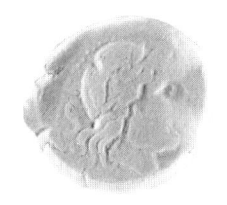

32   The coinages of Carteia and Andalusia

Semis of Carteia:
  Laureate head of Saturn r./Prow r.; above, Q.PEDEC(aeus); before, S   BM
Imitation of semis of Rome probably struck in Andalusia:
  Laureate head of Saturn r.; behind, S/Prow l.; below, retrograde ROMA
                                                                         BMCRR Rome 2206

despite the virtual absence of hoards, to the prolific bronze coinage of Carteia and to the probably first-century imitations of Republican semisses from south-eastern Spain (Fig. 32).[34]

I suspect, though I cannot prove, that the absence of much in the way of Iberian denarius coinage from the most urbanised areas of the north-east (the issues in silver of Kese, for instance, are exiguous) shows that their Roman and Italian population paid little if anything in the way of taxes (Maps 18 and 19). In the case of Baetica, there is independent evidence for the introduction of Roman monetary usages and indeed for their extension to a native environment. Not only are there two silver bowls from this area with their weights in terms of the Roman pound inscribed on them and three uninscribed bowls weighing about a pound each; but there is also a celebrated bowl from La Granjuela with an Iberian inscription and its Roman weight inscribed on it.[35] By way of contrast, late bronzes of Ebusus bear the mark of value 50 in Punic script and clearly owe nothing to Roman units of reckoning (*SNG* (Cop.) 92–8).

The arrival of Roman silver coins in the south of the Iberian peninsula in the last generation of the second century suggests that this was the moment when the men who worked the mines of Spain decided to settle in large numbers, rather than repatriating their profits; for the mines near Nova Carthago must have been worked without a break from the Second Punic War onwards, whatever one thinks of the date when the Sierra Morena and Rio Tinto mines came into operation. The nature of

---

34 L.Villaronga, *AIIN* 29, 1982, 222–6. For a possible hoard from Elche, see *AEA* 26, 1953, 347.
35 K. Raddatz, *Die Schatzfunde der iberischen Halbinsel* (Berlin, 1969) I, 86; 14 and 225 (Pl SC·IIX; P::S SC·IX); F.J. Oroz Arizcuren, *Actas del II Coloquio* (n.2), 283 (bowl from La Granjuela).

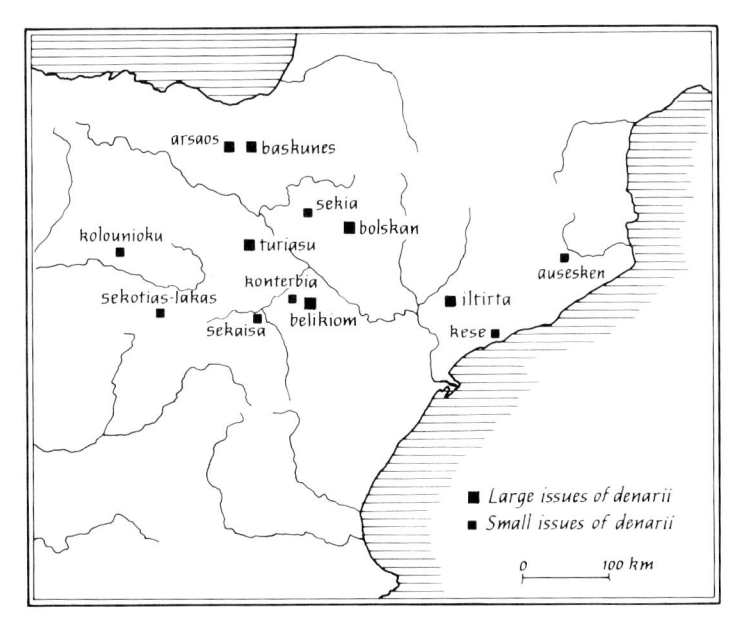

18 The pattern of Iberian silver coinage production
Based on J. Untermann (p.95, n.23), Map 7

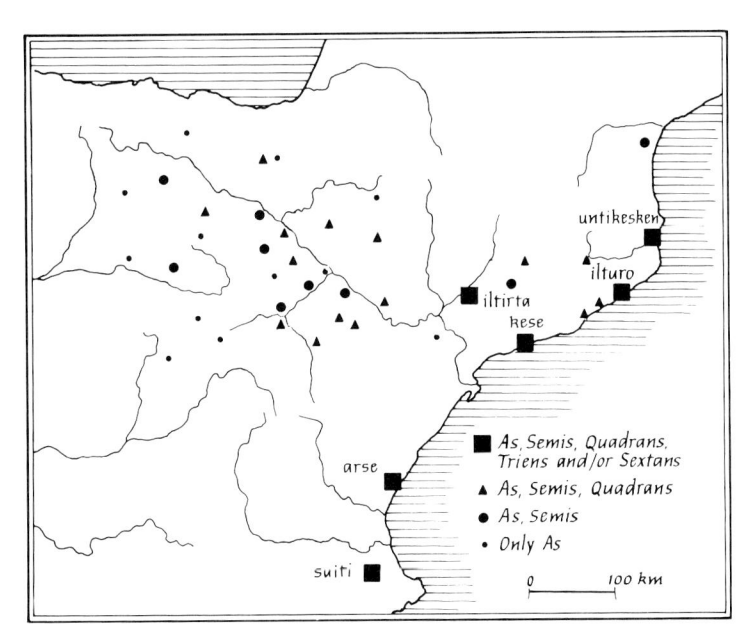

19 The pattern of Iberian bronze coinage production
Based on J. Untermann, op.cit., Map 8

the coin finds from these mining areas seems in any case to show quite clearly that the metal kept by the operators was simply sold on the open market. For the hoards stretch right back to the by now very worn issues of the early denarius coinage; there is no trace of blocks of newly struck coins issued by the mint in return for the metal.

The non-recovery of the numerous hoards of the late second century from the Ebro valley and the Guadalquivir valley naturally poses a problem. It is conventional to regard the loss of the northern hoards as being due to the invasion of the Cimbri and Teutones; but there is no reason to suppose that they got as far as the Guadalquivir valley. It seems to me worth suggesting that the climate of insecurity that they created permitted or encouraged slave revolts in the great mining areas of the south. If it is true that mining in Spain was interrupted towards the end of the second century, this might help to account for the limited issues of silver at Rome in the 90s (p.185).

7

THE ROMANS IN SICILY[1]

The earliest Roman experience of the control of an overseas territory arose from the acquisition of western Sicily, Sardinia and Corsica after the First Punic War (Map 20). Of the administration of these territories by Carthage we know almost nothing, of the Roman administration down to the Second Punic War even less, despite the recent publication of a group of inscriptions of the period of the First Punic War from Entella.[2] Corsica seems to have paid taxes in kind both under Carthage and under Rome (Diod. v, 13, 3–5; Livy xl, 34, 12). In the case of Sardinia we hear of payments in kind under Rome and one may assume that the Carthaginians operated a similar system.[3] The latter produced in Sardinia a substantial bronze coinage both during the First Punic War and during their attempt to recover the island during the Second Punic War; these issues were followed by three Roman issues, to a very large extent overstruck on Punic pieces (*RRC*, nos. 63–5; see also App. D). But the third-century hoards from the island (App. 33) do not include any coinage that is not Carthaginian or Roman (apart from one bronze of Syracuse); after these hoards there is nothing till the end of the second century, though presumably some Roman coinage circulated, since there were usurers on the island for M.Cato to expel in 198 (Livy xxxii, 27, 3). As for Corsica, no coinage was ever struck there and there are no hoards before the

---

1 I am in substantial agreement with G. Clemente, *Kokalos* 26–27, 1, 1980–81, 192, 'Considerazioni sulla Sicilia nell'Impero romano'; M. Mazza, ibid., 292, 'Economia e società nella Sicilia romana', by way of contrast, is a fairy story, e.g. at 306, 'l'inserimento del piccolo regno siracusano nel grande circuito dell'economia ellenistica'.

2 G. Nenci, *ASNP* 1982, 771, 'Materiali e contributi per lo studio degli otto decreti da Entella': Ti. Claudius C.f. of Antium as *epimeletes* of Entella after 254.

3 The remark in Ps. Arist., *On remarkable things heard* 100, that the Carthaginians forbade the Sardinians to grow 'crops useful for revenue', is incomprehensible as it stands. The data presented by R. J. Rowland, *AJAH* (forthcoming), 'Beyond the frontier in Punic Sardinia', suggest that the Carthaginians created a territorial empire in the south-west, presumably to tax the native inhabitants thereof.

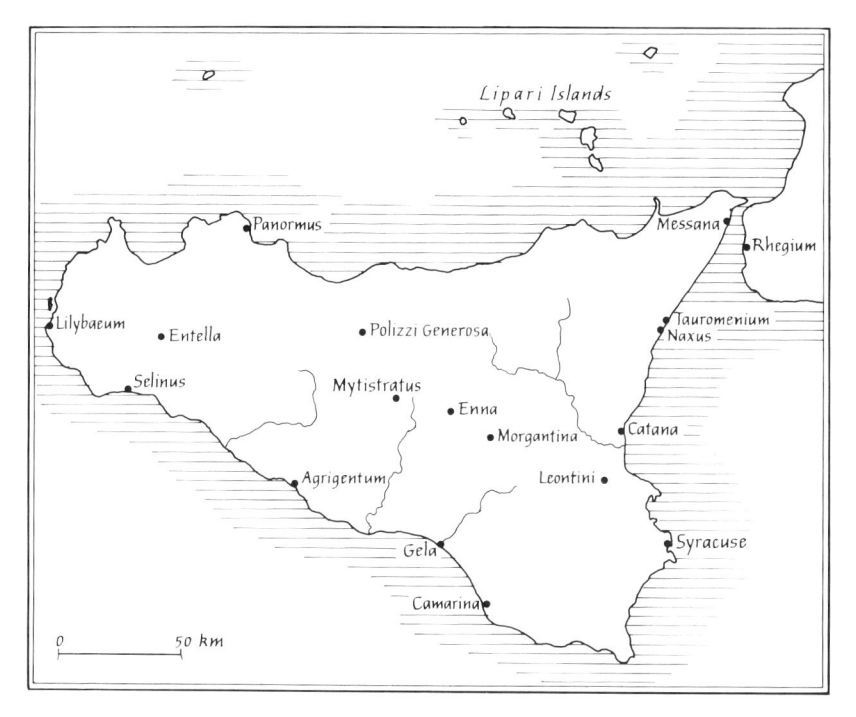

20 Sicily

end of the first century, though the evidence of site finds suggests that some coinage circulated at any rate at Alalia (see App. 34).

The situation in Sicily is obviously much more complex. The sheer quantity of silver coinage produced there by the Carthaginians suggests very strongly that they organised a system of taxation in money;[4] and indeed one of their last issues was produced under the authority of one or more MHSBM, who are clearly treasury officials of some kind.[5] A Roman quaestor was presumably sent annually to the west of the island from 240, based at Lilybaeum, and a praetor was certainly sent annually from 227. I should *guess* that between 240 and the Second Punic War the Romans followed the Carthaginian example and raised taxation in money (compare Appian, *Sic.* 2, 2 with Livy xxiii, 48, 7).

In the east of the island, Hieron not only organised the well-known system of the tithe in corn, which the Romans took over and extended to the west, but also produced a substantial gold and especially silver coinage, the last flowering of the Sicilian

---

4 Cicero, *II in Verr.* 3, 13, cannot in any case be taken to prove the opposite.
5 G.K. Jenkins, *SNR* 1978, 5, 'Coins of Punic Sicily. Part 4'; G. Coacci Polselli, *Studi Maghrebini* 12, 1980, 83, 'I mhsbm cartaginesi', for the meaning of the word.

numismatic tradition.[6] It seems to me very likely that Hieron acquired at any rate part of the silver required for his coinage by the export of grain and that he thus created for the Romans a further precedent to stand beside the tithe. The Romans also, in marked contrast to the position in Spain, not only imported their own coinage to the island on a very large scale during the Second Punic War, but also produced a considerable quantity of coinage there. At this point it suffices to note that the Romans inherited with the capture of Syracuse a fiscal system of which coinage was an integral part and that they themselves became used during the Second Punic War to having their own coinage available in quantity, whether by importing it or by producing it on the spot. It is in fact possible to observe with great clarity the transition from the quadrigatus to the denarius system in the Sicilian hoards of the period of the Second Punic War: the coins of the two systems turn up in sequence, associated with coins of Syracuse and Carthage, with the occasional admixture of coins from the Greek east, which had no doubt arrived in the pockets of Roman soldiers who had served there.[7]

The silver coinage in circulation in Sicily at the beginning of the Hellenistic period seems to have consisted largely of *pegasi*, both imported and local,[8] Siculo-Punic silver and Syracusan silver; a few hoards contain isolated examples of much earlier issues of Camarina (*IGCH* 2151, 2185), Gela (*IGCH* 2184), Leontini (*IGCH* 2145, 2146), Messana (*IGCH* 2145, 2151, 2183, 2185), Rhegium (*IGCH* 2185), Selinus (*IGCH* 2182). In addition, a fair amount of Macedonian and Athenian silver seems to have reached Sicily. Beside the hoards of silver there are also hoards of gold and electrum, Carthaginian and Syracusan, with some Macedonian; and there are a number of mixed gold or electrum and silver hoards. Within the sequence of Syracusan issues, silver and gold of Agathocles and gold of Hicetas appear in due course.

As far as bronze coinage is concerned, Carthage and Syracuse both produced it in very large quantities; bronzes of Agrigentum (*IGCH* 2162 – also Syracuse and one much earlier piece of Himera; 2203 – also Syracuse) and Gela are also well represented in the hoards.[9] The Gela evidence is instructive and shows that we should be cautious in arguing from the absence of particular kinds of hoards. For it is only at Gela, an urban site which has been carefully excavated and which suffered two destructions in the period in question (at the hands of Agathocles and Phintias), that we find hoards

6 G. de Sensi Sestito, *Helikon* 1975–76, 187, 'Relazioni commerciali e politica finanziaria di Gerone II', involves the phantasmagorical construction of relationships between coinages which never had anything to do with each other; nor is there any evidence for the 'politica commerciale a vasto raggio' attributed to Hieron by id., *Gerone II* (Palermo, 1977), totally misunderstanding the nature of Greek coinage and the military context in which Syracusan issues reached Italy at the end of the third century.

7 *IGCH* 2217; 2230; 2232; 2234; 2242. Note also eleven bronzes of Rhodes from Catania, G. Manganaro, *Archivio Storico della Sicilia Orientale* 65, 1969, 283.

8 For their imposition by Timoleon, see *La moneta in Grecia e a Roma* (Bari, 1982), 58–9.

9 Note also bronzes perhaps of Catana from Naxus, *IGCH* 2161.

33 The Sicilian coinage of Carthage during the First Punic War

Tetradrachm of Carthage struck in Sicily, G.K. Jenkins, *SNR* 1978, 5, Series 5:
   Head of Heracles r./Horse's head l.; behind, palm; below, *mhsbm*   Sandeman 265
Five-shekel piece of Carthage struck in Sicily, Series 6:
   Head of Tanit l./Pegasus r.; below, *brst*   *SNG* (Cam.) 1512

of gold or electrum or silver and bronze together (*IGCH* 2164, 2190, 2197; 2195 and 2199 are of bronze only, the former including a much earlier piece of Messana). It is clearly legitimate to hold that precious and base metal coinages circulated together, but were only hoarded together in an emergency.

When we come to the period of the First Punic War, it seems that the Carthaginian war effort in Sicily was paid for by the large electrum and large silver issues which form the later part of G.K. Jenkins' Series 6. It is noticeable that the coins turn up only in Carthaginian territory (Fig. 33). When the war settled into stalemate by land, the issues apparently ceased. From Selinunte there also comes a hoard of the coins of the Libyans who rebelled against Carthage after the war and two hoards of Carthaginian bronzes struck in Sardinia during the war (*IGCH* 2213; 2212 (*SNG* (Cop.) 192); 2214 (*SNG* (Cop.) 226)); they presumably reached Selinunte via North Africa. A hoard of issues of Magna Graecia from the Lipari islands clearly also reflects the turbulent vicissitudes of these years (*IGCH* 2210); so also the bronzes from Campania which occur in some quantity, for instance at Selinunte and Morgantina.

It is when we turn to the issues of Hieron II of Syracuse (275/4–215) that the trouble begins (Fig. 34). Enormous issues of silver in his own name, that of his consort Philistis and that of his son Gelon II were produced; also two enormous issues of bronze, with the types Head of Hieron/Horseman, and Head of Poseidon/Trident. Hoards of hundreds of pieces of silver are not uncommon and one bronze hoard of 60,000 pieces is attested, all of the Head of Poseidon/Trident type.[10]

10 *IGCH* 2217 perhaps contained Ptolemaic as well as Syracusan silver. Ptolemaic bronzes also turn up in small numbers in Sicily; they are the same size as the Head of Hieron/Horseman issue.

34 The coinage of Syracuse

Sixteen-litra piece of Philistis:
 Veiled head of Philistis l./Nike in quadriga r.; above, ΒΑΣΙΛΙΣΣΑΣ and crescent; before, Α; in exergue, ΦΙΛΙΣΤΙΔΟΣ
 Naville 5, 1223
Eight-litra piece of Gelon:
 Diademed head of Gelon l.; behind, eagle/Nike in biga r.; above, ΣΥΡΑΚΟΣΙΟΙ; between horses, Α; in exergue, ΓΕΛΩΝΟΣ
 Naville 16, 879
Bronze of Hieron II:
 Diademed head of Hieron l.; behind, shell/Horseman r.; below, monogram; in exergue, ΙΕΡΩΝΟΣ
 Naville 16, 888
Bronze of Hieron II:
 Diademed head of Poseidon l./Trident with dolphin on either side; below, ΙΕΡΩ ΝΟΣ and Ο Φ
 Naville 5, 1240

There are two pieces of evidence which suggest that much of the bronze coinage of Hieron II belongs to the period of the First Punic War, though its production obviously continued down to the end of his reign.[11] The first piece of evidence is provided by the Polizzi Generosa hoard of bronze coins (*IGCH* 2259), which clearly reflects Roman military activity in Sicily. It contains a good run of Syracusan material down to Hieron II, with fourth-century issues of Mytistratus and Tauromenium and a piece of Phintias of Agrigentum, also examples of the issue of Tauromenium with Head of Dionysus/Tripod and the issue of Agrigentum with Head of Apollo/Two

---

11 See App. D for an overstrike of Neapolis on a Head of Poseidon/Trident bronze.

35 The Sicilian coinage of Carthage during the Second Punic War

Ten-litra piece of Hieronymus:
 Diademed head of Hieronymus l./Thunderbolt; above, ΒΑΣΙΛΕΩΣ; below, ΙΕΡΩΝΥΜΟΥ
Naville 4, 419

Twelve-litra piece of Syracusan Democracy:
 Helmeted head of Athena l./Artemis l. with dog; on l. ΣΩ; on r., ΣΥΡΑΚΟΣΙΩΝ
Enna hoard

Half-shekel of Carthage struck in Sicily:
 Diademed male head l./Elephant r.; below, *a* Enna hoard

Half-shekel of Carthage struck in Sicily:
 Male head r., wearing corn-wreath/Horse r.; below, *h*; laurel-wreath around
Enna hoard

Half-shekel of Agrigentum:
 Laureate head of Zeus r./Eagle r.; on r., A; around, ΑΚΡΑΓΑΝΤΙΝ BM

eagles, finally some Carthaginian pieces and a group of issues of the Mamertini of Messana; most important of all, the hoard contains bronzes of Neapolis with ΙΣ, of Cales, of the earliest issue of Paestum and of Arpi with Bull/Horse, all First Punic War issues. It looks very much as if we are dealing with a First Punic War hoard. The second piece of evidence is provided by the material from Agrigentum; for it is very hard to think of a context for the vast numbers of Head of Poseidon/Trident bronzes of Hieron II hoarded and lost there except for the Roman tenure of the town between

261 and 255 and its loss to the Carthaginians in the latter year. If this is right, it follows that the indemnity which Hieron II paid from 263 to 248 was paid in bronze coinage which went directly to pay Roman troops (compare p.41). The tiny issue of bronzes with Minerva/Eagle ROMANO (*RRC*, no. 23), perhaps struck at Messana towards the end of the war, was an insignificant part of the process whereby the Roman war effort in Sicily in the First Punic War was financed. It remains likely that part of the coinage of the Mamertini served Roman ends.

The pattern in the Second Punic War was very different. The revolts of Syracuse *and* of Agrigentum threw the Romans largely back on their own resources, though it seems worth floating the hypothesis that the late gold and silver of Tauromenium belong to the years after 214, when Tauromenium prudently detached herself from Syracuse. As far as silver is concerned, Syracuse struck substantial issues in silver for her own purposes under Hieronymus and under the Democracy which succeeded him, Agrigentum struck substantial issues of half- and quarter-shekels before her recapture by Rome. At the same time, Carthage struck two large issues for use in Sicily (Fig. 35).[12]

Meanwhile the Romans both imported substantial quantities of quadrigati and later silver into the island and actually produced coinage there to a progressively increasing extent. Indeed the Enna hoard and two new hoards capture perfectly the circulating medium of the island in 212–211:[13]

ENNA	WALKER	MANGANARO
Syracuse (Hieron II to Democracy, with one *pegasus*)	Syracuse (Democracy)	Syracuse (Hieron II to Democracy)
Acragas	Acragas	Acragas
Carthage (Elephant issue) (Horse issue)	Carthage (Elephant issue) (Horse issue)	Carthage (Elephant issue) (Horse issue)
'Sikeliotan'[14]	'Sikeliotan'	'Sikeliotan'
Material from the east		
Rome Quadrigati	Rome Quadrigati Denarii, etc. Victoriati Neapolis and Velia	Rome Quadrigati Denarii, etc. Victoriati

12 R. Ross Holloway, *The Thirteen-months Coinage of Hieronymos of Syracuse* (Berlin, 1969); A. Burnett (n.13); R. Ross Holloway, *AIIN* 7–8, 1960–1, 35, 'Monete già attribuite a Hiempsal II'.

13 *IGCH* 2232 with A. Burnett, *SNR* 1983, 1; A. Walker, in *Studies L. Mildenberg* (forthcoming); G. Manganaro, *JNG* 1981–82, 37.

14 E. Sjoquist, *MusN* 1960, 53, 'The ΣΙΚΕΛΙΩΤΑΝ coinage'. The issue is clearly contemporary with those of the Syracusan Democracy, but there is no good reason to suppose it struck at Morgantina.

Between them, these hoards reveal the scale both of the Carthaginian and, more especially, of the Roman war effort in Sicily. The Carthaginian issue of shekels with Head with corn-ears/Horse was perhaps produced at Agrigentum; it suffered a reduction in weight towards the end. The issue with Laureate head/Elephant was either produced at Carthage, for Sicily, or by workmen from Carthage in Sicily; given the fact that a half-shekel of this issue was overstruck on a denarius (App. D), the latter alternative is perhaps more likely.

During the period before the introduction of the denarius coinage, the only Roman silver issue produced on the island seems to have been a small issue of quadrigati with corn-ear (*RRC*, no. 42); with the introduction of the denarius system at least two mints, one at Catana, struck silver on an enormous scale and a little gold (*RRC*, nos. 67–82, Fig. 36). In addition, quadrigati, denarii, quinarii, sestertii and victoriati were shipped from Rome to Sicily in massive quantities.

The Romans also produced a substantial bronze coinage in Sicily, beginning with a cast bronze issue, which must have surprised the Sicilians (*RRC*, no. 40; App. 35); struck bronze issues followed, still within the period of the quadrigatus system. The two mints which we have seen operating for the production of silver of the denarius system, one at Catana, also produced bronze coinage. If one examines the hoards of this period, it becomes apparent that they contain a number of local issues which are certainly to be regarded as having been evoked by the Second Punic War (see Table 4); their tally can indeed be increased by the inclusion of issues which appear to belong with those which turn up in the hoards or which bear a close stylistic similarity to Roman issues produced in Sicily in this period. Most of the issues in question seem to have been produced by communities on the side of Rome. Within the overall pattern, it is clear that the Mamertini and Rhegium played a substantial role (Fig. 37). The Romans also seem to have used halved Poseidon/Trident bronzes of Hieron II as unciae.[15]

TABLE 4. Sicilian hoards of the Second Punic War

For bibliography see App. 36.

The numbers appearing below each mint are those of the issues in question in *BMCSicily*, unless otherwise indicated.

The Villarosa, Barrafranca and Megara Hyblaea hoards are omitted as containing only Rome and, among Sicilian mints, Syracuse, the Adrano hoard and the hoard mentioned by G. Manganaro, *JNG* 1981–2, 52, as containing only Rome and, among Sicilian mints, the Mamertini.

---

[15] The weight standards of the Mamertini and Rhegium are local, not Roman, *contra* P. Marchetti, 494; for the Roman use of Syracusan coins see R. Ross Holloway, *MusN* 1960, 61, 'Half-coins of Hieron II'.

Tripi	Aidone 1908–1909	Mandanici
Rome to post-semilibral	Rome to post-semilibral	Rome to post-semilibral
		Victoriatus
Syracuse to Hieron II	Syracuse to Democracy	Syracuse Hieron II
Mamertini 3, 22	Mamertini 22	Mamertini 24, Särström III
Rhegium 45, 60, 72	Rhegium 45, 72, 84, 97	Rhegium 45, 71, 72, 84, 87
	Carthage Tanit l./Horse r. looking back *SNG* (Cop.) 307	
	Menaenum 10	

Montagna di Marzo	San Marco d'Alunzio	Grammichele
Rome to sextantal	Rome to sextantal	Rome to sextantal
Syracuse to Democracy	Syracuse Hieron II	Syracuse to Democracy *SNG* (Cop.) 901 *SNG* (Euelp.) 601
Mamertini 25	Mamertini 27	Mamertini 14, 25, 46
Rhegium 45, 71		
Ptolemy II		
Carthage *SNG* (Cop.) 381		Carthage Tanit l./Horse and palm Palm/Horse's head r. Head l./Horse galloping r.
	Haluntium 2, 4, Male head l./ Butting bull l.	Haluntium 2, Male head l./Butting bull l.
		Menaenum 10
		Catana 65

36 The Sicilian issues of Rome during the Second Punic War

Cast quadrans with corn-ear, *RRC*, no. 40/1b:
  Head of Hercules l.; behind, two (out of three) dots/Prow l.; above, corn-ear; below, three dots
  Syracuse 31950

Quadrigatus with corn-ear, *RRC*, no. 42/1:
  Janiform heads of Dioscuri/Jupiter with thunderbolt and sceptre in quadriga r. driven by Victory; below, corn-ear; in frame, ROMA
  BMCRR Romano-Campanian 108

Uncia with corn-ear, *RRC*, no. 42/4:
  Helmeted head of Roma r.; behind, dot/Prow r.; above, corn-ear and ROMA; below, dot
  Oxford

Denarius with corn-ear, *RRC*, no. 68/1a:
  Helmeted head of Roma r.; behind, X/Dioscuri r.; below, corn-ear, in frame, ROMA
  Oxford

Sextans with corn-ear and KA, *RRC*, no. 69/6a:
  Head of Mercury r.; above, two dots/Prow r.; above, corn-ear; before, KA; below, ROMA
  Oxford

Victoriatus with corn-ear, *RRC*, no. 72/1:
  Laureate head of Jupiter r./Victory r. crowning trophy; between, corn-ear; in exergue, ROMA
  BMCRR Italy 138

It seems that the coinage of independent Syracuse, not only in gold and silver, but also in bronze, disappeared from circulation almost immediately after the fall of the city and one must at least ask whether this disappearance is not the result of Roman policy, perhaps implemented by M. Valerius Laevinus, perhaps implemented later; we know of Roman intervention in 193 to settle the composition of the council of Agrigentum. This is a question to which I shall return. What is clear is that at a certain point the Romans organised or allowed a monetary system for Sicily which in some way related locally produced bronze to Roman silver and bronze.

The system was certainly in existence by the time of the Verrines of Cicero, where

37 The coinages of the Sicilian allies of Rome of the Second Punic War

Semis with corn-ear, *RRC*, no. 72/5:
    Laureate head of Saturn r.; behind, S/Prow r.; above, corn-ear and ROMA; below, S
                                                                                                                                 Berlin
Four uncia bronze piece of Centuripae:
    Laureate head of Jupiter r.; behind, eagle/Thunderbolt; above KENT[O]; below,
    ΡIΠINΩN and Δ   Naville 5, 860
Five uncia bronze piece of Mamertini:
    Laureate head of Ares l.; behind, sword in scabbard/Warrior with horse l.; before, Π;
    around, ΜΑΜΕΡΤΙΝΩΝ   Naville 5, 970
Four uncia piece of Rhegium:
    Jugate heads of Apollo, laureate, and Artemis, diademed, r.; behind, Θ/Tripod; on l.
    ΡΗΓΙ; on r. ΝΩΝ and four dots   Naville 16, 633

114 COINAGE AND MONEY UNDER THE ROMAN REPUBLIC

we read (*II in Verr.* 3, 181) 'For how can there be an agio when everyone uses the same kind of coins?' Since local bronzes were produced in Sicily at least down to the time of Augustus 'the same kind of coins' must refer to the unitary nature of the monetary system and not to the origins of the coins themselves. The Roman character of the monetary system of Sicily emerges from the fact that in the Verrines Cicero always calculates in sestertii (compare Quint. vi, 3, 80, for the victoriatus = quinarius used as a unit of reckoning under Augustus). But the inscribed accounts from Tauromenium, which are certainly later than the Verrines, reckon in talents, *nomoi*, *heminoma*, *tetralitra* and *litrai* (see App. L). It is clear that this system must have been compatible with the sestertius as a unit of reckoning, perhaps with a *tetralitron* as the equivalent of a sestertius and a *litra* as the equivalent of an as. The evidence of the coins fills out

38   The coinage of Sicily under Roman rule

Bronzes of Caleacte:
   Helmeted head of Athena r.; behind, poppy-head/Owl on amphora; on either side,
     KA ΛA
     KTI NΩ[N]   BM
   Head of Dionysus r. wearing ivy-wreath/Bunch of grapes; on l. ΚΑΛΑ; on r., ΚΤΙΝΩΝ
                                                                                                                         BM
   Laureate head of Apollo r./Lyre; legend similar   BM
   Head of Mercury r./Caduceus; legend similar   BM
As struck under Roman authority:
   Laureate head of Janus; above, I/Bird in laurel-wreath   BM
Semis struck under Roman authority:
   Laureate head of Saturn l./Warrior l. holding spear; on r., shield; on l., CATO and
   monogram of Panormus   BM

the picture of a symbiosis between local units and Roman units and perhaps provides some evidence for when this symbiosis came into existence (see App. 37).

Sicilian hoards of the first half of the second century, where they do contain local bronzes, contain only insignificant relics of the circulating medium of the third century. It is only towards the end of the second century that the new issues, whether of the Roman authorities at Panormus or elsewhere or of the Greek cities, begin to appear. My guess would be that the new dispensation formed part of the reorganisation of the province after the First Slave Revolt and involved a deliberate encouragement of local autonomies (Fig. 38).[16] At least one substantial issue, that of Caleacte, certainly seems to belong in this period; for the largest piece is clearly copied from the new-style tetradrachms of Athens.

But the large-scale circulation of Roman coinage in Sicily which was one of the factors which made possible a symbiosis of Roman and native systems of reckoning and coins was in a certain sense the result of an accident. For Roman coinage continued to flow to Sicily in substantial quantities *after* the end of the Second Punic War, in clear contrast to what happened in Spain. No doubt this was in part the result of the presence of Romans and Italians as men of business from soon after the fall of Syracuse.[17] But the principal cause surely lies in the fact that the Romans not only took over the tithe system from Hieron II, but also by *buying* a second tithe followed his practice of shipping grain out of the island in exchange for silver.[18] The difference is that under Roman rule the denarii which arrived were not melted down to make new coinage, but circulated as denarii. Thus Sicily rapidly became a zone of denarius circulation, but a zone where native systems of reckoning survived; the eventual result was a system of reckoning and of coinage which can only be described as Romano-Sicilian.

16 Compare the survival of the Greek calendars of the Sicilian cities, Cicero, *II in Verr.* 2, 129; Tauromenium adopted the Roman calendar after 44.
17 A. Fraschetti, in *Società Romana* I, 51, 'Romani e Italici in Sicilia'.
18 In the period after the Second Punic War covered by Livy, the Romans bought a second tithe in 191, 190 and 189, and again in 171. Denarii perhaps also arrived in Sicily in return for slaves, whose export from Sicily is envisaged in the *lex censoria portus* and case law arising therefrom, *D.* 50, 19, 203. Wool was also produced in Sicily, Strabo vi, 2, 7 (273), and perhaps served to clothe Roman armies, *II in Verr.* 2, 5.

8

FROM THE FREEDOM OF THE GREEKS TO THE SACK OF CORINTH

In 199, the Roman army based at Apollonia penetrated briefly across the mountains into Macedonia, and in the same year the Roman fleet operated in the Aegean; but it was not until 198 that T. Quinctius Flamininus forced Philip V, encamped in the gorge of Aoi Stena, to retreat; Flamininus then moved through Epirus into Thessaly, to defeat Philip at the battle of Cynoscephalae in the following year (Map 21).[1] Between 199 and 30, Roman armies operated east of the mountain spine of the Balkan peninsula in 135 out of 170 years; in 167 L. Aemilius Paullus put an end to the kingdom of Macedonia, which became a province in 148; the independence of Greece came to an end in 146 and after 133 the kingdom of Pergamum also became a province. By 63, Pompey had brought almost the whole of the east outside the kingdom of Egypt under direct Roman rule.

Yet Roman coinage hardly circulated in Greece before Sulla, in Asia and Syria before the age of Augustus or even later; and when Egypt became a province it was deliberately isolated from the monetary systems of the rest of the Mediterranean. How did Rome pay for her presence in the east? And what was the impact of that presence on the patterns of coinage and monetary usages of the Greek world?

1 N.G.L. Hammond, *JRS* 1966, 39, 'The opening campaigns of the Second Macedonian War'.

21   Macedonia and Greece

One might suppose *a priori* that until booty became available, the Romans adopted one or other of two approaches in order to acquire the necessities of life, whether as individuals or as groups acting through their command structure: they presumably either used denarii, which were then treated as bullion and melted down, or they took the precaution of acquiring in advance the currency of the localities where they were operating, either in exchange for bullion or in exchange for denarii which were again then treated as bullion and melted down.

Plutarch's account of the movement of the Roman army south through Epirus after the battle of Aoi Stena, presumably deriving from Polybius, certainly implies that at that period Roman armies operating in Greece sometimes followed the normal practice of Greek armies and relied on the local provision of market facilities: 'although they were far from their supply ships and the sea and had not been supplied with their monthly rations and did not have access to a well-stocked market, they kept their hands off the surrounding countryside, although it was full of good things' (Plutarch, *Titus* 5). A similar inference may be drawn from the account of Polybius (xx, 7, 3) of the events in Boeotia following the murder of Brachyllas.

It is in any case quite clear that Roman operations east of the mountain spine of the Balkan peninsula in this period left virtually no trace in the shape of Roman coinage of any sort. An isolated bronze of the pre-denarius coinage from Elatea was presumably a piece which travelled thither casually with a soldier serving under Flamininus and was then lost or thrown away;[2] in the Italy from which it came it had already passed out of currency and it was presumably no *more* useful in Greece. An as in the Makrakomi hoard from near Lamia in Thessaly is presumably likewise an escapee from a Roman soldier passing through the area.[3] It is interesting to note that a number of bronzes of Greek mints of Italy and Sicily of the late third century turn up in the Peloponnese, Attica, Boeotia and Euboea (App. 38); they no doubt arrived in Greece in the context of Roman and allied troop movements.

A small hoard of denarii from Calauria in the Saronic Gulf, closing in the 180s, *may* be connected with Roman movements after the end of the war against Antiochus III (*RRCH* 121). And a single denarius of about 170 in a hoard from Thebes may be connected with the war against Perseus (*RRCH* 233). That is all there is before 146 and there is precious little thereafter.

The occurrence of stray Greek bronzes of Italy and Sicily in larger quantities than stray Roman bronzes invites the hypothesis that their owners, whether Romans or allies, consciously attempted to spend them in Greece and in some measure succeeded. This hypothesis, if acceptable, perhaps in turn lends support to the view that Roman armies in the course of their campaigns east of the Adriatic regularly used local currencies for that part of the *stipendium* of the soldiers which was not held back for payment on their return (see p.94). Presumably they obtained them through normal banking channels and presumably at any rate in theory the demand might stimulate increased output by a local mint, though I know of no certain example. It is this background which helps in part to explain the fact that when the Romans found themselves obliged after 167 to organise a coinage for one area of the Greek world after another they produced coinages which were on a Greek model, though identifiably Roman in

---

2 A Head of Mars/Horse ROMA piece (information from Alan Walker).

3 *IGCH* 214; compare an early sextans (*RRC*, no. 69/6) from Cythera or Anticythera, *JIAN* 10, 1907, 178–80.

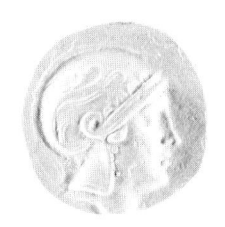

39 The coinage of Athens

Old-style tetradrachm of Athens:
  Helmeted head of Athena r./Owl r.; above, crescent; on r., AΘE Lockett 1878
Transitional style tetradrachm of Athens:
  Helmeted head of Athena r./Owl r.; above, olive-spray; on l., forepart of horse and
  monogram; on r., AΘE Sitochoro hoard

origin;[4] the first of these coinages is of course that of Macedonia itself, followed after 133 by the cistophoric coinage of Asia and in due course by the coinage of Syria, Egypt and Cappadocia,[5] to name the most important.

The monetary situations to which the Romans had to adapt in their use of local currencies were very varied, and to these situations we must now turn in order to appreciate the effect of the Roman presence.[6] For the fact that the Romans did not import their own coinage into the Greek world does not mean that their presence had no effect on existing monetary patterns (App. 39).

As far as Attica is concerned, coin hoards provide almost no evidence for the whole of the period from 250 to 150; there is no reason to doubt, however, that Athenian coinage provided the bulk, perhaps the virtual totality, of the circulating medium, both in silver and in bronze (Fig. 39). The inscriptions of Attica of this period certainly reflect only the use of Attic coinage.[7]

The most conspicuous feature of the coin finds from Euboea, apart from their number, is the prominence, not simply of coins struck on the island, but of coins struck there in the distant past (Fig. 40). With the drachms of the Euboean League and the Euboean cities of the Hellenistic period, their weight oscillating around 3.60 gm., are

---

4 See A. Giovannini, *Rome et la circulation monétaire en Grèce au IIe siècle avant Jésus-Christ* (Basle, 1978), 35, attributing to the Romans too much respect for Greek liberty.
5 The gold issue of Flamininus (p.124) hardly forms part of a pattern of providing a coinage for the Greek world; for the anomalous issue bearing the name of Q. Sura on Thasos and the equally anomalous Sullan issues of the same period, see p.197.
6 The résumé given by A. Giovannini (n.4), 12–13, is wildly inaccurate.
7 *IGCH* 218 consists of 8 pieces of Histiaea; the earliest hoards of new-style Athenian silver from Athens (*IGCH* 250) or Delos (*IGCH* 256, 272, 284) are of the 120s or later.

40 The coinage of Euboea

Drachm of Euboean League:
   Head of nymph r./Head of bull r. decorated with fillets; above, EY   Naville 14, 251
Drachm of Chalcis:
   Head of nymph r./Eagle with snake l.; on r., torch and XAΛ   Lockett 785

found Parian and Rhodian pieces on roughly the same weight standard and Boeotian drachms of about 5.25 gm.; but also early didrachms of Aeginetic weight and tetradrachms of Attic weight of the Euboean League, and Locrian, Phocian and Boeotian issues of Aeginetic weight of the fourth century. Athenian silver and royal silver of Attic weight form a significant element of the first two hoards, a large consignment of Ptolemaic silver of the first hoard, all three coinages to disappear thereafter.

   Other developments are more or less what one would expect. The turbulent years of the Second Macedonian War are reflected in the arrival of some other island coinages of Rhodian weight. The events of the Third Macedonian War are reflected, not surprisingly, in the arrival of a consignment of Macedonian issues (Philip V, Perseus, Macedonia *in genere*, with an early issue of Larissa), together with an enormous consignment of pieces of Rhodian type (see below) and a few strays from Aetolia and the Peloponnese, based on a drachm of 5.25 to 5.00 gm.

   The situation in Boeotia and Phocis is similar to that in Euboea (except for the absence of pieces from Euboea itself), as far as the exiguous evidence permits conclusions; unfortunately, one never quite knows how far the epigraphically attested offerings at shrines such as that of Oropus reflect circulation. The Abae hoard contains a substantial admixture of Peloponnesian pieces and one piece of Aetolian bronze; one Theban hoard contains a few of the pieces of Rhodian type which seem to belong to the period of the Third Macedonian War (see below); the new-style tetradrachms of Eretria and Chalcis, struck in the 170s, appear along with the new-style tetradrachms of Athens in the Anthedon hoard.

   For Thessaly, the evidence is again inadequate; an appendage of Macedonia till after the Second Macedonian War, it presumably shared in the circulation pattern

FROM THE FREEDOM OF THE GREEKS TO THE SACK OF CORINTH 121

41   The coinages of the Sitochoro hoard

Tetradrachm of Philip V:
  Head of the hero Perseus l. in centre of Macedonian shield/Club r. in oak-wreath; on l., star; above club, monogram and ΒΑΣΙΛΕΩΣ; below club, ΦΙΛΙΠΠΟΥ and two monograms
  Sitochoro hoard
Tetradrachm of Perseus:
  Diademed head of Perseus r./Eagle on thunderbolt in oak-wreath; above and on r. of eagle, two monograms; on either side of eagle,   ΒΑΣΙ ΛΕΩΣ
                          ΠΕΡ ΣΕΩΣ; below wreath, torch
  Sitochoro hoard
Imitation of drachm of Rhodes:
  Facing head of Helios/Rose; above, ΕΡΜΙΑΣ   Sitochoro hoard
Tetrobol of Histiaea:
  Head of nymph r./Nymph on prow r.; below, trident and monogram; around, ΙΣΤΙΑΕΩΝ   Lockett 1799

of Macedonia; not much may be inferred from the miserable fragment of a hoard comprising three Seleucid and seven Boeotian pieces; the Grammenon hoard from near Larissa contains one drachm of Philip V, tetrobols of Macedonia and Histiaea, and drachms of Rhodes. We then move to hoards which reflect the events of the Third Macedonian War; two consist exclusively or almost exclusively of tetrobols of Histiaea (see below); the Sitochoro hoard from near Pharsalus, apart from some earlier regal material (along with one third-century tetradrachm of Aetolia and eleven old-style tetradrachms of Athens), contains 600 tetradrachms of the last issue of Perseus, struck

42 The coinages in circulation in the Peloponnese
Tetradrachm of Antiochus III:
 Diademed head of Antiochus r./Apollo seated on *omphalos* l.; on r., ΒΑΣΙΛΕΩΣ; on l.,
 ΑΝΤΙΟΧΟΥ and monogram; in exergue, H   Naville 10, 985
Tetradrachm of Ptolemy III:
 Diademed head of Ptolemy I r./Eagle on thunderbolt; on l., ΠΗ; around,
 ΠΤΟΛΕΜΑΙΟΥ ΣΩΤΗΡΟΣ   Naville 7, 1849

on a weight standard of about 14.00 gm., instead of 17.50 gm.,[8] and up to 2000 pieces of Rhodian type, almost certainly also produced by Perseus (see below), and finally the first issue of Macedonia as a Republic (Fig. 41). Two hoards show what was available in the way of large silver and small silver later in the century, tetradrachms of Perseus in substantial quantities along with tetradrachms of Athens, on the one hand, an assortment of old and new, including issues of the Magnetes and the Thessalian League, on the other.

Macedonia depended during the period of its independence on the silver of its own kings, with some tetradrachms from elsewhere, notably Athens; the Yeniköy (Yenikeui) hoard from Amphipolis combines regal silver along with small silver of Macedonia *in genere*, Histiaea and Rhodes; the first two form the content of an enormous hoard found in the early nineteenth century, the first that of a small hoard from Pella; we then move down into the middle of the second century, when the new-style coinage of Athens is dominant, alongside earlier regal issues and the new coinage of Macedonia as a republic.

The silver hoards of Epirus in the late third century are dominated by the issues of Corinth and her colonies,[9] at first with an admixture of Corcyra, Dyrrachium,

8 The assertion of P.R. Franke, *JNG* 1957, 31–46, 'Zur Finanzpolitik des Perseus', that Perseus wished to relate the weight standard of his silver to those of Rhodes, Egypt and Rome is unreasonable; Perseus wished to save silver.

9 For the continued dominance of Corinthian silver in the late third century see *I.Magnesia* 44, line 32 (relating to Apollonia); 46, line 41 (relating to Epidamnus (later Dyrrachium)).

Apollonia, Acarnania (and Caulonia in Italy) and the early issues of the Epirote Republic (*IGCH* 207 (with one piece of Sicyon), 212, 236). The Republic itself struck substantial quantities of drachms weighing 3.40 gm. in the context of the Third Macedonian War; one issue was struck by the Cephalus of Polybius xxx, 7, 2. But one hoard still consists almost entirely of issues of Corinth and her colonies (with a posthumous tetrobol of Philip II, an early triobol of Boeotia and a coin probably of Corcyra); the batch of coins of Histiaea (*IGCH* 248) clearly arrived in the early 160s; three other hoards with material brought from Macedonia in this period lie close to the route taken by Perseus in his march to Aetolia in 169.[10] The systematic devastation of this area by the Romans after 168 ensured that the numismatic record stopped at that point for a generation.

Of Aetolia almost nothing can be said; the League, between 220/19 and 146/5, struck tetradrachms of Attic weight and then didrachms, drachms and hemidrachms based on a drachm of 5.25 gm.;[11] local coinage seems to have predominated in the late third and early second centuries, with a little material from Boeotia and the Peloponnese.[12] A similar predominance of local material characterises the only relevant hoard from Acarnania.[13]

The coinage in use in the Peloponnese in the last generation of the third century comprised, apart from local issues, predominantly issues of Athens, of the kings of Macedon, of the Seleucids and of the Ptolemies, the last category in very substantial quantities, together with material from Chalcis and a little from elsewhere in central Greece (Fig. 42); this material perhaps arrived via the Macedonian garrison of Corinth, since there was also a Macedonian garrison in Chalcis. The appearance of Rhodian material (with two pieces from Ephesus) in the Corinth hoard, along with Athenian and regal issues, Macedonian, Seleucid and Ptolemaic, should in my view be associated with the Second Macedonian War, even if it is true that no coin in the hoard is later than about 215. The problem which arises for the years after 200 is that there are no hoards of large silver; if this represents the true state of affairs rather than merely resulting from a gap in the evidence, one can see regal issues, here as in Euboea, disappearing from 200 onwards.

On balance, it seems reasonable to accept the disappearance from circulation around 200 of Macedonian and other regal silver, in areas where it had circulated before, with the obvious exception of Macedonia itself. The precise significance of this

---

10 See A. Giovannini (n.4), 103–7, for the coins of Epirus; the hoards are *IGCH* 231, 235, 309; N.G.L. Hammond, *Epirus* (Oxford, 1967), 281–2, describes Perseus' route.

11 R.A. de Laix, *Calif.St.Class.Ant.* 1973, 47, 'The silver coinage of the Aetolian League'.

12 *IGCH* 196, 224; nothing useful can be said of *Coin Hoards* 2, 74.

13 *Coin Hoards* 4, 43; note that *IG* ix², 1, 3A, line 39, a treaty between Aetolia and Acarnania of about 262, specifies Corinthian silver in the payment of troops; by the end of the century *I.Magnesia* 31, line 35, refers to unspecified drachms, presumably Acarnanian.

phenomenon is uncertain and two approaches to a solution are possible. One approach starts from the observation that it is not only regal silver, but also Attic silver which disappears from circulation and one might speculate that both categories, consisting of large denominations, were sucked in by Macedonia as part of the process of collecting the wherewithal to pay the indemnity imposed by Rome.

On the other hand, Athenian silver reappears in Boeotia and Aetolia, whereas Macedonian silver never reappears outside Macedonia, except in Thessaly, which was occupied by Perseus. One might therefore suggest that the absence of Attic silver from hoards in Greece in the first generation of the second century is accidental, whereas the permanent disappearance of regal silver is the result of a deliberate decision. If this is so, one can go on to ask whether the decision is that of Flamininus. The disappearance of regal silver must be considered in the light of another monetary phenomenon of this period, namely the overstriking in Boeotia of thousands of coins of Macedonia (App. 40). The only certain fact about this phenomenon is that it occurred between the late third century and 168; we have no idea how the coins in question reached Boeotia. But the process of overstriking is perhaps evidence of a desire on the part of someone to remove from circulation a substantial block of Macedonian coinage.

There are also grounds for supposing at least that Flamininus would have wished to encourage the disappearance of Macedonian silver from Greece. I was wrong to write that the gold coinage of Flamininus was produced simply to pay homage to Flamininus, not by Flamininus;[14] for not only is the legend T. QVINCTI in Latin, which is perhaps not all that important, but it also consists of *praenomen* and *nomen*, which Greek inscriptions in this period almost never use to designate Romans. (Greeks believed for many years that Romans could be identified by their *praenomen* alone.) We do not *need* to suppose that Flamininus actually issued an order to suppress the circulation of Macedonian silver and to produce gold in his name; as with the assassination of Brachyllas, an indication of his wishes will have sufficed.

But I should like to argue for a compromise between the two approaches, and suggest that the disappearance of large silver from Greece after 196 was the result of the need of Macedonia for the wherewithal to pay the Roman indemnity; the failure of Macedonian silver to reappear in Greece results from the isolation of Greece from Macedonia which Rome was able to orchestrate.[15] The contrast with the situation after 167 is in any case striking. I do not need here to document the Roman 'solutions' to the problems which faced them over Macedonia, Epirus, Greece, Rhodes. But the approach to monetary affairs is quite different and does not seem to involve suppression of Macedonian issues, despite the fact that Perseus had produced not only enormous issues of a traditional kind, but had also organised the production of

14 *RRC*, p. 544.
15 Note that in 189 Athenian coinage served as a standard in the treaties with Aetolia and Antiochus, Pol. xxi, 32, 8; 43, 19.

substantial issues in Epirus and had struck imitations of the coins of Histiaea and of Rhodes, for reasons which remain unclear (App. M, compare p.221 for Illyria).[16]

The monetary sequel in Greece of the Roman settlement of 167 involves consideration of the new-style silver coinage of Athens, which now bore a wreath round the reverse type (the term *stephanephoron* is only attested for Athens [17]) and, in the north, of the tetradrachms of Maronea, Thasos and of two of the four regions of Macedonia; the Magnetes and the Thessalians also struck silver in the period after 167. Thessalian staters are mentioned in the new inscription dealing with the despatch of corn to Rome in about 150.[18]

A few years ago, when the Athenian and other new-style issues were dated to the years after the Roman victory of Cynoscephalae in 197, it was easy to see the new start in the minting of large silver by the cities concerned as a consequence of the freeing of Greece by Flamininus. But it is now clear that the coinages in question belong about 20 to 30 years later. And Greece as a whole did not view the defeat of Perseus altogether favourably (Pol. xxviii, 6). Athens was of course a conspicuous beneficiary of the settlement of 167, notably as a result of the acquisition of Delos, and it may be possible to see the wreath on her new-style coinage in part as reflecting a sense of gratitude for the Roman victory over the Macedonian monarchy, if it is dated after the victory.[19] It is in any case impossible to avoid the conclusion that the existence at Athens of a substantial tetradrachm coinage for nearly a hundred years was evoked in large part by the needs of her administration of Delos, where a large number of the pieces now known have been found (Fig. 43); the mechanism by which the administration of Delos evoked the new-style silver coinage of Athens is not attested; but it emerges from the accounts of the Athenian administration of the temple that coinages other than the new-style coinage of Athens were withdrawn from circulation as they came into the temple treasury;[20] and presumably all those who came to do business on Delos had to acquire and use Athenian coinage. The development of the port then explains the scale on which the Athenian new-style coinage was produced (compare p.196).

16 For the history of the coinage of Epirus in these years see A. Giovannini (n.4), 103–7.
17 H. Nicolet-Pierre, *Studia P. Naster* I (Louvain, 1982), 105, 'De l'ancien au nouveau style'; O. Mørkholm, *MusN* 1984, 29, 'The chronology of the new style coinage of Athens'; compare p.156.
18 P. Garnsey, *JRS* 1984 (forthcoming), 'Thessaly and the grain-supply of Rome'.
19 It is impossible to agree with the view of A. Giovannini (n.4), 100, that the coinage was produced at the behest of the Romans.
20 A. Giovannini (n.4), 51–62; also L. Robert, *RN* 1962, 1, 'Monnaies dans les inscriptions grecques', at 18, for the withdrawal of the coinage of Delos itself. Romans on Delos clearly exchanged their denarii for local coinage; the small hoard of a denarius of C. Fonteius and thirteen asses, *BCH* 1947–48, 392 (with information from M. Oeconomidou), is wholly exceptional (for the first century see p.197); see also *Exploration archéologique de Delos* XXVII, 387, two Roman coins, 28 Delian, 378 Athenian, compare the table; denarii, half-pieces and asses occasionally appear in the temple offertory boxes after 166.

43   The new-style coinage of Athens

New-style tetradrachm of Athens, Thompson 50a:
   Helmeted head of Athena r./Owl on amphora in olive-wreath; above A ΘE; on either
   side, monogram; on l., corn-ear   Lockett 1904
New-style tetradrachm of Athens, Thompson 409b:
   Helmeted head of Athena r./Owl on amphora in olive-wreath; above, A ΘE; on l., ΘEO;
   on r., ΦPA, ΣΩTA, AMΦIK; on l., thunderbolt; on amphora, K; below, ME
                                                                     Naville 7, 1126 = ANS

The other major currency of central and southern Greece in the first half of the second century consists of the triobols weighing just over 2.50 gm. and associated denominations, produced in large quantities by Boeotia, the Aetolian and Achaean 'leagues' (the latter including Megara), and a number of *poleis* in the Peloponnese (including Megalopolis) (Fig. 44); the coinage of the Achaeans is described with pride by Polybius (ii, 37, 10): they observed the same laws and used the same weights, measures and coinage, were indeed almost a *polis*. This and the other coinages are described in a number of inscriptions of the second and first centuries as *argyrion symmachikon*.[21]

The coinages also occur in a large number of hoards (compare p.119), occasionally with drachms of Chalcis or other mints or tetrobols of Histiaea or other odds and ends (see App. 39); the hoards come without exception from the Peloponnese or north-western Greece and are clearly to be related to the disaster of 146.

Meanwhile, it is also clear that issues of bronze coinage were being produced on a vast scale in Greece towards the middle and end of the second century. The hoard evidence is scattered and incomplete, but it serves to show that the prevailing tendency

---

21 A. Giovannini (n.4), 43–51, with list of testimonia, argues oddly that the coinages were not so described because they were 'league' coinages, but because one of them, the Achaean, had been a 'league' coinage before the loss of independence in 146; the essential point was made by U. von Wilamowitz-Moellendorf, *Hermes* 1873, 431, 'Abrechnung eines Hipparchen'. Hesychius, *MSR* I, 323, 22, seems not to be relevant to this coinage.

44 The coinages of the 'leagues'

Triobol of Achaean 'league' of Patras:
  Laureate head of Zeus r./Monogram of AX in laurel-wreath; above, monogram; on either
  side, Δ 1; below, trident r.   Naville 7, 1126
Triobol of Megalopolis:
  Laureate head of Zeus l./Pan seated l. on rock; before, eagle; behind, MEΓ
                                                                           Naville 5, 2257
Triobol of Aetolian 'league':
  Head of Aetolia l./Boar r.; above ΑΙΤΩΛΩΝ; below, two monograms   Naville 1, 1333

was for such issues to circulate locally. The pattern is the same, on Crete, on Delos, on Paros, at Delphi, in Thessaly, on Corcyra, in Acarnania, in Aetolia, at Elis, at Tegea, above all at Corinth, where the destruction level of 146 provides ample material for study (App. 41).

But as far as silver is concerned, after 146, Athens was the only mint active south of Thessaly, apart from a tiny issue of Chalcis. The result was the final acceptance in the Greek world of the silver coinage of Athens as a sort of international currency. The process by which this occurred can perhaps be observed in the inscription recording the votes at the end of the investigation at Delphi of the financial scandal of 125; some votes expressed the missing sum in *talanta*, some in *symmachika talanta*, some in *sterea talanta*, some in *talanta attika*, the last two both being treated as *sterea talanta* in the final summation (*SIG* 826 D). *Talanta symmachika* were apparently of a different weight from *talanta attika*;[22] for the most plausible interpretation of the sums in *argyrion symmachikon* in *IG* v, 2, 345, involves a mina of 70 drachms; such a mina, composed of drachms weighing about 5.00 gm., weighs about five-sixths as much as an Attic mina. The Delphi inscription seems then to reflect the developing role of the silver coinage of Athens. The late second-century Amphictyonic decree enjoining its use was the natural consequence.[23]

[22] G. Colin, *BCH* 1903, 104, 'Inscriptions de Delphes', at 138–40; compare the 'big' talents of Plautus, *Rudens* 1307–1416; Pol. xxviii, 13, 13; *ORF*, C.Gracchus XII.

[23] *La moneta in Grecia e a Roma* (Bari, 1982), 32; note the use of Attic reckoning at Tanagra in the 80s, M.Calvet and P.Roesch, *RA* 1966, 297.

The late second-century Athenian decree on weights and measures probably also reflects the monetary history of these years; one of its clauses prescribed that the commercial mina should consist of 138 + 12 drachms, the equivalent of two Roman pounds (*IG* ii-iii², 1013 = *Epigraphica* I, 14). The weight is already attested in the fifth century, but it is likely that its endorsement or re-establishment is due to Roman influence;[24] in demanding so many talents, Rome was accustomed to ensure that the talents were of full weight by specifying that they must contain 80 Roman pounds (Pol. xxi, 43, 19).

Three hoards also finally attest the very beginning of the arrival of Roman coinage in the Greek world, from Agrinium, Stobi and Naupactus. The first (*IGCH* 271) is an odd assemblage of material, since its three principal blocks of coinage have different terminal dates: the Achaean material about 155, the Athenian about 130, the Roman somewhere in between. The Stobi hoard, consisting of one Athenian tetradrachm, one victoriatus and 504 denarii, was perhaps lost on the occasion of the raid of the Scordisci in 119, and perhaps indeed arrived in Macedonia with a member of the Roman provincial administration.[25] The Naupactus hoard (*IGCH* 317), with one Athenian tetradrachm and three denarii, is fundamentally similar in composition. It would be extremely rash to argue for meaningful circulation of the denarius in Greece on the basis of these three hoards.

Let us turn to northern Greece. Here, as we have seen (p. 120), despite their reduced weight, the coins of Perseus continued to circulate in Macedonia and in Thessaly (whither they had arrived during the reign of Perseus) and one cannot therefore see either the coins of Maronea and Thasos or the coins of the first two regions of Macedonia as coinages organised by Rome to replace the issues of the kings of Macedon.[26] They are, however, almost by definition in some sense Roman creations.

In 167, the Romans divided Macedonia into four separate regions possessing internal autonomy (Map 22): the first lay east of the Strymon, with its capital at Amphipolis, the second between Strymon and Axius, with its capital at Thessalonica, the third between Axius and Peneus, with its capital at Pella, the fourth consisted of Upper Macedonia, Lyncestis, Orestis and Elimiotis, with its capital at Heraclea (Pelagonia); all the regions paid to Rome half of what the monarchy had levied. *Conubium* and *commercium* between the different regions was forbidden, as was the exploitation of the gold and silver mines of the area;[27] at the same time, the importation of salt was

---

24 O. Viedebannt, *Hermes* 1916, 120, 'Der athenische Volksbeschluss über Mass und Gewicht'.

25 *Studies in the Antiquities of Stobi* 1, 1973, 1.

26 A. Giovannini (n.4), 19 and 41, esp. n.69, is simply wrong when he asserts that Alexanders and Macedonian issues were generally suppressed at this point; note also coins of Perseus as offerings on Delos in the 140s, *I.Delos* 1443 A I, line 148; 1449 Aab II, line 22; 1450 A, lines 101 and 112, with P. Roussel, *Delos colonie athénienne* (Paris, 1916), 166–8.

27 See *RRC*, p.74; L. Perelli, *RFIC* 1975, 403, 'La chiusura delle miniere macedoni', is wrong on the history of the Macedonian coinage and offers an impossible translation of Livy.

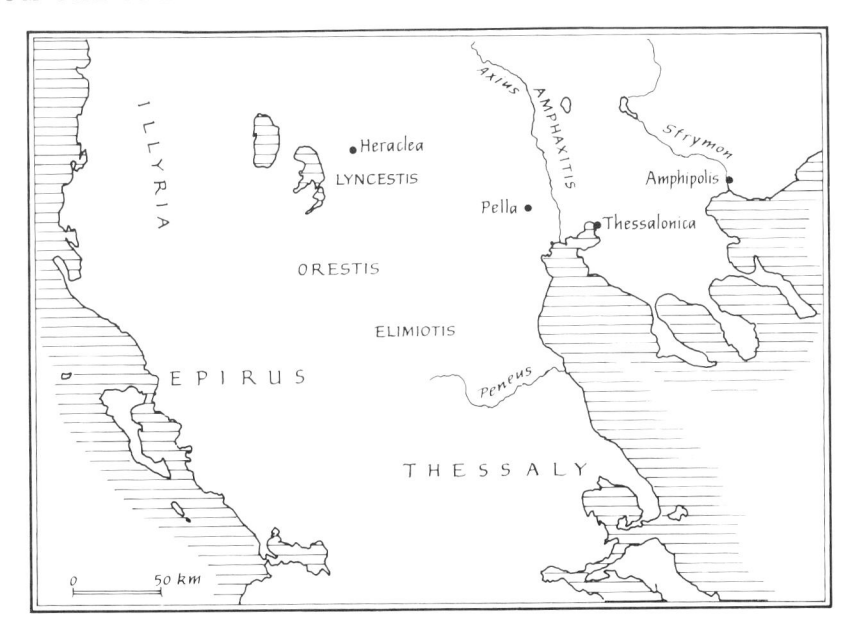

22   The Macedonian regions

forbidden, presumably from one region to another as well as into Macedonia from elsewhere, and there is no doubt that this measure is related to the ban on mining.[28]

The principal elements of the coinage of Macedonia after the creation of the four regions are the similar tetradrachms of the First and the Second Regions, with the types Head of Artemis/Club in oak-wreath (Fig. 45). In addition, there is the small issue of the First Region, which appears for the first time in the Sitochoro hoard (p. 121), with the types Head of Zeus/Artemis Tauropolos, and a small issue with the types Head of Artemis/Club in oak-wreath, above ΜΑΚΕΔΟΝΩΝ, below ΑΜΦΑΞΙΩΝ. The area known as Amphaxitis lay on either side of the Axius,[29] and the coinage may in principle therefore be regarded as a coinage of the Second or the Third Regions. It is perhaps best to regard it as the equivalent for the Second Region of the preliminary issue for the First Region with the types Head of Zeus/Artemis.

What is one then to make of the likelihood that the two regions which produced silver coinage between 167 and 148 are precisely the regions with access to the silver mines of the area? And of the fact that since the Third Region was a particularly large producer of salt (Livy xlv, 29, 13), the ban on its transfer was presumably

28 H. Kuthmann, *Arch.Anz.* 1966, 407, 'Salz zum Würzen'.
29 Strabo vii, fr.11 (329); fr.23 (330); Pol. v, 97, 4; Livy xlv, 29, 5–9. For the coinage see C. Boehringer, *SNR* 1975, 37, 'Hellenistischer Münzschatz aus Trapezunt', at 60, with earlier bibliography.

45 The coinage of Macedon

Tetradrachm of First Region:
    Head of Zeus wearing oak-wreath r./Artemis Tauropolos r.; above, ΜΑΚΕΔΟΝΩΝ;
    below, ΠΡΩΤΗΣ and three monograms   Sitochoro hoard
Tetradrachm of Macedonia Amphaxitis:
    Macedonian shield/Club r. in oak-wreath; above club, two monograms and
    ΜΑΚΕΔΟΝΩΝ; below club, ΑΜΦΑΞΙΩΝ   Naville 16, 1053
Tetradrachm of First Region:
    Bust of Artemis r. in centre of Macedonian shield/Club r. in oak-wreath; above club,
    monogram and ΜΑΚΕΔΟΝΩΝ; below club, ΠΡΩΤΗΣ and two monograms; on l.,
    thunderbolt   Naville 1, 997
Tetradrachm of Second Region:
    Bust of Artemis r. in centre of Macedonian shield/Club r. in oak-wreath; above club,
    monogram and ΜΑΚΕΔΟΝΩΝ; below club, ΔΕΥΤΕΡΑΣ and monogram; on l.,
    thunderbolt   Lockett 1538

46   The coinage of Thasos and Maronea

Tetradrachm of Thasos:
   Head of Dionysus r. wearing ivy-wreath/Heracles standing l.; on r., ΗΡΑΚΛΕΟΥΣ; on l.,
   ΣΩΤΗΡΟΣ and monogram; in exergue, ΘΑΣΙΩΝ   Naville 16, 1074
Tetradrachm of Maronea:
   Head of Dionysus l. wearing ivy-wreath/Dionysus standing l.; on r., ΔΙΟΝΥΣΟΥ;
   on l., ΣΩΤΗΡΟΣ; below, two monograms and ΜΑΡΩΝΙΤΩΝ   Naville 1, 1056

intended to complement the ban on the processing of silver in the First and Second Regions? I do not know the answer but suspect that some extraction and processing of silver went on after 167; the apparent resumption of production with Roman approval in 158 may be the result of a recognition that it was impossible to prevent production if access was open to Macedonians; the Romans no doubt decided that if they could not be stopped they might as well be fleeced. It may also be that Thasos (and perhaps also Maronea) was at this point given access to the mines; at all events, the silver coinage of Thasos seems to resume in about 158 in parallel to that of the First and Second Regions (Fig. 46).[30]

By contrast, the structure of the bronze coinage of this period in Macedonia appears relatively simple, produced at Amphipolis, Thessalonica and Pella, but not in the backward and isolated Fourth Region. A fragment of a hoard from Philippi (*IGCH* 483; compare Mirnik 22 from Dojran) reflects the currency of the three mints. There are in addition issues in bronze with the names of the Roman quaestors of Macedonia, which cannot at the moment be closely dated.

The chief problem involved in an attempt to assess the significance of the post-167 coinages of Maronea, Thasos and the Macedonian regions lies in our uncertainty about how big these coinages were. If one peruses the pages of the *Inventory of Greek Coin Hoards*,

30 F.S. Kleiner, *MusN* 1972, 17, 'The dated cistophori of Ephesus', at 30, n.25.

one gets the impression that the coinages of Thasos and of the First Region of Macedonia were enormous. However, almost all the hoards in question come from the territories of Bulgaria and Romania and I have no doubt, after inspecting many of the hoards myself, that virtually all the Macedonian and Thasian issues in these hoards are local imitations. (It remains unclear why precisely *these* issues were chosen for imitation.)

If none of the coinages under discussion was large, it is reasonable to regard at least the city coinages of Maronea and Thasos as purely local phenomena; I should guess that there is a political element involved in their production as well as a financial element, namely the attempt to fill the gap, for a time and at a local level, left by the end of the tetradrachm coinage of the kingdom of Macedonia.

Similar reasons no doubt also in part explain the tetradrachm coinages of the first two regions of Macedonia, self-assertion of a new political entity and financial need. But we are also dealing with the issues of new, Rome-created entities, which form a sort of bridge to the Roman coinages of the province after 148. Given the careful way in which Rome regulated the relationship between the different regions of Macedonia, I find it hard to see the production of silver coinage as actually contrary to Roman wishes. But it was a Greek coinage which the Romans thus permitted.

It is, in fact, I think, the Greek world which provides the key to understanding the monetary history of the other two areas which fell earlier into the Roman orbit. I have discussed the possibility that Flamininus orchestrated the suppression of regal silver in the Greek world. It seems to me in any case likely that the disappearance of Carthaginian coinage in Spain, of Carthaginian and Syracusan coinage in Sicily was willed by Rome.

A generation later, however, Rome, while ruthlessly eradicating the Macedonian monarchy, and enslaving Epirus, attempted to organise Macedonia into self-governing regions with Greek institutions, including coinage, and provided Athens, in the island of Delos, with the financial basis on which she was able to create one of the last great Greek coinages of large silver. Roman perceptions of the need at least outwardly to respect Greek aspirations and of the need to achieve a *modus vivendi* clearly lie behind both decisions. I suspect that the Roman experience in Greece led them to the fusion of native and Roman traditions in the Iberian denarius coinage and the creation of what I have described as a Romano-Sicilian monetary system (pp.97 and 113). The divorce between Roman imperialism in east and west was perhaps not as great as is sometimes suggested.

9

AFRICA UNDER CARTHAGE AND ROME

The limited use made by Carthage of coinage in North Africa is reflected in the small number of recorded hoards of the early Hellenistic period; there are a few hoards of gold or electrum (sometimes including Cyrenaican or Ptolemaic issues) and a few of bronze. The latter consist for the most part of Sicilian and Sardinian issues, and it may naturally be doubted whether these issues had any real monetary function in North Africa.[1] Their real homes are in Sicily or Sardinia.

The relative compartmentalisation of Carthaginian minting activity emerges not only from the behaviour of the coinage produced in Sicily and Sardinia, but also from a curious bronze issue consisting of at least two denominations, both with Head of Tanit l./Horse galloping r. The issue was apparently produced at Kerkouane on Cape Bon, in the course of the Carthaginian resistance to the invasion of Regulus; all known specimens come from the destruction layer of the settlement (Map 23).[2]

The precious metal coinage of Carthage also reflects the events of the First Punic War, since it is possible to identify the issues which were struck to finance it (Fig. 47):

260–256	Jenkins and Lewis Group VII	Electrum	Silver
256–255	Jenkins and Lewis Group VIII	Electrum	Silver
	Jenkins and Lewis Group IX	Gold	Silver
255–241	Jenkins and Lewis Group X	Electrum	Silver

1 *IGCH* 2276, silver of Cyrene with one Ptolemaic piece and one piece of Alexander, from Algeria, probably has nothing to do with Carthage, though Carthaginian influence on the coastal strip between Carthage and Tangier (ancient Tingis) was considerable.

2 J.-P. Morel, *MEFR* 1969, 473, 'Kerkouane, ville punique du Cap Bon', at 511.

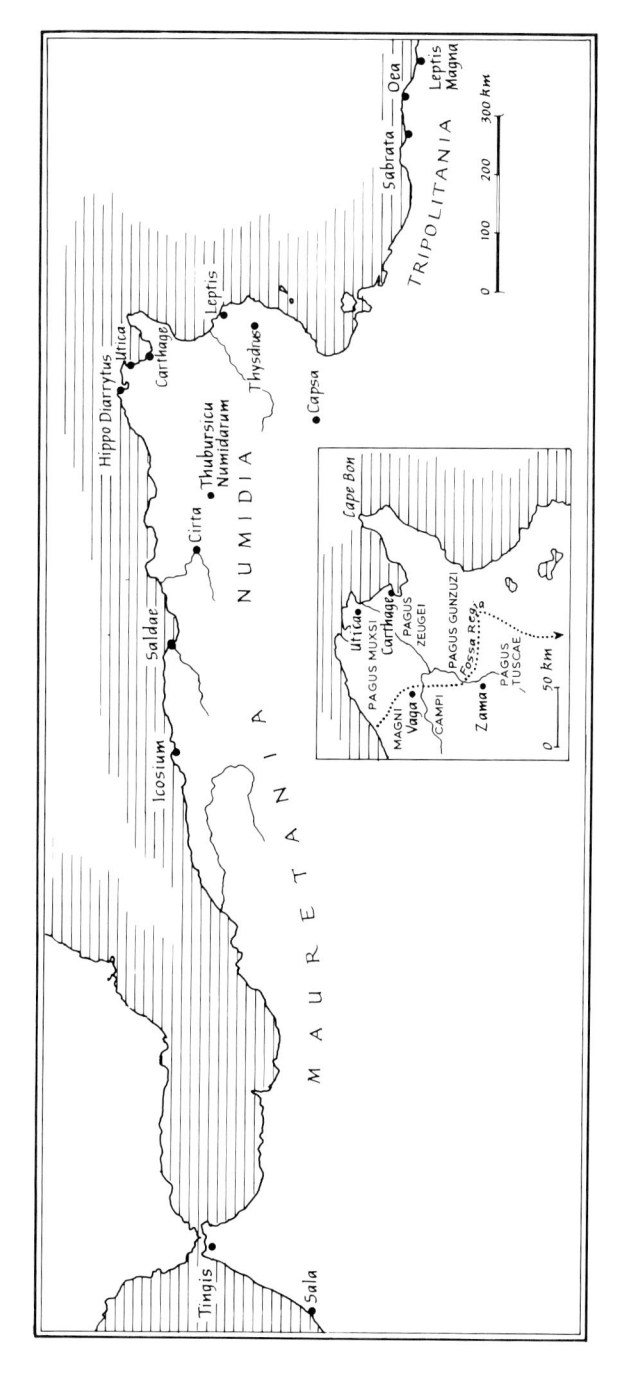

23 Africa

47 The coinage of Carthage during the First Punic War

Electrum shekel, Jenkins and Lewis Group VII:
  Head of Tanit l./Horse r.   Naville 10, 371
Gold one and two-thirds shekel, Jenkins and Lewis Group IX:
  Head of Tanit l./Horse r. with head turned back   BM cast
Electrum shekel, Jenkins and Lewis Group Xa:
  Head of Tanit l./Horse r.; above, *uraeus*   Naville 6, 600
Silver double shekel, after 255:
  Head of Tanit l./Horse r.; above, star   BM cast

Group VIII and its associated silver were struck in Sicily in order to help out the mint of Carthage in the emergency created by the invasion of Regulus in 256–255.[3]

With the closing years of the First Punic War the numismatic evidence sheds further light on the financial history of Carthage, with the production of a very substantial group of coinage for the mercenaries in revolt (Fig. 48). The precise definition of this coinage is not easy;[4] it is clear that some coinage with purely Carthaginian types and no legend belongs with the coinage with ΛIBYΩN, but it is not clear where the line is to be drawn; furthermore, given the nonchalant attitude of Carthage to the types of her coinage, it does not seem to me possible to exclude the possibility that some issues with ΛIBYΩN were struck by Carthage.

In 256–255, as we have seen, Carthage was striking gold, one-and-two-thirds-shekel pieces and fractions, with Head of Tanit l./Horse r. (Jenkins and Lewis Group IX).

---

3 H.R. Baldus, *Chiron* 1982, 163, 'Unerkannte Reflexe der römischen Nordafrika-Expedition'.

4 E.S.G. Robinson, *NC* 1943, 1, 'The coinage of the Libyans'; 1953, 27, 'A hoard of coins of the Libyans'; 1956, 9, 'The Libyan hoard'.

48 The coinage of the Libyans

Double-shekel:
  Laureate head of Zeus r.; before, ΛΙΒΥΩΝ; behind, *mem*/Bull butting r.; above, *mem*;
  below, *alpha*; in exergue, ΛΙΒΥΩΝ   BM cast
Shekel:
  Head of Melqart l./Lion r.; above, *mem*; in exergue, ΛΙΒΥΩΝ   BM cast

These were followed by electrum pieces with the same types, some of which were certainly of light weight (Jenkins and Lewis Group X). We are told by Polybius (i, 66, 6) that in 241 Carthage paid each mercenary one *chrysous*, probably in the sense simply of gold or electrum coin, and it is tempting to identify these with the light-weight electrum pieces, two of which were in a hoard found in Tunisia in 1952 (*IGCH* 2282); imitations in electrum of the gold pieces of Jenkins and Lewis Group IX are also known. The Tunisia hoard also contained triple shekels, double shekels and shekels of base silver, some of the last of which were certainly produced for the Libyans. Whatever one makes of the electrum, it is clear that the silver of Carthage at the end of the First Punic War was heavily debased and that the issues for the Libyans flow naturally on from this coinage and are themselves equally debased (despite Pol. i, 71, 6, with its optimistic account of Libyan finances). Their coinage, beginning with the base silver shekels, is laid out in Table 5; it is characterised by the systematic overstriking of later on earlier issues; the most prolific element in the coinage appears to be that with non-Carthaginian types.

Not surprisingly, the coinage of Carthage between the two wars consisted entirely of bronze issues, apart from the coinage produced by the Barcids in Spain (p. 87). It is no doubt the resources derived from Spain which explain in part the resumption of precious metal coinage with the outbreak of the Second Punic War, though booty was also no doubt used for the coinages struck in Italy and Sicily. The difficulties of the closing years of the Second Punic War are reflected in the production of a very substantial issue of bronze at Carthage (*SNG* (Cop.) 302–29), in part overstruck on

TABLE 5. The coinage of the Libyans

I. CARTHAGINIAN TYPES

Shekels	*Obv.* Head of Tanit l. *Rev.* (1) *mem.* (2) *alpha, mem.* (3) ∴, *mem.* Nos. 5, 1–3, and 4 in second lot of Tunisia hoard, also nos. 11–16 in first lot.	*Rev.* Horse standing r.
Half-shekel	*Rev. zayin, mem.* No. 6 in second lot of hoard.	
Shekels (1) (2)	*Obv.* Behind head, torch. No difference mark (on one perhaps no torch either). *Obv.* ΛΙΒΥΩΝ. Nos. 7–9 in second lot of hoard.	*Rev.* Similar. *Rev. alpha, mem.*
Bronze (1)	*Obv.* Head of Tanit l. No difference mark. (2) *zayin*. *NC* 1943, Pl.II, 7–8.	*Rev.* Plough.
Bronze (1) (2)	*Obv.* Behind head, torch. No difference mark, and perhaps no torch. *Obv.* ΛΙΒΥΩΝ. Ibid., 5–6.	*Rev.* Corn-ear. *Rev.* No difference mark.

II. NATIVE TYPES

Double-shekels (1) (2)	*Obv.* Head of Zeus laureate; in front, ΛΙΒΥΩΝ. *mem/mem.* *mem/alpha, mem.* *NC* 1953, Pl.III, 17–19 and 20.	*Rev.* Charging bull; in exergue, ΛΙΒΥΩΝ.
Shekels (1) (2) (3) (4)	*Obv.* Head of Herakles in lionskin. Without ethnic or difference mark. With *mem* on *rev*. With ΛΙΒΥΩΝ and *mem* on *rev*. With ΛΙΒΥΩΝ, *mu* and *mem* on *rev*. Nos. 14 and 11–13 in second lot of hoard; also *NC* 1953, Pl.III, 23–28; Müller I, p.1310, no. 348.	*Rev.* Lion prowling.
Half-shekels (1) (2)	*Obv.* Head of Herakles, diademed, club lying along neck. No difference mark. *Obv.* A, *mu*. Müller, nos. 345–6.	*Rev.* Lion prowling; above, club; no ethnic.
	Obv. Head of Herakles in lionskin.	*Rev.* Bull charging.

(*cont.*)

Bronze unit	*Rev.* (1) *mem.* (2) *mem, mu.*
	NC 1943, p.2, nos. 9 and 10.
Bronze half	*Rev. mem.*
	Ibid., no. 11.
	Obv. Head of Athena; *Rev.* Bull standing; above,
	in front, ΛΙΒΥΩΝ; above, *mu*. *mem*; in exergue, ΛΙΒΥΩΝ.
Bronze unit	Ibid., no. 8.

bronzes of Hieron II (Fig. 49). One is inclined to regard the hoard of these coins from Bougie (ancient Saldae) (*IGCH* 2296) as Numidian booty.[5] After the war, Carthage was only capable of producing base silver, a large hoard of which turned up at El Djem (ancient Thysdrus) (*IGCH* 2300); an attempt was indeed made to pass it off on the Romans (Livy xxxii, 2, 1–2; compare Gellius vii, 5). But Carthaginian recovery, organised by Hannibal (Livy xxxiii, 46, 8–47, 3), as well as being obvious to the Romans, is reflected in the coinage. The last silver issue of Carthage, found in a hoard from the island of Cani near Bizerta (ancient Hippo Diarrhytus) (*IGCH* 2301), is of pure silver (Fig. 50).

It remains extraordinarily hard to establish what sort of fiscal structure the Carthaginians had established in the North African territory under their control.[6] Nor is it clear how far the use of coinage had spread into the interior. Insofar as they are precisely localised, the hoards come exclusively from Carthage or from the coast to west or south; this leads one to suspect that the Carthaginians levied a surplus in kind, which was exported in exchange for the precious metal used for the coinage of Carthage, in turn used for the payment of troops, mercenaries and others.[7]

But we have seen not only that the Carthaginians produced coinage to pay their troops, which may not be very indicative of monetary usage among the Libyan element within these forces, but also that the rebel troops after the First Punic War absorbed relatively substantial issues of coinage, which were produced specially for and partly by them. The larger the role assigned to Libyans in the Carthaginian armies, the more puzzling the absence of coinage from the *chora* becomes.

Nor is it clear how the Romans organised the taxation of Africa. Within the province there was of course the land of the seven *civitates liberae et immunes*; in addition, some land was granted to the heirs of Massinissa, both in 146 and later (*Lex Agr.* 81; Cicero, *de leg. ag.* 1, 10–11; 2, 58). The rest of the territory was either *ager publicus populi Romani*

---

5 I assume that a new hoard from Tangier, containing (along with Spanish and eastern issues) quadrigati and Punic pieces (including Second Punic War issues of Tarentum) is also booty.

6 For the territorial divisions created by Carthage see G.Ch. Picard, in *Mélanges A. Piganiol* (Paris, 1966), 1257, 'L'administration territoriale de Carthage'; one must not be put off by the careless mistakes.

7 For Carthaginian taxation, see Pol. i, 72, 2, with commentary of F.W. Walbank; C.R. Whittaker, *Klio* 1978, 331, 'Land and labour in North Africa'; for a balanced account of the Carthaginian army, G.T. Griffith, *Mercenaries of the Hellenistic World* (Cambridge, 1935), 207.

49 The coinage of Carthage before and during the Second Punic War

Bronze of Carthage, 241–221, *SNG* (Cop.), 255–9:
   Head of Tanit l./Horse r.; above, *uraeus*; before, control-letter   BM cast
Bronze of Carthage, 241–221, *SNG* (Cop.), 260:
   Head of Tanit l./Horse r.; above, *uraeus*; before, control-letter   BM cast
Bronze of Carthage, after 221, *SNG* (Cop.), 302–6:
   Head of Tanit l./Horse walking r. with head turned back; below, control-letter   BM cast
Base silver piece of Carthage, *SNG* (Cop.), 390–6:
   Head of Tanit l./Horse walking r. with head turned back   El Djem hoard

50 The issues of the Cani hoard

Tetradrachm of Carthage with serrate edge:
   Head of Tanit l./Horse r.; below, control-letter   Cani hoard

or was occupied by Carthaginian and Libyan renegades, the latter of whom paid a land-tax and a poll-tax (Appian, *Lib.* 135, 641; Cicero, *II in Verr.* 3, 12; *Lex Agr.* 77–8, 80–1). We cannot I think be certain that these taxes were paid in money, let alone in coin; we also have no idea how they were collected, since such isolated attestations as there are of *publicani* may simply reflect the collection of harbour dues.

The only coinage which might have been used after 146 was Roman coin; how might one suppose that this arrived in Africa? The Romans struck no coinage in Africa before the age of Caesar and it is hard to imagine the Roman provincial administration putting much coinage into circulation in normal times. Some of the *ager publicus* in Africa was sold off after 146, presumably to Romans and Italians, and some was perhaps leased out; some was then occupied by the settlers sent by C. Gracchus; men of business were present in Utica during the Jugurthine War. The father of M. Caelius Rufus was no doubt one Roman landowner among many in Africa. It is thus possible that Roman and Italian involvement in Africa generated a supply of coin. By the time we get to the first century there is no problem; coinage was officially shipped over to Africa in 111 and 110 (Sallust, *BJ* 27, 5; 36, 1) and again in 82 (Plutarch, *Pomp.* 11); a flourishing market developed in the Roman camp in the early stages of the Jugurthine War (Sallust, *BJ* 44, 5). But I suspect that in the beginning the revenue of the province of Africa was collected at least in bullion if not in kind. The two ingots in the Cani hoard (not of any particular weight) may perhaps be taken as some indication of the use of bullion.

Certainly the evidence for the arrival of the denarius is thin, but this no doubt reflects the level of publication as much as anything else. Apart from the Cani hoard, there is another in the late second century and then one of the age of Caesar. Three other hoards are known to have been discovered, but nothing is known of their dates (App. 42). There is some evidence that some of the population of the province of Africa was treated by the Romans as a dependent labour force;[8] this fact is not incompatible with the introduction and diffusion by an immigrant elite of Roman monetary usages.

If we are ill informed about Carthage, we are catastrophically ignorant about Numidia. A certain fiscal structure is implied by the fact that Capsa is described as free of taxes under Jugurtha (Sallust, *BJ* 89, 4). All the Numidian kings no doubt exported wheat and barley; they apparently imported on the whole luxuries, and their tombs and other archaeological indications reveal their wealth. Their coinage, on the other hand, although produced on an enormous scale, is only of bronze, which does not suggest that the 'state' aspect of the monarchy was very developed; the principal denomination bears the types Bearded head l./Horse galloping l. and weighs between about 10.00 and 15.00 gm. (Fig. 51). Three hoards are known from Africa; a vast quantity of the coinage, along with hundreds of pieces of Carthage, found its way to a small area of Dalmatia, for reasons which are largely mysterious (p.222). As for

---

8 C.R. Whittaker (n.7), at 341–2.

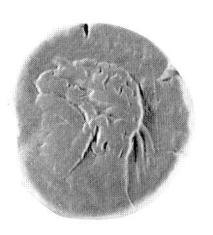

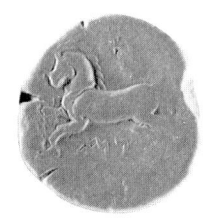

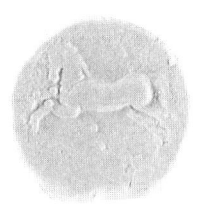

51   The coinage of Numidia

Bronzes of Numidia:
  Bearded and diademed head l./Horse l.; below, control-letter   Glasgow
  Bearded and diademed head l./Horse l.; below, dot   Paris, Seymour de Ricci

chronology, the hoard from Constantine (ancient Cirta) (*IGCH* 2304) contains only coins of Numidia, the hoard from Algiers (ancient Icosium) (P. Salama, no. 100), only coins of Numidia and Icosium itself; the hoard from Teboursouk (ancient Thubursicu Numidarum) (*IGCH* 2305) contains also coins of Carthage, which would suggest an early date, but is extraordinarily ill known. Nonetheless, since none of the material in the Dalmatian hoards need be much later than the middle of the second century, I cannot see any positive grounds for supposing that *any* Numidian coinage was produced after the fall of Carthage. It may be significant that Jugurtha was called upon to provide specified weights of silver and gold to Rome (Sallust, *BJ* 29, 6; 62, 5).

The presence of Roman men of business at Cirta and Vaga at the outbreak of the Jugurthine War is well known, and they presumably returned after the war. Their presence may explain the presence of a mixed hoard of drachms of Massalia, Iberian denarii, tetradrachms of Athens and Roman denarii down to the late second or early first century (not 79) (*IGCH* 2306). But it is necessary to add that the hoard probably reflects the travels of its owner rather than economic activity at Cirta; it may indeed belong to a mercenary rather than a man of business. The state of the evidence allows one to believe almost anything one wishes about relations of production;[9] I note that Juba I settled down quite happily to produce denarii as an ally of the Pompeians in 48 and suspect that the use of Roman coinage had by that stage taken root in the area. Unfortunately, the only hoard evidence from Numidia is of one unspecified Republican hoard (App. 42).

The monetary history of Tripolitania, Carthaginian territory down to the Second

---

9 Discussed by C.R. Whittaker (n.7), at 340–1.

Punic War, then Numidian, is even more mysterious. The area seems to have been settled originally from Phoenicia, rather than by Carthage, but its later history is reflected in the coin finds – Carthaginian pieces, then Numidian bronzes. The cities of Tripolitania, Leptis Magna, Oea and Sabrata produced no coinage till the end of the Republic, when all began to strike bronze; Leptis Magna produced an exiguous issue of denarii, which may perhaps be seen as evoked by circumstances similar to those which lie behind the large issue of Juba I. All three mints struck under Augustus.[10] Despite the Romanisation of the monetary system implied by the striking of denarii, the monetary terms in use under the Roman Empire seem to have been not simply not Roman, but actually Phoenician.[11]

10 G.K. Jenkins, *Libyan Studies* 1973–74, 29, 'Some ancient coins of Libya'.

11 A.F. Elmayer, *Libyan Studies* 1983, 91, on *IRT* 893: a sum of 200 *tibas* = pieces of Tyre = drachms = denarii.

10

THE IMPERIAL REPUBLIC

The conquest of the Mediterranean brought untold riches to Rome and Italy; individuals were able to make their fortunes as men of business, large sums fell into private hands as booty, the indemnities and tribute payments which came to Rome were apparently recycled almost immediately. This emerges from two considerations, the willingness of the senate in 179 to spend the entire revenue for one year over a five-year period on public works and the fact that the *aerarium* had in 157 only 24,000,000 denarii in hand, in gold, silver and coin, although the booty which came to the state from the defeat of Perseus V alone amounted to 30,000,000 denarii. Yet, as we have seen (p.72), most of Rome's expenditure between the end of the Second Punic War and the 160s was in bronze coin. Rome presumably alienated large quantities of gold and silver bullion in exchange for bronze for coinage. In 167, along with the decision not to exploit the Macedonian mines (p.128), there began a period of even greater concentration on bronze coinage (Fig. 52). In addition, Rome seems sometimes to have spent bullion rather than coin. In 180 she allotted the unfortunate Ligurians transferred to Samnium 150,000 pounds of silver, presumably leaving them to spend it or acquire coin with it as best they could (Livy xl, 38, 6).[1] Cn. Manlius Vulso distributed precisely half a pound of silver to his soldiers, perhaps actually as bullion, although the sum in Livy is 42 denarii; and Paullus gave five pounds of silver out of the booty of Pydna to Q. Aelius Tubero (Valerius Maximus iv, 4, 9).

Such conduct was hardly rational. And, in fact, in 158 the mines in Macedonia were restored to life; and in 157 the production of silver coinage was resumed. After a few years, the as ceased to be produced and relatively restricted issues of bronze fractions alone accompanied gigantic issues of silver. At this point, with Rome (*RRCH* 131), Lacco Ameno on Ischia (*RRCH* 147), Petacciato near Termoli (*RRCH* 149),

---

[1] Not the trivial sum of 150,000 denarii, as H. Zehnacker, in *Les dévaluations* 2 (Paris, 1980), 31, 'Monnaies de compte et prix à Rome', at 41.

52 Roman bronze coinage of the middle of the second century

As of A. Cae(cilius), *RRC*, no. 174/1:
  Laureate head of Janus; above, I/Prow r.; above, A.CAE (in monogram); before, I;
  below, ROMA   Paris, A5324
Semis with wolf and twins, *RRC*, no. 183/2:
  Laureate head of Saturn r.; behind, S/Prow r.; above, wolf and twins; before, S; below,
  ROMA   Rochetta à Volturno hoard
Quadrans of Pae(tus):
  Head of Hercules r.; behind, three dots/Prow r.; above, PAE (in monogram); before,
  three dots; below, ROMA   Paris, AF
As with gryphon, *RRC*, no. 182/2:
  Laureate head of Janus; above, I/Prow r.; above, gryphon; before, I; below, ROMA
                                                                             Paris, A2341

there begins the long series of hoards which reflect accurately the dominance of the denarius as the silver coin of Republican Italy; the denarius was from now on also the principal element in the pay of the Roman soldier; and it became almost overnight the most important silver coin in the Mediterranean. Before long, the legend ROMA disappeared from the denarius: the coinage of the ruling power no longer needed to be identified (Fig. 53).

Two developments followed and perhaps flowed from the change in the pattern of monetary circulation in Italy. These developments are the retariffing of the denarius

53 Roman silver coinage of the middle of the second century

Denarius of L. Atilius Nomentanus, *RRC*, no. 225/1:
  Helmeted head of Roma; behind, XVI/Victory in biga r.; below, L.ATILI (in monogram); in exergue, NOM
  Paris, A4945

Denarius of Ti.Veturius, *RRC*, no. 234/1:
  Helmeted bust of Mars r.; behind, X and TI.VET (in monogram)/Oath-taking scene; above, ROMA
  Copenhagen (obv.), Hannover 2207 (rev.)

at 16 instead of 10 asses and the adoption of the sestertius as the official unit of reckoning instead of the as.

The name of the denarius derives precisely from the fact that when it was created it was worth ten asses; in due course it was retariffed at sixteen asses, with the result that the quinarius, or half, was worth eight asses, the sestertius, or quarter, was worth four asses. This scale of values underlies the monetary history of the late Republic and the early Empire. The change is briefly recorded by Pliny (*NH* xxxiii, 45), 'and it was decided that a denarius should exchange for sixteen asses', and it has with negligible exceptions always been associated with the ephemeral appearance of the mark of value XVI on Republican denarii around 140.[2] T.V. Buttrey was clearly right to argue that the retariffing did not impose a new relationship between denarius and as, but accepted a relationship which had developed in the open market.[3] The relative reduction in the value of the as is to be ascribed to the fact that it had for some years been de facto uncial in standard and had ceased to be struck in 146, with the result that the stock in circulation was becoming progressively more worn and less desirable. The silver:bronze ratio implied by the retariffing is 1:110.

Linked by Pliny with the retariffing of the denarius is the question of the pay of the Roman soldier, since he continues, 'but in paying soldiers a denarius has always been given for each ten asses due to them'. This implies that at the moment of the retariffing army pay was computed in asses, but (mostly) paid in denarii, which fits

[2] Against P. Marchetti, 174, see the elegant demonstration of H. Zehnacker (n.1), 40, that the denarius was still worth ten asses in 177.

[3] *MusN* 1957, 57, 'On the retariffing of the Roman denarius'.

well with the switch we have observed from production of bronze coinage to production of silver coinage. Despite Pliny, it is in fact clear that once the objective of paying the soldiers the same number of denarii as before had been secured, their pay was converted to an appropriate number of asses at the rate of sixteen to a denarius. Army pay was certainly computed in asses at this rate in the age of Tiberius (Tac., *Ann.* i, 17, 6 with Suet., *Dom.* 7).

How much pay was actually due to a soldier Pliny does not say, but a well-known passage of Polybius (vi, 39, 12) records that in his time a Roman legionary was paid two obols a day, a centurion double and a cavalry man a drachm. Since Polybius clearly meant by two obols a third of a drachm, the question arises of which drachm. There is in my view no real doubt but that Polybius was talking in terms of the Attic drachm (explicitly cited at xxxiv, 8, 7–8) and that therefore a Roman soldier was paid a third of a drachm = a third of a denarius.

H. Mattingly originally argued that Polybius was not here talking in terms of the Attic drachm, but of the Aeginetic drachm, since this was the unit used by the Achaean League.[4] F.W. Walbank, commenting on ii, 15, 1, objected that Polybius at xxxiv, 8, 7–8 used the Attic drachm; but this argument has been stood on its head with the assertion that where Polybius does not specify Attic drachms he presumably means some other drachms.[5]

Quite apart from the fact that the minae of Pol. ii, 58, 5 are almost certainly Attic minae;[6] and that the unspecified drachms of vi, 23, 15 are even more certainly Attic drachms equal in value to the denarius of ten asses, this argument does not seem strong; if I were writing about British history and sometimes spoke of pounds and at other times of pounds sterling, only a lunatic would suppose that in the former case I referred to pounds scots.

P. Marchetti opts in fact not for the Aeginetic drachm as the drachm of Polybius vi, 39, 12, but for a drachm weighing only three-quarters of a denarius. The mode of argument is essentially the same as that of Mattingly, and involves the equivalence of a semis and a quarter of an obol which occurs at Pol. ii, 15, 6. Two obols of legionary pay are thus not simply a third of a drachm, but also four asses. Before the retariffing, in the reconstruction of Mattingly, the result is a drachm of 12 asses (or $12\frac{1}{2}$ asses, if Polybius was not being precise), hence more than a denarius; after the retariffing,

---

4 *JRS* 1937, 99, 'The property qualifications of the Roman *classes*', at 101–2.
5 P. Marchetti, 197. A. Giovannini, *MH* 1978, 258, 'La solde des troupes romaines', produces a bizarre theory all his own, which attributes to the cavalryman four times the pay of the infantryman; why then did the former always receive three times the booty allotted to the latter? The comment of P. Marchetti, *RBN* 1978, 49, 'Sur la valeur en denier de la drachma polybéenne', is only of historiographical interest. H.C. Boren, *Historia* 1983, 421, 'Studies relating to the *stipendium*', combines partial citation of the evidence with flights of speculation.
6 See *RRC*, p.630; the questions posed by P. Marchetti, 196, n.46, expecting a negative answer, may readily be answered in the affirmative.

in the reconstruction of Marchetti, the result is a drachm of 12 asses, now less than a denarius, in fact three-quarters.

Marchetti also argues that figures in Greek sources relating to Roman valuations work out better with a denarius equivalent to a drachm and a third. The argument is irrelevant. For Greek sources had to operate with whatever equivalence existed and if the Roman denarius was the equivalent of a drachm and fractions did not work out very neatly that was just too bad.

The question is fundamentally boring, since it cannot be resolved with certainty and inscriptional evidence may one day emerge which will settle the level of legionary pay in the time of Polybius. I continue in the meanwhile to regard a third of a denarius as what Polybius meant. If when Polybius wrote the denarius had not been retariffed *and* the conversion of legionary pay to asses at sixteen to the denarius instituted, a third of a denarius would have equalled three asses and a third; if those changes had taken place, a third of a denarius would have equalled five asses and a third. Since the retariffing took place in *c.*141 and since Polybius probably drew on his experience in the Third Carthaginian War in writing about legionary pay,[7] the former view is more probable. One may go on to suppose that the actual figure was three asses and that Polybius was not being precise. Two texts perhaps suggest that in the second century a legionary was paid 3 asses a day (3 asses = 1.80 obols, rounded off by Polybius to 2 obols; similarly, 1 semis = 0.30 obols, rounded off by Polybius to a quarter of an obol). They are Plutarch, *Ti. Gr.* 13, where Nasica probably offers the agrarian commissioners 3 asses a day each, presumably the lowest daily wage paid out by the Roman state,[8] and Plautus, *Most.* 357, where 3 nummi are regarded as an appropriate wage for a soldier;[9] the figure is not a standard Hellenistic one;[10] it is perhaps the equivalent of 3 asses.

The second development to be considered is the change from the use of the as to the use of the sestertius as the unit of reckoning. Obviously small sums such as corn prices could still be expressed in asses. The shift can be placed very precisely thanks to the existence of a sequence of literary and epigraphical references. The practice of reckoning in asses clearly developed from reckoning in pounds of bronze (p. 19); amounts in asses, amounts of *aes* or amounts of *aes grave* are dominant in the pages of Livy throughout. The actual period of transition is best represented in tabular form (Table 6).

The shift to reckoning in sestertii was no doubt undertaken immediately after the

---

7 F.W. Walbank, *Commentary on Polybius* I (Oxford, 1957), 6.
8 For the use by Plutarch of obol to translate as see *Pob.* 11 with Gellius xi, 1, 2, etc. (on the equivalences between sheep and cattle, and bronze).
9 The passage is cited by A.J. Letronne, *Considérations générales sur l'évaluation des monnaies grecques et romaines* (Paris, 1817), 27, following le Beau, *Mémoires de littérature tirés des registres de l'Académie Royale des Inscriptions et Belles-Lettres* 41, 1780, 186, but not in recent literature.
10 G.T. Griffith, *Mercenaries of the Hellenistic World* (Cambridge, 1935), 294–306.

TABLE 6. Asses and sestertii

ASSES

Plutarch, *Cato Maior* 4; Seneca, *Epist.* 94, 27	See App. N
Livy xlv, 42, 12	Gift to embassy in 167
Macrobius, *Sat.* iii, 17, 5; Gellius ii, 24, 3; Lucilius 72 M; Tertullian, *Apol.* 6, 1	Lex Fannia of 161[1]
Gellius ii, 24, 2	SC of 161
Livy, *Epit.* xlviii	Cost of funeral in 152
Macrobius, *Sat.* iii, 7, 9; Gellius ii, 24, 7; Festus, s.v. *Centenariae*	Lex Licinia of after 143
Pliny, *NH* xxxiii, 45	Retariffing of denarius

SESTERTII

SIG 674 = Sherk 9, line 69	SC of 140
Gellius vi, 11, 9	Speech of 140
Frontinus, *Aq.* i, 7	Cost of Aqua Marcia, finished and presumably costed after 140
Livy, *Epit.* lv	Sale in 138
SIG 688 = Sherk 10, B, line 13	SC of 135

1 The calculation of Athenaeus vi, 108 in sestertii ($2\frac{1}{2}$ drachms = 10 sestertii) is clearly an aberration.

retariffing of the denarius, perhaps to disguise the fact that the as, the previous unit of reckoning, had in effect been devalued from a tenth to a sixteenth of a denarius. The term *libella*, the diminutive of *libra*, had no doubt come into use in the early second century to mean an as equal to a tenth of a denarius, because the as of this period was a pale shadow of the as weighing a pound. The term *libella* was presumably now transferred in the sense of a tenth to the system used for calculating the fractions of the sestertius.[11]

11 It certainly does not follow from the existence of a system of decimal subdivision of the sestertius (Volusius Maecianus 65, 73, 76, cf. 74–5) that the sestertius was used as a unit of reckoning while the denarius was still worth ten asses; the system is exposed as a late construction (so also A. Nagl, *Die Rechentafel* (Vienna, 1914), 74–7, for different reasons) by the symbols it uses – I for 1/10 instead of for one as, Σ for 1/20 instead of for one semuncia. I cannot believe with E. Lo Cascio (p.31, n.9, not citing these considerations) that five *libellae*, represented by S, means anything other than half a sestertius at *CIL* iv, 3340, CXLIII).

THE IMPERIAL REPUBLIC 149

The problem which remains to be considered is the expression in sestertii of assessments earlier expressed in asses; the evidence is best displayed in tabular form (see Table 7 below, where the figures in drachms and asses record the state of affairs before *c*.141, the figures in sestertii the state of affairs thereafter).

It seems to me far more plausible to assume that the same figure was transferred

TABLE 7. As and sestertius

Certain passages, which have sometimes been thought to provide equivalences, but which do not in fact do so, have been ignored in the creation of this table: Livy xxxiv, 46, 3, with Plutarch, *Cato Maior* 10 (cf. R. Thomsen (p.43, n.23), 152–3); Livy, *Epit.* xlviii, with Polybius xxxi, 28, 5–6; also all figures relating to the Ludi Romani (p.55, n.5).

The equestrian census in the late Republic was 400,000 sestertii; before *c*.141 it will have been 400,000 asses; unless it had been altered, it cannot be represented by the census level of 1,000,000 asses recorded for 214 in Livy xxiv, 11, 7–8 (*contra* Cl. Nicolet, *L'Ordre Equestre* (Paris, 1966), 46–48; hesitating in *Les dévaluations* 1 (Rome, 1978), 248; for other arguments against his view see P.A. Brunt, *Italian Manpower* (Oxford, 1971), 700; P. Marchetti, 213–19). I see no way of deciding whether the *sponsio* of the Lex Crepereia (125 sestertii, Gaius iv, 95) bore any relation to either of the two primitive *poenae sacramenti* (50 and 500 asses, Gaius iv, 14).

	DRACHMS OR ASSES	SESTERTII
Census qualification for *prima classis*	10,000 drachms Dion. Hal. iv, 16, 2 Pol. vi, 23, 15	
	100,000 asses Livy i, 43, 1	100,000[1] Gaius iii, 42 *Inst.* iii, 7, 2 (qualification of *locupletiores liberti*)
Limit of application of Lex Voconia	100,000 asses Gaius ii, 274	100,000 Ps.-Asc. 247 St Dio lvi, 10[2]
Fine for *iniuria*	25 asses Gell. xx, 1, 12–13[3] cf. xvi, 10, 8 Gaius iii, 223 Festus 508 L	25 *Coll. Mos. Rom.* ii, 5, 5
Basic daily wage	3 asses (see p. 147)	3 Cic., *Rosc. Com.* 28

(*cont.*)

	DRACHMS OR ASSES	SESTERTII
Nominal assessment	1 as (rent) Livy xxxi, 13, 7	1 (fine) Plut., *Mar.* 38[4] Val. Max. viii, 2, 3 (sale of *hereditas*) Gaius ii, 252 (sale of property) Livy, *Epit.* lv Lucilius 656 W Cic., *Rab. Post.* 45, etc. (prize in games) Gellius xviii, 13, 3

---

1 Compare the 100,000 sestertii owned by Vergil, Donatus, *Vit. Verg.* 13; cf. *Vit. Prob.*
2 25,000 drachms = 25,000 denarii = 100,000 sestertii.
3 The early origin of the passage is vouched for by the occurrence of the word *crumena* (p.151, n.16).
4 4 chalkoi = 4 asses = 1 sestertius.

I remain persuaded, despite the arguments of Cl. Nicolet cited above, that 100,000 HS was after 141 the level for the *prima classis*, 'locupletiores liberti' and the Lex Voconia; and that this and the other figures in sestertii in the table were before 141 the same quantity of asses; special pleading may eliminate one or two texts, but not the whole complex. Nicolet discusses only those texts relating to the *prima classis*, etc., not those relating to other valuations transferred from asses to sestertii. (I apologise for the aberration of citing Cicero, *de re pub.* iii, 17, for the level for the Lex Voconia in *RRC*.)

It also seems worth drawing attention to the Forma Idiologi (now known to date to the early first century AD in more or less its complete form, *P. Oxy.* 3014), where a Roman with 100,000 HS if neither married nor with children may not inherit, and to the 100,000 HS mentioned by Laberius (Gellius vi (vii), 9, 3).

It still seems plausible to maintain therefore that the *liberti* at issue in Livy xlv, 15, 2 (168 BC), possessed the wealth of the *prima classis*, and (*RRC*, p.631) that this was at that moment 120,000 asses. The figure of 120,000 asses as the qualification for the *prima classis* cannot be later than the figure of 100,000 asses (attested by Polybius *inter alios*), since 120,000 asses is almost certainly the figure known to Timaeus (*FGH* 566 fr. 61).

I conclude that the level for the *prima classis* was initially 120,000 asses and that it was reduced at some point after 168 to 100,000 asses. The level for the Lex Voconia of 169 is shown to be the same as that for the *prima classis* by Gellius vi (vii), 13; if the latter was changed, consequential legislation obviously changed the former.

from assessments in asses to assessments in sestertii than to argue, with Mommsen,[12] that the sestertius (weighing a scruple of silver) and the libral as were originally equivalent and that figures could be expressed indifferently in one or the other; that figures so expressed were perpetuated unchanged when with the creation of the denarius system the sestertius was fixed at 2.5 asses; and that whenever figures involve the equivalence 2.5 asses = 1 sestertius = 0.25 denarii (an equivalence which came in with the denarius system) they must have been *fixed* after the as ceased to be libral.[13] Against Mommsen's first point may be urged the high silver:bronze ratio of 1:240 which it implies, against the whole theory the fact that there is a gap between the end of the libral as in 217 and the first appearance of the coin and hence of the word sestertius in 211.[14] It is not, by contrast, unreasonable to suppose that the effort of converting assessments in asses to assessments in sestertii when the retariffing took place seemed too great and that it was decided simply to write the assessments across from so many asses to the same number of sestertii; the decision was doubtless also politically convenient, since it would have had the effect of reducing the size of the *prima classis* doubtless swelling out of all proportion because of the effect of the influx of wealth to Rome from the east (compare Aristotle, *Pol.* 1306b 9; 1308a 35).

It has been objected that a multiplication of census levels by 2.5 represents a 'bouleversement', which can only be explained as a reaction to a period of inflation.[15] Yet this is precisely what the other evidence reveals for the first half of the second century; it reveals moreover that men perceived and reacted to the decline in the value of money. There is first the jolly story of L. Veratius (Gellius xx, 1, 12–13), who observed that the penalty of 25 asses imposed by the Twelve Tables for hitting someone was now derisory and amused himself by going round hitting people, accompanied by a slave with the cash necessary to make amends.[16] Then there is the argument marshalled by A.M. Honoré which explains the Lex Silia, the Lex Calpurnia and the Lex Aquilia, which probably belong to the first half of the second century, precisely in terms of inflation.[17] And, as far as I know, the earliest Roman reference to the relationship between supply and price occurs in Lucilius (221–2 W); his awareness may well have been sharpened by the influx of wealth and consequent inflation of the first two generations of the second century.

12 *RMw*, 302–6 (starting from the false premise that the denarius and the triental standard were contemporary), cf. 197, 206 and 292–4.
13 *RMw*, 304, cf. 302, n.40.
14 Varro, *LL* v, 173; Festus, s.v. *Trientem tertium*; Vitruvius iii, 1, *nostri quartam denarii partem, quod efficiebatur ex duobus assibus et tertio semisse, sestertium nominaverunt*.
15 Cl. Nicolet, in *Les dévaluations* 1 (Rome, 1978), 249, 'Mutations monétaires et organisation censitaire'.
16 The early source of the story is assured by the occurrence of the word *crumena*, see A. Watson, *JRS* 1970, 105, 'The development of the praetor's edict', at 112; the episode belongs before the adoption of the sestertius as the official unit of reckoning. For the rich not (no longer) carrying their own money see Lucilius 278–81 W. Note also P. Birks, in *Daube Noster* (Edinburgh and London, 1974), 39, 'Lucius Veratius and the Lex Aebutia'.
17 *The Irish Jurist* 1972, 138, 'Linguistic and social context of the Lex Aquilia'.

II

THE LEGACY OF ATTALUS

The involvement of the Roman state in the affairs of Asia Minor began with the links established with the kingdom of Pergamum in the course of the First Macedonian War. The expedition of Philip V of Macedon to Caria in 201 was followed by the Second Macedonian War, this in turn by the direct Roman confrontation with Antiochus III, culminating in the battle of Magnesia in 190 and the withdrawal of the Seleucids from Asia Minor west of the Taurus Mountains. But the Roman forces left Asia Minor after the campaign of Cn. Manlius Vulso against the Gauls of the central plateau, not to return before 131.

The direct monetary consequences of the Roman involvement in the affairs of Asia Minor are negligible, though occasionally amusing, like the presence of a cast Prow triens of libral standard at Priene;[1] one wonders what the people there made of it. Among indirect consequences of the Second Macedonian War one may note a hoard of silver of Ptolemy IV and Ptolemy V from Cos (*Coin Hoards* 6, 32).

But certain aspects of the monetary history of Asia Minor need to be considered, not only because they reflect indirectly events in which Rome was involved, but also because they help us to understand the legacy of Attalus and the creation of the Roman province (Map 24).

The years 220–218 had seen the restoration of Seleucid control over the whole of southern Asia Minor, along with Phrygia, initially in the person of Achaeus, from 216 in the person of the legitimate king, his nephew Antiochus III. There followed immediately the production at Phaselis, Perge, Sillyum and Aspendus of four series

---

1 K. Regling, *Die Münzen von Priene* (Berlin, 1927), 183.

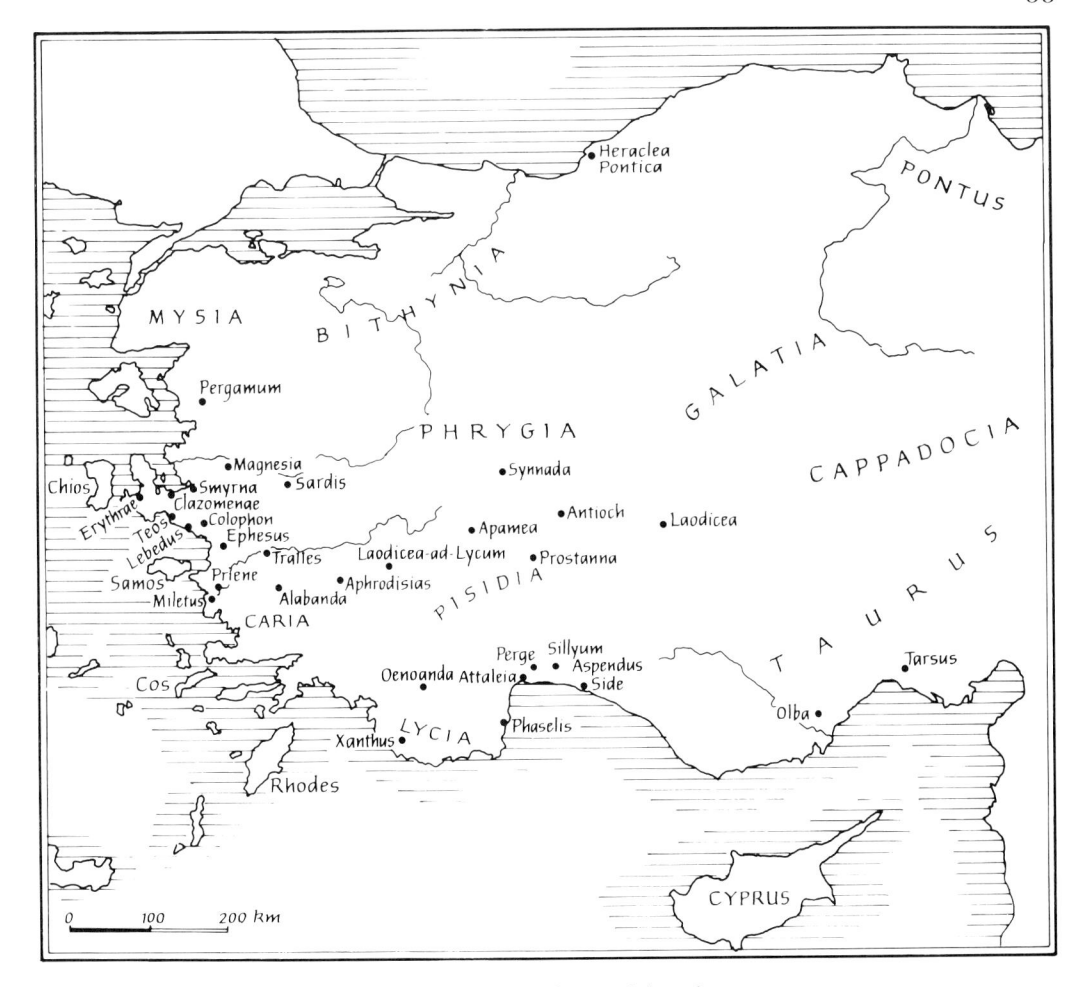

24   The kingdom of Attalus

of tetradrachms with the types of Alexander III, Head of Hercules r./Seated Zeus (Fig. 54); all the series except that of Sillyum were produced in substantial quantities.[2]

These four series mark the resurrection of the types of Alexander III for the production of coinage in Asia Minor. On and near the west coast, the Greek cities produced at various times issues of small silver on an Attic, Rhodian or Persian standard and issues of bronze. But from the late third century onwards, mints from Heraclea Pontica in the north to Rhodes in the south also produced Alexander tetradrachms;

2 O. Mørkholm, *MusN* 1978, 69, 'The era of the Pamphylian Alexanders', with earlier bibliography, argues against Chr. Boehringer, *Zur Chronologie mittelhellenistischer Münzserien* (Berlin, 1972), 52, that all four series began in 221/0; *contra*, Th. Fischer, *Berichte* 125 (November 1981), 1457.

54 The Alexander issues of Asia Minor

Posthumous tetradrachm of Alexander of Aspendus:
  Head of Heracles r./Zeus seated l. holding eagle and sceptre; behind, ΑΛΕΞΑΝΔΡΟΥ;
  before, ΑΣ and ΙΒ   Naville 5, 1432
Posthumous tetradrachm of Alexander of Sillyum:
  Head of Heracles r./Zeus seated l. holding eagle and sceptre; behind, ΑΛΕΞΑΝΔΡΟΥ;
  before, (Year 26)   Naville 5, 1433

the issues of Heraclea, Pergamum, Chios, Erythrae, Samos, Miletus and Rhodes were very large.

It seems to me necessary to suppose that, *as a whole*, the phenomenon is to be related to the military activities in western Asia Minor of Achaeus, Antiochus III, Philip V and, in opposition to Rome, Antiochus III once more. Hoards from Asia Minor in this period include substantial quantities of Seleucid silver and, in addition, Alexander tetradrachms of Aradus in Phoenicia. There are also two further Asia Minor mints to be considered, Alabanda, which bore in this period the name of Antiochia and produced a prolific issue of tetradrachms, with the types Head of Apollo l./Pegasus l., and Side, which lay close to Aspendus and the other Pamphylian mints, and produced a large issue of tetradrachms with the types Head of Athena r./Victory l. (Fig. 55). In the case of Alabanda-Antiochia it seems only natural to regard the coinage under discussion as produced for Antiochus III (for the resources available to him after his eastern expedition of 209 see Pol. x, 27). And given the presence of Philip V at Samos and Miletus and his attempt on Chios in the course of his Carian expedition, it seems equally natural to see the Alexander tetradrachms of those three mints as evoked by military exigencies on one side or the other.[3]

3 See F.S. Kleiner, *MusN* 1971, 95, 'The Alexander tetradrachms of Pergamum and Rhodes', dealing with Pergamum and Rhodes acting and striking in concert against Philip V; the different chronology of Chr. Boehringer (n.2), 42, does not face the arguments deployed by Kleiner; R. Bauslaugh, *MusN* 1979, 1, 'The posthumous Alexander coinage of Chios', at 21.

55   The issues of Alabanda and Side

Tetradrachm of Alabanda:
Laureate head of Apollo l./Pegasus l.; above, ΑΝΤΙΟΧΕΩΝ; below, ΔΗΜΗΤΡΙΟΣ
BM cast

Tetradrachm of Side:
Helmeted head of Athena r./Nike l. holding wreath; before pomegranate; on either side, ΚΛΕ ΥΧ
Naville 7, 1602

The consequence of the defeat of Antiochus III was the imposition of a substantial indemnity to be paid to Rome; and it is not surprising that there is little new Seleucid silver in the following two decades. Bronze indeed largely replaced silver between 173 and 171, and such silver as there was was reduced in weight. The gap left by the shortage of new Seleucid silver was in part filled by the movement into Seleucid territory — I decline to speculate on the mechanism — of the Alexanders of Phaselis, Perge and Aspendus and of the tetradrachms of Side; Alexanders from further west did not share in this movement.[4] Once arrived, many of the coins were countermarked with the Seleucid anchor, presumably as they passed through the hands of the Seleucid administration. The level of awareness of its officials is very striking, since they never countermarked the Alexander tetradrachms of Aradus, which remained in the Seleucid sphere.

Meanwhile, the cities of Asia Minor freed by Rome after the defeat of Antiochus III almost all produced some coinage, a clear mark of their status.[5] It emerges that the production of Alexander tetradrachms was not in any sense a step which bore an ideological significance, since Alabanda proceeded to strike them after it ceased

---

4 O. Mørkholm, *Historia* 1982, 290, 'Some reflections on coinage in ancient Greece', at 302, for the coinage of Syria; for the movement of coinage eastwards, see Chr. Boehringer (n.2), 20: vast numbers of Alexanders of Phaselis, Perge, Aspendus; only 13 from eight other mints. For the movement of coinage eastwards in the second half of the second century, perhaps in connection with the slave trade, see *La moneta in Grecia e a Roma* (Bari, 1982), 82 and 85.

5 R.E. Allen, *The Attalid Kingdom* (Oxford, 1983), 109–11.

56 The wreathed issues of Asia Minor

Tetradrachm of Magnesia:
  Bust of Artemis r./Apollo standing l. holding garland; behind, tripod on which rests quiver; below, maeander pattern; on r., ΜΑΓΝΗΤΩΝ; on l., ΠΑΥΣΑΝΙΑΣ ΠΑΥΣΑΝΙΟΥ; all in laurel-wreath   Naville 1, 2460

Tetradrachm of Cyme:
  Female head r., hair tied with ribbon/Horse r.; before, pail and ΚΥΜΑΙΩΝ; in exergue, ΚΑΛΛΙΑΣ; all in laurel-wreath   BM cast

in 190 to form part of the Seleucid sphere. They were simply a standard form of large silver, often struck in the context of military activity, but not exclusively so.

Equally, no general significance is to be attached to the shift to tetradrachms bearing a wreath round the reverse type. We have already had occasion to consider the wreathed tetradrachms of Athens (p.125); some of the issues in Asia Minor may be earlier and the adoption and spread of the device seem to be no more than the result of a decorative fashion (Fig. 56). The significance of each wreathed coinage must be assessed separately;[6] one cannot apply the name *argyrion stephanephoron* to any coinage except the Athenian and one cannot generalise the explanation which seems to account for the development of the Athenian issue, namely the possession of the port of Delos.[7] Nor can one suppose that the wreathed coinages were instituted by Rome to replace the coinages of the Hellenistic monarchs.[8]

The wreathed issues, apart from those of Athens, were short-lived; but in general the second quarter of the second century saw the emergence of the pattern of coinage which lasted until and in some cases beyond the establishment of Roman rule in the

6 L. Robert, *RN* 1977, 34, 'L'argent d'Athènes stéphanéphore'.
7 *Contra*, Chr. Boehringer (n.2), 22–39, with at the end a truly extraordinary account of the 'Revolt' of Aristonicus.
8 So, rightly, O. Mørkholm, *QTic* 1980, 145, 'Chronology and meaning of the wreath coinages of the early second century BC'; J.H. Oakley, *MusN* 1982, 1, 'The autonomous wreathed tetradrachms of Kyme, Aeolis'; O. Picard, *AIIN* 29, 1982, 245, 'Les Romains et les émissions aux types d'Alexandre'.

57 The coinages of Rhodes, Cappadocia, Pontus and Bithynia

Drachm of Rhodes:
 Facing head of Helios/Rose; above, ΑΡΤΕΜΩΝ; on either side, Ρ Ο; below on l., head-dress of Isis   Naville 1, 2713

Drachm of Ariarathes:
 Diademed head r./Athena l.; on either side, monogram; on r., ΒΑΣΙΛΕΩΣ; on l., ΑΡΙΑΡΑΘΟΥ; below, ΕΥΣΕΒΟΥΣ
  ΙΚ   Lockett 3084

Tetradrachm of Mithridates VI:
 Diademed head of Mithridates r./Deer l.; on l., star and crescent and monogram; on r., two monograms; above, ΒΑΣΙΛΕΩΣ; below, ΜΙΘΡΙΔΑΤΟΥ
  ΕΥΠΑΤΟΡΟΣ
  Θ; all in ivy-wreath   Naville 14, 295

Tetradrachm of Nicomedes:
 Diademed head of Nicomedes r./Zeus standing l.; before, eagle and two monograms; on r., ΒΑΣΙΛΕΩΣ; on l., ΕΠΙΦΑΝΟΥΣ
  ΝΙΚΟΜΗΔΟΥ   Naville 4, 690

west of Asia Minor. Already after Magnesia, Rhodes had begun the production of silver with the reverse type, the rose, set in a square frame. To the east, Cappadocia became the major producer of silver between Rhodes and Syria. In the north, the great coinages of the last century of independence were those of Pontus and Bithynia (Fig. 57).[9]

9 See F.S. Kleiner, *MusN* 1974, 3, 'The Giresun hoard'.

58 The cistophoric coinage of Pergamum

Cistophoric tetradrachm:
  Cista mystica in ivy-wreath/Two snakes and bow-case; above, A K; on l., EΦE; on r.,
  two cornucopiae   BM cast
Cistophoric drachm:
  Club and lion-skin in double laurel-wreath/Bunch of grapes; below, TPAΛ, monogram
  and head of Helios   Newnham Davis 311

But it is in the kingdom of Pergamum that the most crucial development took place. At some point between 180 and 160,[10] the tetradrachms of Attic weight which had been struck up to that point were replaced by coins which weighed only as much as three Attic drachms, but which within Attalid territory had the face value of tetradrachms, and were accompanied by their own half and quarter pieces (Fig. 58). There is no doubt that the Attalid monarchy, in order to save silver, was deliberately creating an isolated monetary zone and enforcing the circulation of a silver coinage with a face value four-thirds of its metal value.[11]

Naturally, the new cistophoric coinage of Pergamum was characterised, like the Ptolemaic coinage, by the fact that it did not normally circulate outside Pergamene territory; nor did foreign silver now circulate in Pergamene territory. And the association in hoards of cistophoric and other silver is very rare. One early cistophoric hoard, probably from Pergamene territory, still contains silver of Attic weight (*IGCH* 1453) and there is one cistophorus from a late second-century hoard from Proconnesus

---

10 O. Mørkholm, *MusN* 1979, 47, 'Some reflections on the early cistophoric coinage'; F.S. Kleiner, *MusN* 1980, 'Further reflections on the early cistophoric coinage'; the mention of cistophori by Livy (xxxiv, 52, 6) in the year 194 must be discounted.

11 H. Seyrig, *RN* 1963, 22, 'Questions cistophoriques'; F.S. Kleiner and S.P. Noe, *The Early Cistophoric Coinage* (New York, 1977); O.

Mørkholm (n.4), 300–1, for the countermarking of earlier silver; R.E. Allen (n.5), 112–4, with whom I disagree over date. W. Szaivert's curious idea, *Litterae Numismaticae Vindobonenses* 2, 1983, 29, 'Stephanephoren und Kistophoren', that the cistophoric coinage was an independent city coinage, may be ruled out of court.

59 The cistophoric coinage of Aristonicus and Rome

Cistophoric tetradrachm:
  Cista mystica in ivy-wreath/Two snakes and bow-case; above, BA and head; on l., ΘΥΑ; on lower l. and r., BA EY; below, B
  BM cast

Cistophoric tetradrachm:
  Cista mystica in ivy-wreath/Two snakes and bow-case; above, Δ; on l., ΕΦΕ; on r., torch
  BM cast

(*IGCH* 1336); otherwise, it was only the turmoil of the Mithridatic Wars or the civil wars of the Roman Republic which carried cistophori to alien environments.

The organisation of the cistophoric coinage is interesting: the mint of Pergamum struck for itself, as well as for Sardis, Synnada and Apamea (not to mention two small, perhaps ceremonial issues, with KOP and BA – ΣY – AP), Ephesus struck for itself, Tralles struck for itself and for Laodicea. The coinage was clearly centrally controlled, since it was Tralles which struck virtually all fractions. It looks very much as if we have the coinage of a centrally controlled fiscal system, with regal appropriation of revenue and redistribution of resources.

The last Attalid king of Pergamum left his kingdom to the Romans, who accepted the legacy with alacrity and suppressed the attempt of Aristonicus to claim what he regarded as his rightful heritage. Despite the fact that he continued, naturally enough, the cistophoric coinage of his ancestors, claiming the title of Ba(sileus) Eu(menes),[12] his and his ancestors' coinage became the coinage of the Roman province of Asia, struck for the Romans for the most part by the mints which had struck earlier for the Attalids (Fig. 59).

The case of Ephesus is particularly interesting. The city was freed in the will of Attalus III and adopted 134/3 as the first year of a new era, to symbolise its newly acquired freedom.[13] Yet it is precisely in the years after 134/3 that Ephesus becomes

12 E.S.G. Robinson, *NC* 1954, 1, 'Cistophori in the name of King Eumenes'; M. Kampmann, *RN* 1978, 38, 'Aristonicos à Thyatire'.

13 K.J. Rigsby, *Phoenix* 1979, 39, 'The era of the province of Asia'; see also F.S. Kleiner, *MusN* 1972, 17, 'The dated cistophori of Ephesus'; *MusN* 1978, 77, 'Hoard evidence and the late cistophori of Pergamum'.

for the first time a major cistophoric mint, obviously to finance the war against Aristonicus and then the Roman presence in Asia. Ephesus had indeed produced its own drachms of Attic weight throughout the period of Pergamene rule; the whole monetary history of Ephesus in this period should caution against any facile linking of freedom and the production of silver coinage.

The Romans obviously took over from the Attalids other institutions than their coinage, first and foremost no doubt the basic system of taxation. The column and door tax attested by Caesar (*BC* ii, 32, 2), may be an Attalid institution. And the nail tax now attested at Aphrodisias in the age of Hadrian may likewise go back to the earlier rulers of the area.[14] Who these were is indeed for the period immediately before 134/3 not altogether clear. Nor is it beyond dispute that Caria fell to Rome at the same time as the kingdom of Pergamum, rather than in the age of Sulla, though I incline to the view that it did, given the road built by Mn. Aquillius from Pergamum to Attaleia via Laodicea-ad-Lycum and the fact that Q. Mucius Scaevola, Cos. 120 or 95, was patron and benefactor of Oenoanda. Certainly a small hoard of cistophori from Aphrodisias suggests that the area became an area of cistophorus circulation.[15]

But the most astonishing feature of the monetary history of Asia under Roman rule is the evidence it provides of the absence of an interventionist approach on the part of the Romans. Despite the fact that the cistophoric coinage was now the Roman coinage of a Roman province, even Roman governors had to pay bankers' commission to change cistophori into denarii (Cicero, *ad Att.* xii, 6, 1 (*sed certe in collybo est detrimenti satis*)). It is hard to suppose that the economic interests of Roman citizens were very close to the heart of the Roman government.

14 R.S. Bagnall, *The Administration of the Ptolemaic Possessions outside Egypt* (Leiden, 1976), 108–9; J.M. Reynolds, *Aphrodisias and Rome* (London, 1982), Doc. 15.

15 For a contrary view on Caria see T. Drew-Bear, *BCH* 1972, 437, 'Deux décrets hellénistiques d'Asie Mineure', at 471, n.224; I owe knowledge of the inscription from Oenoanda to Alan Hall; *I.Delos* 1603, honouring M. Antonius quaestor pro praetore of Asia in 113, *may* be taken to imply that Prostanna in Pisidia was then part of the province of Asia, note the tentative formulation of L. Robert, *Hellenica* 13, 83, n.1; the hoard contained *SNG* (von Aulock) 7463, Pergamum, before 134/3, worn; *SNG* (Cop.) 657, Tralles, *c*.100, fresh (two specimens).

12

FROM NANNUS TO CAESAR

Of all the western peoples absorbed into the Roman empire, the Gauls who lived beyond the Alps were probably the people who had reached the highest level of development by the time the process of conquest began. Settled in tribal groups at least by 600 BC, they occupied between the Mediterranean, the Pyrenees, the Atlantic, the Rhine and the Alps an area vast in extent and of enormous potential wealth. It is also of the highest interest because the archaeological evidence for economic relations with Italy during the Republic is better than for any other area of the Mediterranean. Against a general background of incipient urbanisation with differentiated sacred buildings,[1] of Mediterranean imports and locally produced monumental sculpture, certain areas stand out.[2] The area richest in Mediterranean imports in the sixth century was that centring on Mont Lassois near Vix. In the following centuries, primacy passed to the area between the Seine and the Rhine, characterised by a process of rapid social differentiation and imports on a large scale. In the third and second centuries, the greatest concentration of wealth, as evidenced by burials, is to be found in the territory of the Bituriges Cubi, where also the earliest gold and silver coinage of central Gaul was produced.[3] In contemplating all these areas, it is important to remember that contact with the Mediterranean took the form not only, perhaps even not principally, of trade, but also of service abroad by Gallic mercenaries, who returned with the

---

1 For the sophisticated calendar of the Gauls, see P.-M. Duval, *Mélanges J. Carcopino* (Paris, 1966), 295, 'Les Gaulois et le calendrier'.
2 A convenient recent survey may be found in F.R. Hodson and R.M. Rowlett, in S. Piggott, G. Daniel and C. McBurney (eds), *France before the Romans* (London, 1973), 157, 'From 600 BC to the Roman conquest'. Compare P.S. Wells, *Culture Contact and Culture Change* (Cambridge, 1980), for the Württemberg area.
3 D. Nash, *Settlement and Coinage in Central Gaul* (Oxford: BAR, 1978), 15.

rewards of their hire and the booty which they had accumulated. It is also important to realise that in the third and second centuries the surplus generated in central Gaul went into the creation of urban centres and state structures, rather than being immobilised in burials.

This was also no doubt true of the area with which we are in the first instance concerned, the southern coastal zone (Map 25). From Mailhac and Ensérune in the west (Ruscino belonged in the Iberian sphere) through Montlaurès on the route which later became the Via Domitia, to the edge of the territory of Massalia in the east, with Entremont and Roquepertuse, the area was dotted with urban centres, to which the use of writing had certainly penetrated by the third century BC.[4]

Active Roman intervention in the area began with the war waged from 125 against the Salluvii, Allobroges and Arverni, undertaken at the behest of Massalia; the first two were annexed to form the nucleus of the province of Gallia Transalpina, while alliances were made with the Aedui and the Volcae; direct rule was extended to the latter towards the end of the century. The defeat of the Salluvii, Allobroges and Arverni was followed almost immediately by the laying out of the Via Domitia and the foundation in 118 of the colony of Narbo Martius near Ensérune.

But it is to Massalia that one must first turn in order to understand the economic history of Gaul in the Hellenistic period. From her foundation by Phocaea around 600, with the help of a local king called Nannus, down to the fourth century, Massalia appears to have grown rich by acting as middleman in the shipment to central Gaul of the luxury imports from the Mediterranean mentioned above. But these imports dry up in the Hellenistic period and are not replaced either by Massaliot pottery or by Massaliot wine amphorae. The natural supposition is that Massalia became a 'normal' *polis* living off its *chora* and this still seems to me the best solution, though I should not want to exclude the brilliant suggestion of C. Goudineau,[5] that Massalia in the Hellenistic period lived in part off the export of military and other technology. The picture of a Massalia barely able to resist the pressure of the barbarian tribes around her smacks too strongly of (pro-Roman) apologia to be credible in its entirety, and should not be used as an argument for the view that Massalia possessed no significant *chora*. There are clear cases elsewhere of the colonial exploitation of an indigenous population which has left almost no archaeological traces, so that the 'native' character of the material culture of the settlements close to Massalia does not prove that they did not pay some of their surplus to Massalia. Nor is such a position of economic dependence on Massalia incompatible with the outbreak of hostilities in

---

4 D. Nash, in B. Cunliffe and T. Rowley (eds), *Oppida* (Oxford, 1976), 95, 'The growth of urban society in France' (on central Gaul); P.A. Fevrier, *JRS* 1973, 1, 'The cities of southern Gaul'; for the use of writing, Strabo iv, 1, 5 (181), with C. Goudineau, in P. Garnsey et al. (p.99, n.33), 76, 'Marseille, Rome and Gaul', at 83.

5 Ibid., 82; for the *chora* of Massalia see C. Goudineau, in Cl. Nicolet, *Rome et la conquête du monde méditerranéen* 2 (Paris, 1978), 684–5 and 693.

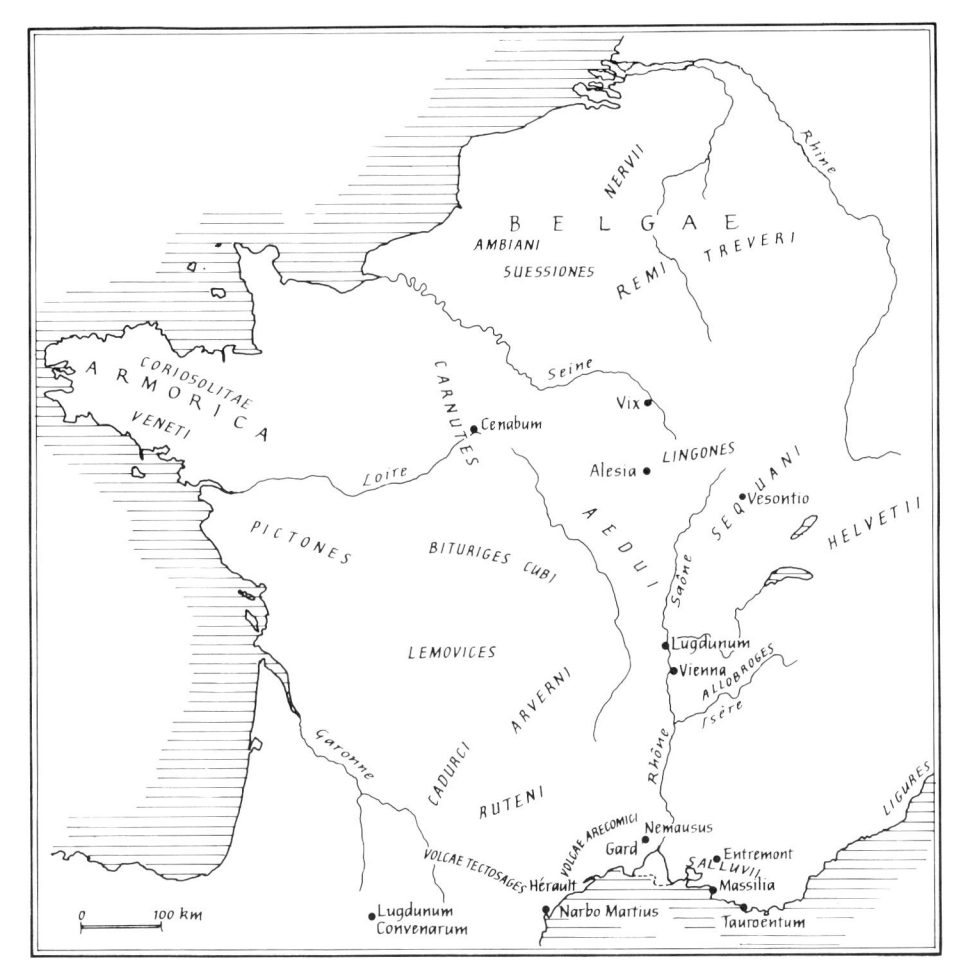

25 Gaul

125 (perhaps in response to an attempt to tighten the screw). The precise forms which the trade-offs between Massalia and her neighbours took are largely unknown; but the presence of Craton in the capital of the Sallyes (Salluvii) (Diod. xxxiv, 23) and the ownership of land by Charmolaos among the Ligures show that peaceful – and, to Massalia, profitable – coexistence was at some times and in some places certainly possible. What is clear is that only *with* the creation of the Roman province does one see an explosion of exports of pottery and wine amphorae, both from Italy, to Transalpine Gaul.

Meanwhile, the distribution of Massaliot coinage offers some support to the notion of an extended *chora*. The later coinage of Massalia consisted essentially of a silver drachm and silver and bronze fractions (Fig. 60): the drachm coinage began about

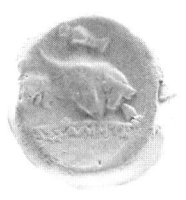

60 The coinage of Massalia

Drachm of Massalia:
  Bust of Artemis r./Lion l.; above, ΜΑΣΣΑ; below, monogram   Lockett 24
Bronze of Massalia:
  Laureate head of Apollo l.; behind, uncertain symbol/Bull butting r.; above, uncertain
  symbol; below, ΜΑΣΣΑΛΙΗΤΩΝ   BM
Obol of Massalia:
  Male head l./Wheel; between spokes, MA   Naville 5, 26

350 with a weight of 3.75 gm.;[6] it was followed by an enormous issue of obols, then about 225 by a drachm coinage with a weight of 2.65 gm., initially with the same types as before. There is no doubt that the production of these drachms is to be related to the Massaliot war effort as an ally of Rome against Hannibal. The beginning of the bronze coinage of Massalia is approximately contemporary. This seems to come to an end early in the first century, to be replaced by diobols and then a further issue of obols.

As far as circulation is concerned, bronze occurs in Massalia itself and in the immediately surrounding territory (App. 43); it apparently circulated for all practical purposes by itself: for instance, the La Cloche hoard contains one Roman bronze, a hoard from Massalia two, in both cases clearly assimilated to Massaliot bronzes; one Entremont hoard of Massaliot bronze contains one obol of Massalia and one Gallic drachm, attributed to the Allobroges.

Massaliot silver was the principal silver to circulate in a rather more extensive territory; a curious phenomenon is the presence of large numbers of the obols of the third century in the Hérault, up the Rhone valley as far as Vienna and up the Isère valley, often in hoards numbering many thousand pieces. I am unable to say why Massalia produced large issues of tiny coins, which were then hoarded en bloc, or how they reached Gallic territory. As Cl. Brenot has observed to me, the burial of the hoards may in part reflect the march of Hannibal, though a hoard from Tourdan

---

6 J.-N. Barrandon, Cl. Brenot, *MEFRA* 1978, 637, 'Le monnayage de Marseille'; Cl. Brenot, *Studia P. Naster* (Louvain, 1982), 35, 'La drachme lourde de Marseille'; *9 Cong.Num.*, 187, 'Le monnayage d'argent de Marseille'.

near Vienna (with Gallic drachms and diobols) includes one tetrobol of Histiaea, which along with the examples forming the Nice hoard presumably came west after the Third Macedonian War.

Massalia thus provided part of the silver coinage used in southern Gaul as a whole in the second century, supplemented by drachms produced by nearby Gallic communities, three of which, Avenio, the Kainiketes and the Glanikoi, signed their issues in Greek. Some local communities also produced bronze, conspicuously the Longostaletes; their issues, with the types Head of Hermes/Tripod, are of good style and accurate lettering; the principal legend is in Greek, the subsidiary legends in Greek or Iberian.

The hoard record discussed so far suggests that (despite the issue of denarii produced for Narbo in 118, *RRC*, no. 282) Massaliot coinage was *the* coinage of southern Gaul down to and indeed even after the governorship of C. Valerius Flaccus in 83. For Massalia continued to strike silver in the age of Cicero, coinage which was apparently produced from the revenues attributed to Massalia in the territory of the Volcae Arecomici. For the metal of these last issues of drachms of Massalia is that of the earlier coinage of the Volcae Arecomici.

But this is not quite the whole story. The sites of Mailhac and Ensérune, and to a lesser extent Ruscino, have a high percentage of Republican issues because of their proximity to Narbo.[7] There is one early second-century hoard of Massaliot and Roman silver from Entremont (*RRCH* 110 = *IGCH* 2371) and large numbers of denarii were found below the 123 destruction level (*RRCH* 560). (The hoard from St. Cyr-sur-mer, ancient Tauroentum, *Coin Hoards* 5, 91, may have been buried at any time down to Augustus.) I suspect that more hoard evidence may one day accrue; but the numismatic dominance of Massalia is clear,[8] and lies behind the use of the mint by Flaccus, albeit to strike denarii (*RRC*, no. 365, Fig. 61).

Such evidence as there is in fact suggests a rather different context for the arrival of Roman silver coinage.[9] A single hoard from Aime, perhaps of the late second century and consisting solely of denarii, is followed by four which associate a few Roman silver coins with Gallic quinarii of the area between the Rhone and the Alps, St. Rémy, Cheverny, Gerbay, Migne, one which associates denarii with 'monnaies à la croix', Bompas, and three of Roman coins alone, Noyer, Peyriac-sur-mer and Bessan (App. 44, Map 26). It is in fact in the period after Flaccus that the penetration of Roman coinage begins; and it was no doubt greatly facilitated by the earlier development of a native coinage of quinarii on the Roman model, partly by the Allobroges in the area

---

7 J.-C. Richard, *II Simposi Numismatic*, 46, 'La circulation des monnaies pre-augustéennes en Languedoc-Roussillon'; J.-L. Hygounet, *Acta Num.* 1982, 31, 'Un exemple d'emploi d'un modèle statistique', adds nothing.

8 J. Chamesson et al., *II Simposi Numismatic*, 97, 'La circulation monétaire dans le nord-est du Gard', document the overwhelming dominance of Massalia in the area.

9 The Brusc hoard, *RRCH* 284, comes from a shipwreck and was not necessarily ever intended to reach Gaul.

61 The issue of Flaccus at Massalia

Late drachm of Massalia:
   Bust of Artemis r./Lion l.; above, ΜΑΣΣΑ; in exergue, Γ   Lockett 29
Denarius of C. Valerius Flaccus:
   Bust of Victory r.; before, palm-branch/*Aquila* between two standards; on l.,
   C.VAL.FLA (in monogram); on r., IMPERAT; below, EX.S.C   *BMCRR* Gaul 4

which later formed part of the province, partly by the Aedui, Sequani and Lingones outside it (Fig. 62).

The earliest of these Rhone valley coinages, with Horse's head, Horse, Ibex and Sea-horse reverses, are rather heavier than Roman quinarii and are presumably light copies of the second-century drachms of Massalia. The first three groups occur in the Tourdan hoard (p.164) and should be regarded as beginning in the middle of the second century, the Sea-horse issue has been found at Entremont and therefore antedates 123. The latest issue, with Horseman reverse, weighs much the same as Roman quinarii.[10]

One further coinage remains to be considered before we can turn to the literary and other evidence for the developing Roman presence in southern Gaul, the so-called 'monnaies à la croix' (Fig. 63).[11] Imitations of the drachms of Rhode in Spain, they belong for the most part to the territory of the Volcae Tectosages, in part also to that of the Volcae Arecomici, Cadurci and Ruteni. An enormous coinage, based initially on a drachm of 3.40 gm., then on a lighter drachm, examples occur in the three Spanish hoards of Drieves, Valera and La Plana de Utiel; all the *datable* pieces in these hoards belong to the period of the Second Punic War.[12] But I remain puzzled that the only

---

10 J.-C. Richard, in M. R.-Alföldi (ed.), *Studien zu Fundmünzen der Antike* (Berlin, 1979), 197, 'Les monnaies au cavalier de la vallée du Rhone'. See D.F. Allen, *The Coins of the Ancient Celts* (Edinburgh, 1980), 35, for the use of melted down denarii for this coinage. For the finds from Entremont see *RN* 1959–60, 37; A. Deroc, *Les monnaies gauloises d'argent de la vallée du Rhone* (Paris, 1983), 57, rejects the evidence of excavation in order to follow the chronology of J.B. Colbert de Beaulieu for Gallic coinage as a whole.

11 D.F. Allen, *NC* 1969, 33, '*Monnaies-à-la-croix*', esp. 39, n.5; the imitation of drachms of Emporiae in the territory of the Lemovices was on a very small scale.

12 P.P. Ripollés, L. Villaronga, *Acta Num*. 1981, 29, 'La chronologie des monnaies à la croix', with earlier bibliography.

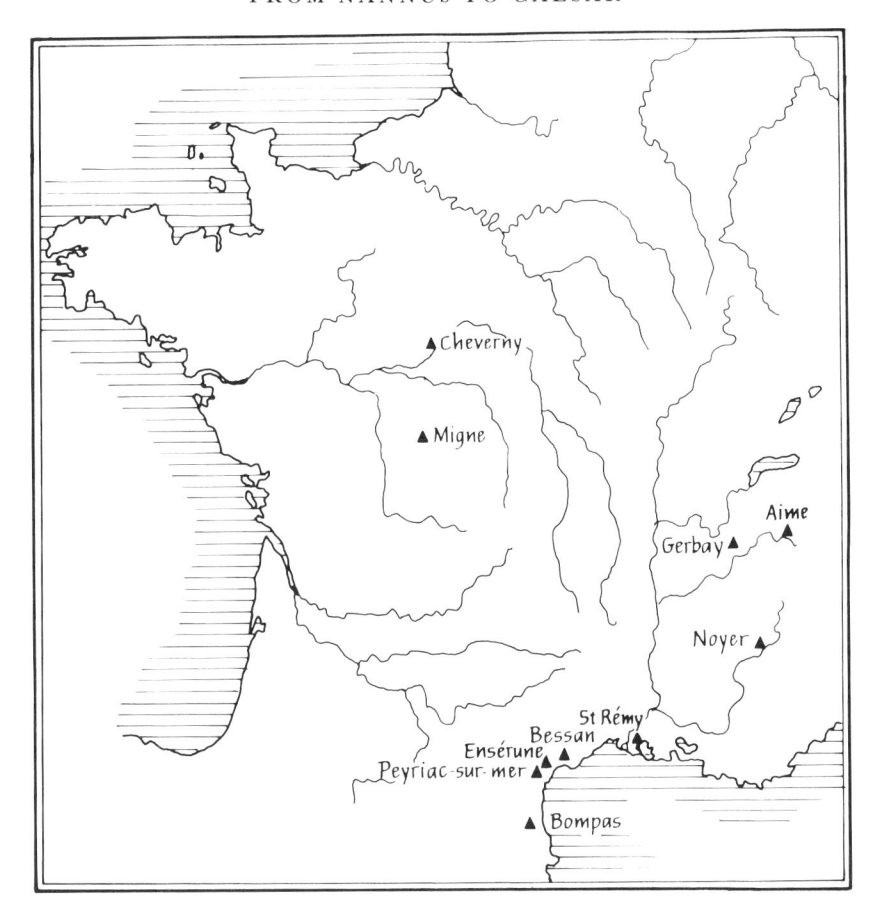

26 Early hoards with Roman coins in southern Gaul
See App. 44

62 Quinarii of southern Gaul

Female head r./Horse's head r.; below, IALIKOVESI — Glasgow
Laureate head r./Ibex r. — Naville 4, 1
Helmeted head r.; before, BR/Horseman r. with spear — BM

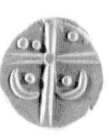

63   Monnaies-à-la-croix

Female head l.; before, blundered legend/Rose   Glasgow
Head l.; before, branch/'Cross'   Glasgow

other securely dated material with which the 'monnaies à la croix' turn up consists of Roman denarii in the Bompas hoard of the seventies BC. Fortunately, the early history of the 'monnaies à la croix' is in a sense marginal, since it is clear that the later issues were assimilated to the weight standard of the quinarius coinages to the east; together the two coinages provided much of the circulating medium of Gallia Narbonensis in the two generations before Caesar.

It is of course to the period after Flaccus that the well-known passage of the *pro Fonteio* of Cicero relates (11–12):

Gaul is full of men of business, full of Roman citizens. None of the Gauls ever does business without the presence of a Roman citizen, no coin changes hands in Gaul without being entered in the accounts of a Roman citizen .... Let [the accusers] produce one witness from among so large a number of men of business, colonists [of Narbo], *publicani*, farmers, ranchers ...

Even allowing for some exaggeration by Cicero, the picture is an astonishing one; and it is equally remarkable that, if the evidence we have been considering is reliable, Romans in southern Gaul carried on many of their business activities in a variety of local currencies, a fact reflected in the use of the quinarius as a unit of reckoning (*pro Font.* 19) and in the high proportion of Roman quinarii in the Peyriac-sur-mer and Bessan hoards.

If Roman coinage barely penetrated southern Gaul before Caesar, the same cannot be said of Italian pottery and amphorae, and to these imports we must now turn, before moving on to consider the monetary history of the rest of Gaul before the governorship of Caesar. From the last quarter of the second century onwards Italian black-slip pottery and Dressel 1 wine amphorae appeared in substantial quantities in certain areas of Gaul; the pottery provoked some imitation. Two points require emphasis: there is no substantial presence of imports from Italy before 125,[13] which

13 R. Lequément and B. Liou, *Cahiers Ligures* 1975, 76, 'Les épaves de la côte de Transalpine'; A. Tchernia, in P. Garnsey et al. (p.99, n.33), 87, 'Italian wine in Gaul'.

means that talk of trade preparing the way for conquest is inappropriate; and neither pottery nor wine amphorae replace imports from elsewhere.

Unless one supposes that for some odd reason Italian wine systematically travelled some way in amphorae and was then transferred to barrels, the principal areas of importation seem to have been two, the territory of the Volcae Tectosages within the Roman province and the territory of the Arverni and Aedui immediately to the north. These peoples should, however, probably be regarded as forming in effect part of the Roman world. It was the defeat of the Arverni which led to the establishment of the Roman province and the Aedui were early friends of the Roman people. It is in fact possible to see the areas of importation as those within reach of the sea, but not within the area where the coinage of Massalia circulated.

It is easier to draw attention to weaknesses in explanatory hypotheses of the phenomenon than it is to produce one of one's own that is entirely convincing; I suspect in the end that a variety of factors was at work. In the first place, a model drawn from the relationship which existed between modern imperial powers and their dependencies, where industrial goods were (in effect) exchanged in protected markets for cheap primary products, seems quite inappropriate. It would be hard to think of many products more primary in the ancient world than pottery and wine. And there is no trace in the case of Gaul under the Republic of measures designed to ensure a captive market for Italian exports; Cicero, *de re pub*. iii, 16, which has sometimes been taken as recording a Roman attempt to prevent local production of wine and hence competition with Italian produce, has been shown beyond all reasonable doubt to have nothing whatever to do with Gaul at all.[14]

Two aspects of the problem are in principle separable; what commodities were exchanged for the pottery and wine? And how was the exchange stimulated? The conventional wisdom is that the principal commodity which left Gaul was slaves,[15] mentioned by Cicero (*pro Quinctio* 24), Afranius (232–3 Ribbeck) and Diodorus (v, 26, 3), rather than minerals or agricultural produce. The trade will on this view have been generated by the Roman demand for slaves, and the objects traded by them not have met a concrete pre-existing demand.

Of course there was some trade in slaves from Gaul, and Poseidonius had already observed that wine satisfied a craving for luxury among the Gallic aristocracy (compare Caesar, *BG* iv, 2, 2 for the import of fine horses). And there is a fair amount of literary evidence for traders in Gaul outside the province in the time of Caesar, at Vesontio (*BG* i, 39, 1), at Cenabum in the territory of the Carnutes (vii, 3, 1–2) and in the territory of the Aedui (vii, 42, 1–6; 55, 5), though it must be said that some of these

---

14 J. Paterson, *CQ* 1978, 452, 'Transalpinae gentes' (ignored by B. van Rinsveld, *Latomus* 1981, 280, 'Cicero, *De re publica* iii, 9, 15–16'); the objection of A. Tchernia (n.13), n.43, misses the point made by Paterson at 457–8.

15 A. Tchernia (n.13), 97. Given its location, it is rather hard to see the graffito from Olbia cited by C. Goudineau (n.4), n.5, as having anything to do with the slave trade.

men may as in Germany (iv, 2, 1) have been interested in buying up booty (other than slaves) acquired in inter-tribal fighting or may have been attracted by the presence of the Roman army (see vi, 37, 2).

But there are difficulties in the way of supposing that the slave trade provides the whole answer. Enslavement within a Roman province was illegal; no doubt it occurred, but I find it hard to suppose that it occurred to a sufficient extent to explain the level of imports among the Volcae Tectosages. Nor do I find it easy to suppose either that relatively developed states such as those of the Arverni and the Aedui were busy selling off their own people or that a great deal of slave-raiding elsewhere is compatible with the relatively stable tribal network of pre-Roman Gaul.

I suspect that *part* of the answer is to be found in the Roman presence *in* Gaul rather than in a Roman demand for slaves *from* Gaul. Some pottery and wine surely went to Roman armies in the area;[16] this notion is suggested very strongly by the fact that in the period immediately after Caesar, the bulk of the imports flows to the military presence on the frontier, Arretine pottery being replaced in due course by Gallic products.[17] (*Some* imports of course continued to flow into Gaul proper, supplemented by local products.) Against the notion that military supply accounts for part of the imported material may be set the fact that much of it occurs in native *oppida*; this objection is not altogether cogent, since we do not know to what extent Roman troops were billeted in native communities in friendly areas.[18]

It is also clear from Cicero, *pro Quinctio* 12 and *pro Fonteio* 12, that there were numerous Roman farmers in the province;[19] it seems likely that they were the destination of some Italian imports to Gaul. Some of these imports may indeed have been bartered for the land which they had come to own. But neither army nor Roman residents can explain, for instance, imports to the area of the Aedui before the time of Caesar; I should argue that a major factor here and elsewhere is likely to have been the simple one of a local aristocracy exchanging an agricultural surplus for desirable foreign luxuries. Pottery from Italy is well represented among the grave goods of the warrior aristocracy of the Volcae Arecomici in the late second and the first century.[20] (Strabo's ecstatic account (iii, 4, 11 (162)) of the marketing of hams from

---

16 As I have already argued in *Società Romana* III, 271–83; the remarks of A. Carandini and M. Torelli, in *Opus* 1, 1982, 2, 422 and 435, read as if they thought they owned the data on the interpretation of which we disagree.

17 P. Middleton, in B.C. Burnham and H. Johnson (eds), *Invasion and Response* (Oxford, 1979), 81, 'Army supply in Roman Gaul', though with the bizarre view that Gallic pottery was supplied in lieu of tax.

18 E. Wightman, *Helinium* 1977, 105, 'Military arrangements in early Roman Gaul', mounts a powerful argument that many Roman units were still based in native settlements for a generation or so after 50.

19 R. Syme, *Ktema* 2, 1977, 373, 'La richesse des aristocraties de Bétique et de Narbonnaise' for the attractive view that the great landed families of the turn of the era were the descendants of settlers of the second century BC.

20 G. Barruol and G. Sauzade, in *Hommages F. Benoit = Rev.Et.Lig.* 1969, 15, 'Une tombe de guerrier à St. Laurent-des-Arbres'.

the central Pyrenees seems likely to reflect simply the foundation of the city of Lugdunum Convenarum by Pompey in 72.)

A further element in the explanation may be furnished by the mining areas of the Ruteni, where Dressel 1 amphorae appear at the turn of the second and first centuries, and by those just to the south-east around Ceilhes and Camarès; Roman interest in these areas and a consequential Roman presence are very likely (compare p.99 for Spain);[21] it is worth noting that *someone* conveyed a small group of the coins of the Ruteni to Modena, probably during the second century (App. 24).

If the picture advanced here is correct, the province in the late Republic emerges as already a highly Romanised area; it comes as no surprise that Caesar was able to recruit there (*BG* i, 7 (probably); iii, 20; vii, 65), while the paradox of the non-arrival of Roman coinage is enhanced (p.168).

But the coinages of the Aedui, Sequani and Lingones suggest that some parts of the rest of Gaul were also relatively advanced on the eve of the governorship of Caesar. What other elements did the Romans have to build on in creating a province, with in due course a Roman monetary framework? Quite apart from the evidence of their coinages, it is clear that the tribes of central Gaul had developed relatively complex city-based administrative structures before the arrival of Caesar. (The Belgae were in a different position; note the exclusion of merchants and luxuries such as wine from the territory of the Nervii, *BG* ii, 15, 4; iv, 2, 6; cf. i, 1, 3; also their ignorance of the Greek alphabet, v, 48, 4.) The Gauls in general and the Helvetii in particular are attested as making use of the Greek alphabet (*BG* vi, 14, 3; i, 29, 1), and we hear of tolls on the River Saône contested between the Sequani and the Aedui (Strabo iv, 3, 2 (192)), of *portoria* and other taxes of the Aedui (*BG* i, 18, 3); even in the more backward north-west, the Veneti levied *portoria* (*BG* iii, 8, 1; Strabo iv, 2, 1 (190), on the south-west, has, alas, nothing to do with taxation). Given the existence of coinage, all these taxes were presumably computed in monetary terms and levied at least in part in cash. And even the Belgic tribes had a substantial gold coinage before Caesar.

All the major central Gaulish tribes had complex coinages before Caesar, the Arverni in gold, silver and base metal, the Bituriges Cubi likewise,[22] the Pictones in gold and silver, the Carnutes and Lemovices likewise (Fig. 64). In at least two cases, the Bituriges Cubi and the Pictones, minting took place at more than one centre, and it seems preferable to believe that this reflects the existence within the tribe of city-based fiscal systems, rather than that coinage was produced by private enterprise, along the lines

---

21 A. Tchernia (n.13), 95 and 90.
22 D. Nash, in *Essays H. Sutherland* (London, 1978), 12, 'Plus ça change: currency in central Gaul from Julius Caesar to Nero'. Much of the work of J.B. Colbert de Beaulieu and S. Scheers is vitiated by their belief in an Arvernian hegemony, which prevented other tribes coining before 121, see D. Nash, *NC* 1975, 204, 'The chronology of Celtic coinage in Gaul'; in fact the Arverni produced no coinage before the first century, D. Nash (n.3), 138.

64 The coinage of central Gaul before Caesar

Gold piece of Bituriges Cubi:
  Head l.; before, uncertain symbol/Horse l.; above, bird; below, three circles and
  ABVD[OS]   Oxford (obv.), BM (rev.)
Quinarius of Bituriges Cubi:
  Head l./Horse l.; above, uncertain symbol; below, circle and branch   Paris
Bronze of Bituriges Cubi:
  Head l./Horse l.; above, three circles; below, ABVDO[S]   Paris
Potin of Aedui:
  Head l./Ibex l.   Oxford
Potin of Togirix:
  Helmeted head r., before, TOC/Lion r.; below, TOC   BM

suggested for Britain by J.R. Collis.[23] The notion of a city-based coinage is supported by the existence of a base-metal coinage precisely where urbanisation had progressed furthest before Caesar, among the Aedui, Sequani and Lingones. It is unlikely that coinage appeared in Gaul in response to commercial needs, but in order to provide a vehicle for display and for large payments such as fines, dowries and ransoms.[24] But it is clear that by 58 the Celtic tribes of Gaul possessed complex and sophisticated coinages which were a far cry from the almost entirely non-functional coinages of pre-Roman Dacia (p.228).

23. *World Archaeology*, 3, 1971–72, 71, 'Functional and theoretical interpretations of British coinage', with interesting reflections on the ways in which Celtic coinage spread.

24. D.F. Allen, *Essays S. Piggott* (London, 1976), 199, 'Wealth, money and coinage in a Celtic society', cites booty and mercenaries' pay as the principal source of metal.

13

THE YEARS OF CRISIS: ITALY

The second great phase of Roman territorial expansion ended with the annexation of southern Gaul. The effect of this expansion was of course enormously to increase the financial resources at the disposition of the Roman Republic and to extend to the whole of the Mediterranean world, apart from its eastern extremity, the economic structures generated by the process of exploitation.

To take the latter point first, much of the annual tribute to Rome must in the long run have come back to the provinces concerned with the same regularity with which it left them; the alternative would be to suppose (once available stocks of coin or bullion had been removed) continuous new production by the mines in the tax-paying provinces of enough metal to pay the annual tribute, and at the same time replace the metal lost by hoarding, etc. Furthermore, the tribute must have come back in return for goods and services of one sort or another; financial gifts to the provinces are almost exclusively an imperial phenomenon.[1]

There are two possible means by which the Roman state may have returned the annual tribute to the provinces, either by itself purchasing goods and services or by distributing its revenues to Romans or Italians, with the result that they could buy goods and services from the provincials. Of these two possibilities, it seems that the second is what actually happened. There are no traces under the Republic of large-scale

---

1 For a fuller statement of the argument, see *Ec.Hist.Rev.* 1977, 42, 'Rome and the Greek world: economic relationships'; also K. Hopkins, *JRS* 1980, 101, 'Taxes and trade in the Roman Empire'. Note the building activities of Ap. Claudius Pulcher at Eleusis, which anticipate imperial gifts (*ILLRP* 401; Cicero, *ad Att.* vi, 1, 26; 6, 2); also the restoration of statues by P. Servilius Isauricus on Calymnos (*OGIS* 449, n.2; L. Robert, *Hellenica* VI, 38, n.4), Tenos and perhaps at Aegae (*ILLRP* 403–4).

state purchases from the provinces, apart from Sicily (p.115), nor is there any likelihood that these occurred.[2] On the other hand, it is likely that the amount of coinage issued by the Republic year by year from 157 down to Sulla corresponds fairly closely with what can be argued on other grounds to have been the expenditure of the Republic on three main items, army stipends, official salaries and public works (p. 187); it seems reasonable to argue that during the period in question, no doubt for accounting purposes, Rome normally paid her expenses in new coin. It follows that the surplus tribute of the provinces, which was not necessary for the pay of soldiers and officials on the spot, came to Rome and was returned to the countries in which it originated via the pockets of Roman citizens and their Italian associates, many of them no doubt engaged in the execution of public works. It is important to observe that the process did not necessarily lead to the export to the provinces of Roman coinage, rather than goods or bullion; in the east, for instance, Roman and Italian traders regularly converted their money into Athenian tetradrachms.[3]

Perhaps the most obvious way to return to the provinces the wealth which had been removed in the form of tribute was by making loans to provincial communities or needy individuals; but all that this achieved was to increase the flow to Rome. The best-known example of this process is to be found in what happened as a result of the indemnity levied by Sulla from the province of Asia; the provincial communities borrowed the sum needed from the *publicani* and found themselves paying to the limit of their capacity each year without ever managing to pay all the interest charges due,[4] an example of a short-term levy transformed into a standing obligation. The indebtedness of Spain in 62–61 and Gaul in 63 are almost equally notorious.

What then were the goods which Romans and Italians acquired in exchange for the wealth which returned to the provinces so that they could pay the next round of tribute, exactions, fees to *publicani* and interest charges? Three categories seem to be particularly relevant: works of art (in the east), land, and slaves. The trade is naturally best documented for the east, but can be observed or surmised elsewhere.[5]

What of the effects of the flow of wealth to the provinces in return for land and slaves? The basic structure of the economy, of course, remained unchanged, with peasants producing what they needed to feed themselves together with a surplus to support the cities and the upper classes and, ultimately, part of the structure of the

---

2 For Miletus building ten ships for Rome *ex pecunia vectigali* see Cicero, *II in Verr.* 1, 89; money for ships seems normally to have been an extra levy, *pro Flac.* 27–33, compare *in Pis.* 90. Lucullus refused money from Rome for a fleet in the Mithridatic War and relied wholly on the allies, Plutarch, *Luc.* 13.

3 For the surplus of income from Asia over expenditure for Asia see Cicero, *de imp. Pomp.* 14. For a rare mention of coin travelling to Greece, see L. Pomponius, frr.115–16 Ribbeck, where the speaker takes 10,000 victoriati with him to exchange for *Graeca merces*.

4 Cicero, *ad Q.fr.* i, 1, 33 with Plutarch, *Luc.* 7 and 20; Appian, *Mith.* 83, 376.

5 See also D. Musti, in *Società Romana* I, 243, 'Modi di produzione e reperimento di manodopera schiavile'; and p.169, for Gaul, whither Roman and Italian wealth travelled in the form of wine and pottery.

Roman government; one must assume that they sold part of their corn to those who were the recipients of wealth from trade with Romans and Italians. But if one of the things sold on a large scale was human beings, we should expect evidence of substantial depopulation.[6] Of this there is a great deal of talk apropos of the east; early Imperial writers on Greece state or imply that the country was depopulated and given over to herding.[7] But it is clear that behind their remarks lies primarily a refusal to believe that cities as small as Greek cities could have achieved the glorious deeds about which they read in Herodotus and Thucydides; unfortunately there is little hard evidence to suggest that depopulation had occurred.

For Greece, there is only the isolated and useless piece of information that Pompey settled some reformed pirates at Dyme, because it was underpopulated.[8] There is even less evidence for the rest of the Mediterranean. Otherwise the result of the circular flow of tribute from the provinces to Rome and back again was twofold: to remove from the east to Italy moveable objects such as works of art, that constituted together with coin and plate (largely removed as booty) the inherited capital of the Greek east; and to place Romans and Italians as large-scale landowners in the provinces as a whole, a phenomenon well-attested in the east (compare pp. 97 and 170 for Spain and Gaul).

What happened with the end of the Republic? In the first place, the absolute amount taken was reduced; the tribute of Asia was reduced by a third by Caesar, who also took its collection out of the hands of the *publicani*;[9] we have no information for the rest of the empire, but perhaps less was taken elsewhere also; furthermore, once the Empire was established, it was in the Emperor's interest to ensure that revenues came primarily to the central treasury, rather than into the pockets of individual members of the upper classes. At the same time money began to flow back to the provinces in the shape of Imperial gifts; more important than this is the fact that the establishment of the Empire brought with it the permanent stationing of four legions in Syria, of eight legions in Germany, for instance, together with the setting up of a network of Imperial officials; to a greater extent than before, revenues will have flowed out of the provinces as tribute and back as payment for an agricultural surplus used to support Roman soldiers and officials. One must postulate a certain amount of trade between provinces, since Asia and parts of Gaul and Spain, for instance, produced tribute, but normally had no soldiers.[10]

---

6 There is no relevant early evidence: Polybius xxxvi, 17, 5, talks of a decline in population because of wilful childlessness; Polybius xxxvi, 17, 13, on Macedon under Roman rule and Zonaras ix, 31, on Greece under Roman rule (both favourable) are about the advantages of *political* stability, not about economic conditions.

7 T.R.S. Broughton, in *ESAR* IV, 467–8.

8 Plutarch, *Pomp.* 28; the foundation of colonies in Greece by Augustus is equally useless as evidence. The reflections of Servius Sulpicius Rufus, (Cicero) *ad fam.* iv, 5, 4 are perhaps suggestive: once flourishing cities now in ruins.

9 T.R.S. Broughton, in *ESAR* IV, 538, n.17.

10 For corn going from Asia to Syria in the third century AD see G. Bean and T.B. Mitford, *Journeys in Rough Cilicia* (Vienna, 1970), nos. 19–21.

65 The growth in the Roman money supply

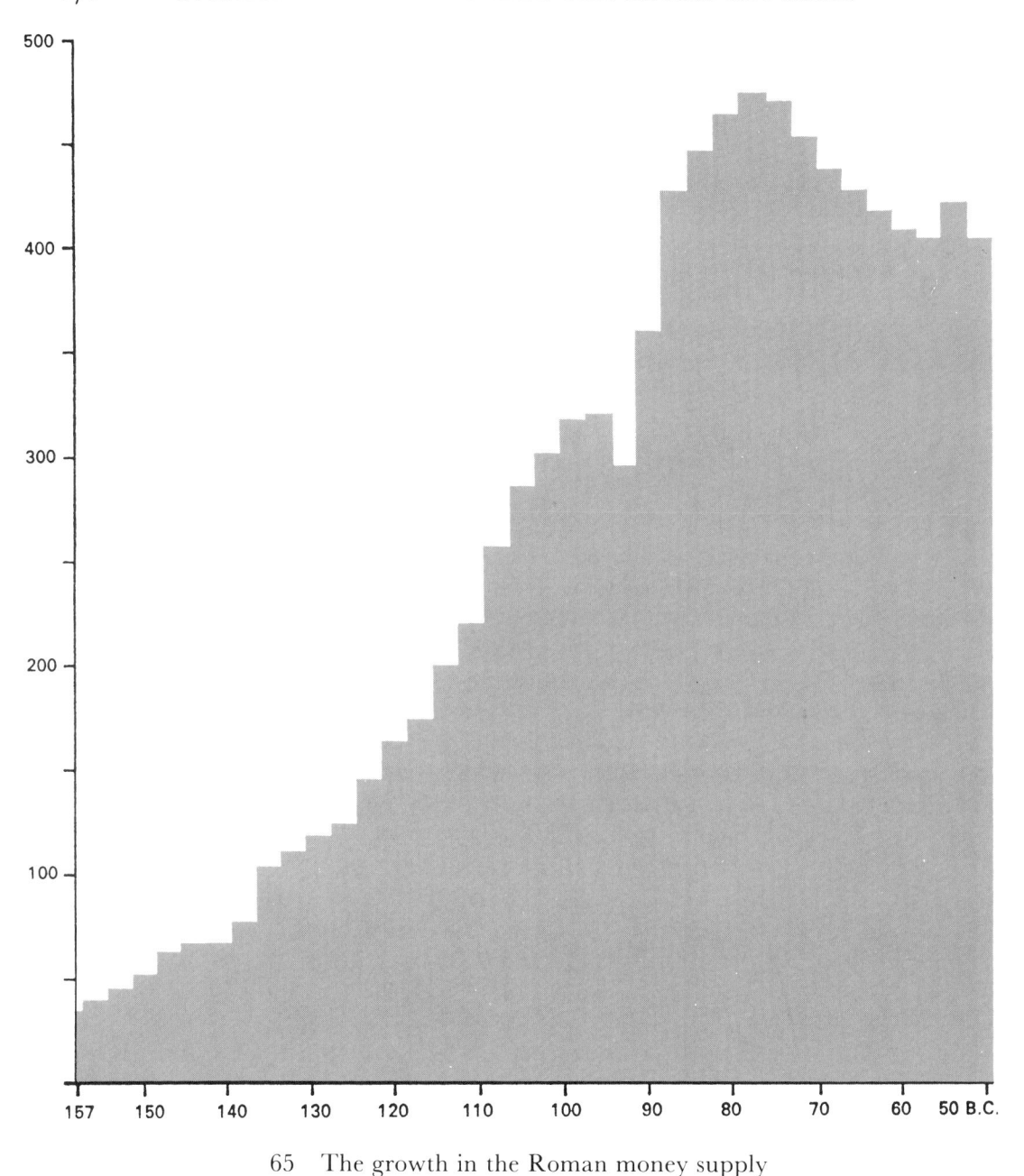

Roman silver coins in circulation 157–50 BC, in millions of denarii, by three-year periods
(from K. Hopkins, *JRS* 1980, 109, Fig. 2)

Secondly, the Roman demand for works of art and for what one might call works of sub-art, elegant furniture, etc., could not in the end be satisfied by acquiring what already existed. The demand thus stimulated a revival of artistic production and of manufacture in the eastern part of the empire.[11] In the west, there developed, for instance, the export of wine from Spain to Italy. Finally, it has long been noticed that the Roman and Italian businessmen active in the east in the late Republic settled and became absorbed in the early Empire, families such as the Crepereii of Attaleia and Pisidian Antioch and the Plancii of Perge; benefactors of their adopted cities, they served to transfer back at least some of the wealth which their ancestors had removed.[12] The same process undoubtedly took place in the west.

As far as the volume of coinage produced by the Roman Republic is concerned, we have seen that it was substantial from 157 onwards (p.143). The result was a steady growth in the money supply throughout the second half of the second century (Fig. 65). Some of this growth was absorbed by areas which had had little or no Roman coinage earlier, such as the Po valley and Spain. But much must have been absorbed by the monetisation of the Italian economy, an impression borne out by the size, number and distribution of coin hoards in Italy between the fall of Carthage and the Social War (Map 27 with App. 45) (Fig. 66). It appears, at any rate, that the inflation rate was remarkably slow during the second half of the second century: the smallest denomination normally struck from 157 onwards was the sextans, which was not replaced by the quadrans until 91/90 (Fig. 67); the numismatic evidence is borne out by the testimony of Cicero, *de oratore* ii, 254, where the late second-century Q. Granius is made to say of something that it was not worth a sextans; in the first century the quadrans is used in similar phrases (Cicero, *pro Cael.* 62; Horace, *Sat.* i, 3, 137). The only area where inflation did occur is in the prices paid by members of the elite for luxury goods. But no general pattern may be inferred from this.

Despite the fact that denarii are present throughout Italy in large numbers from 146 onwards, and have indeed become the only silver circulating in Italy, serving as a standard of value and as a store of wealth as well as a means of exchange,[13] the spread of Roman weights and measures to replace local units (p.15) seems to have been rather slow. A set of *pondera* installed at once Oscan Capua in 98 (*ILLRP* 718) may mark the moment of transition there. At Pompeii it did not come till the age

---

11 Activity in this field goes back to the second century BC; note the Cossutii, E. Rawson, 'Architecture and sculpture: the activities of the Cossutii', *PBSR* 43, 1975, 36. For the first century BC note the Attic workshop of C. Avianius Evander, Cicero, *ad fam.* xiii, 2; compare vii, 23, 1–3.

12 *Exempli gratia*, see a recently published inscription (bibliography in J. and L. Robert, *Bulletin Epigraphique* 1971, no.342), recording the gift by Sex. Tempsonius A.f. of a building for the agoranomoi to Acraephia.

13 Foreign silver in this period is to be regarded as booty, perhaps sometimes stored as a bullion equivalent, but certainly not circulating (App. 45). Cicero, *ad Att.* ii, 6, 2; 16, 4, do not prove that cistophori came back to the Roman treasury.

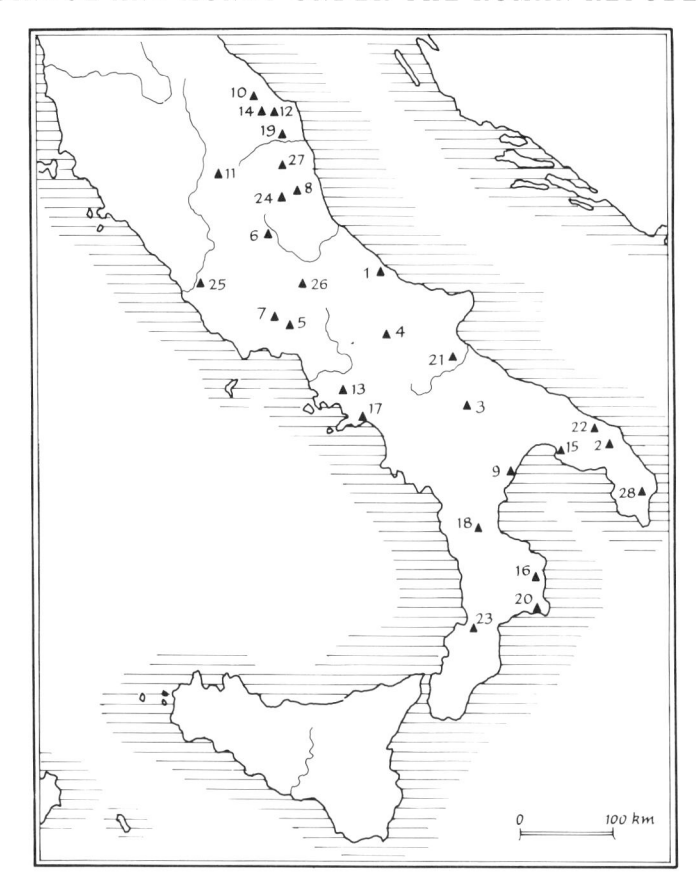

27 Hoards in Italy between 146 and 91
See App. 45

of Augustus (Vetter 22 = Poccetti 109 = *CIL* x, 793). Yet the coinage of the Italian insurgents in 91–88 consisted essentially of denarii, with one issue of gold (Fig. 68).

The period between the middle of the second century and the Social War was indeed a boom period for Appennine Italy. The wealth acquired in the east and elsewhere in the empire by men of business from the area was applied to the development of urban centres, as at Bovianum or Monte Vairano, and the construction of monumental sanctuary complexes, as at Pietrabbondante or Schiavi d'Abruzzo. The range of Mediterranean contacts of men from these areas is illustrated to perfection by the bronzes from the four corners of the globe brought back and lost or thrown away as useless (App. 46). Such bronzes were of course perhaps in part acquired by serving soldiers; but the phenomenon seems not to be attested in the period of the great wars in the east and it is better to regard it as evidence in the second half of the second

66 Roman silver coinage of the late second century

Denarius of M. Herennius, *RRC*, no. 308/1b:
 Diademed head of Pietas r.; behind, PIETAS (in monogram)/Catanaean brother r.; on
 l., M.HERENNI (in monogram); on r., control-letter   *BMCRR* Rome 1259

Denarius of C. Sulpicius, *RRC*, no. 312/1:
 Jugate, laureate heads of Dei Penates l.; before, D(ei) P(enates) P(ublici)/Two male
 figures and sow of Lavinium; above, control-letter; in exergue, C.SVLPICI.C.F (in
 monogram)   Oxford

Denarius of Q. Thermus, *RRC*, no. 319/1:
 Helmeted head of Mars l./Roman soldier fighting barbarian soldier in protection of
 fallen comrade; in exergue, Q.THERM.M.F (in monogram)   BM, Clark

Denarius of C. Fabius, *RRC*, no. 322/1b:
 Bust of Cybele r.; behind, EX.A.PV/Victory in biga r.; below, control-letter and bird;
 in exergue, C.FABI.C.F   BM 1949-4-3-31

Denarius of Piso, Caepio, *RRC*, no. 330/1b:
 Head of Saturn r.; behind, PISO.CAEPIO.Q/Two male figures seated on bench; on l.
 and r., corn-ear; in exergue, AD.FRV.EMV
           EX.S.C   *BMCRR* Rome 1218

Denarius of L. Pomponius Molo, *RRC*, no. 334/1:
 Laureate head of Apollo r.; around, L.POMPON.MOLO/Numa, altar and *victimarius*
 with goat; in exergue, NVMA.POMPIL (in monogram)   *BMCRR* Italy 735

century for the movements of men of business. Such men also brought back or had shipped the Rhodian wine with which they had become familiar in the east.[14]

The growing wealth of Appennine Italy underlies two further crucial developments in the history of Republican Italy, the Social War and the penetration of the Roman governing class by men of municipal origin. The Social War is unthinkable without

14 Larino, *Sannio*, 306; Monte Vairano, *Sannio*, 342; *SE* 1981, 454.

67 Roman bronze coinage of the late second century

As of L. Memmius, *RRC*, no. 131/2:
  Laureate head of Janus; above, I/Prow r., stem decorated with head of Venus; above, L.MEMMI (in monogram); before, Cupid crowning stem; below, ROMA
  Vatican 6804

As of Lentulus Marcelli f., *RRC*, no. 329/2:
  Laureate head of Janus; above, I/Prow r.; above, LENT.MAR.F (in monogram); before, *triskeles*; below, [ROMA]
  Corpus Christi College, Cambridge

Quadrans of L. Memmius, *RRC*, no. 313/4:
  Head of Hercules r.; behind, three dots/Prow r., stem decorated with head of Venus; above, three dots and L.MEMMI (in monogram); before, Cupid crowning stem; below, [ROMA]
  Rome, Capitol 2188

Semis of L. Pomponius, *RRC*, no. 334/3b:
  Laureate head of Saturn r.; before, S/Prow r.; above, L.POMP (in monogram); before, S; below, ROMA
  BMCRR Italy 741

Semis of C. Malleolus, *RRC*, no. 335/5b:
  Laureate head of Saturn r.; before, S/Prow r.; above, hammer; below, ROMA
  BMCRR Italy 710

68 Denarii of the insurgents in the Social War

Laureate head of Apollo l.; behind, *viteliu*/Warrior and bull; in exergue, *a*　　　BM cast
Helmeted head of Minerva l. crowned by Victory/Figure greeting second figure alighting from ship; in exergue, III　　　BM cast
Helmeted head of Minerva l.; around, *Mutil embratur*/Oath-taking scene; in exergue, *C. Paapi*　　　BM cast

the wealth that flowed into Samnium and other areas in the second century and the expressions of local pride that this wealth made possible. The same wealth allowed men of municipal origin to compete for office at Rome once they had acquired Roman citizenship.[15] The conspicuous absence of Samnites from the ranks of such men before Augustus may be explained in two ways: the ruin of Samnium brought about by Sulla, but perhaps also the proud independence of the men who formed the core of the movement against Rome in 91.

Two major changes took place in the structure of the Republican coinage in the period shortly before the Social War, the revival of the quinarius and the adoption of a semuncial standard for the bronze coinage. In circulation, the three-quarter piece of the denarius, the victoriatus, had by now acquired the value of the half of the denarius (App. N). The new quinarius was clearly designed as the successor of this piece, since it took over, with minor variations, its typology; it has also recently become clear that the new quinarius was, like the old victoriatus, deliberately debased (Fig. 69).[16]

The principal problem faced by any attempt to understand the revival of the quinarius lies in the ambiguous nature of Pliny's account (*NH* xxxiii, 46), *is qui nunc victoriatus appellatur lege Clodia percussus est*, the coin (the quinarius) which is now called the victoriatus is struck under the Lex Clodia. This does not make it clear whether the Lex Clodia, which made official the equivalence of victoriati and quinarii,

15 T.P. Wiseman, *New Men in the Roman Senate* (Oxford, 1971).
16 Denarius 97 per cent, quinarius 94 per cent, according to D.R. Walker (p.33, n.11), 61; quinarius 80 per cent, according to P. Petrillo Serafin, *Arch.Class.* 1976, 99, 'Ripostigli repubblicani sottoposti ad analisi', supplemented by verbal information: *very* doubtful.

69 The revival of the quinarius

Quinarius of C. Fundanius, *RRC*, no. 326/2:
   Laureate head of Jupiter r.; behind, control-letter/Victory crowning Gallic trophy with kneeling captive before; on r., C.FVNDA; in exergue, Q
   Oxford

Quinarius of P. Sabinus, *RRC*, no. 331/1:
   Laureate head of Jupiter r.; behind, control-letter/Victory crowning trophy; between, P.SABIN; on r., control-letter; in exergue, Q
   BMCRR Rome 1565

Quinarius of T. Cloulius, *RRC*, no. 332/1b:
   Laureate head of Jupiter r.; below, control-letter/Victory r. crowning trophy with seated captive before; between, T.CLOVLI (in monogram); in exergue, Q
   BMCRR Rome 1102

Quinarius of C. Egnatuleius, *RRC*, no. 333/1:
   Laureate head of Apollo r.; behind, C.EGNATVLEI.C.F (in monogram)/ Victory l. placing shield on Gallic trophy; between, Q; in exergue, ROMA
   BMCRR Rome 1077

permitted or ordered the striking of quinarii. It is better to concentrate on the other evidence.

It is noticeable that the victoriatus as a unit of reckoning is particularly characteristic of the Rhone valley and of one area of the Italian peninsula, Cisalpine Gaul (pp.165 and 81). It is also of the same weight as the native currency of the two areas.

If we look at the occasions on which Rome struck quinarii, a significant link with Gaul is apparent. Supplies and recruits came from Cisalpine Gaul in 90–89, years of large issues of quinarii (Plutarch, *Sert.* 4; Appian, *BC* i, 42, 188, cf. Sisenna, frr. 29 and 72 P);[17] Marian forces, for whom perhaps the issue of quinarii, *RRC*, no. 373, was struck, concentrated in Cisalpine Gaul at the end of 82 (Appian, *BC* i, 89–91, 410, 415, 418 and 422, with commentary of E. Gabba on last two passages). In 43–42 Antony and Lepidus were in Gaul or were governors in absence and part of their coinage alludes specifically to Lugdunum. It is not surprising to find them striking

---

17 There is no evidence that Cisalpine Gaul aided the Italian side, U. Ewins, *PBSR* 23, 1955, 73, 'The enfranchisement of Cisalpine Gaul', at 74–5.

the local denomination. In 39 and 29, again years of large issues of quinarii, there were veterans to be settled, partly in Cisalpine Gaul. I should argue that the issues of 101 and 99–97 are to be linked with Marius' colonising activity and with Saturninus' *leges agrariae*. The moderate issue of 101 suggests that Eporedia was by then envisaged for settlement, the enormous issues of 99–97 that the *lex agraria* of 100 was put into effect and that Rome struck money specially for the purpose, to finance the viritane settlement of Marius' veterans.[18] Only if this took place is the tranquillity of the 90s comprehensible.[19] (For one consequence of the volume of the victoriatus coinage after 101, see n.3 above.)

The adoption of the semuncial standard for the bronze coinage of the Republic is also problematic. After the as ceased to be produced in 146, the weight standard of the fractions which were being produced gradually drifted downwards. By the 120s, the weight standard of the bronze coinage was *de facto* semuncial. Then, in 116 or 115, it was restored to an uncial level, and a few years later the production of the as was resumed; the two-stage nature of the process makes it look as if administrative action, rather than legislation, is involved; as and fractions, on an uncial weight standard, continued in production down to the mid-90s. But from 93/2 or 91/0, a semuncial weight standard was officially adopted by virtue of a Lex Papiria: *mox lege Papiria asses semunciarii facti*, next the as was fixed at a semuncial level by the Lex Papiria (Pliny, *NH* xxxiii, 46). The bronze coinage itself corroborates the account given by Pliny, bearing as it does the legend *l(ege) P(apiria) d(e) a(ssis) p(ondere)*. Contemporaneously, sestertii were struck for the first time for over a century, *e l(ege) P(apiria)*, as their legends announce, a numismatic fact which finds no echo in the literary tradition (Fig. 70).

Again, we do not know whether the Lex Papiria simply placed the semuncial as and the sestertius on the list of authorised denominations or whether it also ordered their production. Given that the Lex Papiria must be later than the date of the last uncial as in the mid-90s and given that both semuncial as and sestertius were in production by 91, the second possibility seems to me on balance the more economical hypothesis. But why did Rome decide to produce semuncial asses and sestertii?

The conventional explanation for the adoption of the semuncial weight standard sees it as an attempt to save metal. But it is very hard to take this suggestion seriously, although Roman issues of *silver* did become somewhat less frequent in the course of the 90s and the outbreak of the Social War undoubtedly caused severe financial difficulties (p.185). For the amount saved in relation to the total expenditure of Rome

---

18 For the Lex Agraria of 100 see Appian, *BC* i, 29, 130, with commentary of E. Gabba; the hereditary connection of Antony with Bononia, Suetonius, *Aug.* 17, perhaps arose from an involvement of his grandfather with land distribution in the area in 99.

19 The negotiations between Marius and the leading men of Plutarch, *Mar.* 30, were doubtless over precisely this question. I do not share the doubts of P.A. Brunt, *Italian Manpower* (Oxford, 1971), 412–13.

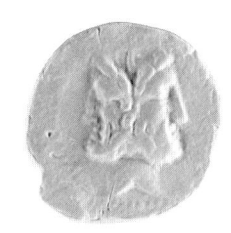

70 The semuncial bronze coinage and the sestertius

Denarius of D. Silanus, *RRC*, no. 337/3:
  Helmeted head of Roma r.; behind, control-letter/Victory in biga r.; above, control-numeral; in exergue, D.SILANVS.L.F
                    ROMA   Carbonara hoard
Sestertius of D. Silanus, *RRC*, no. 337/4:
  Helmeted head of Roma r.; behind, E.L.P/Victory in biga r.; in exergue, D.SILANVS.L.F   Berlin
As of D. Silanus, *RRC*, no. 337/5:
  Laureate head of Janus; above, I/Prow r.; above, D.SILANVS.L.F
                                                                     BMCRR Rome 1857

in these years by producing a rather small quantity of bronze coinage at half the previous weight standard would have been absolutely trivial. The same objection weighs against Elio Lo Cascio's suggestion that the aim was to facilitate the provision of small denominations in order to serve the market economy of the city of Rome.[20] I do not regard this ultimate objective as being even a conceivable one; but even without taking so extreme a view, the particular position advocated by Elio Lo Cascio does not make sense; for Rome could have produced enormously more uncial asses without more than a tiny addition to the annual budget, quite apart from the possibility of increasing the proportion of lead which they contained. The suggestion that the semuncial reduction was intended to facilitate the production of small change forms part of an interpretation which sees the resumption of production of the quinarius and the sestertius in the same light. I have argued above, however, that the production of the quinarius, certainly on a very large scale, either side of 100 is a phenomenon very specifically linked to Cisalpine Gaul; and I am unable to see a few diminutive issues of sestertii as a serious contribution to the provision of small change. It is striking that the only periods in the late Republic when the silver sestertius was produced, now and in the 40s, were periods of war; but no very obvious mechanism suggests itself whereby a war economy might have evoked the production of the

20 *Ath.* 1979, 215, 'Carbone, Druso e Gratidiano'; C.T. Barlow, *AJP* 1980, 202, 'The Roman government and the Roman economy, 92–80 BC', avoids direct contact with the evidence.

denomination; and *if* it is true that the Lex Papiria actually ordered the production of the silver sestertius one would have to suppose that it was passed at a moment when the Social War was foreseen for an explanation along these lines to be plausible.

As far as the production of semuncial bronze is concerned it seems to me most elegant to suppose simply that the author of the Lex Papiria supposed the reversion to an uncial standard to have been a mistake and wished to establish what had been a *de facto* semuncial standard officially. We have already seen that the retariffing of the denarius and the Lex Clodia were measures which involved the official recognition of what had come about (pp.144 and 181). All that one can really say about the production of silver sestertii from 91 is that the experiment was rapidly abandoned.

The later history of the Republican bronze coinage is curious. Semuncial asses and fractions were struck for some years and there are a few hoards; but at any rate as far as asses are concerned, which is really all that there is evidence for, semuncial pieces did not survive in circulation, whereas light uncial and better pieces of the third and second centuries did; and hoards continued to include them down to the end of the first century AD, whereas there are no semuncial pieces in hoards later than the 80s. Indeed, it appears that the official adoption of the semuncial standard was itself regarded as a mistake at one stage; for the asses of L. Sulla were more or less uncial in standard. After this issue, no mainstream bronze was struck by Rome till Caesar. One is left with an image of a state which did not give a damn for the provision of small change. The gap was in fact remedied by the production in Italy and to a lesser extent in Spain (p.100) of unofficial imitations of bronze fractions.[21]

The last problem to be faced before the Social War is posed by the brief notice of Pliny, *NH* xxxiii, 46, *Livius Drusus in tribunatu plebis octavam partem aeris argento miscuit*, Livius Drusus in his tribunate of the plebs mixed an eighth part of bronze into the silver. Since the notice is sandwiched between notices of the Lex Papiria and the Lex Clodia, we are probably dealing with the younger Drusus, tribune in 91. Beyond that, controversy reigns (p.187).

With the outbreak of the Social War, Rome was forced to raise more legions than at any time since the Hannibalic War. Initially, their cost seems to have been met without undue difficulty, although Rome had produced relatively little silver coinage in the 90s and may for a time have been short of metal (p.102); more coinage was produced in 90 than in any other year in the history of the Republic (Fig. 71). But in 89–87, the silver content of the denarius was reduced to about 94.5 per cent.[22]

---

21 M.H. Crawford, *AIIN* 29, 1982, 139, 'Unofficial imitations and small change under the Roman Republic'.

22 *RRC*, pp. 569–72; G. Fortina et al., *Sibrium* 11, 1971–2, 465, 'Indagini su denari di epoca repubblicana', a denarius of Cn. Lentulus with 89.96 per cent Ar; J.-B. Colbert de Beaulieu, 218, n.349, a quinarius of Cn. Lentulus with 83.50 per cent Ar; D.R. Walker (p.33, n.11), 62 (the later issues of 90, those of Q.Titius and C.Vibius Pansa, were perhaps already somewhat debased; the quinarii of the former are of peculiarly poor quality).

71 The issues of L. Piso and his colleagues

Denarius of L. Piso Frugi, *RRC*, no. 340/1:
  Laureate head of Apollo r.; behind, control-numeral/Horseman with palm r.; above, control-numeral; below, L.PISO FRVGI
                    R(om)A   BM 1949–4–3–153
Quinarius of L. Piso Frugi, *RRC*, no. 340/2a:
  Laureate head of Apollo r.; behind, control-symbol/Victory walking r. holding wreath and spear; on l., L.PI; on r., SO   *BMCRR* Rome 2176
Denarius of Q. Titius, *RRC*, no. 341/1:
  Bearded head r. wearing winged diadem/Pegasus r.; in frame, Q.TITI
                                                          BMCRR Rome 2220
Denarius of Q. Titius, *RRC*, no. 341/2:
  Head of Liber r. wearing ivy-wreath/Pegasus r.; in frame, Q.TITI   *BMCRR* Rome 2226
Quinarius of Q. Titius, *RRC*, no. 341/3:
  Bust of Victory r./Pegasus r.; below, Q.TITI   *BMCRR* Rome 2229
Denarius of C. Vibius Pansa, *RRC*, no. 342/3b:
  Laureate head of Apollo r.; behind, PANSA; before, control-letter/ Ceres walking r.; before, pig; behind, C.VIBIVS.C.F   *BMCRR* Rome 2241
Denarius of C. Vibius Pansa, *RRC*, no. 342/5b:
  Laureate head of Apollo r.; behind, PANSA; before, control-symbol/ Minerva in quadriga r. holding trophy; in exergue, C.VIBIVS.C.F   BM 1926–10–2–28

The most immediate consequence of the financial stringency of the period, worsened of course by Mithridates' invasion of the province of Asia in 88, was that Rome took the first steps towards the takeover of Cyrene, willed to her by Ptolemy Apion in 96; an embassy was sent in 86 to collect what was available in ready cash,[23] with the result that the purity of the denarius was restored almost to its original level in 86.

But the Social War not only caused short-term financial difficulties. As Cl. Nicolet has shown,[24] the Italian allies of Rome, down to the Social War, raised local *tributum* in order to pay the wages of the soldiers they sent to fight for Rome; Roman citizens of course had since 167 been relieved of their *tributum* by the revenues of empire and the different position of the Italians clearly caused resentment (compare p.97). But with the enfranchisement of Italy in 88, all men were now Roman citizens and therefore paid no *tributum* and all soldiers were Roman soldiers and paid by Rome. The result of this latter fact was that the Roman treasury was in permanent difficulties from which only the conquests of Pompey relieved it (p.241).[25] With Sulla the mint abandoned the wasteful practice of paying the great bulk of the year's expenses in new coin;[26] the military issues of Sulla himself, as well as those with Q.C.M.P.I, Q and EX S.C had indeed been of reduced fineness (Fig. 72).[27] A perhaps Marian issue of anonymous quinarii of the same period was also debased (*RRC*, no. 373, see p.182).

The Sullan period is marked in other ways as a period of transition in the history of the finances of the Roman Republic. For, as E. Gabba has shown,[28] one of the purposes of the Lex Cornelia de XX quaestoribus was to ensure control of the staff of the treasury by the new regime, as well as to reorganise its working for the future. It is almost certain that when Sulla came to power he replaced the moneyers in office and organised the production of an issue whose types and legends were derived from an issue of the 120s (*RRC*, nos. 369–71, Fig. 73). It is not surprising that when M. Cato acquired for his own information copies of the financial records of the Republic, he did not go back beyond Sulla (Plutarch, *Cato Minor* 18).

The Social War and concomitant events also caused monetary disturbances which were more short-term in effect.[29] Cicero records (*de off*. iii, 80) that, probably in 85, the tribunes called on the praetors 'to get together to deal with the coinage; for at that time the *nummus* was being tossed about in such a way that no one could know how much he possessed'. So the praetors produced an edict with *poena* and *iudicium*, which they were to proclaim together. However, M. Marius Gratidianus, one of the praetors, proclaimed the edict by himself and was almost deified by a grateful populace, which presumably now knew what it had.

---

23 E. Badian, *RhM* 1967, 178, 'The testament of Ptolemy Alexander'.
24 *PBSR* 46, 1978, 1, 'Le stipendium des alliés italiens'.
25 *RRC*, pp. 637–8.
26 *RRC*, ch.7, with the comments of E. Lo Cascio, in *AIIN* 29, 1982, 252–61.
27 D.R. Walker (p.33, n.11), 66.
28 *Ath*. 1983, 47, 'Lineamenti di un commento alla *Lex Cornelia de XX quaestoribus*'.
29 I here reproduce with revisions *PCPhS* 1968, 1, 'The edict of M. Marius Gratidianus'.

72 The issues of Sulla and his associates

Aureus of L. Sulla, *RRC*, no. 359/1:
  Diademed head of Venus r.; before, Cupid with palm-branch; below, L.SVLLA/Jug and *lituus* between two trophies; above, IMPER; below, ITERVM   *BMCRR* East 1

Aureus of L. Sulla, *RRC*, no. 367/2:
  Helmeted head of Roma r.; before, L.MANLI and T; behind, PRO.Q/*Triumphator* in quadriga r. crowned by flying Victory; in exergue, L.SVLLA IMP   Glasgow

As of L. Sulla, *RRC*, no. 368/1:
  Laureate head of Janus; above, I/Prow r.; above, L.SVL (in monogram); below, IMPE
      Hague

Denarius of Q. Caecilius Metellus Pius, *RRC*, no. 374/1:
  Diademed head of Pietas r.; before, stork/Elephant l.; in exergue, Q.C.M.P.I   Oxford

Denarius of Q. Caecilius Metellus Pius, *RRC*, no. 374/2:
  Diademed head of Pietas r.; before, stork/Jug and *lituus*; in exergue, IMPER; all in laurel-wreath   *BMCRR* Spain 49

Aureus with Q, *RRC*, no. 375/1:
  Diademed head of Venus r./Double cornucopiae; below, Q   Paris, AF

73 The restored issues of Sulla

Denarius ostensibly of M. Metellus, *RRC*, no. 369/1:
    Head of Apollo r., hair tied with ribbon; behind, ROMA, before, X/ Head of elephant in centre of Macedonian shield; around, M.METELLVS.Q.F; all in laurel-wreath
                                    BMCRR Rome 1148

Denarius ostensibly of C. Serveilius, *RRC*, no. 370/1a:
    Laureate head of Apollo r.; behind, A and *lituus*; before, X; below, ROMA/ Combat on horseback; in exergue, C.SERVEIL (in monogram)   *BMCRR* Rome 1168

Denarius ostensibly of Q. Maximus, *RRC*, no. 371/1:
    Laureate head of Apollo r.; behind, ROMA, before, lyre and X; below, Q.MAX (in monogram)/Cornucopiae on thunderbolt in wreath of barley, wheat and fruit
                                    BMCRR Rome 1154

It is not immediately obvious what Cicero meant when he said that the *nummus* was being tossed about and the passage has always been interpreted in the light of what Pliny has to say about Gratidianus. According to Pliny (*NH* xxxiii, 132; compare xxxiv, 27), as a result of reductions in fineness or weight, *ars facta denarios probare*, the testing of denarii became a science, by a law of Gratidianus. On the basis of this information, it has been assumed that the problem facing Gratidianus and his colleagues was that of plated coins, which had become so prevalent that money no longer meant anything.[30]

An entire house of cards has been built on this assumption. It is held that the problem of plated coins was brought to a head by M. Livius Drusus, who instituted the issue by the state of plated coins (p.185). The optimates thus, in the early first century, advocated a silver coinage of reduced intrinsic value, their opponents a pure silver coinage. The astonishing conclusion is that the optimate Lex Cornelia de falsis was intended to enforce the acceptance of plated coins.[31] The only evidence cited in support of this conclusion is [Julius Paulus], *Sent.* 5, 25 (*FIRA* II, 410), which proves the exact opposite, namely that one was entitled to reject a false coin.

It is most unlikely that Pliny's story about Drusus refers to plated coins. It should be considered with another passage of Pliny (*NH* xxxiii, 132), *miscuit denario triumvir*

---

30 See, for instance, C.M. Bulst, *Historia* 1964, 330–7, '*Cinnanum tempus*'.

31 Th.Mommsen, *RMw*, 387–9.

Antonius ferrum. In both stories, *miscere* might be expected to refer to the mixing of base metal with silver. But iron and silver are virtually immiscible. In the story about Antony, therefore, either Pliny wrote *ferrum* instead of some other metal or he meant to describe the process of plating. The fact that the legionary issue as a whole was struck from debased silver suggests that Pliny meant to talk of debasement with bronze and simply wrote *ferrum* in error.[32]

If, therefore, *miscere* can keep its natural reference to debasement in the story about Antony, it should keep it also in the story about Drusus.

It is clear, however, from the recent analyses of D.R. Walker that the silver coinage was not debased in 91 or early 90 and the notice as it stands cannot then be true. It was probably perverse to suggest that Pliny or his source garbled a notice relating to relief of debt;[33] one is left to suppose either that the notice misplaced the undoubted debasement of 89–87 or that it recorded a measure never put into effect. Neither solution seems very satisfactory; but in any case there is no reason to suppose that Gratidianus had to cope with the effects of a measure of Drusus concerning plated coins.

I believe that all Republican plated coins are ancient forgeries.[34] But even if well executed plated coins are accepted as official, the traditional view of the monetary history of the nineties and eighties cannot stand. If a measure of Drusus requiring that one-eighth of each issue be plated had been put into effect, we should expect to find a particularly large number of plated coins of the years immediately after 91.

We do not.

Tenney Frank's suggested explanation, that Gratidianus succeeded in eliminating plated coins, is not acceptable.[35] There exists a very large number of well-executed plated coins of about 100 and it seems most improbable either that the edict of Gratidianus could have dealt only with issues of 91 and later or that if it had done so it would have reduced the number of plated coins in existence enough to have any effect.

There is thus no reason whatever to suppose that the problem facing Gratidianus and his colleagues was posed by a flood of plated coins.[36] It is, furthermore, hardly

---

32 The denarius of Antony plated on iron, published in *NC* 1843–44, 67–8, and now in the Ashmolean Museum, is a palpable modern forgery.

33 *The Roman Republic* (London, 1978), 140.

34 *RRC*, pp. 560–5; the arguments there advanced cannot be refuted by an appeal to the authority of Th. Mommsen, *contra* H. Chantraine, *Novaesium* VIII (Berlin, 1982), 40–2: Epictetus, *Diss.* iii, 3, 3, is irrelevant precisely because a plated coin was not *to tou Kaisaros nomisma*; for *debasement* of the coinage by the state, a different matter altogether, see p.52.

35 In *ESAR* I, 267.

36 *Contra* B. Santalucia, *AIIN* 29, 1982, 47, 'La legislazione sillana in materia di falso nummario': even if one discounts the fact that testing of denarii existed before Gratidianus and the fact that Pliny talks of a *lex* where Cicero talks of an *edictum*, the testimony of Pliny is clearly worthless. The reason why (according to Cicero) 'iactabatur nummus' cannot be the prevalence of plated coins, for the consequence 'ut nemo posset scire quid haberet' *cannot* apply; it was by that date easy to find out if a coin was plated.

possible that the testing of denarii became a science only with Gratidianus, as Pliny states; for the earliest dated *tessera* recording the testing of denarii is of 96 (*ILLRP* 1001, see p.241). Nor can Pliny's account of Gratidianus be saved by R. Herzog's odd suggestion that testing did not take place between Livius Drusus and Gratidianus,[37] quite apart from the fact that he has to date Gratidianus' first praetorship to 86 (although 85 is more likely),[38] since a *tessera* of 5 February 86 is recorded (*ILLRP* 1004).

If Pliny's account of Gratidianus is therefore rejected as a hopelessly confused record, a reasonable interpretation of Cicero's text is possible. The *nummus* is surely the denarius, the standard coin, and if it is being tossed about, the reference can only be to its value. Since an edict on prices is hardly conceivable, the edict of Gratidianus should be regarded as an attempt to prescribe a given relationship between the denarius and the as. Taken thus, it forms an intelligible part of the monetary history of the Roman world and of the history of the *Cinnae dominatio*.

Republican monetary history can only be understood if it is accepted that the state was prepared to exchange silver and bronze coinage at the official rate. But there is nothing strange about the existence at the same time of unofficial rates of exchange. The convenience of not having to deal with the government and sheer ignorance will both have played their part in bringing this about. Official and unofficial rates existed side by side in Roman Egypt and a variety of rates are recorded in Greek cities under Roman rule, sometimes in the same place at the same time.[39] In Rome itself, the retariffing of the denarius in the mid-second century had become necessary when the official and unofficial rates of exchange drifted too far apart (p.145).

The as had been reduced from a weight of an ounce to one of half an ounce in 91, an entirely acceptable operation, provided that the state continued to honour the old exchange rate between denarius and as. But it is hardly surprising if the chaotic conditions at Rome between 88 and 86 caused violent fluctuations in the unofficial exchange rate, in fact caused the *nummus* to be tossed about.[40] The proper solution was not another retariffing of the denarius. An edict of Gratidianus reasserting the old exchange rate and threatening speculators with punishment forms a natural part of a return to stability in the first consulship of Cinna and Carbo. It also marks the final success of the state in persuading people to accept a token bronze coinage. The weight of the as in the 80s was roughly that adopted by Augustus (p.260).

Finally, if it is agreed that no measure of Drusus concerning plated coins was ever

---

37 *RE* XVII, 1441.
38 *RE* XIV, 1826.
39 *La moneta in Grecia e a Roma* (Bari, 1982), 112–13.
40 If *aeraria ratio* is taken to refer to the exchange rate between silver and bronze, a reasonable meaning can be assigned to Cicero, *pro Quinctio* 17, *cum pecuniam C. Quinctius P. Scapulae debuisset, per te, C. Aquili, decidit P. Quinctius quid liberis eius dissolveret. Hoc eo per te agebatur quod propter aerariam rationem non satis erat in tabulis inspexisse quantum deberetur, nisi ad Castoris quaesisses quantum solveretur*. The use of the official rate of exchange seems to have been universal in computing interest, though not necessarily in paying it.

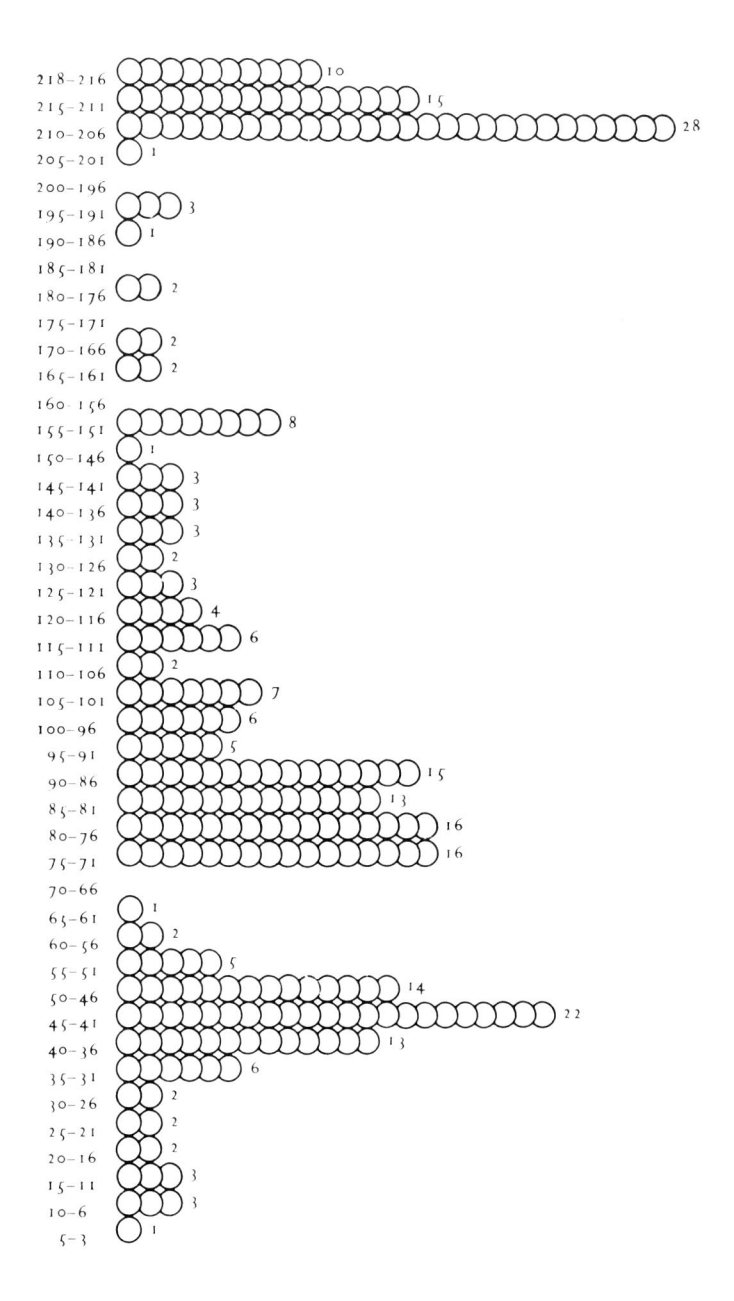

74 The pattern of hoarding in Roman Italy

The closing dates of known coin hoards from Italy, Corsica, Sardinia and Sicily, plotted in five-year periods (from *PBSR* 1969, 79)

put into effect and that the Lex Cornelia de falsis simply made illegal the production of false, i.e. plated, coins, the notion of a difference of opinion between two parties at Rome over the merits of plated coins can disappear. Both probability and the ancient evidence support the view that they were held in execration by all except the criminals who made them.

But the most abiding impression left by the monetary history of the 80s and 70s is the numismatic evidence for the scale of devastation.[41] The hoards lost in this period are more numerous than at any other time. A glance at Fig. 74 shows that major concentrations of hoards correspond to major wars of the late Republic: the Second Punic War, the Social War, the First Civil War, the war between Caesar and Pompey and the wars between the Pompeians, Antony and Octavian. The simple view that fighting in Italy itself was directly responsible for the loss of the hoards will not always stand. Doubtless it sometimes was. The widespread fighting in Italy between the outbreak of the Second Punic War in 218 and the battle of the Metaurus in 207 had a disastrous effect on the civilian population, as also did the wars of the 80s and 70s, the Perusine War and the war against Sextus Pompey.

But the large number of hoards falling between 50 and 46 cannot be explained in this way. When Caesar crossed the Rubicon he left a Cisalpine Gaul that was firmly in his hands. Two months later he was in control of Italy almost without a fight. Italy remained at peace during his lifetime apart from the minor disturbance caused by Caelius and Milo. Yet we have fourteen hoards spread evenly over the period and the explanation seems to be that they are the property of men who left to join one or the other of the opposing armies. The flight of the Pompeians from Rome in 49 is well known and there seems to have been at the same time considerable displacement of population elsewhere in Italy.[42] Correlation of hoards with recruiting attested in the area of the hoards would require more precise and more complete information than we possess. But it should be observed that four of the six hoards of 49 (two very large and two small) are from Gallia Cisalpina, where Caesar recruited. And Caesar's battles against his citizen enemies were bloody affairs.

The same explanation may *perhaps* apply to three much smaller concentrations of hoards, those of 155 to 151, 115 to 111 and 105 to 101. In none of these periods is there any trace of war in Italy (the slave war in Sicily might be invoked to explain the one Sicilian hoard in the last period). The hoards may therefore be the property of casualties among unusually large levies for the Spanish Wars, the Fourth Macedonian War, the Achaean War and the Third Carthaginian War and for the wars in Africa and the north from 114. The Romans incurred in these some heavy defeats, notably at Arausio.

---

41 For a fuller discussion see *PBSR* 37, 1969, 76, 'Coin hoards and the pattern of violence in the late Republic'.

42 Plutarch, *Caes.* 33, 1; Appian, *BC* ii, 35, 141.

On recruiting in the late Republic, see P.A. Brunt, *JRS* 1962, 69, 'The army and the land in the Roman revolution'. See also *D* 41, 2, 44, pr., *peregre profecturus pecuniam in terra condiderat*.

A further explanation may be suggested for at least some Italian hoards. Thirteen of the hoards which close between 45 and 41 belong precisely to the end of 43 and the beginning of 42, the period of the Triumviral proscriptions. Some of the hoards of 81 and 80 are perhaps a legacy of the Sullan proscriptions.

If concentrations of hoards in the late Republic are rightly regarded as the direct or indirect result of foreign or civil war, they provide dramatic evidence of the recurring violence of the period, in the 80s and 70s on a truly cataclysmic scale. An important consequence of this level of hoarding was a progressive decline in liquidity, leading in the end to the crisis of 63 (p.240).

14

THE YEARS OF CRISIS: THE EMPIRE

The story that I have tried to tell so far has on the whole been a story of relatively separate developments in Italy on the one hand and in the ever increasing area of the Mediterranean world ruled by Rome on the other hand. From the beginning of the first century onwards it becomes hard to tell separate stories in this way. In the first place, the unfolding of the Roman Revolution involved the forging of ever closer links between the political and military histories of different parts of the Roman empire; in the second place, more importantly, the first century sees the extension to the whole of that empire of a single monetary system and to much of it of a single coinage.[1]

I have argued (p.173) that much of the tribute which the east paid to Rome, Macedonia from 167, much of Greece from 146, the province of Asia from 129, was regularly returned in exchange for slaves, land and works of art, whereby the individuals who sold these commodities acquired the wherewithal to pay the next round of tribute, and so on. But it is likely that stored wealth will have been used in addition, whence a general loss of liquidity; and in fact the century between Ti. Gracchus and Actium sees the virtual disappearance of independent silver coinages in the Greek world.

The first intimation that Rome was not entirely in control of her empire and the client states around came with the war against King Jugurtha of Numidia (p.140). Even before the war with Jugurtha had begun, Rome had in 113 suffered her first defeat at the hands of the Cimbri and their allies, migrating German tribes who ravaged southern Gaul and northern Spain (p.102) until they were finally defeated by C. Marius

---

1 I hope that this chapter identifies at least some of the structures which F. Millar seeks, *Past and Present* 1984, 3, 'The Mediterranean and the Roman Revolution. Politics, war and the economy'.

in 102–101. The Social War (p.183) was, it is true, relatively rapidly resolved in Rome's favour; but, as we shall see in a moment, its aftermath had grave repercussions in some of the provinces of the empire. And in 88 there befell the greatest disaster of all, the invasion of the province of Asia by Mithridates VI of Pontus. His success there encouraged him to cross the Aegean in 87; Athens and much of Greece went over to him. At the same time, his fleet attacked and plundered Delos; and it was with his encouragement that the pirates of the eastern Mediterranean directed their attention in the 70s and 60s to the civilised lands around the Aegean theoretically under Roman protection (for the coinage of Mithridates see p.201). The scale of human misery in Greece alone in these years emerges from the fifty-five hoards whose non-recovery may be attributed to the devastation caused by Mithridates and the pirates; at the same time Roman military action to recover lost territory had equally unpleasant consequences, conspicuously the sack of Athens in 86 (App. 47).

In monetary terms, the consequence of a decade of war and revolution in the east, with the burial and non-recovery often of substantial quantities of silver, was to reduce even further an already low level of liquidity. As a result, the cities of Asia found themselves in terrible financial difficulties when they had to pay the indemnity imposed by Sulla after the defeat of Mithridates (Map 24). A number of communities attempted to raise money by total or partial re-coinages; existing bronze coinage was called in and either melted down and re-struck or overstruck or countermarked, at Smyrna, Lebedus, Colophon, Teos, Erythrae, Clazomenae at least; we do not know what percentage of the value of the new coinage was levied as a charge, but it may have been substantial.[2] In the case of Athens, it was the second sack of Delos, by the pirates, which virtually put an end to her new-style coinage (p.125); although this continued to be produced down to Caesar, these later issues formed an insignificant trickle.

Meanwhile, one of the Roman generals in Asia had probably been responsible for a curious issue which introduced a new monetary metal into the Roman coinage system (Fig. 75). The man in question is Q. Oppius, captured at Laodicea-ad-Lycum in 88; it is probably to him that an issue of orichalcum with the types Head of Venus/Victory (*RRC*, no. 550) is to be attributed. What has become apparent as a result of recent metal analyses is that the metal, an alloy of copper and zinc, which was used by Caesar and then on an enormous scale by Augustus (p.258), was widely used in Bithynia, Mysia and Phrygia from the time of Mithridates, though not, as far as we know at the moment, at Laodicea and not, again as far as we know at the moment, earlier than about 80.[3]

2 J.G. Milne, *NC* 1934, 31, 'Notes on the Aberdeen University collections', with further information from P. Kinns.
3 J.M. Reynolds, *Aphrodisias and Rome* (London, 1982), Docs. 2–3, for Q. Oppius; the account in *RRC* of the provenances attested for the issue should have been explicit in rejecting what might be taken as a reference to it by G. Spano, *Bull.Arch.Sard.* 4, 1858, 199–201. P.T. Craddock, A.M. Burnett and K. Preston, in W.A. Oddy (ed.), *Scientific Studies in Numismatics* (London, 1980), 53, 'Hellenistic copper-base coinage and the origins of brass'; eid., *9 Cong. Num.*, 263, 'New light on the origins of orichalcum'.

75   The issue of Q. Oppius

Bronze of Q. Oppius, *RRC*, no. 550/2d:
  Diademed head of Venus r.; behind, capricorn/Victory holding bowl of fruit and
  palm-branch; on l., Q.OPPIVS.PR   Oxford

In general, however, the period of the First Mithridatic War involved little change in the pattern established in Asia with the settlement of 129 (p.159), the continuing production of the issues of existing Greek mints and the production of the cistophori of the Roman province. In Greece, on the other hand, this period is the one which witnesses the beginning of the transformation of the area into one where the denarius was the standard silver coin.

Sulla had struck imitations of the tetradrachms of Athens in the course of his campaigns (Fig. 76) and, as we have seen, Athens continued to strike some silver issues down to Caesar. Thessaly and Thasos also struck silver in this period and there was one last group of four issues of tetradrachms of Roman Macedonia: all bear the legend ΜΑΚΕΔΟΝΩΝ; three bear in addition the legends LEG, SVVRA PROQ and AESILLAS Q; one has no differentiating legend. The issue of Aesillas is very large; my own view is that it was produced from the mid-80s to the mid-70s, though it is not easy to see why the legend was immobilised in this way (Fig. 77).[4]

But the conspicuous feature of first-century hoards in Greece is the penetration of the denarius, circulating either alone, or with one or more of the Greek coinages just mentioned (see Apps. 47–8). It seems likely that the penetration of the denarius is to be ascribed to Roman military activities; the fact that this penetration occurred in Greece, but not in Asia Minor, is presumably to be ascribed to the fact that there was in Greece a monetary vacuum, compared with Asia Minor. An example of what is probably a Roman military presence is provided by Corinth, where a denarius of Q. Cerco and two of C. Censorinus turn up with late second- and early first-century

---

[4] For Athens, see *RRC*, p.80, n.1; C. Habicht, *Chiron* 1976, 127, 'Zur Geschichte Athens in der Zeit Mithridates VI'; for Macedonia, A.M. Burnett, *Coin Hoards* 7, forthcoming, with different conclusions; Q. Bruttius Sura also struck on Thasos.

76   The Sullan imitations of the tetradrachms of Athens and the post-Sullan issues of Athens

New-style tetradrachm of Sulla, Thompson, 1285b:
  Helmeted head of Athena r./Owl on amphora in olive-wreath; on either side, monogram; on amphora, A   Locker Lampson 215
New-style tetradrachm of Athens, Thompson, 1265b:
  Helmeted head of Athena r./Owl on amphora in olive-wreath; above, A ΘE; on either side, ΦΙΛΟ ΚΡΑ
    ΤΗΣ
    ΚΑΛΛΙ
    ΦΩΝ; on r., Nike; uncertain letter(s) on amphora; below, ΣΩ   Lockett 1941

material;[5] the site was perhaps used as a base by Sulla. The total disappearance of Greek gold coinage from normal circulation is illustrated by the purchase of gold coins at Tanagra to make crowns for a festival at the very high gold:silver ratio of 1:15 (*RA* 1966, 297); Greek silver coinage was shortly to follow Greek gold coinage into oblivion.

Elsewhere in the east, the course of the Third Mithridatic War (74–63) saw the inexorable progress of direct Roman control over more and more provinces. We have already observed the Roman acceptance of the bequest of Cyrenaica and the seizure of the liquid assets of the last king during the Social War (p.187). It may be that Rome took an interest in the administration of the erstwhile royal lands from an early date,[6] but it was only in 75 or 74, in the aftermath of a period of disturbance, that Cyrenaica was made a province, including the cities which had originally been given their freedom; they had perhaps proved incapable of controlling the native populations in their territories.[7]

There were Roman men of business present by 67, who probably requested further

5 C.K. Williams, *Hesp.* 1978, 21, 'Corinth: 146 BC to 44 BC.'
6 R.S. Bagnall (p.160, n.14), 32–3 and 36–7, with earlier bibliography (the argument is speculative).
7 J.M. Reynolds, *Arch.Class.* 1973–74, 622, 'A civic decree from Tocra'; for the disturbances, ead., in *Sidi Krebish* I (London, 1975), 234, no.3.

77 The last silver coinages of Macedon

Tetradrachm of Macedonia:
    Bust of Artemis r. in centre of Macedonian shield/Club r.; above, MAKE and
    monogram; below, ΔΟΝΩΝ; all in oak-wreath; on l., thunderbolt   Naville 1, 1000

Tetradrachm of Macedonia:
    Bust of Artemis r. in centre of Macedonian shield/Club r.; above, LEG and hand with
    branch; below, ΜΑΚΕΔΟΝΩΝ   Locker Lampson 170

Tetradrachm of Sura:
    Head of Alexander r.; behind, Θ; below, ΜΑΚΕΔΟΝΩΝ/*Fiscus* and *sella* on either side of
    club; above, SVVRA.LEG
        PRO   Q; all in laurel-wreath   Naville 13, 571

Tetradrachm of Aesillas:
    Head of Alexander r.; below, ΜΑΚΕΔΟΝΩΝ/*Fiscus* and *sella* on either side of club; above,
    AESILLAS
        Q; all in laurel-wreath   Naville 5, 1501

Roman regulation of the affairs of the province in that year; names familiar from Campania and Delos turn up later in the first century.[8] It may also be that the *publicani* who had the contract for the exploitation of the pasture land of Cyrenaica in the first century AD (Pliny, *NH* xix, 38–9) had been there from the start. There is, however, little evidence that Roman coinage circulated in Cyrenaica before the age of revolution; the area presumably went on using the small bronzes produced in the last period of

---

8 J.M. Reynolds, *JRS* 1962, 97, 'Cyrenaica, Pompey and Cn. Lentulus Marcellinus'.

78   The bronze coinage of Cyrenaica

Bronze of Ptolemy VII:
Head of Ptolemy I r./Head of Libya r.; around, ΠΤΟΛΕΜΑΙΟΥ ΒΑΣΙΛΕΩΣ; below, monogram
BMCCyrenaica, pp. 86–9, no. 76

independence (*BMCCyrenaica*, pp.86–9; note that the monetary system of Cyrenaica is no longer in any way related to that of Egypt)(Fig. 78).

The most conspicuous feature of the monetary history of Crete is its isolation from that of the rest of the eastern Mediterranean, though Crete seems to have reckoned in Alexander coinage in the normal way (*SIG* 712, etc.). Coins brought to the island were systematically overstruck. To the period just before the Third Mithridatic War belongs the Limani-Chersonisou hoard, including Cretan coins overstruck on Seleucid pieces, Lysimachi of Byzantium and Athenian tetradrachms. The Seleucid, Byzantine and Athenian issues may have come by way of piracy or the slave trade; the presence of the Byzantine and Athenian coins without being overstruck perhaps shows isolation in the process of breaking down (Fig. 79). But the Cretan issues in question are the last silver issues of the island, which was rash enough to help Mithridates VI in his final bid for independence from Rome. Cnossus was sacked by Metellus in 68/7 and the island became a province, and was in due course combined with Cyrenaica.[9] There is no more evidence here than in Cyrenaica for the circulation of Roman coinage or the adoption of Roman monetary usages before the age of revolution.

One of the problems faced by Cyrenaica in the early years of Roman rule had been that posed by pirate raids; the year 67 saw not only measures specific to Cyrenaica, but also the command given to Pompey to eradicate piracy from the Mediterranean. A feature of this command was the right of access granted to Pompey to all provincial treasuries (Plutarch, *Pomp.* 25); one result of this facility was the interruption of the cistophoric coinage of the province of Asia.[10]

9 G. Perl, *Klio* 1970, 319, 'Die römischen Provinzbeamten in Cyrenae und Creta'; 1971, 369, 'Nachtrag'.
10 The interruption had nothing to do with a need for silver in Rome, *contra* T.S.R. Broughton, *AJA* 1937, 248, 'A significant break in the cistophoric coinage of Asia'; by 62, Flaccus felt it necessary to prevent even Jewish offerings to the Temple from leaving Asia, Cic., *pro Flac.* 66–9, with A.J. Marshall, *Phoenix* 1975, 139, 'Flaccus and the Jews of Asia'.

79   The issues of the Limani hoard

Tetradrachm of Cnossus:
  Diademed head of Zeus r./Labyrinth; above, on either side and below, ΚΝΩΣΙΩΝ

  Naville 7, 1292

Tetradrachm of Byzantium:
  Diademed head of Alexander r./Athena seated l. holding Nike; before, monogram;
  below seat, BY; below, trident

  BM 66-12-1-858

Pompey of course succeeded in suppressing piracy in the Mediterranean and went on in the course of the next few years to acquire for Rome Pontus and Bithynia, the remnants of the Seleucid kingdom, Judaea and much else besides.[11] In the case of Bithynia and Pontus, much of their silver coinage is no doubt to be explained in terms of the demands made by the military policies of their rulers (Fig. 80). With the end of independence, the cities of the joint province went on striking bronze, some of which is of considerable interest (p.243), but Rome took no steps to organise a provincial coinage in silver.

The story in Syria is rather different (Map 28, Fig. 81). The last effective ruler of an ever more fragmented kingdom had been Philip Philadelphus; his rule was followed by that of Tigranes of Armenia (83–69), then of Antiochus XIII, Philip II and Antiochus XIII once more. This last appealed to Pompey for recognition, but saw his kingdom made into a province instead.[12]

As far as the monetary history of the area is concerned, the last two generations of the Seleucid monarchy had seen city after city 'freed' and producing its own silver coinage; Aradus had resumed the production of large silver in 138/7, Tyre in 126/5, followed by Sidon, Seleucia Pieria, Tripolis, Ascalon, Laodicea-ad-Mare. All of these mints except for Seleucia Pieria and Tripolis were still functioning when Syria became

11 For Pompey in Armenia see *La moneta in Grecia e a Roma* (Bari, 1982), 78.

12 A.R. Bellinger, *Trans. Connecticut Acad. Arts and Sciences* 38, 1948–52, 51–102, 'The end of the Seleucids'.

Corpus of dated Tetradrachms of Mithradates VI

96/5	ΒΣ							Η	Θ	Ι	ΙΑ		
95/4	ΓΣ		Β										
94/3	ΔΣ										ΙΒ		
93/2	ΕΣ	Α		Γ			Ϛ	Ζ	Η				
92/1	ϚΣ	Α		Γ		Ε	Ϛ	Ζ	Η				
91/0	ΖΣ								Η				
90/89	ΗΣ		Β					Ζ	Η	Θ	Ι		
89/8	ΘΣ	Α				Ε					ΙΑ	ΙΓ	No month
	Α	Α	Β	Γ	Δ		Ϛ	Ζ					No month
88/7	ΙΣ	Α	Β		Δ	Ε		Ζ		Θ			
	Β												No month
87/6	ΑΙΣ							Ζ		Θ	Ι	ΙΑ	
	Γ												No month
86/5	ΒΙΣ	Α		Γ	Δ	Ε		Ζ			Ι	ΙΑ	ΙΒ
	Δ												No month
85/4	ΓΙΣ	Α	Β	Γ		Ε	Ϛ					ΙΑ	
84/3	ΔΙΣ	Α								Θ			
83/2	ΕΙΣ												
82/1	ϚΙΣ											ΙΑ	
81/0	ΖΙΣ												
80/79	ΗΙΣ					Ε						ΙΒ	
79/8	ΘΙΣ	Α								Θ	Ι	ΒΙ	
78/7	ΚΣ												No month
77/6	ΑΚΣ	Α											
76/5	ΒΚΣ					Ε	Ϛ	Ζ	Η	Θ	Ι	ΑΙ	
75/4	ΓΚΣ			Γ	Δ	Ε				Θ	Ι	ΙΑ	ΙΒ ΙΓ No month
74/3	ΔΚΣ		Β	Γ								ΙΑ	
73/2	ΕΚΣ	Α	Β		Δ				Η		Ι		
72/1	ϚΚΣ	Α								Θ			
71/0	ΖΚΣ										Ι	ΑΙ	
70/69	ΗΚΣ												No month
69/8	ΘΚΣ												
68/7	ΛΣ												
67/6	ΑΛΣ												No month

80 The issues of Mithridates VI

The table shows the issues of each month or without any indication of month, with very heavy minting during the First Mithridatic War (88–85) and again just before and just after the outbreak of the Third Mithridatic War in 74   *MusN* 1974, 25

28 Syria

a province (Fig. 82). Meanwhile, the silver coinage of the Seleucid kingdom had both diminished in quantity and declined in quality; the last issues were small and debased. With the creation of the province of Syria, the production of Seleucid silver ceased altogether.[13]

The creation of a silver coinage for the province of Syria was the work of A. Gabinius, who in 57 revived the production of tetradrachms with the types of Philip Philadelphus (Fig. 83). His example was followed by M. Crassus in 53 and C. Cassius Longinus in 51, then by Caesar in 47, who abandoned the Seleucid era as a means of dating the coins and instituted a new era. Bronze was also struck in 54–51 and by Caesar.[14] It

13 A.R. Bellinger, *Studies A.C. Johnson* (Princeton, 1951), 58, 'The early coinage of Roman Syria', at 64 n.25. For Philip II being dunned for the repayment of a loan in 67/6, see G. Downey, *CQ* 1937, 144, 'Q. Marcius Rex at Antioch'.

14 A.R. Bellinger, *NC* 1944, 59, 'Crassus and Cassius at Antioch' (corrected by the article cited in n.12); D.R. Walker, *The Metrology of the Roman Silver Coinage* I (Oxford, 1976), 67. See O. Mørkholm, *MusN* 1983, 89, 'The autonomous tetradrachms of Laodicea-ad-Mare', for the impact of Caesar and L. Cassius on the coinage of that city.

81 The issues of the last Seleucid kings

Tetradrachm of Tigranes I:
  Bust of Tigranes r. wearing tiara; bead and reel border/Tyche of Antioch seated r. holding palm-branch; at her feet, Orontes swimming r.; on r. and below on l., two monograms; on either side, ΒΑΣΙΛΕΩΣ ΤΙΓΡΑΝΟΥ; all in laurel-wreath   Naville 10, 1559
Drachm of Tigranes I:
  Bust of Tigranes r. wearing tiara/Tyche of Antioch seated r. holding palm-branch; at her feet, Orontes swimming r.; on r., ΖΛ; below, ΞΚ; on either side, ΒΑΣΙΛΕΩΣ ΤΙΓΡΑΝΟΥ
  Naville 10, 1570

82 The coinages of the Syrian cities

Tetradrachm of Tyre, 77/6 BC:
  Bust of Melqart r./Eagle on ram of ship l.; on l., club and (Year 50); on r., palm-branch and Α; around, ΤΥΡΟΥ ΙΕΡΑΣ ΚΑΙ ΑΣΥΛΟΥ   Naville 7, 1747
Tetradrachm of Sidon, 58/7 BC:
  Bust of Tyche r./Eagle on ram of ship l.; on l., (Year 50); on r., palm-branch and monogram; around, ΣΙΔΩΝΟΣ ΤΗΣ ΙΕΡΑΣ ΚΑΙ ΑΣΥΛΟΥ   Naville 7, 1738

83 The Roman coinage of Syria

Posthumous tetradrachm of Philip Philadelphus:
 Diademed head r.; bead and reel border/Zeus seated l. holding Nike; before, monogram;
 in exergue, ΚΑ; on r., ΒΑΣΙΛΕΩΣ ΦΙΛΙΠΠΟΥ; on l., ΕΠΙΦΑΝΟΥΣ ΦΙΛΑΔΕΛΦΟΥ
Naville 10, 1523

was no doubt the decision of Gabinius which ensured that reckoning in tetradrachms remained the norm in the province. Although Roman men of business are attested at Antioch at least by 48 (Caesar, *BC* iii, 102, 6), L. Cassius in 43 gave Cicero the price of *triticum* in tetradrachms (Cicero, *ad fam.* xii, 13, 4).

In order to see the initiative of Gabinius in its context, it is necessary to look at the history of the areas near the province of Syria and indeed further afield also. It is clear that Judaea, although not directly ruled by Rome after 63, came then under Roman control; it matters little for present purposes whether Hyrcanus was simply high priest from 63 or was also allowed the title of ethnarch, which would imply a greater degree of independence. Judaea in any case certainly paid tribute of some kind to Rome after 63 (Josephus *AJ* xiv, 74; *BJ* i, 154);[15] the alleged sufferings of the *publicani* in Judaea at the hands of Gabinius show that his writ as governor of Syria ran in Judaea (Cicero, *de prov. cons.* 10–12); despite his supposed sympathy for the Jews, he levied money from them to pay for his Egyptian campaign (Dio xxxix, 56, 6; Josephus, *AJ* xiv, 98–9; *BJ* i, 175).

What exactly did he do? The text of Cicero provides no warrant for the view originally propounded by A. Momigliano that he removed the *publicani* from the collection of taxes in Judaea and Syria, in which they were already engaged in 59 (Cicero, *pro Flac.* 69).[16] And nothing that Cicero says positively demands that we accept a reform of fiscal procedure in Syria and Judaea, rather than simply an attempt to

---

15 Schürer I[2], 240–1; compare perhaps Emesa, for which taxation is implied by Cicero, *ad Att.* ii, 16, 2.

16 D.C. Braund, *Klio* 65, 1983, 241, 'Gabinius, Caesar, and the *publicani* of Judaea'.

control the *publicani* on a day-to-day basis, perhaps as a result of the removal of such secular power as Hyrcanus possessed in Judaea. But Cicero's venomous hostility might be more easily explained on the assumption that Gabinius had attempted to reform the fiscal system of Syria on a long-term basis.

Let us look elsewhere. The years 58–57 saw the incorporation in the Roman empire of Cyprus, hitherto part of the Ptolemaic kingdom or ruled independently by a member of the Ptolemaic royal family. As R.S. Bagnall observes, it is unfortunate that we know so little of how the mines, forests and agricultural land of Cyprus were administered and taxed by the Ptolemies. There was probably an overall financial administrator, an *oikonomos*, and a separate mines official; in general the taxation of forests or farmland is likely to have been simplified by the fact that Cyprus was, perhaps increasingly, a land of large estates.[17] One document suggests that there was on Ptolemaic Cyprus, as in Ptolemaic Egypt, a substantial variety of taxes. The Ptolemies also produced substantial issues of coinage on the island.

What is clear is that Ptolemaic rule in Cyprus was in disarray from the late second century onwards. Although sent to Cyprus as *strategos*, the younger brother of Ptolemy IX Soter II regarded himself as king of Cyprus from 114/3; in 107/6 he returned to Egypt with the title of Ptolemy X Alexander I, while his brother went to Cyprus. From 88 to 80 Soter II controlled Egypt and Cyprus, but the two were separated on his death; Ptolemy XII Auletes, an illegitimate son of Soter II, whom we shall meet again in a moment, held Egypt, while another illegitimate son held Cyprus. Auletes in 59 persuaded the Romans to recognise him as king of Egypt, but in 58 P. Clodius passed a law providing for the annexation of Cyprus, which was put into effect by M. Cato as quaestor pro praetore.[18] Cyprus formed thereafter part of the province of Cilicia; it had no provincial coinage before Augustus (p.267). In contrast to the fate of Cyprus, the destiny of Egypt was at any rate temporarily settled in a different fashion when Gabinius forcibly restored Auletes to his throne against the will of his subjects. As a result, Auletes was forced to raise the money to repay the loan he had raised in order to bribe his Roman 'friends' to take action; one of the means he adopted was the debasement of his silver coinage (Fig. 84).[19]

It is in Asia Minor, however, that there occur the crucial developments which may make possible an understanding of the events which I have been describing. In Asia from 58 and in Cilicia from 56, in two of the three *conventus* temporarily transferred from Asia to Cilicia, there began the production of cistophori bearing the names of provincial governors (see Table 8 and Fig. 85); the sequence comes to an end with the issue of Q. Caecilius Metellus Pius Scipio, actually governor of Syria, but active in Asia in the

17 T.B. Mitford, *The Nymphaeum of Kafizin* (Berlin, 1980), in part superseding the valuable overall account of R.S. Bagnall (p.160, n.14), 73–8 (who goes beyond the evidence in postulating tied farmers on Cyprus).

18 E. Badian, *JRS* 1965, 110, 'M. Cato and the annexation of Cyprus'; I. Nicolaou and O. Mørkholm, *A Ptolemaic Coin Hoard* (Nicosia, 1976), with M.H. Crawford, *Gnomon* 1981, 401.

19 M.H. Crawford (n.11), 91.

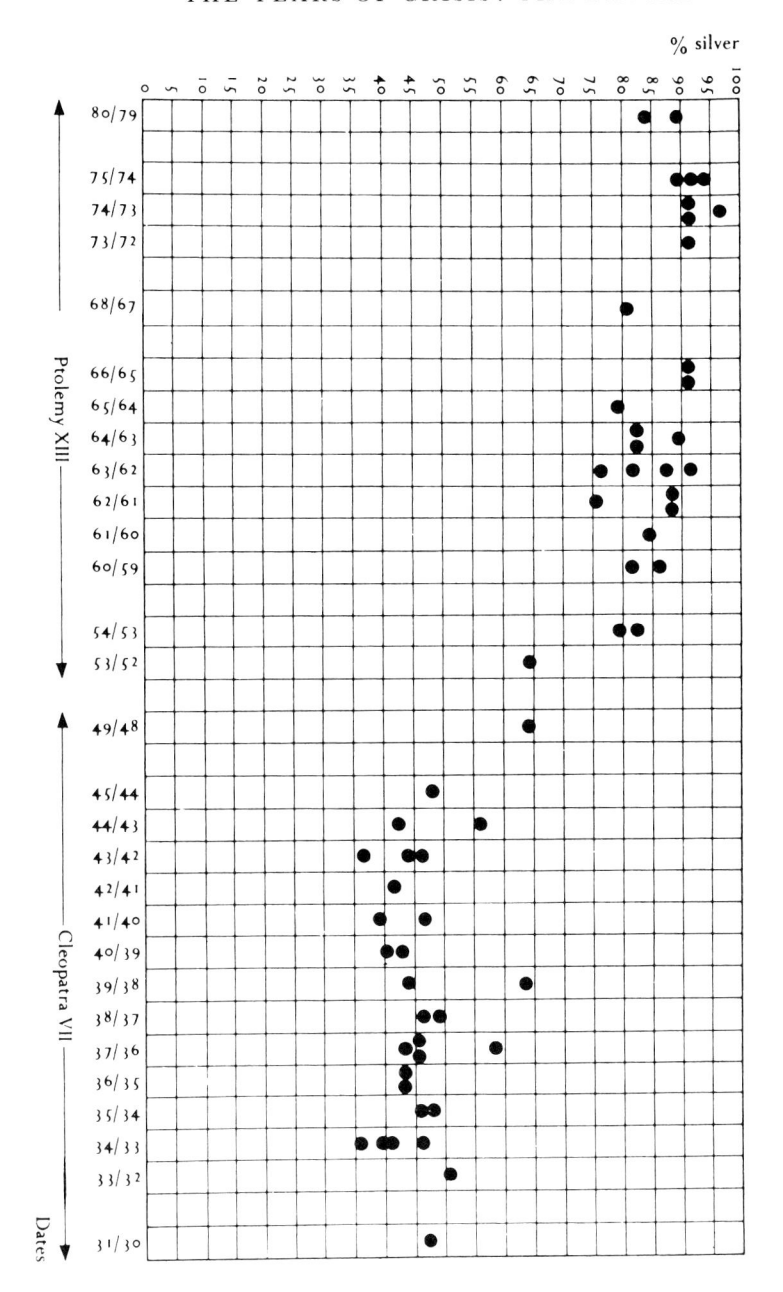

84 The debasement of the coinage of Egypt

The decline coincides with the attempt by Ptolemy XII Auletes to repay the loan which he had raised to fund his bribery of members of the Roman oligarchy (from D.R. Walker (p.271, n.27), 151)

TABLE 8. Mints of the proconsular cistophori

NAME AND RANK OF GOVERNOR	MINT CITIES AND REFERENCES				
	Ephesus	Pergamum	Tralles	Laodicea	Apamea
T. Ampius Balbus Procos. Asia, 58	*BMCIonia* 67		*Inv. Wadd.* 6997 f.	Pinder 568.180	
C. Fabius Procos. Asia, 57	*BMCIonia* 67	Bunbury, *NC* 1883, 186	*BMCLydia* 333–334	*Inv. Wadd.* 7030	*Inv. Wadd.* 7016
C. Septimius Procos. Asia, 56			*BMCLydia* 334		
C. Claudius Pulcher Procos. Asia, 55–53	Head, *Ephesus* 72	Pinder 569	*BMCLydia* 334		
L. Antonius Quaestor, Pro-q. Asia, 50–49	*BMCIonia* 68	Wroth, *NC* 1893, 10			
C. Fannius Propr.(?) Asia, 49	*BMCIonia* 68		*BMCLydia* 334	*Inv. Wadd.* 7031	*BMCPhrygia* 73
Q. Caecilius Metellus Pius Scipio Procos. Syria, 49		Bf. I, 64; III, 29			
P. Cornelius Lentulus Spinther Procos. Cilicia, 56–53				*BMCPhrygia* 281–282	*BMCPhrygia* 72–73
Ap. Claudius Pulcher Procos. Cilicia, 53–51				*BMCPhrygia* 282	*BMCPhrygia* 73
M. Tullius Cicero Procos. Cilicia, 51				Imhoof-Blumer 263	Pinder 571

The table is constructed on the basis of that of J.M. Cody, *AJA* 1973, 43, 'New evidence for the Republican Aedes Vestae'.

The issue of T. Ampius Balbus was first published by B. Borghesi, *Oeuvres* I, 271.

For a new piece of M. Tullius Cicero see *RBN* 1975, 5.

There are in addition unassignable pieces of a Lepidus (W. Caland, *ZfN* 1885, 113); a Fimbria (perhaps to be put in 40s, according to C.A. Hersh); and an Atra(tinus) Q(uaestor).

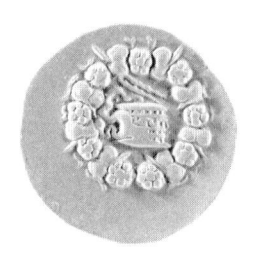

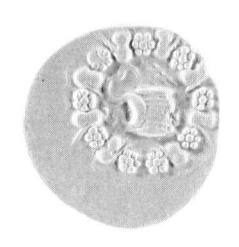

85 The proconsular cistophori

Cistophoric tetradrachm of C. Pulcher
   Cista mystica in ivy-wreath/Two snakes and bow-case; above, C.PVLCHER
                                                                   PROCOS; on l.,
   monogram of Pergamum; on r., staff of Asclepius; below, ΜΗΝΟΔΩΡΟC   Naville 16, 1368
Cistophoric tetradrachm of Q. Metellus:
   Cista mystica in ivy-wreath/Two snakes and *aquila*; above, Q.METELLVS PIVS; on l.,
   monogram of Pergamum; below, SCIPIO IMPER   Naville 12, 1736

opening year of the First Civil War. The innovation is the more striking in that the production of cistophori in Asia had been suspended after 68/7 (p.200).

Probably at about the same time as the resumption of issues of cistophori, the mints of Amphipolis and Thessalonica in Macedonia also instituted the production of coinages which reveal the influence of Rome (Fig. 86). These consist of asses with the head of Janus and semisses with the head of Zeus, the latter very similar to the head of Saturn on Roman semisses. At Thessalonica, there was a sequence of issues of reduced weight, which it is very tempting to associate with the outbreak of civil war in 49.

The annexation of Cyprus and the restoration of Auletes, the acts of men who can be treated as political associates, have often been regarded as motivated by greed, greed for the wealth of Cyprus and greed to recover the money advanced to Auletes; but if the man who restored Auletes was also responsible for the creation of a coinage for Syria and perhaps for fiscal reform there; if the year 58, which saw the decision to annex Cyprus, saw also a decision to reform the coinage of the Roman province of Asia and the production of a bronze coinage in Macedonia based on the Roman as, one should perhaps wonder if there was not a group of men in Rome prepared to undertake measures of reform, which were in some cases extremely detailed, relating to the eastern provinces.

Meanwhile, in the west, the last generation of the Republic was also a period of major change in monetary patterns. The control of Spain by Q. Sertorius, in opposition to L. Sulla and his successors in power, meant that Spain was for a number of years

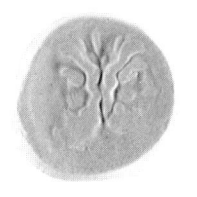

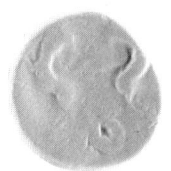

86 The bronze coinage of Thessalonica

As of Thessalonica:
  Laureate head of Janus; above, I/Two centaurs riding apart; in exergue, ΘΕΣΣΑΛΟ
                                                                          ΝΙΚΗΣ   BM
Semis of Thessalonica:
  Laureate head of Zeus r.; behind, monogram/Bull r.; above, ΘΕΣΣΑ; below, two
  monograms and ΛΟΝΙΚΗΣ   BM
As of Thessalonica:
  Laureate head of Janus/Two centaurs riding apart; no legend visible   BM

politically separate from the rest of the Roman empire, but subject to more intensive Roman influence (Map 15).[20] Given this and given the production in Spain just before the effective arrival of Sertorius of a very substantial issue of Roman denarii (Fig. 87), it is the more remarkable that the monetary history of Spain under Sertorius shows him as responsible for the last burst of production of the Iberian denarius coinage (Fig. 88). The evidence of the hoards makes it clear that the latest Iberian denarius issues are of the time of Sertorius (App. 29) and there can be little doubt that they were struck for Sertorius. Not only did he have his headquarters at Osca (Plutarch, *Sert.* 14, 2, cf. 25, 4; Strabo iii, 4, 10; Velleius ii, 30, 1), one of the mints producing Iberian denarii in this period,[21] but he was also in command of a plentiful supply of money for most of the war, in striking contrast to his opponents. Despite his (presumably partial) remission of taxes (Plutarch, *Sert.* 6, 4), he was able in the early stages of the war, before the arrival of Perperna in the winter of 77/6 with a plentiful supply of money (Plutarch, *Sert.* 15, 1), to squander precious metals in display (Plutarch, *Sert.* 14, 1). From Contrebia in 77 he exacted only a moderate sum of money (Livy xci, fr.2; note also the pay for his cavalry). He ran short of money in the later stages of the war; for Pompey's letter (see below) suggests that Sertorius' army was not then being paid any more than his own. To this last period belong the negotiations with Mithridates for a subsidy (Plutarch, *Sert.* 24, 2) and the confiscations recorded by Diodorus (xxxvii

20 For Spaniards as soldiers in these years, see J.M. Roldan Hervas, *Hispania y el Ejercito Romano* (Salamanca, 1974), 31.

21 G. Gaggero, *RIN* 1976, 55, 'Aspetti monetari della rivolta sertoriana in Spagna', exaggerates the importance of Osca as a mint.

87 The issues of C. Annius

Denarius of C. Annius, *RRC*, no. 366/2a:
  Diademed female bust r.; below, control-letter; around C.ANNI.T.F.T.N.PRO.COS.S.C/
  Victory in quadriga r.; above, Q; in exergue, L.FABI.L.F.HISP.Q   *BMCRR* Spain 26

Denarius of C. Annius, *RRC*, no. 366/4:
  Diademed female head r.; around, C.ANNIVS.T.F.T.N.PRO.COS.EX.S.C/ Victory in
  biga r.; above, control-numeral; below, Q; in exergue, C.TARQVITI.P.F   Cambridge

(xxxviii), 22a),[22] perhaps also a shift from silver to bronze coinage. It seems to me likely that the L. Appuleius Decianus who struck as quaestor at Urso, Baelo and Myrtilis was striking for Sertorius (App. H).

His opponents, Metellus in Hispania Ulterior from 79, Pompey in Citerior from 76, were short of money throughout. The speech of the consul C. Aurelius Cotta in 75 records their lack of money (Sallust, *Hist.* ii, 47M, 6) and Pompey's letter in the winter of 75/4 claims in addition that in 76 Metellus had had money only from Gaul (Sallust, *Hist.* ii, 98M, 9) and that he himself had not had even this and had been forced to use his personal assets and to borrow as well (Sallust, *Hist.* ii, 98M, 2 and 9; cf. ii, 97M; Cicero, *pro Balbo* 40). The issue of Cn. Lentulus (*RRC*, no. 393) *may* represent the money provided by Gaul and Sallust (*Hist.* ii, 34M) *may* provide a reference to its production, *quae pecunia ad Hispaniense bellum Metello facta erat* (Fig. 89). Since Corduba was Metellus' base, it seems to me very likely that the quadrantes struck there by Cn. Iulius L.f. as quaestor were struck for him in this period (App. O); the coinage of Saguntum and Valentia should be regarded as struck for Sertorius (App. P, Fig. 90). An indication of the monetary exigencies of these years in Spain may be found in the prevalence of the practice of overstriking (App. Q).

Pompey's letter ended with the celebrated threat to return to Rome if his demands were not met. They were (Plutarch, *Pomp.* 20, 1; *Sert.* 21, 5; *Luc.* 5, 2). The only really large issue of the 70s, that of C. Postumius (*RRC*, no. 394), may be dated to 74 and

---

22 I am not persuaded by any of the points made by G. Gaggero, *Contributi A. Garzetti* (Genoa, 1977), 125, 'Sertorio e gli Iberi'.

88   The Iberian coinage in the Sertorian period

Denarius of Turiasu:
    Male head r.; behind, control-letter/Horseman r.; below, *turiasu*   BM
Denarius of Areikoratikos:
    Male head r.; behind, control-letter/Horseman r.; below and in exergue, *arekoratos*   BM
Denarius of Belikiom:
    Male head r.; behind, control-letter/Horseman r.; below, *belikiom*   BM
Denarius of Bolskan:
    Male head r.; behind, control-letter/Horseman r.; below, *bolskan*   BM
As of Urso:
    Male head r./Sphinx r.; above, VRSONE; below, L.AP.DEC.Q (in monogram)   Paris
As of Ilerda:
    Male head r.; around, dolphins/Horseman r.; below, *iltirta*   BM
Semis of Ilerda:
    Male head r./Horse r.; above, *iltirta*   BM

89 The issue of Cn. Lentulus

Denarius of Cn. Lentulus, *RRC*, no. 393/1a:
  Bust of Genius populi Romani r.; above, G.P.R/Sceptre with wreath, globe and rudder; on either side, EX S.C; below, CN.LEN.Q
  Oxford

90 The issues of the Spanish cities in the Sertorian period

As of Saguntum:
  Helmeted head of Roma r.; around, SAGVNTINV/Prow r.; above, Victory; before, caduceus; below, *arse*
  BM
As of Valentia:
  Helmeted head of Roma r.; around, T.AHI.T.F.L.TRINI.L.F.Q/ Cornucopiae on thunderbolt in laurel-wreath; below, VALENTIA
  BM

regarded as the response to the threat. Several Spanish or Portuguese hoards close with precisely this issue. Pompey and Metellus went on to defeat Sertorius and after his murder, his murderer Perperna. The Iberian followers of Sertorius, thus leaderless, made their peace with Rome and their silver coinage, doubtless identified with their support of Sertorius, came to an end. Their taxes were henceforth paid in Roman denarii.

The production of bronze coinage in Spain seems also to have diminished in volume in the course of the first century. A small bilingual issue of Osicerda in Hispania Citerior imitates the Elephant reverse type of Caesar and therefore belongs in or after 49; but otherwise the Iberian bronze coinage of the north had probably ceased to be produced, while major mints such as Emporiae and Tarraco were by now producing issues of Roman type with Latin legend. The extent of private indebtedness in Spain during the governorship of Caesar in 61 was perhaps accompanied by a shortage of city revenues and a consequent decline in the production of coinage.

The principal difficulty in assessing the bronze currency of the north lies in our uncertainty over the dating of the Azaila hoards. These have traditionally been assigned to the 70s, but M. Beltran Lloris has argued recently for an association with the battle of Ilerda, fought nearby in 49.[23] But there is no good evidence that Period III at Azaila, to which the hoards belong, goes down to 50; certainly neither the thin-walled ware nor the Campana B pottery demands such a conclusion. It is to my mind much more plausible to attribute the massive late issues of Ilerda, well represented in Azaila II (App. 32), to the fact that the city was a base of Sertorius than to the First Civil War, in which Ilerda played no real part. It would have been a gratuitous act of madness for Caesar to destroy Azaila. I regard the Iberian bronze coinage of the north, like the silver, as ending for all practical purposes with Sertorius.

As far as the south is concerned, the Guadix hoard, dated by an as of Cn. Pompeius the younger, contained on the whole late second- or early first-century issues, with some pieces which perhaps belong to the generation between Sertorius and the First Civil War (App. H). But here too, there seems to be a gap before the resumption of production under Augustus.

The last generation of the Republic also saw the progressive extension of Roman control over the west of Spain, apart from the north-west, and indeed the beginnings of Romanisation. In southern Lusitania the population used a native language and script, both of which remain mysterious to us. Further north, an Iberian substratum was overlaid by a Celtic presence; but it was only with the spread of knowledge of the Latin alphabet that inscriptions began to be put up. Much Roman penetration before 50, evidenced by the presence of Campana B pottery, clearly took place in the context of military activity or of Roman exploitation of the mines of the area;[24] but particularly in the south-west the finds show a much wider distribution. In one case, the numismatic evidence allows us to see what seems to be a case of settlement in the west of a presumably partly Romanised group of Iberians, at Salacia; they produced coins with an Iberian legend, alien to the area, and types borrowed from the coinage of Gades (Fig. 91). In general, it is developments of this kind that lie behind the flourishing of city coinage in this area in the age of Augustus (p.271).

The last great act of Roman imperialism was Caesar's conquest of Gaul (Map 25). In terms of monetary history, there were three principal consequences, two ephemeral, the other long-lasting. The latter was the appearance, for the first time in central Gaul, of Roman denarii in quantity; although Caesar struck no denarii till he crossed the

---

23 *Arqueologia e historia de Azaila* (Zaragoza, 1976), 207 (thin-walled ware), 315, 447 (Campana B); *Numisma* 1978, 93, 'La cronologia de los tesoros monetarios de Azaila'.

24 I owe this point to J.C. Edmondson.

91   The coinage of Ketouibon

Bronze of Ketouibon:
   Laureate head of Jupiter l.; before, SISBE.SISCRA/Two tunny-fish; between, *ketouibon*
   Paris (obv.), Vienna (rev.)
Bronze of Gades:
   Head of Melqart l./Two tunny-fish; around, Punic legend   Madrid

Rubicon in 49, the finds of Roman with Gallic coins at Alesia are eloquent testimony to the penetration of Roman coinage (*RRCH* 565; the hoard from Civaux near Poitiers, *Corpus* I, p.8, perhaps belongs in this context).

The Gallic War also saw an upsurge in production by those native mints striking quinarii, obviously to pay troops, whether on the Roman side like the Aedui or engaged against them like the Bituriges Cubi. In the north-west, the gold coinages of the Veneti, Coriosolitae and Redones were replaced by silver issues; these are perhaps to be seen as fiduciary substitutes for the gold, since they were in their turn rapidly replaced by debased silver. In the case of the Coriosolitae, there is a large number of hoards containing these late phases of their coinage, which are almost certainly to be explained by the victory of Caesar in 56. Much of the first-century coinage of the Arverni is no doubt to be attributed to the final attempt at resistance; the gold issue of Vercingetorix is represented in the finds from Gergovia, the bronze issue in those from Alesia.[25] Meanwhile, the Belgic tribes, in opposition to Caesar, also produced a substantial volume of gold coinage; here too, financial difficulties rapidly brought about reduction in weight and debasement and in some cases the replacement of gold by silver (Fig. 92).[26] At the same time, the course of the war brought about a quite untypical dispersal of these coinages far from their places of origin.[27]

But the life of native coinages in Gaul was to be finite, although it is clear that the

25 J.B. Colbert de Beaulieu, 126 (Coriosolitae), 124 (Vercingetorix).
26 S. Scheers, *BNJ* 1972, 1, 'Coinage and currency of the Belgic tribes during the Gallic War'.
27 E.M. Wightman, *11 Cong. Frontier Studies*, 75, 'Soldier and civilian in early Roman Gaul'; *Helinium* 1977, 105, 'Military arrangements in early Roman Gaul', at 117, though the suggested link with the winter quarters for Caesar's troops does not work.

92   The gold and silver coinages of Gaul in the age of Caesar

Quinarius of Togirix:
    Head l.; before, TOCIRIX/Horse l.; above, TO[BM
Gold piece of Suessiones:
    Head r./Horse r.   BM
Gold piece of Coriosolitae:
    Head r./Horse r.   Oxford
Gold piece of Arverni:
    Head of Vercingetorix l.; around, VERCINGETORIX/Horse l.; below, amphora   Paris

conquest did not in any way lead to their prohibition; the Arverni produced some silver and some bronze after 52, the Bituriges Cubi some bronze and perhaps some silver, the Pictones some silver of a new type and some bronze; one particularly large silver issue is that with the legends ATEVLA/VLATOS, produced by one of the Belgic tribes. Other Belgic tribes and perhaps even the peoples of Armorica may have gone on producing debased gold or silver coinages.[28]

Within a generation of the conquest, however, the production of Gallic precious metal coinage had ceased, perhaps in part because of the opening of a mint for the production of Roman gold and silver (and bronze) (p.264), but perhaps principally because the various *civitates* were no longer independent fiscal units and simply no longer needed precious metal coinages. Bronze issues went on being produced into the reign of Tiberius. It is interesting that these issues contain no lead or silver traces; there are thus clearly no contemporary silver coinages produced by the same authorities. But although there are some purely Gallic bronze issues which are both large and late, such

28 S. Scheers, *8 Cong.Num.*, 197, 'L'histoire monétaire de la Gaule Belgique après Caesar'; ead., in B. Cunliffe (ed.), *Coinage and Society in Britain and Gaul* (London: CBA, 1981), 18, 'Coinage in Belgic Gaul', at 20; ead., in *Antike Fundmünzen* (p.166, n.10), 225, 'Le Tetelbierg et la circulation monétaire sur le territoire des Treveri'.

as those with ARDA for the Treviri and AVAVCIA for one of the Belgic tribes, they came eventually to an end, replaced in part by rather small quantities of Roman issues and in greater part by local imitations of these issues (Fig. 93).

Two points are worth making about the bronze issues of Gaul in the period after Caesar. In the first place, they became increasingly Roman in character. A number

93 The coinages of Gaul after Caesar

Quinarius of Q. Iulius Togirix:
   Head l./Q.IVL   BM
Quinarius of Cambotri:
   Laureate head l./Horse l.; above, sword; below, [CA]MBOTRI   BM
Quinarius of Epasnactus:
   Laureate head of Apollo r.; before, EPAD/Facing warrior; on l., winged caduceus and helmet   Paris
Bronze of Epasnactus:
   Head r.; behind, star/Horseman r.; below, waves and EPAD   Paris
Quinarius of Arivos Santonos:
   Helmeted head l.; before, ARIVO[S]/Horse r.; below, star; before, SANT[ONOS]   Oxford
Quinarius of Ateula Ulatos:
   Head of Cupid l.; before, ATEVLA/Horse r.; above, uncertain symbol; below, flower; in exergue, corn-ear; before, VLATOS   BM
Bronze of Arda:
   Terminal bust of Jupiter r.; before, ARDA/Horseman r.   BM
   Veiled head r.; before, ARDA/Horse r.; behind, ARDA   BM

(cont.)

93 The coinages of Gaul after Caesar (*cont.*)

Quadrans of Germanus Indutilli l.:
 Diademed head r./Bull butting l.; above, GERMANV[S]; in exergue, INDVTILLI.L
 Oxford

Semis of Lexovio:
 Eagle l.; around, CISIAMBOS CATTOS VERGOBRETO/Cross; around, SIMISSOS PVBLICOS LEXOVIO
 Oxford

are apparently quadrantes, one issue is actually marked SIMISSOS PVBLICOS for semis; another issue is marked EX.S.C, probably without the people responsible for its production having understood quite what the significance was.[29] Another feature of the coinage of Gaul in this period is the production of pieces with Roman names, the Elephant issue with that of A. Hirtius among the Treviri from 49 – with that of Carrinas in addition in 30 – the issue of Germanus Indutilli l. after 15–12. Some issues bear Roman and Gallic names, a further issue of A. Hirtius among the Remi, an issue of L. Munatius Plancus in 44–43.

It is thus, secondly, not surprising if native quadrantes circulated with Roman coinages, as at Meilleraie-Tillay, where quadrantes of Poitou and Saintonges turn up with small bronzes of the mint of Lugdunum, or at the Tetelbierg, where a similar quadrans turns up with a bronze of Germanus Indutilli l. and a range of Roman issues, from Gallic and Italian mints.[30] At least two issues, that with CONTOVTOS and that of Germanus Indutilli l., were actually made from Roman orichalcum.[31]

A nice piece of evidence of the spread of Roman monetary practices may be seen in a find from near Bonn: one gold bracelet, two gold torques, twenty gold staters of the Ambiani and twenty-six Regenbogenschüsselchen of the Vindelici (p.277) weighing just 321.84 gm., close to the Roman pound of 324 gm., way above the Celtic pound of 310 gm.[32]

29 D.F. Allen (p.166, n.10), 37; 128; compare p. 83.
30 J. Hiernard, *9 Cong..Num.*, 633, 'La circulation des dernières monnaies celtiques en Poitou et Saintonges'; *Pub.Sect.Hist.Inst.Luxembourg* 91, 1971, 120, 128 and 156 (Tetelbierg).
31 D.F. Allen (n.29), 35; S. Scheers, 208.
32 *Die Kelten in Mitteleuropa* (Salzburg, 1980), no. 267; D.F. Allen (n.29), 32.

15

THE BALKAN QUESTION

Although the first Roman expeditionary force to cross the Adriatic did so in order to deal with what was perceived as a problem of Illyrian piracy and although from the early second century Rome controlled, *de iure* or *de facto*, the area round Aquileia on the one hand and Epirus, Greece and Macedonia on the other hand, the establishment of Roman control over Dalmatia and the Danube basin was a long drawn out process. The First Illyrian War in 230 led to the establishment of friendly relations with Corcyra, Apollonia and Dyrrachium (formerly Epidamnus), as well as with Issa and the Parthini and Atintani; but Pharos, the power-base of the Demetrius who first served the Illyrian kingdom, then went over to the Romans, remained in the Illyrian sphere when Demetrius was left in *de facto* control by the Romans; Pharos was attacked by the Romans when Demetrius' alleged misbehaviour provoked the Second Illyrian War, but was not removed from the realm of his successors; the Parthini were also attacked in 220 and had presumably also misbehaved; they remained in the Roman sphere; the Atintani were abandoned to Macedonia in 205. It was not till 167 that Illyria from Rizon to Lissus was reduced to tribute-paying subjection (Map 29).

The mountain chain which forms the south-eastern continuation of the Alps runs in an unbroken chain as far as the Gulf of Corinth: there is an easy route through the range from Aquileia to Emona (now Ljubljana), but thereafter few easy passes until one reaches the line followed by the Via Egnatia east from Dyrrachium and Apollonia. Few rivers of any size flow west into the Adriatic; and the economy of the mountain area must always have been essentially pastoral.[1]

The natural geographical divisions of the region were eventually enshrined in the Roman provincial system: the coastal area formed the province of Dalmatia, the Sava and Drava valleys belonged to Pannonia, the lower Danube basin formed the provinces of Moesia (Superior and Inferior) and (eventually) Dacia. Of more immediate interest

---

1 J.J. Wilkes, *Dalmatia* (London, 1969), 178–80.

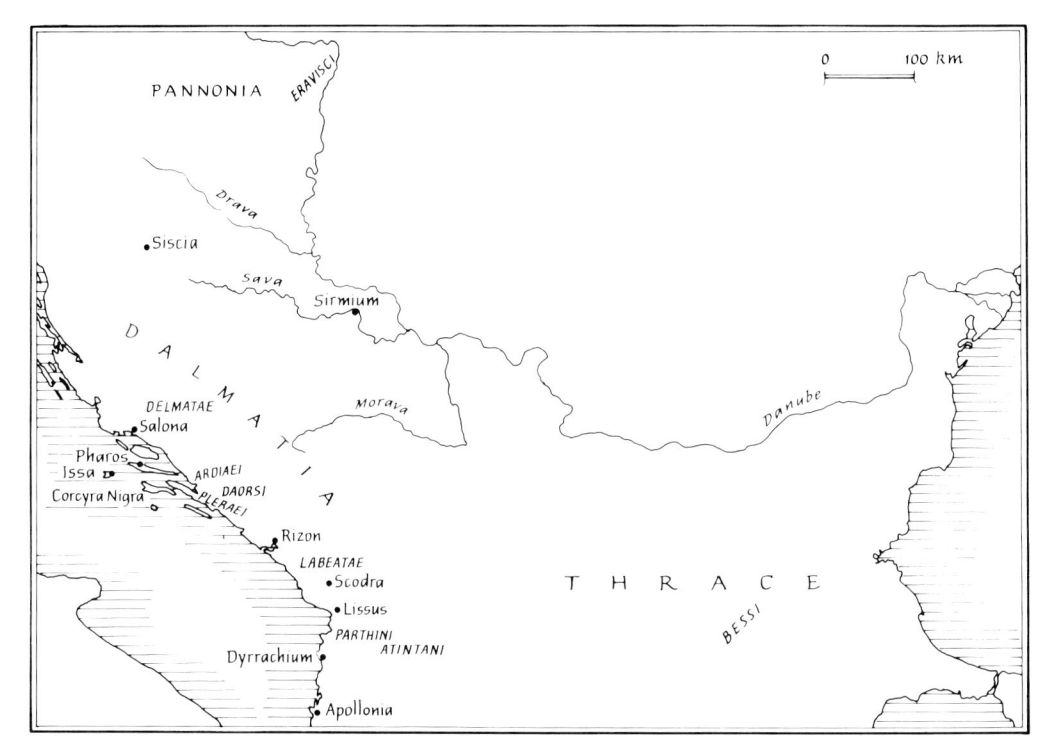

29 Illyria

is the fact that the Roman conquest of the region, when it took place, involved the encircling of the coastal area from the north and the south. This does not mean, however, that Roman forays in the coastal area were without significance or consequence.

North of the long-established Greek colonies of Apollonia and Dyrrachium lay the later foundations of Pharos, Corcyra Nigra and Issa, with Heraclea on Pharos. Just as in the south the presence of Apollonia and Dyrrachium led to the beginning of a process of urbanisation among the Illyrian tribes in the hinterland, so further north the Daorsi on the mainland opposite Pharos acquired an urban centre at Osanić, the Delmatae at Delminium.

Leaving aside the prolific fourth-century silver coinage from the inland mint of Damastion, Apollonia and Dyrrhachium possessed normal Greek coinages from the classical period onwards. Pharos struck a small issue of silver in the fourth century, Heraclea, Pharos and Issa bronze from the fourth century onwards, Corcyra Nigra a small issue of bronze in the third century.[2] Some of the native communities also began

2 The coins with the legend IONIO(Σ) were produced by Issa, those with ΔI by Pharos.

to produce coinage, in the Hellenistic period, two 'kings' called Monounios and Mytilos reigning in the hinterland of Apollonia and Dyrrachium (the former silver, the latter bronze), Rhizon (silver as well as bronze), Lissus,[3] Scodra, Olympa[4] and Lychnus, and the Daorsi and the Labeatae, in the late third or early second centuries. Silver as well as bronze issues are attested for a second-century king called Ballaeus, bronze issues for one called Genthius; some of their issues seem to have been struck at the Greek city of Pharos, others at Scodra or Lissus. Genthius is a well-known figure of the time of the Third Macedonian War, Ballaeus is known only from his coins, but they appear to belong in the same general period.[5] It is interesting that silver seems to have been struck for Genthius by Perseus at Pella (Livy xliv, 27, 8–12); I suppose that it was all seized by L. Anicius Gallus (Livy xlv, 43, 5).

We should not exaggerate the extent to which the use of coinage spread to the native communities of Dalmatia. Certainly the emergence of the kingdom of Illyria under Agron from 240 onwards did not lead to the production of an organised coinage, though it is probably significant that all the native communities which produced coinage in their own name rather than or as well as for Genthius or Ballaeus were at some time part of the kingdom of Illyria (for Lychnus see Pol. xviii, 47); we do not know enough about the coinages to be sure, but it seems to me likely that they were all in effect coinages of the kingdom of Illyria. The basis for a royal coinage certainly existed since it emerges from the Roman settlement of Illyria in 167 that the area had previously paid tribute to its kings.[6]

Nor does the evidence of hoards suggest a very widespread use of coinage in the area, or even its presence as bullion.[7] There is one hoard from Risan (ancient Rhizon) of the late fourth century, which *may* represent booty or the accumulation of a mercenary (*IGCH* 391 = Mirnik 9), otherwise one silver hoard from Risan (Mirnik 39), one mixed hoard from Selce near ancient Scodra (*IGCH* 560), one bronze hoard from Pharos and one of coins of Heraclea from Murter (*IGCH* 418–420 = Mirnik 11–12 with P. Visonà; *IGCH* 421 = Mirnik 7). Not surprisingly, a fair number of Syracusan coins seem to have reached the area of Pharos and Issa in and after the period of Dionysius' interest in the region.[8]

3 Not a Greek colony, J.J. Wilkes (n.1), 9.

4 H.Ceka, *Questions de numismatique illyrienne* (Tirana, 1972), 145.

5 Z. Dukat and I. Mirnik, *BIArch* 13, 1976, 175, 'Pre-Roman coinage on the territory of modern Yugoslavia', with bibliography; G. Gorini, in *Atti delle Tornate di Studio nel cinquantesimo anniversario della fondazione in Zara* (Società Dalmata di Storia Patria. Sezione Veneta, 1976), 67, 'Aspetti della monetazione greca nell'antica Dalmazia'. See also p.224.

6 Compare Theopompus fr.39 Jacoby for the helots of the Ardiaei.

7 The fact that the interior of Dalmatia did not use coinage (Strabo vii, 5, 5 (315) (compare Polybius xxxii, 9, 4, for neighbouring tribes paying the Delmatae tribute in kind) does not militate against the possibility that the area accepted coinage as bullion.

8 P. Visonà, *9 Cong.Num.*, 147, 'Early Greek bronze coinage in Dalmatia'; note that *IGCH* 417 = Mirnik 4 is not a hoard; that Mirnik 35 is not a hoard (see App.50). I have no idea what to make of the coins composing Mirnik 27.

222   COINAGE AND MONEY UNDER THE ROMAN REPUBLIC

In the only area in which coinage penetrated into the interior before the age of Augustus it did so in a context which remains almost wholly obscure (see Map 30). The Mazin hoard consists of *aes rude* and currency bars and cast bronze coinage, none of which is likely to have been available in circulation in Italy after the late third century, one early struck piece with ROMANO and a scatter of Italian and Sicilian pieces, to which the same consideration on the whole applies, and one piece from Caphyae in Arcadia, together with much Egyptian, Carthaginian and Numidian

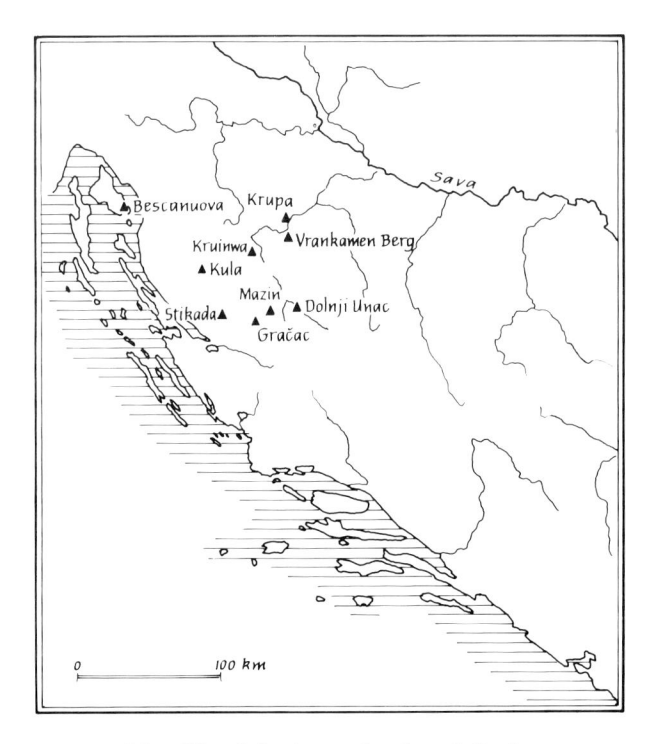

30   The Mazin and related finds
See App. 49

material and pieces of the denarius coinage down to about 150. Comparable assemblages including Roman material come from Gračac, Vrankamen Berg and Štikada; comparable assemblages not including Roman material come from Dolnji Unac, Kruinwa, Krupa and Kula; a related hoard is that of cast bronze coinage alone from Bescanuova (= Baška) on the island of Curicta (modern Veglia = Krk); this hoard by itself shows Roman coinage moving to the area during the third century, a process which may in any case be inferred from the content of the Mazin hoard and its kin. The Bescanuova hoard also suggests that the coinages in question arrived by way of the coastal area, an inference supported by other find material (App. 49).⁹ The latest dated material in the hoards under discussion is perhaps of the middle of the second century, they are perhaps to be regarded as having been undisturbed since about 100;¹⁰ but it is inconceivable that at either date the earliest material was in circulation anywhere. It remains to me wholly baffling why this relatively small area sucked in bronze predominantly from Rome and North Africa from the middle of the third century onwards and then on the whole simply kept it in its original form for up to a century and a half,¹¹ though some isolated coins travelled further north and east (App. 49).

To return to the coastal areas further south, they had of course long been in close contact with the opposite shore of the Adriatic,¹² contact for which the numismatic material provides some evidence. This evidence is not, as we have seen, evidence of the large-scale influx of coins from elsewhere; nor does the pattern change with the Roman period.

It follows that if trade between Italy and the western part of the Balkan peninsula between the Roman establishment of hegemony in Italy and the end of the Republic was conducted with coinage as an object of trade, this has left little trace; given the likelihood that trade in slaves between Italy and Dacia in the late Republic did leave substantial traces in the form of hoards of Roman Republican denarii from Dacia, it is the more economical hypothesis to suppose that trade across the Adriatic between the mid-third century and the mid-first century was not conducted with coinage as an object of trade.¹³

On the other hand, there is a fair amount of evidence throughout this period for the movement of isolated pieces across the Adriatic, mostly pieces of low value (App. 50); they cannot be regarded as in any sense objects of trade, but are presumably evidence for the movement of individuals; these may be pilgrims, tourists, diplomats, soldiers or pirates as readily as traders; a single coin can easily be lost by anyone. But some of the movement may be of traders and the numismatic evidence is worth recalling,

9 See F. Lo Schiavo, *MAL* 1969–70, 363, 'Il gruppo liburno-japodico', for other evidence for contact with Italy. The material culture of the area remained substantially unchanged between the fifth and first centuries.

10 So K. Kurz, *Situla* 14–15, 1974, 155, 'Zur neuen datierung des Mazinfundes', wrongly attributing to me a belief in an earlier date and then refuting it.

11 K. Kurz, *Arh.Vestnik* 1969, 27, 'Zum Charakter der Geldwirtschaft im Japodengebiet', after considering the extent of Celtic admixture in Illyria, argues that coins in the area of the Mazin group of hoards came in as objects of trade and were then treated as money and not as raw material. But all is supposition; and a hoard of gold of Carthage from the area (*IGCH* 549) does not help; it is perhaps the property of a mercenary.

12 S. Batović, *Diadora* 6, 1973, 5, 'Les vestiges préhistoriques sur l'archipel de Zadar'; map 12, for Apulian geometric pottery, compare p.163. P. Lisičar, *Arch.Jug.* 14, 1973, 3, 'Cenni sulla ceramica antica', at 15, for Gnathia ware.

13 For trade in slaves between Dacia and Italy, see p.226. Nothing useful can be deduced from the report (deriving from Theopompus) of a hill near the Adriatic whence the Black Sea could be seen and of an agora where goods from the Adriatic and the Black Sea were exchanged: Strabo vii, 5, 1 (313); 5, 9 (317); [Aristotle], *de mir. ausc.* 104, with P.M. Fraser, *Ptolemaic Alexandria* (Oxford, 1972), 160, with n.226.

in order to set it beside the evidence of Polybius for trade across the Straits of Otranto, interference with which by Illyrian privateers was regarded by Polybius as provoking the Romans into fighting the First Illyrian War.

Our knowledge of Illyria between 167 and the late Republic is minimal; we hear of military intervention in 156–155 against the Delmatae, in 135 against the Ardiaei and Pleraei, in 119–118 and in 78–76 against the Delmatae. The coinage of Ballaeus may belong to the period after 167;[14] but nothing whatever is known of the ruler concerned or of the person represented by another name which appears on the same coins, MVN. A rather different phenomenon requires attention, and highlights the absence of coinage from the area as a whole before the Augustan conquest.

94   The coinage of Apollonia and Dyrrachium

Drachm of Apollonia:
  Cow suckling calf; above, ΑΙΒΑΤΙΟΣ; in exergue, corn-ear/Fire and *pedum* in square;
  above, ΑΠΟΛ; around, ΧΑΙΡΗΝΟΣ   Naville 5, 1802
Drachm of Dyrrachium:
  Cow suckling calf; above, head of Helios and ΕΧΕΦΡΩΝ; on r., owl/Patterned square;
  above, ΔΥΡ; around, ΖΩΠΥΡΟΥ   Naville 1, 1273

Let us begin with the coinage of Apollonia and Dyrrachium (Fig. 94), mints which produced in the late third, second and first centuries a very large silver coinage, consisting basically of drachms weighing 3.4 gm., exported widely in the Danube basin from about 100 onwards (App. 51). Obviously the position of Apollonia and Dyrrachium as transit towns at the start of the Via Egnatia may help to explain their coinages, but it hardly explains the pattern of their distribution in the first century. It has been argued

14 See p.221. The arguments advanced by A.J. Evans for a date for Ballaeus after 167 are not strong, but they are perhaps supported by the material listed in App. 50, no. 4. The arguments of G. Gorini, in *Il crinale d'Europa* (Rome, 1984), 43, 'Re Ballaios', for a date before 167 are also very weak. For hoards of the coins of Ballaeus see Mirnik 21, 26, 28a, 40; *IGCH* 563. It is not at all clear that the find from Rentje, *IGCH* 562, which might help to date Ballaeus, is actually a hoard at all.

that the mints struck essentially to finance the Roman military presence in Greece on various occasions in the late third and early second centuries;[15] but this is not the whole story. It is clear that the coinages cover the whole period down to 50, not just the late third and early second centuries.[16] It remains true that Roman exigencies explain the later, as well as the earlier, issues of the coinages, but in a different and more sinister fashion.

The most important single fact about the economy of Epirus after 167 is that it was in the hands of great Roman landowners, who exploited its pastures and of whom T. Pomponius Atticus is no more than one example.[17] As Emilio Gabba has suggested to me, it is likely that a large number of the men enslaved by the Romans in 167 (p.123) were left in Epirus to work for the new owners of the land; but a constant supply was necessary and I suggest that some of the surplus acquired by the *latifondisti* of Epirus was in due course converted into coinage by Apollonia and Dyrrachium, to be exported to the Danube basin in order to acquire the slaves and indeed the salt necessary to the functioning of a large-scale pastoral economy. It may be that the metal came from the same mines as had been used for the coinage of Damastion, mines which were probably located north-east of Lake Ohrid.[18]

As a hypothetical model, one may suggest that hides and wool were sold to contractors for the supply of the Roman army (compare Cicero, *in Pis.* 87) and that some of the revenues which accrued were paid to Apolloniate and Dyrrachian slave-traders, who then sought their wares in the Danube basin. It must also be said that at any rate Dyrrachium was notorious for its prostitutes (Plautus, *Men.* 258–64; Catullus 36, 15) and some of the slaves purchased may well have been female.

With this background in mind, we may turn to the area of the Delmatae, whose capital was destroyed in 155 and whose territory was converted to pasture (Strabo vii, 5, 5 (315)), presumably for the benefit of Romans or Italians. The evidence of the coin finds fits this hypothesis. The arrival of the coins in and the deposition of the earliest hoard, the Zasiok hoard, are in my judgement to be linked with the campaigns of L. Caecilius Metellus Delmaticus in 119; but it is clear that from the second quarter of the first century denarii circulated along the central Dalmatian coast (App. 52 and Map 31). This fact is clearly to be associated with the epigraphic evidence for the presence of Romans and Italians in the area, presumably as *latifondisti*:[19]

---

15 A. Giovannini, 113, cf. 34–5, 30, misinterpreting Cicero, *ad fam.* xiii, 29, 4 (for which see p.245).

16 H. Ceka (n.4); the Tangier hoard (p.138, n.5) shows that the coinages began in the late third century, the Bakërr hoard (*IGCH* 559) the point reached in the two sequences by about 160.

17 M. Pasquinucci, 'T. Pomponio Attico e l'allevamento in Epiro' (forthcoming); note that there was a *conventus* of Roman citizens at Lissus in the age of Caesar.

18 J.M.F. May, *The Coinage of Damastion* (Oxford, 1939).

19 For the archaeological evidence for a Roman presence near Narona see *Wiss.Mitt.aus Bosn. Herz.* 1912, 81. The area used coinage in the time of Strabo, vii, 5, 5 (315).

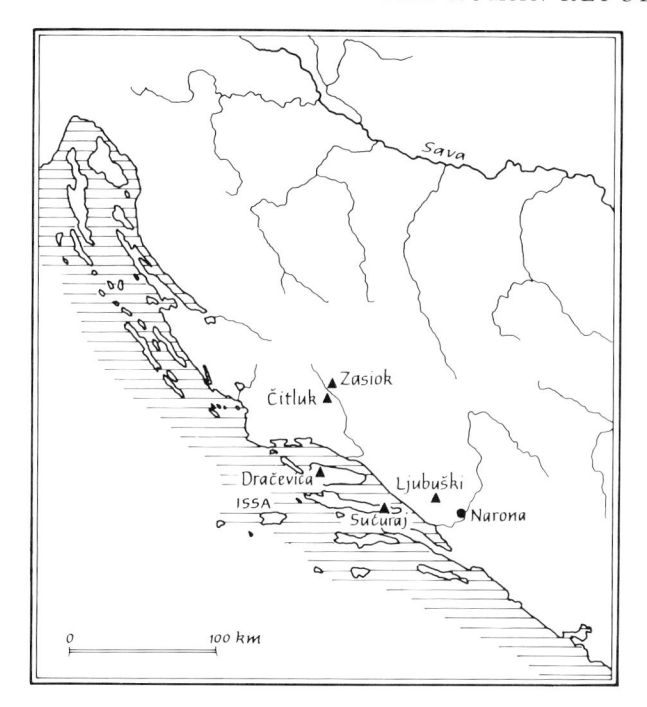

31 Hoards of Republican denarii in Dalmatia
See App. 52

NARONA

CIL i, 2289 = iii, 1784 = *ILS* 3354 = *ILLRP* 206, temple of Liber Pater
CIL i, 2290 = iii, 1785 = *ILLRP* 207 with *add.*, building for Liber Pater
CIL i, 2288 = iii, 1772 with p.1029 = *ILLRP* 87, altar of Diana
CIL iii, 14625 = *ILS* 8893 = *ILLRP* 417, dedication to Octavian
CIL i, 2291 = iii, 1820 + 8423 = *ILS* 7166 = *ILLRP* 629, wall-building
CIL i, 2293, wall-building
CIL i, 2292 = iii, 1821, building
CIL iii, 8446 and 8446a, epistylium with names

ISSA

CIL i, 2295 = iii, 3076 = *ILS* 3189 = *ILLRP* 233, dedication to Mercury
CIL i, 759 with p.839 = iii, 3078 = *ILLRP* 389, rebuilding of portico

It is time to turn from the slave-using to the slave-producing areas of the Balkan peninsula. One of the most remarkable phenomena within the pattern of monetary circulation in antiquity is the presence of large numbers of Roman Republican denarii, for the most part struck between about 130 and 31, on the soil of present-day Romania, roughly ancient Dacia. Absolute figures are impressive; it has been calculated that taking together isolated finds, hoards closing with Republican pieces, nuclei of Republican coins in Roman Imperial hoards and Republican coins in collections in Romania, the total comes to something like 25,000 pieces.[20] But absolute figures are themselves unable to convey fully the uniqueness of the phenomenon; this emerges most clearly from a comparison with neighbouring territories.

There are no known hoards of Republican denarii from the territory of the Moldavian S.S.R.; the territories of Poland, Czechoslovakia and Hungary to the north-west have produced between them a mere handful of Republican hoards; Jugoslavia and Albania to the west and Greece to the south are slightly more productive, but display no trace of the feature characteristic of Romania, a great block of hoards, the latest coin of which belongs in the first century (App. 53).

The only area which may eventually rival Romania, when the level of publication improves, is the Bulgarian side of the lower Danube basin. Such published material as there is shows a pattern in some respects not dissimilar to that characteristic of Romania, and there are numerous brief citations in Bulgarian periodicals of hoards of unspecified Republican coins (App. 54). I shall therefore be considering what may be a single phenomenon, the appearance *en masse* of late Republican denarii in the lower Danube basin, although much of the detailed evidence I shall be discussing is Romanian rather than Bulgarian.

I have so far talked of the presence in rather than of the import into Romania and Bulgaria of Republican denarii; for the possibility must be faced that the bulk of the apparently Republican denarii therefrom are in fact locally produced imitations. I argue elsewhere, however, that the positive reasons for supposing this are entirely without weight and that there are indeed strong grounds for arguing the opposite.[21] I have on present evidence no doubt that it is reasonable to talk of the massive import of Republican denarii into the lower Danube basin, predominantly in the latter part of the first century.

I propose to consider first why the denarii came there at all, then the evidence for the precise moment at which they began to arrive, finally why they began to come then.

The answer to the first question emerges in large measure from a consideration of the existing context into which the denarii of the Republic were inserted. It is clear from the literary and epigraphic evidence that Thrace and the lower Danube basin were in the Hellenistic period as earlier an area hungry for precious metal. The war

---

20 See I. Glodariu, *Acta Mus..Nap.* 1971, 71, 'Consideraţii asupra circulaţiei monedei străine'. I here reproduce with revisions the arguments of *JRS* 1977, 117, 'Republican denarii in Romania: the suppression of piracy and the slave-trade'. For later work see my review in *NC* 1985 (forthcoming).

21 *SCN* 7, 1980, 51, 'Imitations of Roman Republican denarii in Dacia'.

95 The barbarous coinages of the Balkans

Imitation of tetradrachm of Thasos (Fig. 46)   Lockett 39
Geto-Dacian tetradrachm:
  Laureate head of Zeus r./Horseman r.   BM cast

between Rhodes and Byzantium in 220 was provoked by an attempt by Byzantium to impose tolls on traffic sailing into and out of the Black Sea in order to pay tribute to the Gauls settled in her hinterland;[22] the Agathocles inscription from Istria shows that city buying immunity from invasion for 600 gold coins.[23]

The evidence of coin finds shows also that Thrace and the lower Danube basin had by the first century long been used to the large-scale availability of silver: tetradrachms of Philip II (together with imitations in large quantities), tetradrachms of Alexander III, Philip III and Lysimachus (again with imitations), imitations of coins of Larissa, Geto-Dacian tetradrachms (with a very few drachms), coins of Macedonia Prima and Thasos (together with imitations in large quantities), coins of Dyrrachium and Apollonia – each of these coinages for a time, between the fourth and the first centuries, predominated in part or all of the area.

Most of these coinages came from outside the lower Danube basin, the coinages of Philip II and his successors and their imitations from Macedonia or southern Thrace, the coins of Macedonia Prima and Thasos and their imitations from the same area, the coinages of Dyrrachium and Apollonia from the west. Only for a limited period in the third and second centuries did the Geto-Dacian coinage provide Dacia with its own coinage (Fig. 95).[24]

22 Polybius iv, 46, 3. Note that the Thracian kings of the fourth century drew large revenues from customs-dues.
23 S. Lambrino, *Rev.ét.roum.* 5–6, 1960, 180 = *Historia* 11, 1962, 21; see also D.M. Pippidi, *I Greci sul basso Danubio* (Milan, 1971), 104–6.
24 No longer struck in the first century, *contra* C. Preda, *Monedele Geto-Dacilor* (Bucharest, 1973); for Thracian issues of the third/second or of the first centuries, see p.236.

Beside the evidence of coin finds stands the evidence of finds of jewellery; the two are indeed often associated. But just as there are a large number of finds of coins alone, so also there are of jewellery alone.[25]

If one turns to consider the social and economic significance of these finds, it seems likely that the presence of a variety of coinages in the lower Danube basin from the fourth to the first centuries has little to do with the operation of a money economy; this picture does not essentially alter with the arrival of denarii of the Republic.

The virtual absence of any small denominations means that none of the coinages available to the lower Danube basin can have functioned very effectively as a means of exchange in a market economy. And the readiness of the area to use coins of differing areas and differing weight standards without any consistent attempt to produce its own suggests that the coinages functioned perhaps only in a rather rough and ready way as a measure of value.[26]

The answer lies along other lines, I think, with coinage being used rather for exchange of gifts and for payments such as dowries, where the gift element is considerable; its function was presumably to define and enhance the status of a local aristocracy and its retainers. An analogy from Gaul, in the absence of direct evidence for Dacia, may lend plausibility to this view of the role of money in Dacian and proximate societies; the father of King Bituitus of the Arverni displayed his wealth by scattering gold and silver coins from his chariot;[27] one may perhaps suggest that a similar process lies behind isolated finds of Republican denarii and other coins in Romania.

Coinage in fact is to be envisaged as for the most part a fashionable form in which to hold and display wealth, alongside jewellery and other forms of mobile riches; the origin of the fashion perhaps lies in a perception of the power of money in the civilised and fascinating Greco-Macedonian Mediterranean world; there of course the power derived from a real economic function.[28]

Nor is there any reason to suppose that any change took place when Republican

25 The material is catalogued by K. Horedt, *Dacia* 17, 1973, 127; E. and F. Stoicovici, *Acta Mus.Nap.* 1973, 541; 1974, 19, analyse the (small) gold content of selected pieces. For jewellery manufactured from Republican denarii see the Stancuța hoard (*RRCH* 331).

26 The bronzes catalogued by B. Mitrea, *Pontica* 1978, 89, 'Les monnaies pontiques chez les Daco-Getes de Burebista', are a trivial twenty-four in number. Isolated indications of weight on a few pieces of plate, no doubt put there by Greek craftsmen, tell us little (*Thracian Treasures from Bulgaria* (British Museum, 1976), nos. 311, 360, 361).

27 Athenaeus iv, 152d = Posidonius fr. 67 Edelstein-Kidd; Strabo iv, 2, 3 (191); see the important remarks of D. Nash, *NC* 1975, 214–15.

28 My view of Dacian society and economy is thus radically different from that of C. Preda, *Monedele Geto-Dacilor* (n.24), 22–3 = 440, who sees the development of 'Warenaustausch' as leading to the emergence of Geto-Dacian coinage. I should not of course wish to deny that *some* 'Warenaustausch' for coinage took place. The fascination exercised by the typology of the Republican coinage is documented by the terracotta medallion from Gradiștea copying the head of Diana on the obverse of a denarius of Ti. Claudius Ti.f. Ap.n. (*Mat.Arch.* 1959, 396; *Illiri și Daci* (Cluj and Bucharest), 1972, pl. xxxi; I see no reason to suppose that the medallion portrays Bendis).

denarii replaced the assortment of Greek and native issues available earlier. There is still no small change, and it is clear that the arrival of Republican denarii in the lower Danube basin does not mean the extension to that area of existing patterns of circulation elsewhere.[29] In Italy and the other Mediterranean areas to which the circulation of the denarius gradually extended, the hoards usually contain a solid run of issues down to the latest one; the pattern is one of regular contact with the source of supply. Most Dacian hoards consist of a run of issues followed by a few pieces separated by several years from each other and from the hoard as a whole.

There are good reasons in terms of the needs of a relatively primitive society for Republican denarii to have come to the Lower Danube basin, to have remained there and in a restricted sense to have circulated there in the form of coin. But none of these phenomena need have much to do with any development of the Dacian economy. Talk of a first-century Geto-Dacian monetary economy is the purest fantasy.

The problem of the date when the massive import of Republican denarii into Dacia and neighbouring areas began is complicated by a factor which does not affect a consideration of the earlier coinages which entered the area. Unlike these, the Republican coinage remained long in circulation in the Roman world, and it is theoretically possible that none of it entered the area before the imperial age; though it would be in that case exceedingly hard to explain the large number of hoards which contain no coin later than the middle of the first century BC.

It is, however, inconceivable that most of the material did not enter Dacia well before the Roman conquest in the reign of Trajan. By that time there were few Republican denarii in circulation, certainly not enough to account for the pattern of their occurrence in Dacia; we are in any case therefore faced with the phenomenon of massive penetration of non-Roman territory by Roman coinage.

Similarly, I doubt very much whether the availability of Republican denarii in the age of Augustus or immediately thereafter could have allowed penetration on the scale which actually occurred.[30] Further, although Republican denarii were still circulating in the Roman empire under Augustus, and it is possible that some such denarii entered Dacia in that period, one would expect that if the penetration were in general so late it would comprise in addition a far higher proportion of contemporary issues. Moreover, the latest Republican coins in some of the Romanian hoards which close in the first century BC show relatively little wear; it is hard to believe that they came to Romania or were buried many decades later than the date of the latest coins in them. I shall return later to the possibility that *some* Republican denarii came in the Augustan period.

29 *Contra* B. Mitrea and I. Glodariu (cited in n.33 below); for the absence of small change see C. Rodewald (cited in n.53 below), 41–2.
30 Early imperial hoards from Pannonia and Illyria do not show a particularly large proportion of Republican pieces. It has also been argued that Roman Republican denarii in Romania were in large part the booty of Burebista (first by L. Ruzicka, *BSNR* 1922, 5, 'Die Frage der dacischen Münzen', esp. 10); but the areas he plundered were not characterised by extensive circulation of Republican denarii.

On balance, therefore, the beginning of the massive penetration of Republican denarii may be regarded as contemporary with the closing date of the earliest hoards of Republican denarii from the Danube basin (App. 54). For it is implausible to suppose, in view of the large numbers of hoards of non-Roman coins of earlier centuries, that Republican denarii circulated for very long in the Danube basin without being hoarded.[31]

We are faced then with a massive penetration of the lower Danube basin by Republican denarii probably beginning towards the middle of the first century BC and continuing on a considerable scale to the end of the Republic and beyond. A phenomenon so anomalous and so unique can hardly be explained in terms of general trading activity,[32] the existence of which between the lower Danube basin and the Mediterranean world is of course not to be denied. Polybius in the second century records five different commodities – cattle and slaves among necessities, honey, wax and preserved fish among luxuries – as coming from the area round the Black Sea, in exchange for olive-oil and wine, with corn sometimes going one way and sometimes another (Polybius iv, 38, 4–5). The archaeological record shows a variety of goods from the Mediterranean world entering the territory of present-day Romania. But such trade cannot explain the phenomenon in which we are interested.[33]

Some recent work has moved away from the perspective of earlier scholars, simply postulating general trading activity, but is vitiated in my view by concentration on particular parts of the phenomenon rather than on the whole, and by insufficient awareness of the pattern of circulation of the Republican coinage outside Romania.

M. Chiţescu has argued that Republican coins came into the lower Danube basin as a result of being paid out as remuneration to mercenaries hired by Rome.[34] It is of

---

31 B. Mitrea, *SCIV* 1970, 429, 'Un nou tezaur de denari romani', at 434, is quite wrong to suppose that the presence in Romania of many examples of issues of the late second century and of the 80s shows that the coins must have come in during those periods; both periods were characterised by massive issues which remained in circulation in enormous quantities in the first century and were indeed the major component of Italian hoards of the mid-first century.

32 See in any case the fundamental cautionary remarks of P. Grierson, *Trans.Roy.Hist.Soc.* 1959, 123, 'Commerce in the Dark Ages: a critique of the evidence'.

33 B. Mitrea, *Eph.Dac.* 1945, 1, 'Penetrazione commerciale e circolazione monetaria nella Dacia prima della conquista' (concentrating mainly on Transylvania), esp. 113, sees the import of Republican coinage into Dacia purely as a result of general commercial activity, without undertaking any analysis of this concept. Gold, salt and corn are seen (151) as the major exports from Dacia; to suggest corn goes against the evidence of Polybius and Strabo (vii, 4, 6 (311)); salt seems quite implausible as a *major* export from Dacia to Italy; likewise gold, of which Rome had more than she knew what to do with after the victories of Pompey.

I. Glodariu, *Dacian trade with the Hellenistic and Roman World* (Oxford, 1976), operates with a similarly modernising framework. Isolated objects, such as the tools of Aquileian origin at Gradiştea, 211, prove nothing of importance.

34 *Carpica* 1971, 159, 'Monnaies républicaines trouvées en Moldavie'; *DHA* 6, 1980, 123, 'Les monnaies géto-daces', at 130, n.15. *None* of the texts cited supports the argument; the whole point of Cicero, *ad Att.* ix, 10, 3, is that Getae were *not* used, see D.R. Shackleton Bailey *ad loc.*

course true that at various stages of antiquity the area provided mercenaries to the Mediterranean world; but nothing suggests that the Romans used mercenaries from this or indeed any area on any significant scale.[35] And Dr Chiţescu is mistaken in supposing that the wave of coins which she is discussing entered Dacia in the 80s (see p.231). (This is a period when the Roman need for troops *might* have led them to use foreign mercenaries, but in fact almost no such use is attested in a well-documented period.)

Similarly, Dr Chiţescu has also argued that the prevalence of legionary coins of Antony in parts of Dacia is to be explained in terms of military assistance provided for him and the recompense made therefor;[36] Dr Chiţescu has gone on to localise particular Geto-Dacian chiefs on the basis of the coin finds. This seems to me wildly implausible. Dacian hoards closing with legionary coins of Antony do indeed exist, but these coins occur in hoards all over the Mediterranean world soon after 31 in numbers which make the Romanian pattern not particularly striking; and, alone of Republican issues, the legionary issue continued to circulate in enormous numbers under the principate, surviving in some cases until the Severan age; we know nothing of the arrival of these coins in Dacia, except for the relatively small proportion consisting of those pieces in hoards where they form the latest issue.[37]

In considering then the earliest hoards of Republican coins from Dacia, we are dealing with hoards composed for the most part of a block of common coins of the late second century and of the 80s, with normally an isolated terminal coin or scatter of coins of the 70s and 60s; the vast majority of these hoards are not now known in anything like their entirety. Even were it not true that the 70s and 60s are for the most part a period of small issues from the Roman mint, it would clearly be extremely hazardous to argue that the hoards were deposited immediately after the date of the latest coin in them. Even if the hoards were Italian, all we could say is that the group *as a whole* is likely to have been deposited by the mid or late 60s.[38] In the case of Dacia, we perhaps have a time-lag for travel to reckon with as well.[39]

If we may with all due caution posit a beginning to the massive import of Republican denarii into the lower Danube basin from the mid or late 60s onwards, an anomalous and unique phenomenon, as I have already remarked, as well as a sudden one, I cannot think of any satisfactory explanation except in terms of the slave trade, forced in the

---

35 See G.T. Griffith, *Mercenaries of the Hellenistic World* (Cambridge, 1935), 234–5, for the limited use by Rome of mercenaries.
36 *Dacia* 18, 1974, 147, 'A propos des monnaies frappées par Marc-Antoine', esp. nn.52–5 for earlier bibliography.
37 The attempt to refute the argument that worn legionary coins found in Dacia perhaps arrived long after 31 by asserting that worn dies gave the coins a worn appearance from the outset betrays total unfamiliarity with the non-Dacian material.
38 The general methodological point is made quite correctly by M. Babeş, *Dacia* 19, 1975, 125, 'Problèmes de la chronologie de la culture géto-dace', at 132–3 and 139, n.61.
39 Assertions to the contrary without supporting evidence are valueless, as by M. Chiţescu, (n.36), 153.

immediate aftermath of the victorious campaigns of Cn. Pompeius against the pirates in 67 to find an alternative source of supply for Rome and Italy outside the Greco-Macedonian Mediterranean world. The problem was no doubt exacerbated by the fact that not only did 67 see a virtual end to the kidnapping and slave-raiding organised by the pirates, but 63 saw the inclusion within the Roman empire of vast territories which thereby theoretically ceased to be available as sources for the supply of slaves. Caesar's razzias in Gaul (see p.214) did not begin until 58. Italy had also of course in any case suffered severe *losses* of slave manpower in the revolt of Spartacus.

It should not of course be assumed that denarii were the only object imported into the lower Danube basin in exchange for slaves, though it is precisely their massive import from the middle of the first century onwards that is, I think, best explained in terms of a phenomenon such as the slave trade, the scale of which is attested in general terms by Strabo's famous account of Delos.[40] One may suppose that traditional imports into the Black Sea area, such as the wine and oil recorded by Polybius, also came in exchange for slaves; in support one may draw attention to the account of trade in Gaul preserved by Diodorus, where Italian traders take wine to Gaul and exchange a jar of wine for a slave (p.169).

In Dacia, as perhaps also to a limited extent in Gaul, we have a local aristocracy selling perhaps its own humble dependents and certainly the humble dependents of others captured in internal raiding in exchange for the desirable products, from silver to wine, of the Mediterranean world;[41] contact with that world was leading a barbarian elite to define its status in terms of the possession of things presumably perceived as among the characteristic goods of civilisation.[42]

The Black Sea area as a whole is reasonably well documented as a source of slaves. They are highlighted by Polybius among the five commodities exported by the Black Sea area,[43] and M.I. Finley was able to show that there was just enough evidence for an earlier period to show a consistent pattern.[44] I should argue that imports of silver

---

40 Strabo xiv, 5, 2 (668). For Roman involvement on Delos, see p.125. There is a casual mention of slaves at I. Glodariu (n.33), 56.

41 Endemic raiding might indeed help to explain the non-recovery of the large number of Dacian hoards which now form the material for study; the retainers who helped carry it out no doubt received Republican denarii as a status-enhancing reward.

42 I note in passing that, *grosso modo*, amphoras and pots (and their imitations) predominate outside the mountains which surround Transylvania, silver-ware, bronze-ware and coins (and their imitations) predominate within; there is not enough evidence for glass-ware and other assorted objects to detect a pattern; see I.

Glodariu (n.33), summarised in *Crisia* (Oradea) 1, 1972, 45, 'Importuri elenistice-italice (200 BC – AD 100)'. I suppose the difference to correspond to a difference of fashion; within the mountains one threw silver around, without them one got drunk. Burebista eventually attempted to ban wine, Strabo vii, 3, 1, (303–4), and he may also have tried to stop or reduce the slave trade.

43 Polybius iv, 38, 4–5; 50, 2–4; see Strabo xi, 2, 3 (493) for the Crimea, with slaves and skins going one way, clothing and wine the other way. Polybius, with Strabo vii, 4, 6 (311), shows that corn was no longer in the Hellenistic period a major export of the Black Sea area.

44 See App. R.

into the lower Danube basin in the Hellenistic period reflect in part the trade in slaves; knowledge of this trade then suggested in and after 67 to some merchants (whose identity remains unknown) the solution to the problem posed by the suppression of piracy; the result was presumably the substantial monopolisation of the trade by the western market.[45]

The nature of the evidence does not make it possible to point to an upsurge of slaves from the lower Danube basin in the last years of the Republic; one can only draw attention to the fact of their existence. Even if it is not possible to say whether or not the Thracians attested are to be taken as including peoples from further north,[46] Dacians are amply attested at Rome under the early Empire; one even appears under Augustus in Africa.[47]

If it is true that the Roman world moved to replace a lost source for the supply of slaves after 67, it follows that the world was not in any sense glutted with slaves despite the mass enslavements of Cimbri and Teutones and by Sulla in the east, and despite the long-term effects of piracy in producing slaves.[48] Strong demand for slaves in the Roman world in this period is also to be inferred from the lists of Delphic manumissions; foreign slaves seem progressively to disappear over the period from the second century into the first,[49] and the mean release price of an adult male slave rises over the same period.[50] The last generation of the Roman Republic is probably a period of increase in the size of great estates;[51] stable or increasing demand in Italy for slaves over the same period would be no surprise. It is perhaps reasonable to suggest that the *relative* infrequency in the lower Danube basin of coin hoards closing with coins of the 50s is to be connected with the availability of slaves from Caesar's razzias in Gaul,[52] perhaps also with a decision of Burebista to conserve manpower; the penetration of coins of the 40s and 30s into Romania is again on a massive scale.

It is unfortunately not possible to calculate other than very roughly what proportion

---

45 Contact between Italy and the lower Danube basin seems to have been relatively direct, presumably by sea; the maps published by I. Glodariu as pls xii, xiii, xiv show the coins of Macedonia Prima and Thasos on the one hand and of the Republic on the other hand spreading out from the lower Danube; by way of contrast, the coins of Dyrrachium and Apollonia seem to come overland from the west (p.224).

46 See M. Bang, *MDAI(R)* 1910, 223, 'Die Herkunft der römischen Sklaven', esp. 226; G.G. Mateescu, *Eph.Dac.* 1923, 57, 'I Traci nelle epigrafi di Roma', esp. 77ff. for freedmen; M.L. Gordon, *JRS* 1924, 93, 'The nationality of slaves under the early Roman Empire', is a – for our purposes – inconclusive study of nomenclature.

47 See M. Bang, 237 and 230 (*CIL* vi, 7407). The evidence of slave nationality at Laurium is trivial in bulk for this period.

48 See *Ec.Hist.Rev.* 1977, 42, 'Rome and the Greek world: economic relationships', also p.173.

49 W.L. Westermann, *The Slave Systems of Greek and Roman Antiquity* (Philadelphia, 1955), 33.

50 Keith Hopkins, *Conquerors and Slaves* (Cambridge, 1978), 158.

51 See P.A. Brunt, *Italian Manpower* (Oxford, 1971), 301–5; *Latomus* 1975, 619, 'Two great Roman landowners'.

52 W.L. Westermann (n.49), 63, playing down the numbers involved. Precise calculations are speculative.

of the Republican denarii which travelled to Romania is represented by the 25,000 now known. Some hazardous calculations may, however, perhaps be suggestive. If one assumes that one coin in a thousand from an original population may survive, one would have a total of 25,000,000 Republican denarii once circulating in Dacia. There is of course no way of knowing the number of denarii exported to Dacia and instantly melted down because of the special circumstances obtaining there (see above). As a pure hypothesis, one might suggest a total of 50,000,000 denarii once exported to Dacia. One might then hypothesise that a very low sum was paid for a slave at the point of original purchase, comparing the amphora of wine paid for a slave in Gaul, say 50 denarii. Republican denarii exported to Dacia between the mid-60s and 30 might then account for something approaching 30,000 slaves per year. This is a substantial part of the annual requirement of Italy, if one assumes a total slave population of 2,000,000 and an annual requirement of 50,000 by purchase and 50,000 by breeding.

Precise tabulation of Imperial hoards in Romania is not possible for much of the period, since many of the terminal coins are not so precisely datable as is the case with the Republican coinage. But some flow of Roman coins into Dacia continued right down to the conquest of Dacia by Trajan.[53]

It is also possible that the beginning of the principate sees the extension to other areas of a phenomenon peculiar to the lower Danube basin under the Republic. The export of silver coins beyond the Rhine and Danube has been documented by Cosmo Rodewald;[54] Strabo's account of Aquileia leaves no doubt about the importance of slaves among the commodities that came from the north.[55] I suggest that they formed the main commodity in exchange for which silver coins under the Empire passed beyond the northern frontiers.

It is then a possible corollary of this thesis, if true, that one can no longer use one of the arguments for supposing a shift from slavery to tenancy as a mode of production on Italian estates in the early Empire, namely the disappearance of a major source of slaves without any alternative source being found.[56]

The conquest of the lands south of the Danube which were not like central Dalmatia, Macedonia and Greece already under Roman control in the age of Caesar happened with surprising speed. Siscia in the valley of the Sava was seized by Octavian in 35–33.

---

53 C. Rodewald, *Money in the Age of Tiberius* (Manchester, 1976), 45: 24 hoards altogether, closing with Augustus, 3 between Tiberius and Nero, 13 between Vespasian and the conquest. These hoards of course contain some Republican denarii; there is no way of knowing whether any of these came in with the Imperial denarii or not.
54 C. Rodewald, 32–4, for coins crossing the Rhine probably under the Julio-Claudians; 34–7, for coins crossing the Upper Danube under the Flavians.
55 Strabo v, 1, 8 (214); there is no further information in S. Panciera, *Vita economica di Aquileia in età romana* (Aquileia, 1957), 82. Note that Corsica was still a source of (bad) slaves in Strabo's day, v, 2, 7 (224).
56 *Contra*, for instance, N. Brockmeyer, *Arbeitsorganisation und ökonomisches Denken in der Gutswirtschaft des römischen Reiches* (Diss. Bochum, 1968), 152–3.

We hear of M. Licinius Crassus campaigning in the valley of the Morava in 29–28 and apparently pacifying it; at any rate, although we sometimes later hear of troops there, apparently under the control of the governor of Macedonia, we hear of no further fighting; the area became in due course the province of Moesia (Superior), with its first governor attested under Tiberius.[57]

Between 13 and 11 a rising of the Bessi overwhelmed the friendly kingdom of Thrace; it was suppressed, and between 13 and 9 the whole of the area between Thrace and Noricum was subdued, beginning with the seizure of Sirmium in 13, perhaps from the south.[58] The great rebellion of AD 6–9 involved attacks on the coastal cities of Salona and Apollonia, but with its suppression the whole area was definitively secured for Rome.

In the area covered by present-day Jugoslavia, one can see the penetration of Roman coinage following in the wake of the penetration of the Roman armies (Map 32); hoards appear on the route from Aquileia to Carnuntum, at Celeia, Poetovio and Emona (*RRCH* 462, 492, 536; see *ILLRP* 33–4 for a late Republican *vicus* at Nauportus); a hoard closing in 31 appears at Sisak (ancient Siscia) (Mirnik 85), an Augustan hoard at Gomolava near Sirmium (Mirnik 61a); hoards continue to come from the central Dalmatian coast and the immediate hinterland; and a hoard of fifty-three pieces from Valpovo, near modern Osijek, in the Illyrian interior, marks the beginning of the penetration of Roman coinage deep inland from the Dalmatian coast (*RRCH* 547).

Two further points call for comment. First, when the subsequent penetration of Roman coinage into Pannonia occurred, it seems to have been able to build on the pre-Roman coinage of the area, the 'denarii' produced by the Celtic Eravisci in the area north-east of Sisak in the middle of the first century.[59] Second, although the details escape us, it is clear that an oppressive fiscal regime was instituted in the newly conquered inland areas, resentment at which underlay the revolt of AD 6–9 (Dio lvi, 16, 3). The suppression of the revolt was followed by the beginning of the exploitation of the gold mines in Dalmatia (Florus ii, 25 (iv, 12) 12).

The monetary history of the kingdom of Thrace is both different and more complex. The pattern of circulation of Republican denarii south of the Danube, apart from a small area near the Danube itself, was quite different from the pattern in Dacia. What we see in Thrace is not a massive penetration in and after the 60s, but a slow penetration in the years after Caesar. It seems to me that this penetration represents the slow monetisation of the area in the general context of a process of Romanisation. For the

---

57 A. Mocsy, *Pannonia and Upper Moesia* (London, 1974), ch. 1; F. Papazoglou, *The Central Balkan Tribes in Pre-Roman Times* (Amsterdam, 1978), cover this area.

58 R. Syme, *CAH* X, 356–7.

59 For the 'denarii' of the Eravisci, see P. Popović, *NK* 1973–74, 7, 'Hoard of imitations of the Roman Republic denars'; A. Mocsy (n.57), 56–7; K. Biró-Sey, *9 Cong.Num.*, 503, 'Münzverkehr in Pannonien', both dating the 'denarii' too late. 'Denarii' of the Eravisci and Roman denarii occur together in the Bia, Nagykagya and Lagymanyos hoards (*RRCH* 370, 411, 510).

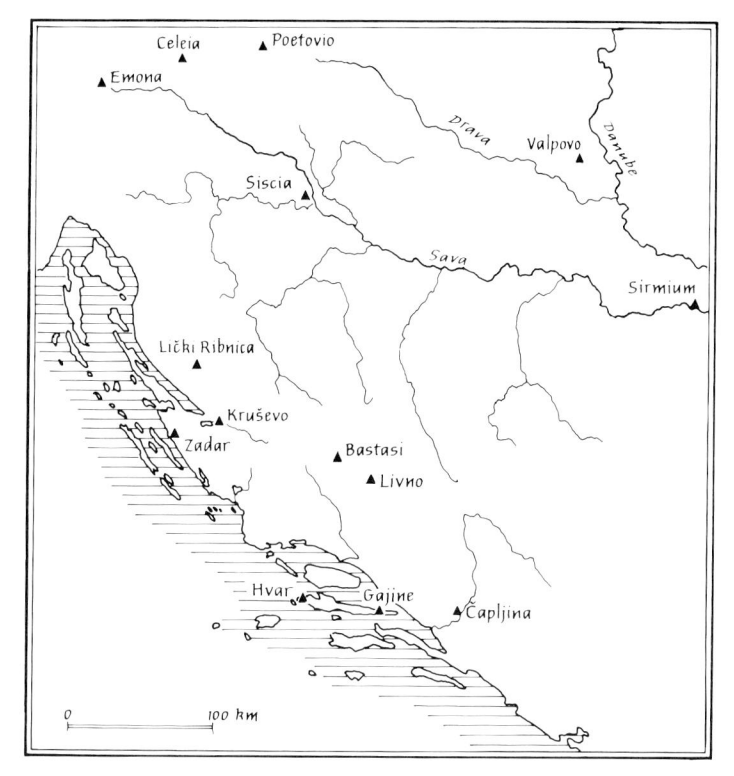

32   Hoards of Augustan denarii in Illyria

See p.236 and Mirnik 68 (Licki Ribnik), 66 (Kruševo), 45 (Bastasi), 69 (Livno), *AIIN* 1971–2, 128 (Zadar), *Archiv für Österreichische Geschichte* 23, 1865, 135 and 142 (Hvar), Mirnik 61 (Gajine), 51 (Capljina)

96   The coinage of Koson

Gold piece of Koson:
   Consul between two lictors l.; on l., monogram; in exergue, ΚΟΣΩΝ/Eagle on sceptre with wreath   Naville 5, 1718

97 The Roman coinage of Thrace

Bronze of Rhoemetalces I:
  Bare head of Augustus r.; around, ΚΑΙΣΑΡΟΣ ΣΕΒΑΣΤΟΥ/Head of Rhoemetalces r., hair tied with ribbon; around, ΒΑΣΙ[ΛΕΩΣ ΡΟΙ]ΜΕΤΑΛΚΟΥ   BM cast

area had already been characterised by the production of a sequence of issues of named and often recognisable rulers and in one case of the Odrysae as a people, from the beginning of the Hellenistic period onwards:

Scostocus	Silver	Bronze
Odrysae		Bronze
Cavarus	Silver	Bronze
Adaeus		Bronze
SECOND CENTURY		
Cotys		Bronze
Mostis	Silver	Bronze
FIRST CENTURY		
Cotys (57–48)	Silver (imitations of Thasos)	Bronze
Sadalas		Bronze
Cotys with Rhaescuporis		Bronze

In contrast to some other areas of the northern barbarian world, in Thrace the process of state formation had clearly produced fiscal structures capable of sustaining complex coinages, with a variety of denominations. A remarkable issue of gold staters, imitated from the denarii of M. Brutus (*RRC*, no. 433/1), may serve as a measure of the difference between Thrace and Dacia. Showy and useless, it was probably produced in the area of modern Transylvania in the second half of the first century (Fig. 96).[60]

60 Y. Youroukova, *Coins of the Ancient Thracians* (Oxford, 1976), 26 and 40; M.A. Halévy, *Stud.Clas*. 1961, 89, 'A propos du statère avec la légende ΚΟΣΩΝ', with earlier bibliography, rejecting any connection with a man called Cotiso attested south of the Danube; I. Winkler, *SCIV* 1972, 173, 'Consideraţii despre moneda "Koson"'.

The monetary patterns of Thrace in the Hellenistic period in due course combined with the Roman model, familiar from the denarii circulating in the country, to produce the coinage of Rhoemetalces I, a denarius coinage with subsidiary bronze (Fig. 97); the latter was produced on a very large scale, as a recent hoard makes clear (*Coin Hoards* 3, 85).[61] His kingdom, however, never achieved stability after his death in AD 12, and was finally made a province in AD 45–6.[62]

61 Compare the hoards from Gruevo (with one Tiberian piece of Mytilene), Plovdiv, Kardjalii, Erma Reka, Y. Youroukova (n.60), 61 and 63 (attributing some issues of Rhoemetalces I to Rhoemetalces II).

62 M.P. Charlesworth, *CAH* X, 645–6; R. Syme, ibid., 806–7.

16

THE END OF THE FREE STATE

The economic history of the late Republic, along with its history in general, is better known than that of any other period of antiquity; whence a need for care to avoid falling into the supposition that a practice attested for the first time is necessarily therefore new. It does seem possible to draw attention, however, to some new and important aspects of the monetary history of the age of Cicero.

First and foremost, the consequences of the staggering rise in the volume of coinage in circulation which we have already considered (p.177). The Roman aristocracy had become dangerously dependent on access to coined money: they needed it to pay for the luxuries that had become an indispensable part of their life-style, and indeed it is precisely in the late Republic that we find an awareness of a rise in prices, at any rate for luxury items, brought about by a combination of insatiable demand and high liquidity;[1] the Roman aristocracy also needed money for the bribery that had become part of the normal practice of political life.

The only problem was that despite the achievement of a certain sophistication in the handling of money, the Romans were unable to guarantee the maintenance of the level of liquidity to which they had become accustomed. This emerges only too clearly from the debt crisis which underlay the conspiracy of Catiline in 63. We have already seen (p.193) that the 80s and 70s were periods when substantial numbers of large hoards were buried and not recovered. The resulting loss of liquidity was then not made good

---

[1] Ath. vi, 274e–275a; much information on prices seems to have been assembled by Varro, whence it passed to Verrius Flaccus and so to Pliny; see in general, Cl. Nicolet, *Annales* 1971, 1203, 'Les variations des prix'; M.H. Crawford, ibid., 1228, 'Le problème des liquidités'; and, importantly, A. Früchtle, *Die Geldgeschäfte bei Cicero* (Erlangen, 1912), 68–92.

in the 60s; the 70s and 60s were indeed, as we have already seen, periods of small issues, the result of the financial difficulties in which Rome found herself between the Social War and the eastern conquests of Pompey. The squeeze on debtors which was the necessary consequence of the drop in liquidity led eventually to the explosion of 63. And however much Cicero might vaunt himself on his suppression of the conspiracy of Catiline, it was the rise in liquidity which followed the eastern conquests of Pompey that restored stability, at any rate for a time; the outbreak of civil war in 49 and again after 44 saw further debt crises.[2]

I have spoken of a certain sophistication in the handling of money in the age of Cicero; the financing of an empire with still a range of diverse systems of reckoning is perhaps sufficient justification for this remark; for it is clear that private individuals could move their wealth from one monetary zone to another without moving coin as easily as the state could transfer its revenues.[3] It is also interesting that when Cicero referred in court (*pro Quinctio* 17) to the procedure for the settlement of debts devised by the praetor Gratidianus (p.191), he did so in a brief, allusive sentence which assumed that his hearers knew exactly what he was talking about.

The widespread evidence from the Ciceronian period for the testing of coins to see if they were plated also deserves consideration. The term *nummularius* need mean no more than banker; but it is likely that one of the functions of a *nummularius* was *spectatio*, the testing of coins, alluded to by Plautus (*Persa* 437) and Cicero (*II in Verr.* 3, 181); it is surely legitimate to suppose that the *nummularii* who are epigraphically attested were engaged *inter alia* in the testing of coins.[4]

The testing of coins was also undertaken by slaves, whose record survives in the *tesserae* which they attached to bags of coins. These *tesserae* normally give name of slave, name of owner, statement of *spectatio* and date, as in *ILLRP* 1002: Piloxen(us) soc(iorum) fer(rariarum) (servus) C. Coil(io) L. Dom(itio) (94 BC) spectavit n(onis) Apr(ilibus). Such men worked for companies, as in this example, for men of business, as in a recently discovered *tessera* (55 BC) of a slave belonging to a Veveius, attested by amphora stamps from the Madrague de Giens wreck, for rich Romans in general.[5]

The world of the late Republic was changed out of all recognition and for ever when Caesar crossed the Rubicon in the course of the winter 50/49. From the beginning of his rebellion, he struck his own coinage in enormous quantities, as an authority

---

2 On the background to the conspiracy of Catiline, see M.H.Crawford (n.1); I now incline to hold that *in Vat.* 12 does record a ban on the export of gold and silver from Italy in 63, in order to prevent a further reduction in liquidity; on later debt crises, M.W. Frederiksen, *JRS* 1966, 128, 'Caesar, Cicero and the problem of debt'.

3 *Ad Att.* v, 13, 2; 15, 2; xi, 1, 2; xv, 15, 4; *ad Q. fr.* i, 3, 7; *ad fam.* iii, 5, 4; contrast the practice cited on p.174, n.3.

4 *ILLRP* 106a (Praeneste); *ILS* 7262 (Antium); *ILS* 7463 (*ager Pomptinus*); *CIL* x, 5689 (Cereatae); for analogous banking activity on Delos, see R. Bogaert, *Banques et Banquiers* (Leiden, 1968), 174–5.

5 R. Herzog, *RE* xvii, 1415, 'Nummularius'; P. Pensabene, *Arch.Laziale* 2, 1979, 70.

98   The issues of Caesar during the First Civil War

Denarius of Caesar, *RRC*, no. 443/1:
  Pontifical implements/Elephant r. trampling dragon; in exergue, CAESAR   Oxford
Denarius of Caesar, *RRC*, no. 452/2:
  Diademed female head r. wearing oak-wreath; behind, LII/Gallic trophy; on r.,
  pontifical axe; below, CAESAR   Oxford
Denarius of Caesar, *RRC*, no. 458/1:
  Diademed head of Venus r./Aeneas r. carrying Anchises and *palladium*; on r.,
  CAESAR   Oxford
Denarius of Caesar, *RRC*, no. 467/1a:
  Head of Ceres r.; on l., COS.TERT; on r., DICT.ITER/Pontifical and augural
  implements; on r., D; above, AVGVR; below, PONT.MAX   Oxford
Denarius of Caesar, *RRC*, no. 468/1:
  Diademed head of Venus r.; behind, Cupid/Gallic trophy with captives below; in
  exergue, CAESAR   Oxford
Denarius of Caesar, *RRC*, no. 468/2:
  Diademed head of Venus l.; before, *lituus* and Cupid; behind, sceptre/Gallic trophy with
  captives below; in exergue, CAESAR   *BMCRR* Spain 87

99   The gold issue of A. Hirtius

Aureus of A. Hirtius, *RRC*, no. 466/1:
  Veiled female head r.; on l., C.CAESAR; on r., COS.TER/*Lituus*, jug and axe; on l.,
  A.HIRTIVS.PR   Oxford

100   The bronze issue of C. Clovius

Dupondius of C. Clovius, *RRC*, no. 476/1a:
  Bust of Victory r.; before, CAESAR.DIC.TER/Minerva walking l.; before, snake and
  C.CLOVI; behind, PRAEF   *BMCRR* Rome 4125

independent of and parallel to that of the state; the first issue, of denarii, bore the emblems of the pontificate on the obverse, an elephant trampling a dragon on the reverse, with the simple legend CAESAR (Fig. 98).

From this point on there is a near continuous sequence of Caesarian issues down to 44; these issues consisted not simply of denarii, but also of the first large gold issues ever produced at Rome; they were presumably, though not certainly, tariffed at the Augustan level of 1 aureus to 25 denarii; the largest was produced for Caesar by A. Hirtius (Fig. 99).[6]

Perhaps more remarkable is the fact that Caesar was also, through C. Clovius, responsible for the resumption of the production of a base metal coinage (Fig. 100). The issue consisted of a single denomination, in orichalcum; given their weight, the pieces are probably dupondii. The demands of military finance may be surmised as the underlying reason for the issue; what is interesting is the choice of orichalcum. This metal was perhaps first used for coinage by Mithridates VI in Pontus (p.196); its use became widespread in Phrygia, perhaps also in Mysia, in the age of Cicero, and spread to Bithynia by 47. The notion of using orichalcum for one of a range of denominations existed already at Apamea in Phrygia in the period between 75 and 67, and it may be that the entire notion of using orichalcum for a double unit was taken over from there by Caesar.[7]

Caesar was not the only military leader to strike his own coinage in this period; military issues were produced by or for Pompey and his supporters, not including gold,

---

6 A moment's glance at the context suffices to show that Suetonius, *Caes.* 54, is worthless as evidence for the gold:silver ratio in this period.

7 P.T. Craddock et al. (p.196, n.3).

101 The issues of Pompey

Denarius of Q. Sicinius and C. Coponius, *RRC*, no. 444/1a:
  Head of Apollo r., hair tied with ribbon; below, star; before, Q.SICINIVS; behind, III.VIR/Club and lion-skin; on r., bow and C.COPONIVS; on l., arrow and PR.S.C.
  Oxford

Denarius of L. Lentulus and C. Marcellus, *RRC*, no. 445/2:
  Head of Apollo r.; before, L.LENT.C.MARC (in monogram); behind, COS/Jupiter facing; on l., Q and star; on r., altar   Oxford

Denarius of Cn. Piso, *RRC*, no. 446/1:
  Head of Numa r.; behind, CN.PISO.PRO.Q/Prow r.; above, MAGN; below, PRO.COS
  Oxford

Denarius of Varro, *RRC*, no. 447/1a:
  Terminal bust of Jupiter r.; behind, VARRO.PRO.Q/Sceptre between dolphin and eagle; in exergue, MAGN.PRO
              COS   Oxford

but including three issues of asses (*RRC*, nos. 471, 478, 479) (Fig. 101). After the death of Caesar, almost all the contenders for power struck their own coinage, in one or more metals.

The consequences for the mint of Rome of the outbreak of civil war were threefold: since Caesar was able to seize Rome at a very early stage of the war, the regular moneyers' issues came in effect to be *his* issues. What is more, their typology came increasingly to reflect Caesarian concerns, until the issues of 44 used his portrait to reflect the *de facto* position of sole ruler which he had achieved (Fig. 102). (For reasons which are not apparent, Caesar also raised the number of moneyers from three to four.) Finally, not surprisingly, it appears that the fineness of the denarius was reduced by about 2 per cent.[8]

8 D.R. Walker (p.33, n.11), 64.

102 The issues of Caesar as dictator

Denarius of L. Aemilius Buca, *RRC*, no. 480/6:
   Head of Caesar r. wearing triumphal wreath; before, CAESAR.DICT; behind, PERPETVO/Fasces on caduceus; above, globe; on l., clasped hands; below, axe; on r., L.BVCA   *BMCRR* Rome 4158
Denarius of M. Mettius, *RRC*, no. 480/17:
   Head of Caesar r. wearing triumphal wreath; before, CAESAR; behind, IMPER/Venus Victrix l.; behind, M.METTIVS; before, control-letter   Oxford

Meanwhile, the different parts of the empire were inexorably drawn into the struggle for its mastery, as spectators, sufferers, participants, and in addition in some cases as producers of coinage. It is likely that the last issues of drachms of Apollonia and Dyrrhachium were evoked by the civil war, those of Apollonia struck first for Pompey, then for Caesar after the town went over to him, those of Dyrrachium for Pompey. Three hoards are now known from the area which reflect the violent events of these years (*IGCH* 665–7). At the same time, one issue of Roman denarii was struck at Apollonia (*RRC*, no. 445/1–2), by the Pompeian quaestor T. Antistius (Cicero, *ad fam.* xiii, 29, 4). At some point during the wars of the age of revolution, Apollonia itself actually struck a small issue of denarii (and fractions).

The case of Thessaly is even more striking; we hear from Caesar (*BC* iii, 80, 3) of a *praetor Thessaliae* called Androsthenes, who supported Pompey; his staters should be regarded as struck in the same cause. The other two Thessalians mentioned by Caesar, his enemy Hegesaretus and his friend Petraeus (*BC* iii, 35, 2), also produced staters in this general period, and it may be that much of the last flurry of Thessalian silver coinage belongs in the context of civil war (Fig. 103). One hoard, from Aidona, contains examples of these issues, with Roman denarii (*IGCH* 351).

In Asia Minor, also, there are coinages which may be regarded as evoked by the preparations of Pompey for resistance against Caesar; perhaps in the province of Asia, where Teos struck reduced-weight Attic drachms in the middle of the first century, Smyrna Attic tetradrachms and drachms, Priene and Chios Attic drachms, though some or all of these issues may belong earlier or even later; certainly in Lycia, whence a substantial problem.

Lycian silver coinage of Rhodian weight came to an end around the time of the First

103   The coinage of the First Civil War in Greece

Stater of Thessaly:
Laureate head of Jupiter r./Athena r.; on l., ΘΕΣΣΑ; on r., ΛΩΝ; above, ΚΥΛΛΟΥ;
below, ΠΕΤΡΑΙΟΣ   Lockett 1623

Mithridatic War; and although Lycia was declared free by Rome in the 80s, silver coinage was not resumed. When it was resumed, it consisted not of local denominations, but of quinarii and sestertii; this despite the fact that Lycia remained formally free till AD 43.[9] The precise occasion of the resumption of coinage in Lycia is not absolutely certain, but it is likely that Lycia was forced to this step by Pompey or Caesar. Certainly the second series of the new model coinage is contemporary with Brutus (see p.251); certainly also Lycia was among the places where Pompey and Caesar raised fleets (Cicero, *ad Att.* ix, 9, 2; [Caesar], *Bell. Alex.* 13). Obviously the choice of denominations may be seen simply as another aspect of the influence of Pompey or Caesar; but I do not think one should exclude the hypothesis that in insisting on it they were appealing to a regulation which was part of the package of measures contemporary with A. Gabinius to which I have already referred (p.209). The new model coinage of Lycia was doubtless used to pay for Lycian soldiers or sailors, rather than handed over directly to one or other of the dynasts. It is noteworthy that the cities which struck the new model Lycian coinage from the beginning were Masicytus and Cragus, which became the centres for the collection of taxes by the Romans when Lycia became a province (Fig. 104).

Apart from restoring Cyprus to Egypt and thus to Cleopatra in 48, Caesar made few administrative changes in the east.[10] In the west, the civil war brought about the incorporation of much of Numidia into the Roman empire. Juba I of Numidia was rash enough to throw in his lot with the Pompeians and indeed struck denarii in much larger

---

9 H. Troxell, *The Coinage of the Lycian League* (New York, 1982), 173–83; but Appian, *BC* i, 102, 474–5, is *not* precisely anchored chronologically and cannot be used to argue that Lycia paid tax from 81, any more than it can be used to argue that Sicily was attacked by Mithridates, *contra* pp.116–17.

10 I. Nicolaou and O. Mørkholm (p.206, n.18), 19, for the mint at Paphos and its issues for Cleopatra.

quantities than they did in order to support their cause. These denarii mark, of course, the entry of Numidia into the Roman monetary system; it is interesting that they turn up in Italian and other western hoards into the reign of Augustus (Fig. 105).

After the battle of Thapsus, Caesar naturally realised the cash value of Juba I's possessions; he also dealt with the *vectigalia regia* ([Caes.], *Bell. Afr.* 97). It is unfortunately not clear what form of taxation Caesar imposed on that part of Numidia which was annexed, since the revenues in oil and corn of which Plutarch speaks (*Caes.* 55) *may* all be accounted for by the punishments imposed on Leptis, Thysdrus

104 The coinage of Lycia

Quinarius of Cragus, Troxell, Series 1:
  Laureate head of Apollo r.; on either side, Λ Y/Cithara; on either side, K P; all in incuse square   Naville 1, 2772
Quinarius of Masicytus, Troxell, Series 4:
  Head of Apollo r., hair tied with ribbon/Cithara; above, ΛYKIΩN; on either side, M A
  Σ I; all in incuse square   Locker Lampson 333
Quinarius of Cragus, Troxell, Series 5:
  Laureate head of Apollo r.; on either side, Λ Y/Cithara; on either side, K P; on l., corn-ear; all in incuse square   Naville 1, 2773
Quinarius of Masicytus, Troxell, Series 6:
  Laureate head of Apollo r.; on either side, Λ Y/Cithara; on either side, M A; on r., tripod; all in incuse square   Lockett 3010
Sestertius of Masicytus, Troxell, p.156:
  Head of Artemis r./Quiver; above, Λ Y; below, M A; on l., branch tied with fillet; all in incuse square   Lockett 3011
As of Masicytus, Troxell, Series E:
  Head of Apollo, r., hair tied with ribbon; on either side, Λ Y/Apollo Patroos facing; on either side, M A   BM cast

105 The issues of Juba I and the Pompeians

Denarius of Juba I:
   Bearded bust of Juba r. with sceptre over shoulder; before, REX IVBA/Temple   Paris

Denarius of Q. Metellus Pius, *RRC*, no. 459/1:
   Laureate head of Jupiter r.; above, Q.METEL; below, PIVS/Elephant r.; above, SCIPIO; in exergue, IMP   Oxford

Denarius of Q. Metellus Pius, *RRC*, no. 460/3:
   Female head r. wearing turreted crown; on l., corn-ear; on r., caduceus; below, ram of ship; above, uncertain symbol; on r., CRASS.IVN; on l., LEG.PRO.PR/Trophy between *lituus* and jug; on r., METEL.PIVS; on l., SCIP.IMP   *BMCRR* Africa 6

Denarius of Q. Metellus Pius, *RRC*, no. 460/4:
   Lion-headed Genius terrae Africae holding sign of Tanit; above, G.T.A; on r., Q.METEL.PIVS; on l., SCIPIO.IMP/Victory standing and holding caduceus in r. hand and *patera* in l. hand; on r., P.CRASSVS.IVN; on l., LEG.PRO.PR
    BMCRR Africa 8

Denarius of M. Cato, *RRC*, no. 462/1b:
   Draped female bust r., hair tied with ribbon; behind, ROMA (in monogram); before, M.CATO.PRO.PR/Victory seated r.; in exergue, VICTRIX (in monogram)   Oxford

Denarius of Q. Metellus Pius, *RRC*, no. 461/1:
   Head of Africa r.; on r., Q.METELL; on l., SCIPIO.IMP/Hercules facing; on r., EPPIVS; on l., LEG.F.C.   Oxford

Quinarius of M. Cato, *RRC*, no. 462/2:
   Head of Liber r. wearing ivy-wreath; below, M.CATO.PRO.PR (in monogram)/Victory seated r.; in exergue, VICTRIX (in monogram)   ANS, HSA 10500

and perhaps other towns. However, the completeness of the eventual insertion of North Africa into the monetary structures of the Roman world emerges from the fact that Mauretania to the west, which acquired some Numidian territory and which remained independent till AD 40, struck denarii and quinarii, with a bewildering variety of types. It is probably at this stage that Republican and early Imperial denarii arrived in Mauretania (App. 42), perhaps with the veterans settled there by Augustus between 33 and 25.[11] Graffiti from the Magdalensberg (p.278) perhaps record the presence of two traders from Volubilis.

106   The issues of 42

Aureus of L. Mussidius Longus, *RRC*, no. 494/13:
    Head of Lepidus l.; around, M.LEPIDVS.III.VIR.R.P.C/Cornucopiae; on l.,
    L.MVSSIDIVS; on r., LONGVS   *BMCRR* Rome 4232
Aureus of L. Mussidius Longus, *RRC*, no. 494/14:
    Head of Antony r.; around, M.ANTONIVS.III.VIR.R.P.C/Cornucopiae; on l.,
    L.MVSSIDIVS; on r., LONGVS   *BMCRR* Rome 4230
Aureus of Octavian, *RRC*, no. 494/15:
    Head of Octavian r.; around, C.CAESAR.III.VIR.R.P.C/Cornucopiae; on l.,
    L.MVSSIDIVS; on r., LONGVS   *BMCRR* Rome 4231

The uneasy calm which followed the murder of Caesar on 15 March 44 was broken by the unsuccessful attempt to eliminate Antony and by the agreement between Antony, Octavian and Lepidus at the end of 43. Caesar had in effect created a fiscal structure parallel to that of the state and had in due course come to control that of the state as if it were his own (Suet., *Caes.* 76). With his death, existing resources and incoming revenues fell almost exclusively to one or another of the military dynasts contending for power (note Plutarch, *Ant.* 21 for the overall control of Antony, Octavian and Lepidus over the finances of Rome). The regular moneyers of 42 produced a large coinage on behalf of Antony, Octavian and Lepidus (Fig. 106), but within a couple of years the dynasts had ceased to bother with the coinage of the moneyers and simply

---

11 N. Mackie, *Historia* 1983, 332, 'Augustan colonies in Mauretania'.

107   The coinage of the dynasts

Denarius of Lepidus and Octavian, *RRC*, no. 495/2a:
  Head of Lepidus r.; around, LEPIDVS.PONT.MAX.III.V.R.P.C (in monogram)/Head
  of Octavian r.; around, CAESAR.IMP.III.VIR.R.P.C   *BMCRR* Africa 30
Denarius of Antony, *RRC*, no. 496/2:
  Head of Antony r.; behind, *lituus*/Head of Sol r.; around, M.ANTONIVS.III.VIR.R.P.C
                                                               BMCRR Gaul 88
Aureus of Octavian, *RRC*, no. 497/1:
  Head of Octavian r.; around, CAESAR.III.VIR.R.P.C/Equestrian statue l.; in exergue,
  ram of ship between S   C   *BMCRR* Gaul 95
Denarius of M. Brutus, *RRC*, no. 508/3:
  Head of Brutus r.; on l., L.PLAET.CEST; on r., BRVT.IMP/Cap of liberty between
  two daggers; below, EID.MAR   *BMCRR* East 68
Denarius of Q. Cornuficius, *RRC*, no. 509/2:
  Head of Jupiter Ammon l./Juno Sospita crowning Q. Cornuficius; around,
  Q.CORNVFICI.AVGVR.IMP   *BMCRR* Africa 26
Aureus of Sex.Pompey, *RRC*, no. 511/1:
  Head of Sex.Pompey r.; behind, MAG.PIVS; before IMP.ITER; all in oak-wreath/
  Facing heads of Pompey the Great and Cn.Pompey junior; on l., *lituus*; on r., tripod;
  above, PRAEF (in monogram); below, CLAS.ET.ORAE
              MARIT.EX.S.C (in monogram)
                                                              BMCRR Sicily 14

produced their own issues in their own name. After 40, there were only military issues until some years after Augustus had established himself in power (p.256).[12] Within this pattern, one difference between Antony and the eventual victor stands out: down to the end, the former associated the names of his lieutenants with his own on his coinage; after 38, the name of Octavian appears alone (Fig. 107).

12 See *RRC*, ch. 7.1 for the finances of the state in
    this period.

107   The coinage of the dynasts (*cont.*)

Denarius of Cn. Domitius Calvinus, *RRC*, no. 532/1:
   Male head r.; behind, OSCA/Pontifical implements; below, DOM.COS.ITER.IMP
   BMCRR Spain 109

Aureus of Octavian, *RRC*, no. 540/1:
   Head of Octavian r.; around, IMP.CAESAR.DIVI.F.III.VIR.ITER.R.P.C/ Temple with DIVO.IVL on architrave; on l., altar; around, COS.ITER.ET.TER.DESIG
   BMCRR Africa 32

Denarius of Antony, *RRC*, no. 542/1:
   Head of Antony r.; around, ANTON.AVG.IMP.III.COS.DES.III.III.V.R.P.C/ M.SILANVS.AVG
      Q.PRO.COS
   BMCRR East 176

Much of the coinage of the dynasts, like that of Caesar, was in gold and the emergence of this metal as a major element of the Roman monetary system emerges with great clarity from the casual nature of Cicero's reference to L. Antonius distributing *aurei nummi* to the soldiers late in 44 (*Phil.* xii, 20). The story of Augustus giving 40 aurei to each of his companions to spend on Alexandrian goods, because he was pleased with the greetings of the crew of an Alexandrian ship, paints a similar picture (Suet., *Aug.* 98).[13]

Meanwhile, in the east, Brutus and Cassius were assembling the human and financial resources for the struggle against the heirs of Caesar (Cicero, *ad fam.* xii, 14–15). Two hoards from Athens, which probably belong to 42 (*IGCH* 340, 341–3), were no doubt the property of conscript auxiliaries, students or tourists, who fell at Philippi. As for finance, the sack of Rhodes by Cassius and of Xanthos by Brutus or the demands of Cassius at Tarsus or in Judaea (Appian, *BC* iv, 64, 273; Josephus, *BJ* i, 220) were perhaps more typical than the gift by the widow of a Thracian king to Brutus of gold and silver, from which he struck coin (Appian, *BC* iv, 75, 320). With the example of Xanthos before them, Masicytus and Cragus struck for Brutus, as they had for Pompey or Caesar (p.246).

13   P. Veyne, *Annales* 1979, 211, 'Rome devant la prétendue fuite d'or', at 227, misreads the passage.

In general, however, even formally autonomous precious metal coinages in the Greek world were fast coming to an end, as kingdoms, tribes and cities saw their liquid resources seized by Rome. The two hoards from Athens which I have just mentioned are of bronze and few hoards of Greek precious metal coinage post-date the death of Caesar. One such, containing also denarii, comes from Hierapytna (*RRCH* 374; *Coin Hoards* 4, 76), no doubt lost when Antony recovered Crete from the man who was holding it for Brutus (Cicero, *Phil*. ii, 97; Appian, *BC* v, 2, 8).

For it is the period after the death of Caesar which sees the spread for the first time over almost the whole of the Greek east of issues of the mainstream coinage of Rome. A burial from Bestefeler in Turkey includes an aureus of Caesar of 46, a large hoard of aurei down to the late 30s from Antioch in Pisidia passed through the market in the 1970s, likewise a hoard of cistophori and denarii down to 41;[14] a hoard of denarii down to the late 30s from Asia Minor was shown to me at about the same time at the Archaeological Museum in Istanbul. This change in the pattern of monetary circulation in the east is the obvious consequence of the fact that the Liberators, Antony and Octavian all struck issues of denarii and associated denominations in Asia Minor. There is even an issue of aurei and denarii struck by Q. Labienus while leading a Parthian invasion of Asia Minor (*RRC*, no. 524). Only Syria and Egypt still remained outside the sphere where Roman mainstream issues circulated.

The money to pay for the Roman issues struck in the east after the defeat of the Liberators, and indeed probably for some issues struck in the west also, came from the exactions organised by Antony at Ephesus (Appian, *BC* v, 6, 26–7). The proceeds of these exactions went of course also to continue the cistophoric coinage of the province of Asia. For reasons which remain mysterious, an agent of Antony with the name of Kydas, from Gortyn, struck cistophori for Crete, using the title of ΚΡΗΤΑΡΧΑΣ (Svoronos 334, 1). On the whole, however, the influence of Antony on the structure of coinage in the east seems to have been minimal (Map 28),[15] though the types and legends on the issues struck there of course reflect his position and that of Cleopatra.

The lands granted to Cleopatra and her children at various stages seem to have been the following:

    Part of Crete   by 37
    (not Cnossus, where a Roman colony was later founded)
    Cyprus   by 19 November 38[16]
    Phoenicia

---

14 A. Oliver, *Getty Mus. Journ.* 8, 1980, 155, for the Bestefeler hoard; also for an aureus of Antony from an eastern burial (G. Kastner 4, 212); B. Overbeck, *SNR* 1978, 164, for the hoard of cistophori and denarii.

15 See A.M. Rouanet-Liesenfelt, in *Mélanges H. van Effenterre* (Paris, 1984), 343, 'Le crétarque Kydas'; note the arrival in Alexandria, apparently in this period, of Apulian amphorae, E.L. Will, *Yearbook Am.Phil.Soc.* 1962, 647, 'Latin stamped amphorae in the eastern Mediterranean area'.

16 I. Nicolaou and O. Mørkholm (p.206, n.18), 20; see in general Schürer[2] I, 288, n.5.

Coele Syria
Lands in Cilicia, Judaea and Arabia
Cyrenaica

The one possible case where Antony *may* have had some influence on the structure of the local coinage is that of Crete and Cyrenaica. At a certain point, issues on a Roman pattern began to be produced for the two provinces together, with a Greek legend for Cyrenaica and a Latin legend for Crete (Fig. 108):[17]

| L. Lollius | As, semis, quadrans | Uncial |
| Crassus | As, semis, quadrans | Semuncial |

These issues are followed by issues for Cyrenaica alone:

| A. Pupius Rufus | As, semis, quadrans | Semuncial |
| Antony and Cleopatra | As, semis | |

None of the people involved are known until we get to Antony and Cleopatra in 31. The other issues are certainly earlier (note also that another Kydas overstruck bronzes of Crassus when he produced bronze as a magistrate at Cnossus); but how much earlier? The only possible indication derives from the issue of P. Lepidus and P. Licinius, produced on Crete, but alluding by its types to the two provinces. It seems, like a somewhat earlier bronze issue of Roman Crete with the types Head of Roma/Bee, not to fit a Roman denominational structure;[18] it is presumably therefore to be placed before the issue of L. Lollius. If P. Lepidus is the officer of Brutus alluded to by Appian, *BC* v, 2, 8, the sequence of issues on a Roman model may be ascribed to the period of Antonian dominance.

The coinage of Egypt itself bore no allusion to Antony, naturally enough, while Cleopatra struck both silver and bronze in Alexandria, the latter with her portrait. Outside Egypt, however, the two appear as joint rulers of the east, notably on the tetradrachms of Roman Syria produced at Antioch and on a whole range of bronze issues of different cities under their sway: Ptolemais-Ace, Tripolis, Aradus, Balanea, Chalcis-ad-Libanum, Dora (?) (34/33), Cyrene.[19]

---

17 T.V. Buttrey, *Essays P. Grierson* (Cambridge, 1983), 23, 'Roman coinage of the Cyrenaica'; M.J. Price, *INJ* 1982–3, 118, on Crete, is lightweight.

18 A.E. Chapman, *NC* 1968, 13, 'Some bronze coins of Knossos', at 15, n.3; A.(E.) Jackson, *ABSA* 1971, 283, 'The chronology of the bronze coins of Knossos'.

19 O. Mørkholm, *Studia P. Naster* I (Louvain, 1982), 139, 'The Attic coin standard in the Levant during the Hellenistic period', on the tetradrachm issue at Antioch; S. Walker and A.M. Burnett (p.273, n.34), 33, n.2; H.R. Baldus, *JNG* 1973, 19, 'Ein neues Spätporträt der Cleopatra aus Orthosia'; *SM* 1983, 5, 'Eine Münzprägung auf das Ehepaar Mark Anton-Kleopatra VII'. The piece from Dora bears a mark of value of Egyptian type, Π; M. Amandry tells me that there is evidence for the transfer of Alexandrian mint-workers to Corinth. For Cyrene see T.V.Buttrey (n.17), esp. n.12.

108   The issues of Crete and Cyrenaica

Asses of L. Lollius:
   Male head r.; before, sceptre/Curule chair; above, ΛΟΛΛΙΟΥ   Oxford (obv.), BM (rev.)
   Male head r.; before, sceptre/Curule chair; above, L.LOLLIVS   BM
As of Antony·
   ΒΑΣΙΛ/ΑΝΤΩ
    ΘΕΑ/ΥΠΑ
     ΝΕ/Γ   BM
Semis of Antony with identical types   BM

Antony also struck while in the east a curious series of coins conventionally described as a 'Fleet coinage', by reason of its types. It was produced on his behalf by a group of lieutenants, some of it certainly in the Peloponnese. None of the issues seems to have been at all common; their principal interest lies in the fact that they covered the range from sestertius to quadrans, entirely in base metal. They thus anticipate by well over a decade the pattern of the reformed base metal coinage of Augustus (p.257) (Fig. 109).[20]

Perhaps the most striking feature, however, of the coinages of the years from 44 to 31 is the very high fineness maintained by almost all mainstream issues. It was only

---

20 M. Bahrfeldt, *NZ* 37, 1905, 9, 'Die Münzen der Flottenpräfekten des Marcus Antonius'; M. Amandry, *SM* 1983, 82, 'A propos du monnayage de L. Sempronius Atratinus'; *INJ* 1982–3, 1, 'Monnayages émis en Achaïe sous l'autorité d'Antoine'.

109   The issues of Antony and Cleopatra

'Fleet' sestertius of Antony and M. Oppius Capito:
  Facing heads of Antony and Octavia; around, M.ANT.IMP.TERT.COS.DESIG.ITER.
  ET.TERT.III.VIR.R.P.C (in monogram)
  Quadriga of sea-horses r.; on l., HS; below, Δ and rectangle   M. Amandry cast
'Fleet' dupondius of Antony and L. Bibulus:
  Facing heads of Antony and Octavia; around, M.ANT.IMP.TER.COS.DES.ITER.
  ET.TER.III.VIR.R.P.C (in monogram)/Two ships r.; on either side, caps of Dioscuri;
  below, B   M. Amandry cast
Drachm of Antony of Antioch:
  Head of Antony r./Head of Tyche r.; around, ΑΝΤΙΟΧΕΩΝ ΜΗΤΡΟΠΟΛΕΩΣ   BM
Bronze of Antony and Cleopatra perhaps of Dora:
  Jugate busts of Cleopatra and Antony r./Tyche standing l. holding caduceus in l. hand; on
  r., ΑΣΥ (lou), on l., L ΘΙ (Year 19)   SM 1983, 10

at the end, in his penultimate issue and in his final issue of legionary denarii, that Antony was obliged to reduce the percentage of silver to just over 90 per cent. The final conflict was in some contexts devastating in its consequences, witness the number of hoards closing with legionary denarii of Antony (see App. 55); but the monetary structures of the Roman Republic were still in surprisingly good shape, as the victor of Actium surveyed the world at his feet.

17

THE EMPEROR AUGUSTUS

The principal theme of this book so far has been the gradual creation of a single monetary system for the whole of the Roman world and, latterly, the increasing concentration of minting authority in the hands of military commanders and, eventually, of a single individual. Although there were some later developments, both processes were in all essentials complete by the end of the reign of Augustus.

Perhaps the most dramatic development was the emergence of Augustus as in effect the sole minting authority. As we have seen, the denarius, sometimes accompanied by the quinarius and the sestertius, was the standard coin of the Roman Republic from the middle of the second century; the aureus, occasionally accompanied by the half-aureus, was a normal component of the currency of the Roman world from the age of Caesar. Octavian struck both silver and gold unsystematically, but fairly continuously, from 43 down to 35; there then followed a group of issues, including denarius and aureus, with legends consisting of all or part of the title Imp. Caesar Divi f. Neither the relative chronology of the different issues nor their precise apportionment in the period from 34 to 30 is clear.[1] In 29 there begins a sequence of dated issues, none of them very large, the last of gold only, with Imp. VII (29), Cos. VI (28), Cos. VII (27) (Fig. 110).

At this point there is a break in the main sequence of the coinage of Augustus.[2] Dated issues appear again from 14, with Imp. X, but types referring to the Ludi

---

[1] C.H.V. Sutherland, *QTic* 1976, 129, 'Octavian's coinage from c.32 to 27 BC', mechanically assigns issues with Caesar Divi f. to before Actium, issues with Imp. Caesar to after.

[2] Augustus himself produced three small issues in the east, P.Carisius as his *legatus pro praetore* an issue in Spain.

110   The early issues of Augustus

Aureus of Octavian, *RIC* 268:
  Head of Octavian r./Victory standing facing on globe; on either side, IMP CAESAR
                                                                             Guzman Collection
Denarius of Octavian, *RIC* 266:
  Head of Octavian r./IMP.CAESAR on architrave of temple   BM cast
Aureus of Augustus, *RIC* 277:
  Head of Augustus r.; around, CAESAR.COS.VII.CIVIBVS.SERVATEIS/ Eagle on
  oak-wreath; above, AVGVSTVS; below, S C   Morcom Collection

Saeculares presumably belong in 17, types referring to the recovery from Parthia of the standards lost at the battle of Carrhae presumably belong in 19. It would in theory be possible to fill the years between 27 and 19 with a large group of undated issues, traditionally assigned to mints in Spain, but probably struck in Gallia Narbonensis or Lugdunensis. But die-links, similarities of legend and type, and stylistic associations make it clear that these undated issues also all belong in or after 19 (Fig. 111).[3]

It seems clear, therefore, that when Augustus handed back the *res publica* to senate and people in 27, he handed back also the right of coinage, the mark of a sovereign power, usurped in 43 and retained thereafter for seventeen revolutionary years. The resumption of the right of coinage in 19 formed part of the constitutional settlement of that year as described by Dio (liv, 10, 5–6), when Augustus acquired the right to sit between the two consuls of the year and to be preceded by twelve lictors and when he became a source of law, as were all later emperors after him.

But Augustus did more than become the central minting authority of the Roman world, he also completely reorganised the mainstream bronze coinage of Rome. When he resumed the production of coinage in 19, his aureus and denarius were of more or less the same weight and fineness as they had been earlier.[4] His bronze coinage was a radical innovation.

As we have seen, the Roman Republic produced no bronze coinage between Sulla

---

3   I owe this point to T.R. Volk.   4   H. Mattingly, *BMCRE* I, xliv–xlv; D.R. Walker (p.33, n.11), 22.

111   The revival of mainstream coinage under Augustus

Denarius of Augustus, compare *RIC* 42a:
　Head of Augustus r.; around, CAESAR AVGVSTVS/S.P.Q.R.
　　　　　　　　　　　　　　　　　　　　　　　CL.V on shield
　　　　　　　　　　　　　　　　　　　　　　　　　Nordheim Collection

Denarius of Augustus, *RIC* 77a:
　Head of Augustus r.; around, CAESAR AVGVSTVS/   OB
　　　　　　　　　　　　　　　　　　　　　　　CIVIS
　　　　　　　　　　　　　　　　　　　　SERVATOS in oak-wreath
　　　　　　　　　　　　　　　　　　　　　　　　　　BM cast

Denarius of Augustus, *RIC* 82a:
　Head of Augustus r.; around, CAESAR AVGVSTVS/Mars standing l.; on l., SIGNIS;
　on r., RECEPTIS　　　　　　　　　　　　　　　　　Morcom Collection

and Caesar, while a wide variety of standards was in use during the wars of the age of revolution. The Augustan reform consisted not only in the adoption of a fixed standard, but also in the use of two monetary metals almost entirely new to the Roman coinage. Republican bronze coinage had been in principle just that, a mixture of copper and tin; in fact, often large quantities of lead were added to the alloy and some pieces contained no tin at all. Quality control varied from the low to the non-existent.

The Augustan bronze coinage, which was introduced between 23 and 19,[5] consisted of as, semis and quadrans of virtually pure copper, sestertius and dupondius of orichalcum, copper and zinc, although one continues for the sake of convenience to talk of bronze coinage (Fig. 112). We have already seen orichalcum in use for Roman issues, for the issue of Q. Oppius, perhaps produced in Asia Minor in 88 (p.196) and for the issue of C. Clovius, produced for Caesar in Italy in 45 (p.243). But it is only with Augustus that the metal finds a fixed place in the Roman monetary system.[6]

It has become clear as a result of recent analyses that the idea of using two different metals for two different base metal denominations was known at Apamea in Phrygia

---

5 A.M. Burnett, *NC* 1977, 37, 'The authority to coin in the late Republic and early Empire', at 48, with earlier bibliography, opts for 23, probably rightly.

6 For a discussion of the (for our purposes not informative) literary references to the metal see H. Michell, *CR* 1955, 21, 'Oreichalkon'.

112 The reformed bronze coinage of Augustus

Sestertius of T. Quinctius Crispinus Sulpicianus, *RIC* 328:
  Oak-wreath between two laurel-branches; above, OB; within, CIVIS; below,
  SERVATOS/ T.QVINCTIVS.CRISPINVS.SVLPIC.III.VIR.A.A.A.F.F around S.C
  Oxford

Dupondius of C. Asinius Gallus, *RIC* 372:
  AVGVSTVS
  TRIBVNIC
  POTEST within laurel-wreath/C.ASINIVS.GALLVS.III.VIR.A.A.A.F.F around S.C
  BM

As of C. Cassius Celer, *RIC* 376:
  Head of Augustus r.; around, CAESAR.AVGVSTVS.TRIBVNIC.POTEST/
  C.CASSIVS.CELER.III.VIR.A.A.A.F.F around S.C   BM cast

Quadrans of Pulcher, Taurus and Regulus:
  PVLCHER.TAVRVS.REGVLVS around clasped hands with caduceus/III.VIR.
  A.A.A.F.F around S.C   BM

in the generation between Sulla and Caesar and that the idea was taken over for the eastern coinage of Augustus with the legend C.A produced for Asia Minor and Syria after 29 (p.266); presumably the mint of Rome borrowed the idea from this coinage; it had also already been used for the coinage of P. Carisius in Spain (p.264).[7]

Very little else is clear. The new copper asses of Augustus weighed about half an ounce and it seems to me most elegant to suppose that the weight was adopted because it was prescribed by the last law to pronounce on the weight of the as, the Lex Papiria (p.183), rather than for any more complicated reason.[8] The weights of the sestertius and the dupondius, the former attested as being an ounce (*MSR* I, 234, 9), the latter close to that of the as, no doubt followed simply from the intrinsic value of orichalcum as compared with copper. All elements of the new system were no doubt to a certain extent fiduciary and Augustus was no doubt able to effect some savings by making payments in orichalcum rather than in silver sestertii.

But this aspect of the reform should not be exaggerated; for silver sestertii had never been produced in more than minute quantities. Indeed, it seems to me likely that the metal value and the face value of the various denominations of the base metal coinage of Augustus were fairly close. For it is noticeable that when forgeries of Imperial bronze issues were produced they were substantially lighter and baser than the genuine article and were produced outside Italy; this suggests that little profit was to be made from, for instance, sestertii of full weight and purity and that it was necessary to pass poor-quality pieces in areas unfamiliar with Roman coinage. I attach greater weight to this argument than to the fact that the ratio of gold to orichalcum in Diocletian's Prices Edict is 1:720, that implied by the coinage of Augustus 1:320. I see no reason to suppose with A.M. Burnett (n.7) that a metal which the literary sources of the turn of the eras imply to be of great value should still have been so valuable three centuries later.

More striking at first sight is the fact that whereas the ratio of silver to bronze within the coinage after the adoption of the uncial weight standard was 1:110 (p.145), the ratio of silver to copper implied by the Augustan denarius and as was 1:55. But, as we have seen, the Republican bronze coinage was of appalling quality, whereas the Augustan as was of pure copper, more difficult and expensive to produce.

Clearly, Roman struck bronze was always to a certain extent fiduciary, though this did not prevent its being hoarded. But I do not think that this factor was an important element in the Augustan reform, which was motivated rather by the correct belief that the bronze coinage could not be left in the state in which Augustus found it.

The impression that Augustus was principally concerned with a reform of the coinage is strengthened by a probable further measure of Augustus contemporary with the introduction of his new base metal denominations. At that moment, the dominant element in the bronze currency of Rome was still formed by asses struck in the first

---

7 P.T. Craddock et al. (p.196, n.3).

8 *Contra* E. Lo Cascio, *JRS* 1981, 76, 'State and coinage', at 82, n.50.

half of the second century, eloquent testimony of the volume of production in that period. These asses were about twice as heavy (though not twice as valuable) as an Augustan as and bore on the obverse the double head of Janus rather than the single head of Augustus. Large numbers were halved (usually down the line between the two faces of Janus) when Augustus introduced his new asses and there is little doubt that they were being revalued as dupondii.[9] We cannot tell whether this was done officially. I should guess that it was and that Augustus was aware of the conditions which needed to be fulfilled for his new asses and associated denominations to fit into the existing pattern of monetary circulation.

A side effect of this Augustan reform of the bronze coinage, which revalued existing asses as (distinctly fiduciary) dupondii, was thus to increase the stock of bronze coinage in circulation. This was quantitatively a much more important phenomenon than the occasional halving of an Augustan as to produce two semisses, or of a semis to produce two quadrantes, though both did occur.[10] Within a few years, however, even the doubled stock of Republican asses paled into insignificance compared with the growing volume of new Augustan asses.

I have spoken of Augustus as concentrating minting authority in his own hands and as reforming the bronze coinage, for that is what I believe happened. It must be observed, however, that alongside the production of a precious metal coinage, initially in Narbonensis or Lugdunensis and eventually at Lugdunum (Strabo iv, 3, 2 (192)), and a base metal coinage at Lugdunum, the office of moneyer was revived at Rome to produce some precious metal coinage and, above all, the new base metal coinage of Augustus discussed above; hence the possibility of dating it before the constitutional settlement of 19.

More interesting is the fact that the new base metal coinage of Augustus bore the letters S.C. This might at first sight be taken to imply that they were produced by the senate, but the correct reading of the legend was in my view seen by Aase Bay in 1972: since the base metal denominations of Augustus were in effect new, since they had never had this metal composition before, their introduction in Italy (Augustus could do what he liked in the provinces he governed) had to be authorised; the same would have been true for the precious metal coinage if this had been reformed. The authorisation was promulgated in the senate, though not of course on its initiative, and the fact that the new denominations were thus authorised was embodied in their typology.[11] (The absence of S.C on a tiny number of asses which have the head of

9 T.V. Buttrey, *AJA* 1972, 31, 'Halved coins'. For the reservations expressed by H. Chantraine in *Novaesium* VIII (Berlin, 1982), see *JRS* 1985 (forthcoming).

10 E. Ripoll, *Numisma* 120–31, 1973–74, 75, 'Las monedas partidas procedentes de las excavaciones de Emporion'; D. Nash (p.171, n.22), 25–6, has not understood the force of Buttrey's arguments.

11 A. Bay, *JRS* 1972, 111, 'The letters S.C on Augustan bronze coinage'; T. Leidig, *JNG* 1981–82, 55, 'S.C auf kaiserzeitlichen Bronzemünzen', with intervening bibliography (add A.M. Burnett (n.5)), produces the truly amazing theory that the letters S.C were intended to draw attention to the endorsement by the senate of the legitimacy of imperial rule.

113 The cistophori of Augustus

Cistophoric tetradrachm of Augustus, *RIC* 477:
  Head of Augustus r.; below, IMP.CAESAR/Capricorn r.; below, AVGVSTVS; all in
  laurel-wreath   Oxford
Cistophoric tetradrachm of Augustus, *RIC* 507:
  Head of Augustus r.; below, IMP.IX.TR.PO.V/Round temple; on either side,
  MART VLTO   Oxford

Numa instead cannot be pressed; they are on a variety of other grounds anomalous, even if genuine.) There is no cause for surprise in the fact that Augustus chose to work through senate rather than people; it may indeed be that when Festus (468 L) records that the sextantal weight standard was introduced by the senate he does so because his source, Verrius Flaccus, has erroneously retrojected an Augustan innovation. (There is nothing to be made of the bizarre story in Dio lx, 22, 3.) The countermark S.C on bronze of Tarraco in Spain may be a local reaction to the impression made by the Augustan reform.

Augustan measures relating to the mainstream coinage, however, are only part of the story; the period also saw a variety of provisions relating to provincial and local coinages.

As we have seen on a number of occasions, the Republic had both perpetuated existing coinages to serve as the coinages of newly acquired provinces and had also created coinages *ex novo*. The cistophoric coinage of the province of Asia was simply continued by Augustus, who struck a number of substantial issues to circulate beside those of Antony and his predecessors. Obviously, Augustus' principal intention was to provide the monetary wherewithal to run the administration of the province (Fig. 113). At Antioch, tetradrachm issues of Augustus with the types of Philip Philadelphus followed those of Antony and Cleopatra; they were struck for the last time in 17/16; in 5 there appeared tetradrachms with the portrait of Augustus (Fig. 114).[12]

12 C.M. Kraay, *RN* 1965, 58, 'The early imperial
   tetradrachms of Syria'.

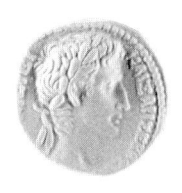

114   The coinage of Syria

Tetradrachm of Augustus of Antioch:
Laureate head of Augustus r.; around, ΚΑΙΣΑΡΟΣ ΣΕΒΑΣΤΟΥ; bead and reel border/
Tyche of Antioch seated r. holding palm-branch; at her feet, Orontes swimming;
before, two monograms; around, ΕΤΟΥΣ ΘΚ ΝΙΚΗΣ (Year 29 = 3/2 BC)   Glasgow

Bronze of Augustus of Antioch:
Laureate head of Augustus r.; around, ΚΑΙΣΑΡΙ ΣΕΒΑΣΤΩ ΑΡΧΙΕΡΕΙ/ Crown
enclosing   ΑΡΧΙΕ
         ΡΑΤΙΚΟΝ
           ΑΝΤΙΟ
            ΧΕΙΣ
              ZK (Year 27 = 5/4 BC)   BM cast

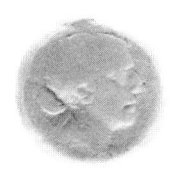

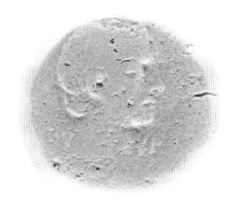

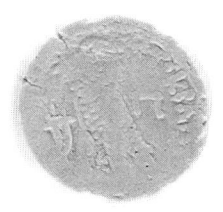

115   The coinage of Egypt

Bronze of Cleopatra:
Head of Cleopatra r./Eagle on thunderbolt l.; on l., cornucopiae; on r., M; around,
ΚΛΕΟΠΑΤΡ[ΑΣ ΒΑΣΙΛΙΣΣΑΣ]   BM cast

Bronze of Augustus:
Head of Octavian r.; on either side, ΘΕΟΥ ΥΙΟΥ/Eagle on thunderbolt l.; on l.,
cornucopiae; on r., Π; around, ΚΑΙΣΑΡΟΣ ΑΥΤΟΚΡΑΤΟΡΟΣ   Fitzwilliam, Leake

116 The mainstream Augustan coinage of Spain

Denarius of P. Carisius, *RIC* 3:
  Head of Augustus r.; around, IMP.CAESAR.AVGVSTVS/Shield between spear and
  curved sword; around, P.CARISIVS.LEG.PRO.PR   Sandars Collection
As of P. Carisius, *RIC* 15a:
  Head of Augustus r.; around, CAESAR.AVG.TRIB.POTEST/P.CARISIVS
                                                           LEG
                                                          AVGVSTI
                                                              BM *PCR* 349

One substantial province, however, began its sequence of issues produced under Roman control with the age of Augustus, Egypt, where it was not the tetradrachm coinage of the Ptolemies (see p.207), but only their bronze coinage which was continued; Augustus' pieces with the marks of value Π and M (80 and 40 units, perhaps bronze drachms) are the direct successors of Cleopatra's similar issues (Fig. 115). We have no way of knowing whether the resources that Herod acquired in 24 by melting down gold and silver plate (Josephus, *AJ* xv, 9, 2) were sent to Egypt (to buy corn) as bullion or were coined first; but they clearly passed into the coffers of the administration of Egypt without affecting the coinage of Egypt. Probably, however, since Tiberius resumed the production of tetradrachms at Alexandria, their absence under Augustus is casual.

Some of the other provincial bronze coinages of Augustus were on the surface simply the coinages of individual cities; but the scale on which they were produced makes it clear that they were for the use of the Roman authorities of the entire area. Thus the asses struck by P. Carisius at Emerita after 23 were clearly intended to provide the administration of Lusitania with currency (Fig. 116). In Gaul, a recent hoard suggests that Narbo produced an issue of asses, perhaps when Octavian was in Gaul in 39. From 28, Nemausus in Narbonensis produced a gigantic series of bronze coins, with the heads of Augustus and Agrippa on the obverse and a crocodile on the reverse; these coins were perhaps asses when the issue began, but became dupondii along with

117 The mainstream Augustan coinage of Gaul

'Dupondius' of Nemausus:
  Helmeted bust r.,/NEM
           COL in wreath   BM cast
As of Nemausus, *RIC* 159:
  Heads of Agrippa and Augustus back to back; above, IMP; below, DIVI.F; on either
  side, P P/Palm-tree decorated with wreath and crocodile; on either side, COL NEM
                                                                    Glasgow
As of Vienna:
  Heads of Caesar and Augustus back to back; on l., DIVI.IVLI; above, IMP; below,
  CAESAR; on r., DIVI.F/Prow r.; above, C.I.V   BM cast
As of Lugdunum:
  Heads of Caesar and Augustus back to back; between, palm-branch; on r.,
  IMP.CAESAR.DIVI.F; on l., DIVI.IVLI/Prow r.; above, globe and *meta*; below,
  COPIA   BM cast
Sestertius of Augustus, *RIC* 231a:
  Laureate head of Augustus r.; around, CAESAR.AVGVSTVS.DIVI.F.PATER.
  PATRIAE/Altar of Lugdunum; below, ROM.ET.AVG   Hall Collection

Republican asses with the Augustan reform (p.257). Vienna and Lugdunum also produced issues of asses, with Prow reverse. Thereafter, at Lugdunum, two issues of quadrantes, with Bull and Eagle reverses, were followed by an issue of asses of the so-called Altar series, then by the whole range of denominations from sestertius to semis of the same series (Fig. 117).[13]

The Augustan coinage of Nemausus is particularly interesting, since it marks the final replacement of the coinage of Massalia by a coinage on the Roman model. The Volcae Arecomici had struck silver around 100 and had also in the early first century struck bronze with the legend NAMASAT; they then perhaps struck no coinage for the generation during which Massalia enjoyed the revenues in their territory attributed to her in 77 (p.165). From 49 onwards, they struck coins which are probably semisses with Standing figure reverse and the legends VOLCAE/AREC and coins which are probably quadrantes with Eagle reverse and the legends AR/VOLC; semisses, clearly identified, and quadrantes, with NEM.COL, followed from 44, accompanied by small silver coins which are probably dupondii. There is a precisely parallel group of issues from Cabellio, sestertius and dupondius in silver, quadrans in bronze. Although the predilection for small silver no doubt derives from the numismatic practice of Massalia, the issues which immediately precede the Augustus and Agrippa asses are in fact an important step towards the Romanisation of the coinage of Narbonensis.[14]

In addition, there are two major coinages which are certainly eastern, one normally with C.A as the reverse legend, one normally with S.C, as well as a number of related issues (Fig. 118).[15] The former group consisted of a full range of denominations from sestertius to semis and was probably struck in Asia during the 20s (the volume of find evidence is inadequate to suggest a more diverse origin); the latter group was struck at Antioch in Syria rather later. It is likely that the first group was evoked at any rate in part by the operations undertaken against Armenia and Parthia which led up to the settlement of 19; the most interesting feature of the group is that it used different metals, orichalcum and bronze, for different denominations, thus anticipating the reform of Augustus at the mint of Rome (p.257).

Antioch had produced bronze down to 23/22 and tetradrachms intermittently down to 17/16 (p.262); thereafter there was a gap until the revival of bronze in two different

---

13 For the asses probably of Narbo, see M. Grant, *FITA*, pl. 2, 10–11 (I owe my information on the hoard to J.-C.M. Richard); for the issues of Nemausus, see C.M. Kraay, *NC* 1955, 75, 'The chronology of the coinage of Colonia Nemausus'; J.-B. Giard, *SM* 1971, 68, 'Nîmes sous Auguste'; id., *Ecole Antique de Nîmes* 1971–72, 47, 'Le monnayage antique de Nîmes'; for their metal content, *Journ.Chem.Soc.* 1852, 222 (leaded bronze).

14 H. Willers, *NZ* 34, 1902, 79, 'Die Münzen der römischen Kolonien Lugdunum, Vienna, Cabellio und Nemausus'; G. Gentric, *Les monnaies de Bollène (Vaucluse)* (Caveirac, 1981).

15 A.M. Burnett (n.5), 46–8; C.J. Howgego, *NC* 1982, 1, 'Coinage and military finance: the imperial bronze coinage of the Augustan east.' The details of the dating and attribution of these issues remain obscure.

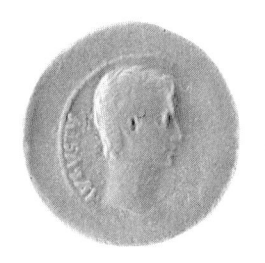

118 The eastern bronze coinages of Augustus

Dupondius with C.A, *RIC* 502:
   Head of Augustus r.; behind, AVGVSTVS/C.A in rostral crown   Berlin
Unit with S.C, *RIC* 528:
   Laureate head of Augustus r.; around, IMP.AVGVST.TR.POT/S.C in laurel-wreath
                                                                                                  Fitzwilliam

series, as well as some tetradrachms, under the governorship of P. Quinctilius Varus in 6–4. The S.C group of bronze issues begins in the same period, with a second issue in AD 4–5; countermarks show that the group circulated in a military context and military needs in relation to Armenia and Parthia should again be regarded as providing the explanation. In general, the level of central concern with the provision of bronze coinage for the eastern provinces emerges from the fact that even Cyprus (p.206) had occasional issues of bronze with Latin legend between 26 and AD 1 (*SNR* (Oxf.) 726–32).

The coinage of the Roman world naturally consisted also of elements other than issues produced directly under Roman authority, though only the states on the fringe of the Roman world produced silver in any volume. We have already had occasion to look at the Roman-style silver coinage of Lycia (p.245); under Augustus, this was joined by bronze issues which are clearly sestertii and dupondii.[16] Elsewhere in Asia Minor, the kingdom of Armenia continued at least under Artavasdes III (AD 2–10) to produce drachms; Amyntas of Galatia (36–25) also struck tetradrachms, though at Side rather than in Galatia proper (Fig. 119). (His gold coins are forgeries.) Cappadocia struck an extensive coinage for as long as it remained independent, which was indeed perpetuated under Roman authority to serve the ends of the Roman administration of the area when Cappadocia came under direct Roman rule in AD 17, with the death of Archelaus (Fig. 120). Further east, the Nabataeans maintained

16 H. Troxell (p.246, n.9), 186.

119 The coinages of the kings

Tetradrachm of Amyntas of Galatia:
  Helmeted head of Athena r.; behind, monogram/Victory l. holding sceptre tied with fillet; between sceptre and fillet, IB; above, ΒΑΣΙΛΕΩΣ; below, ΑΜΥΝΤΟΡΟΣ

  Locker Lampson 262

Denarius of Juba II:
  Diademed head r.; before, REX.IVBA/Head of Africa r.   Paris

Quinarius of Juba II:
  Diademed head r./Boar r.; above, star   Paris, de Luynes

a continuous coinage of ever more debased 'denarii' in the early Empire, from the reign of Obodas II or III (30–9) onwards; the issues of his successor, Aretas IV, were very large indeed (Fig. 121). The picture is completed by the Greek-style coinage of Thrace (p.236), and in the far west by the Roman-style coinage of Mauretania (compare p.249).[17]

In none of the cases so far mentioned should it be supposed that Roman permission was necessary for coinage to be produced. It would have been theoretically possible for Rome to insist on authorising the production of coinage in areas under her direct control, though there is no evidence that she did so systematically.[18] But the Romans possessed no juridical concept of a client state, which is an entirely modern invention; hence they could not even have thought of whether or not such a category possessed

---

17 O. Mørkholm, *NC* 1979, 242, 'The Cappadocians again'; Y. Meshorer, *Nabataean Coins* (Jerusalem, 1971) (opaque); A. Negev, *Palestine Exploration Quarterly* 1982, 119, 'Numismatics and Nabataean chronology'; D. Salzmann, *MDAI(M)* 1974, 174, 'Zur Münzprägung der mauretanischen Könige'.

18 The fact that permission to strike was only occasionally advertised surely implies that it was not normally necessary: Corduba, Ebora, Emerita, Italica and Traducta (*SNR* (Oxf.) 1037, 1040, 1050, 1060, 1067); note also PERM.SIL at Berytus (M.Grant, *FITA*, 260; the legend on the coin discussed at 127–8 divides SILANVS.P and then AVG); PERM.L.VOLVSI PROCOS in Africa (ibid., 232); compare, e.g., *CIL* x, 5393, for a *flamen divi Augusti* appointed *ex auctoritate Ti. Caesaris Augusti et permissu eius*.

120   The coinage of Roman Cappadocia

Drachm of Tiberius:
    Laureate head of Tiberius r.; around, [ΤΙΒΕΡ]ΙΟΣ ΚΑΙΣΑΡ ΣΕΒΑΣΤ[ΟΣ]/Statue of
    Emperor on Mount Argaeus; around, ΘΕΟΥ ΣΕΒΑΣΤΟΥ ΥΙΟΣ   *SNG* (Cam.) 5425

121   The coinage of the Nabataeans

Denarius:
    Laureate bust r./Standing figure   BM cast
Quinarius:
    Jugate busts r./Lyre in wreath   BM cast

the right of coinage. What modern scholars call client states were in fact territory controlled without being ruled directly, like free cities within provinces. As far as these are concerned, it is very hard in the first and second centuries AD to see any difference between the coinage of a provincial capital like Ephesus or a free city like Aphrodisias.

The reasons, therefore, why statelets like Olba or states like Commagene or the Ituraean principalities, between Syria and Judaea, struck only bronze are to be sought in the local monetary traditions of the areas concerned. This is particularly clear in the case of Judaea, where Herod simply picked up the practice of the Maccabees from Alexander Jannaeus onwards when he was given his kingdom in 37.[19]

19 G.M. Stafferi, *La monetazione di Olba* (Lugano, 1978); Y. Meshorer, *Ancient Jewish Coinage* (New York, 1982) (chaotic).

The fact that non-Roman silver coinages gradually died out in the Roman world is then to be attributed, as we have already had occasion to remark on a number of specific occasions, to the end of the fiscal independence of communities within that world. The survival of city coinages in bronze in the first two centuries AD may be explained in terms of civic pride, the desire to fill a perceived need and the wish to profit from supplying small change for local use. By the time of the Jewish revolt of AD 66–74, it was as a matter of fact true that most communities within the Roman world struck only bronze – the silver issues even of Tyre, for instance, die out in this period – and the silver coinage of the revolt was a deliberate act of defiance.

The absence of any attempt by Rome to regulate the actual production of coinage by communities in the Roman world does not mean that Rome was not concerned with such coinage. Steps to ensure that local systems of reckoning and local coinages were compatible with Roman usage accompanied the Augustan organisation of provincial censuses; such action was naturally more necessary in the east than in the west, where the spread of Roman rule had already been accompanied by the spread of Roman monetary usage. As a result the coinage of one city *could* circulate in another, though this does not seem to have happened to any great extent.[20]

Thus the early Imperial inscriptions recording the arrangements for the eight-obol *eisphora* at Messene assess the various properties subject to the tax in talents and so on, but the amount actually due, presumably eventually to Rome, is expressed in denarii, though obols and chalkoi are still used as fractions of the denarius.[21]

Similarly, in Thessaly, there seems to have been early in the reign of Augustus a *diorthoma* laying down that the manumission tax of 15 staters was to be recorded as $22\frac{1}{2}$ denarii; the shift is most clearly attested in *IG* ix, 2, 415b, lines 52–61 (compare lines 84–91; *BCH* 1975, 120, no.1, lines 7–8; *Praktika* 1972 (1974), 47, lines 12–13). Mention of the *diorthoma* is rare and haphazard, but it is perhaps to be dated immediately after Actium;[22] there is no evidence that it concerned itself with the production of coinage. A curiosity is represented by the two inscriptions which use the term *tropaikon* = victoriatus to refer to the half denarius.[23]

It is in any case clearly important for the spread of the Roman denominational system that it was actually used before and during the reign of Augustus for the production of issues of coinage outside Italy (for Lycia and Syria, see pp.267 and 266). Thus,

---

20 Note that those posthumous Lysimachi of Byzantium which passed through Roman hands after Thrace became a province were countermarked, H. Seyrig, *Essays S. Robinson* (Oxford, 1968), 183, 'Monnaies de Byzance', at 199. D.C. Braund, *Rome and the Friendly King* (London, 1984), 123, over-reacts against Th. Mommsen.

For provincial censuses, see P.A. Brunt, *JRS* 1981, 161.

21 *IG* v, 1, 1432–3, compare 1434 (properties of Romans assessed in denarii); A. Wilhelm, *JOAI* 1914, 1, 'Urkunden aus Messene'; M.N. Tod, *ABSA* 1926–27, 151, republishes *IG* v, 1432. See A. Giovannini, 115–22, for the date.

22 H. Kramolisch, *Die Strategen des thessalischen Bundes* (Bonn, 1978), 18–19, 124–5.

23 B. Helly, *9 Cong..Num.*, 165, 'Deux attestations du 'victoriat' dans les listes d'affranchissements de Thessalie'.

the so-called Fleet bronze, struck in the east for Antony, was marked Δ for the sestertius and so on (p.254); the coins of the IIviri of Corinth of 42 or 41 were countermarked with A, S or ∴ to make their values, as, semis or quadrans, explicit. The Augustan and Tiberian issues of Cyrene were clearly Roman in denominational structure (see p. 253):

Scato	dupondius to quadrans
Capito	dupondius and as
Palicanus	dupondius and as
Tiberius	dupondius to semis

In the west, Leptis in Africa (p.247), which struck only under Augustus, at the beginning and end of the reign, used a notation similar to that of the Fleet bronze of Antony.[24] In Sicily, issues of bronze under Augustus and Tiberius consist of dupondii, asses, etc., not of local denominations.

It appears, however, that at any rate in some areas, a decisive step was taken in the course of the reign of Tiberius. The Palmyra customs tariff records that an edict of Germanicus, in the east from AD 18 to 19, insisted on calculation according to the *assarion Italikon*;[25] the coinages of Herod Antipas and Philip seem to have been adjusted to the Roman model in about AD 20;[26] production of the tetradrachm started up again in Egypt in AD 20.[27] Dio lii, 30, 9 should thus be taken not as recommending the banning of local coinages, but as insisting on their compatibility with Roman coinage, as also on the compatibility of local weights and measures with Roman.[28]

There remains the problem of why local coinage nearly died in the east under Tiberius or Gaius and did die in the west. In Spain under Augustus, there were prolific city issues; local coinage, which had largely come to an end in the time of Sertorius (p.213), took on a new lease of life, with over twenty mints active under Augustus (Fig. 122, Map 33). But there are, with one possible exception, no western local coinages

24 D. MacDowall, *NC* 1962, 113, 'Countermarks of early imperial Corinth', at 115–18; M. Amandry, *SM* 1983, 11, 'Le monnayage de Leptis Minor'.
25 J.F. Matthews, *JRS* 1984 (forthcoming); note that the edict of Sex. Sotidius Strabo Libuscidianus from Pisidia, of AD 14–20 (S. Mitchell, *JRS* 1976, 106), reckons the reimbursement for the provision of waggons or mules in asses. Note the rare drachms of Aphrodisias and Plarasa with the mark of value of the denarius (*BMCCaria* (App.) 10a).
26 A. Kindler, *INC Jerusalem*, 180, 'The monetary pattern of Jewish coins', at 191–3; D. Sperber, *Jewish Quarterly Review* 1966, 273, 'Palestinian currency systems during the Second Commonwealth', antedates Roman influence on the coinage of the area by nearly a century.
27 D.R. Walker and C.E. King, in D.R. Walker, *The Metrology of the Roman Silver Coinage* I (Oxford: BAR, 1976), 139, 'Ptolemaic and Augustan silver'; compare II, 114.
28 Compare p.177 (Pompeii) and *IGRR* iii, 864 for the banning of local weights and measures. Note J.M. Reynolds and R. Goodchild, *Libya Antiqua* 2, 1965, 103 = *AE* 1967, 531 (Vespasian), where city-lands are measured in medimn(i)a, but their rent calculated in denarii. Alexander of Aphrodisias, however, observed that different peoples used different weights (on Aristotle, *Top.*, p.210, 9).

122   The Augustan city coinages of Spain

As of Ercavica:
  Laureate head of Augustus r.; around, AVGVSTVS.DIVI.F/Bull r.; above, MVN;
   below, ERCAVICA   Paris
As of Caesaraugusta:
  Laureate head of Augustus r./Ploughman r.; above and before, CAESARAVGVSTA (in
   monogram); in exergue,   II.VIR
                    Q.LVTAT.M.FABI (in monogram)   Paris

later than Gaius;[29] in the Peloponnese, only three pairs of IIviri struck at Corinth under Tiberius, one under Gaius; there is no coinage at all at Patras or Sparta between Augustus and Claudius. In northern Greece, Buthrotum did not strike under Tiberius or Gaius, Dium and (probably) Thessalonica did not strike under Gaius or Claudius, Pella did not strike between Augustus and Hadrian.[30] On balance I incline to the view that the removal of revenues from a number of cities by Tiberius (Suet., *Tib.* 49) almost killed off local coinage.[31] Claudius on the other hand perhaps took steps to organise further the production of coinage in the east. Bronze semisses of Corinth are countermarked SE(mis) in this period, to make their denomination clear; Latin titulature is used on the civic bronzes of Antioch;[32] after a period of experiment, the silver content of the tetradrachm coinage of Alexandria was established at the level at which it remained until the reign of Trajan.[33]

29 J.B. Giard, *RN* 1970, 23, 'Le monnayage de bronze de Claude', at 42, n.2, rejects coinage of Ebusus under Claudius, accepted, however, by M. Campo, *Numisma* 1976, 159, 'Las monedes de Claudio I de Ebusus'.
30 S. Grünauer, *Die Münzprägung der Lakedaimonier* (Berlin, 1978), 108, with much information from M. Amandry.
31 See M. Grant, *FITA*, 203, n.13; his later thoughts in *NC* 1949, 93, 'The decline and fall of city coinage in Spain', are fanciful. For the link between the acquisition of revenues and the beginning of coinage in the case of Stratonicea-Hadrianoupolis, see L. Robert, *Hell.* 11–12, 53, 'AITESAMENOS sur les monnaies'. See also p.252.
32 A. Dieudonné, *RN* 1927, 1, 'Les monnaies grecques de la Syrie', at 38.
33 D.R. Walker and C.E. King (n.27).

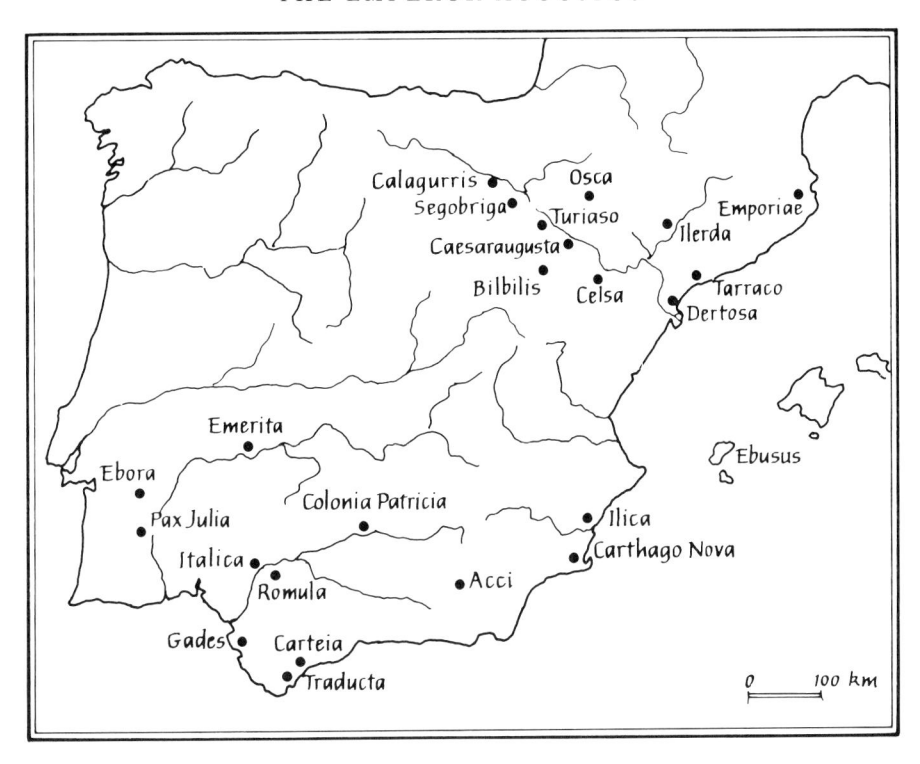

33 Spain under Augustus
Based on L. Villaronga (p.87, n.8), 271

The most dramatic expression, however, on the coinage of the Roman world of the unity of that world under Augustus is the flood of issues bearing his portrait; that the practice is the result of a growing awareness of the position of Augustus and not of any kind of direction is clear from the fact that the practice gradually becomes more common towards the end of Augustus' reign (Fig. 123).[34]

Polemon I, ruler of Pontus and of Colchis (c.38 BC – c.8 BC), did not put Augustus' head on his coins at all. His wife and successor, Pythodoris (c.8 BC – c.AD 33), occasionally did. In Armenia, the Imperial head makes an occasional appearance on the coins of Tigranes III (c.12 BC – c.6 BC). It appears on the coinage of Artavasdes III (c.AD 2 – AD 10). In Olba, the coins of Ajax, son of Teucer (c.AD 10/11 – c.AD 14/15), bear the portrait of Augustus. Zenodorus, ruler in part of the Ituraean principality (c.36 BC – 20 BC), put Augustus' head on his coins. Herod, who took

34 A.M. Burnett and S. Walker, *Augustus* (London: BM, 1981), 23. I owe much to discussion with M. Thomas. For the head of Augustus used as a countermark in the aftermath of Actium, see S. Grünauer (n.30), 55; R. Martini, *RIN* 1981, 27, 'Contromarca su una moneta di Sinope' (at absurd length).

123 The portrait issues of Augustus and Tiberius in the cities

As of Hadrumetum:
  Head of Caesar r.; before, CAESAR/Head of Augustus l.; before, AVGVSTVS; behind, HADR   P.V. Collection

Bronze of Thessalonica:
  Diademed head of Caesar r./Head of Augustus r.; around, ΘΕΣΣΑΛ[ΟΝΙΚΕ]ΩΝ   BM

Dupondius of Cyrenaica:
  Facing heads of Augustus and Agrippa; on l., CAESAR.TR.POT; on r., AGRIPPA/SCATO
       PROCOS in laurel-wreath   BM

Bronze of Corinth:
  Head of Augustus r.; behind, CAESAR; before, CORINTH/Facing busts; between, C.L; around, C.S[ERVILIO.C.F.PRIMO.]M.ANTONIO.HIPPARCHO.II.VIR   Boston

Bronze of Ninica, H. Seyrig, *RN* 1969, 49:
  Head of Augustus r.; around, PRINCEPS.FELIX/Two oxen ploughing l.; above, COLONIA.IVL; below, VE and PET (in monogram) with II.VIR   Levante Collection

Bronze of Olba:
  Laureate head of Tiberius r.; around, ΣΕΒΑΣΤΟΣ ΣΕΒΑΣΤΟΥ ΚΑΙΣΑΡ/ Thunderbolt; above, ΑΡΧΙΕΡΕΩΣ
      ΑΙΑΝΤΟΣ; below, ΤΕΥΚΡΟΥ
          ΤΟΠΑΡΧΟΥ
          ΕΠΙ ΔΙΟΔΩ; on r., ΕΤ
              Ε (Year 5 = AD 14/15)   BM cast

over this principality in 20 BC, discontinued the practice and kept his coinage strictly aniconic. Of his sons (who ruled from 4 BC onwards), Philip, tetrarch in part of the Ituraean principality, put the jugate heads of Augustus and Livia onto his coinage in AD 5/6. In Thrace, the practice started with Rhoemetalces I (c.11 BC – AD 12) and was continued by his successors.

In parallel, portraits of others than members of the Imperial family are common early in the reign of Augustus, a natural consequence of the striking of portrait coins by and under the auspices of the various contenders for power in the Civil Wars. But, gradually, portraits come to be used only for relatives or very close associates of the *princeps* and even the latter category disappears under Tiberius.[35]

The spread of the use of Roman monetary terms and the creation of coinages compatible with Roman money were obviously slow processes. As far as the use of Roman coinage itself is concerned, we have seen its arrival in Spain, Africa, Narbonensis, the Dalmatian coast, Greece during the Republic, in some parts of the east in the age of revolution.

In Cyrenaica, it is the age of Augustus that sees the arrival of Roman coinage (for local issues on the Roman model see p.253). The exiguous number of four Republican denarii in a lot of coins from the whole area makes it clear that they only arrived at the beginning of the Empire,[36] an inference borne out by the total absence of Republican hoards. Augustan bronze is similarly the earliest Roman bronze from Sidi Krebish (Euhesperides).[37] Interestingly, the Augustan practice of halving coins arrived at the same time.[38]

As far as Gallia Lugdunensis and Gallia Belgica are concerned, I doubt the argument of D. Nash that Roman coinage only penetrated in the area of the Roman army camps.[39] It is true that native bronze is still dominant in finds in areas distant from these camps; but we are now in a period where the *pax Augusta* is responsible for the relative absence of gold or silver hoards to fill out the picture (App. 56). Here, as elsewhere, I suspect that the monetary system was fundamentally Roman, with a Roman denominational structure and actual high-value Roman coins circulating alongside low-value local coins. Nor will it do to see the production of imitations of Roman bronze coins as evidence of Celtic continuity; for they occur in precisely the areas where the actual penetration of Roman bronze coins was most intensive.

Meanwhile, one of the earliest concerns of Augustus had been to complete the conquest of Spain, including the rich gold-producing area of the north-west. Despite

---

35 There is no reason to hypothesise with M. Grant, *FITA*, 229, a formal right of coinage for *amici principis*.
36 *NC* 1944, 105.
37 *Sidi Krebish* I (London, 1975), 230: *SNR* (Oxf.) 696, 704 (2), 802, 805 (2).
38 T.V. Buttrey (p.253, n.17), 30.

39 D. Nash (p.171, n.22), 23. The argument is even harder to maintain if E. Wightman, *Helinium* 1977, 105, 'Military arrangements in early Roman Gaul', is right to hold that for the first decades of the Roman occupation many troops were based in native settlements.

the long history of the Roman presence in Spain and despite the level of Roman military activity under Augustus, in Spain as in Gaul, the circulating medium was in part Roman and in part local. Alongside Roman aurei and denarii, much of the bronze in use was city bronze; an Augustan hoard from Ablitas contains pieces of Bilbilis, Caesaraugusta, Calagurris, Celsa (Colonia Lepida), Osca and Turiaso.

The last great area of the west which remained to be assimilated in the early Empire was that of the Alps and the plains extending north to the Danube frontier. A number of the major Alpine passes had of course been frequented from very early times, not simply by the local tribes, but by travellers from further afield. This emerges for instance from the coins left as offerings at the top of the Great St Bernard; it is easier to suppose that the Roman Republican coins, for instance, were left by travellers from Central Italy than that they circulated in the valleys on either side of the pass.[40]

The Augustan conquest of the Alps took place in two stages.[41] The area had only begun to become important to Rome when Caesar reached the Rhine, for it then lay between two areas under Roman control; the territory of the Helvetii was already under Roman rule by the death of Caesar, a rule reinforced by the foundation of colonies at Nyon and Augst. The conquest of the Salassi in the Val d'Aosta in 25 removed the last barrier to Roman movement between Italy and the Rhine.

The Salassi down to that moment had been a tribe of some power and at an advanced stage of state formation.[42] They had initially worked gold mines in the valley, whence endless quarrels with their neighbours lower down over the use of the waters of the Dora Baltea (Strabo iv, 6, 7 (205)), until the Romans drove them out and took over the mines themselves;[43] but they continued to sell water to the *publicani* who worked the mines and perhaps at this stage took to exacting tolls from travellers using the Great St Bernard. Though they produced no coinage themselves, the Salassi perhaps used the gold and silver produced north of the Great St Bernard.[44] But even though we know that the picture given by the literary sources of the extirpation of the Salassi is exaggerated, since some were incorporated in the colony of Aosta (*ILS* 6753), there is no likelihood that there was any continuity of monetary usage from the period of independence to the Roman period. The use of coinage will have been imported afresh by the praetorian soldiers whom Augustus settled at Aosta.

By way of contrast with the Salassi, the Taurini to the south remained loyal to Rome in the face of Hannibal in 218 and indeed thereafter. The evidence for Roman

---

40 See App. 58; no general conclusion may be drawn from the Greek bronzes, chiefly of Corcyra, found in a shrine near Thun, which was not on a route from anywhere to anywhere before the building of the Lötschberg railway tunnel (B. Kapossy, *SM* 1967, 37).

41 C.M. Wells, *The German Policy of Augustus* (Oxford, 1972), chs. 3–4; G. Walser, *Summus Poeninus* (Wiesbaden, 1984); and the impressive work of B. Overbeck (p.277, n.48) I, 169–83.

42 A.M. Cavallaro, in *Archeologia in Valle d'Aosta* (Aosta, 1981), 63.

43 Compare Pliny, *NH* xxxiii, 78 for mints similarly taken over by the Romans in the territory of the Liburni to the east, beyond Eporedia; xxxiii, 66 for gold washing in the Po.

44 A. Pautasso, 137; App. 59 cited below.

penetration and settlement in the Republican period is slim, but it looks as if it followed the pattern characteristic of the Po valley as a whole.[45]

In any case, the conquest of the Salassi undoubtedly led to much increased Roman use of the Great St Bernard and to the progressive Romanisation of the territory of the Helvetii. The area north of the Great St Bernard had indeed a history of the production and use of coinage before the arrival of the Romans. One class of imitations of the drachms of Massalia, found in profusion on the Great St Bernard and at Martigny, was presumably produced in the upper Rhone valley in the middle of the first century (App. 59). Further north, one group of the so-called Bushel series of silver quinarii was produced by the Helvetii, who had earlier produced gold coinage, and was followed by another issue with the legends NINNO or MAVC, certainly post-conquest. One hoard of Roman denarii and Gallic quinarii from Belpberg near Bern is now known.[46] Here, as in the south of the Rhone valley, the transition from pre-Roman to Roman coinage was gentle and easy. Vidy developed in the same period into a major Roman site; Roman coins appear at La Tène, despite its poverty;[47] the scene was set for the conquest of the eastern Alps.

The first steps seem to have been taken in 16, when the Romans moved over the Spluga or one of the neighbouring passes into the upper Rhine valley; Chur was fortified now or later and in 15 the eastern Alps as far as the friendly kingdom of Noricum were conquered in a single easy campaign. This area of the Alps either side of the watershed was inhabited by the Raeti, whose iron-producing centre at Sanzeno we have already had occasion to notice (p.79). The Italian part of the territory of the Raeti had seen in the third to second centuries the penetration of Roman cast coinage and some Greek pieces (p.83), which I should see as the casual filtering north of elements of the pay or booty brought to the Po valley after the Second Punic War by settlers there. There is no evidence that the economy of the area – where no coinage was ever produced – was in any sense monetised before the Augustan conquest. The same is even more true of the upper Rhine valley.[48]

The final Roman push, after the conquest in 14 of the Alpes Maritimes at the other end of the mountain chain, took the legions across the plains north of the Alps to the Danube, the territory of the Vindelici. Unlike the mountainous region further south, this area had a substantial coinage in gold and silver before the arrival of the Romans, a coinage which reveals the Celtic nature of the population.[49] This

---

45 T.R. Volk informs me that imitations of the bronzes of Octavian with DIVVS IVLIVS were perhaps produced in this area.

46 D.F. Allen, *Germania* 1978, 190, 'The coins from the oppidum of Altenburg', at 194 and 198; H.-M. von Kaenel, *SNR* 1980, 15, 'Der Schatzfund vom Belpberg'.

47 D.F. Allen, *Etudes Celtiques* 1972–73, 477, 'The coins found at La Tène' (also on the end of the period of prosperity in the second quarter of the first century).

48 B. Overbeck, *Geschichte des Alpenrheintals* II (Munich, 1973), esp. map 2.

49 D.F. Allen (n.46), 194, for the group of Bushel quinarii struck by the Vindelici.

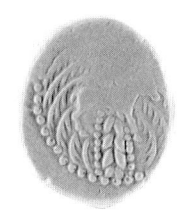

124   The coinage of Noricum

Tetradrachm of Noricum:
  Horse r. before tree/Horseman r.; above, monogram; in exergue, SVICCA   BM
Fraction of Noricum:
  Uncertain type/Cross   Oxford

population had very little contact with the Roman world before the arrival of the legions, as is shown by the limited range of imports at Manching, destroyed by other Celts just before the arrival of the Romans.[50] The Roman conquest seems to have brought coinage to an end and there is no trace of continuity; Roman coinage indeed hardly seems to have penetrated till after the death of Augustus. A curiosity is represented by the presence of gold of the Vindelici in the general area of Vercelli and Novara; I should regard the pieces as buried or lost by veterans who shared in the conquest of the Vindelici and happened to settle around Vercelli and Novara, a process not otherwise attested.[51]

Meanwhile, further east, the kingdom of Noricum had developed by the first century both a complex fiscal structure including the production of coinage on the one hand and friendly relations with the Romans on the other hand. The central point of the kingdom was the area of the Magdalensberg, where around an earlier hill-fort there grew up from say 75 onwards a city producing and marketing ironware on a large scale;[52] and it was no doubt the revenues derived from the export of this iron which enabled the kingdom to produce a substantial coinage of large and small silver between say 75 and Augustus (Fig. 124).[53] Several hoards of Roman silver come from the area

50 W.E. Stöckli, *Die Grob- und Importkeramik von Manching* (Wiesbaden, 1979).
51 A. Pautasso, *RIN* 1975, 99, 'Sui ritrovamenti di stateri vindelici del Vercellese', describes the phenomenon, which includes one piece from Aosta and one from near Brescia; compare C. Robert, *RN* 1860, 203, for coins of the Eravisci (p.236) from near Mortara.
52 G. Piccottini and H. Vetters, *Führer durch die Ausgrabungen auf dem Magdalensberg* (Klagenfurt, 1978).
53 R. Göbl, *Typologie und Chronologie der keltischen Münzprägung in Noricum* (Vienna, 1973); P. Kos, *Keltische Münzen Sloweniens* (Ljubljana, 1977); *Situla* 20–1, 1981, 394, 'Die Rolle der norischen Silbermünzen'. The names on the coinage should be regarded as those of moneyers, not merchants.

round the Magdalensberg and indeed also a number of mixed hoards (App. 60). The transition from pre-Roman to Roman monetary usages was as painless as the absorption of the Norican kingdom into the Roman empire, presumably in 16/15. It comes as no surprise to find the Roman pound early in use near Salzburg.[54]

What then were the mechanisms by which a monetary economy like that of Roman Italy was eventually spread to this and other areas of the Roman empire? First and foremost, at any rate for certain areas, the Roman legions, paid in coin and with enormous spending power in relation to the areas where they were stationed; they bought from and 'married' into these areas, bringing with them the monetary usages to which they were accustomed. Secondly, the imposition of taxes in money, with the consequent necessity, to which Keith Hopkins has drawn attention, to export a surplus for cash in order to acquire the wherewithal to pay the taxes. Finally, the desire of local aristocracies, particularly in the west, to share in the government of the empire; to do this they needed cash to spend in Rome and I do not doubt that this need led to the conversion of the traditional obligations of their dependants in kind to 'rents' in cash.[55] The result of all these factors was an empire that for the next two and a half centuries possessed a monetary unity which covered almost the entire Mediterranean world.

---

54 G. Alfödy, *Noricum* (London, 1974), chs. 1–5, for a general account, though with an altogether fantastic view of the character of Roman commercial activity; F. Moosleitner, *Germania* 1979, 1 = *Die Kelten in Mitteleuropa* (Salzburg, 1980), no. 45, for the weight: 295.15 gm., somewhat worn.

55 *JRS* 1980, 101, 'Taxes and trade in the Roman Empire'; compare E.R. Cregeen, in I.M. Lewis (ed.), *History and Social Anthropology* (London, 1968), 153, 'The changing role of the House of Argyle in the Scottish Highlands', for aristocracies converting traditional obligations into obligations in cash.

APPENDICES

FINDS

App. 1 Finds of Greek coins in Etruria in the classical period (p.3)

Two hoards are attested:
Volterra – *IGCH* 1875; M. Cristofani Martelli, in *Mon.Etr.*, 87; *Coin Hoards* 5, 4.
'Auriol' pieces
The assertion by E. Muret and A. Chabouillet, *Catalogue des monnaies gauloises de la Bibliothèque Nationale* (Paris, 1889), 9, and A. Sambon, p.12, that a number of Etruscan gold coins were found with the Volterra hoard seems to be without foundation.

G. Gorini, in *Mon.Etr.*, 136, mentions a similar find from Campiglia now in the Museo Civico di Livorno; but T.R. Volk informs me that the pieces are in fact Phoenician and do not constitute a find.

Pyrgi – *IGCH* 1905; *Coin Hoards* 2, 22
Late fifth-century Sicilian and Athenian silver

The pattern of stray finds, readily exemplified, suggests that the hoard record is misleading in its sparseness:
Monteriggioni – *RRCH* 555
2 fourth-century didrachms of Neapolis

Volterra – *NSc* 1972, 60
2 late fourth-century didrachms of Neapolis (Sambon 454 and 462)

Near Orvieto – *NSc* 1884, 188 = 340
1 'drachm' (presumably didrachm) of Neapolis

Chiusi and Talamone – *RAL* 1889, 83
2 tetradrachms of Athens

Vitorchiano, Arezzo, Pitigliano, Chiusi and Marzabotto – *Bullettino* 1881, 261; *NSc* 1898, 140; *Mon.Ant.* 30, 1925, 429; E. Cocchi Ercolani, in A. Berselli (ed.), *Storia della Emilia Romagna* I (Bologna, 1975), 202
5 gold staters of Philip II

I doubt whether the fraction of Phocaea from Chiusi now in Florence, G.F. Gamurrini, *Per.di Num.e Sfrag.* 6, 1874, 52; F. Bodenstedt, *Die Elektronmünzen von Phokaia und Mytilene* (Tübingen, 1981), 20, Em.2, Nr. 2, was lost in antiquity. I do not know on what basis L. Breglia asserts, *PdelP* 1970, 158, n.8, that the 'Auriol' or Phocaea piece in Modena (E. Babelon, *Traité* II, 1, 323, no.514) was found in Etruria

It is possible that the pieces of Neapolis form part of the phenomenon documented in App. 18.

App. 2 Finds of 'ramo secco' bars (p.3)

The basic study is that of F. Panvini Rosati, *Emilia Preromana* 6, 1970 (1971), 15, 'Il ripostiglio di Castelfranco Emilia' (one must go back to Haeberlin, p.10, for a list of the bars without type); for Pontecagnano see *AIIN* 1971–2, 305 (a piece of a bar with 'ramo secco' found with lumps of bronze and a cake ingot, perhaps also with sixth- to fifth-century votive offerings); for Stabiae see Haeberlin, p.16.

The relevant bar from Este is published by A. Callegari, *BPI* 1929, 65. The bar from Grammichele is published in *BPI* 1900, 276. E. Cocchi Ercolani, *RIN* 1975, 7, 'Ritrovamenti di pani di rame', reintroduces confusion by treating all types of bronze bar together indiscriminately.

For Gorizia see App. 49.

App. 3 Hoards in Magna Graecia around 300 (p.25)

Pegasi – *IGCH* 1948, 1949, 1952, 1958 (?)
Gold of Tarentum, Metapontum or Locri – *IGCH* 1937, 1950, 1956–8
Gold of Tarentum and Macedon – *IGCH* 1932
Gold of Macedon and Ptolemy I – *IGCH* 1955

Sala Consilina – *IGCH* 1936
Metapontum – *IGCH* 1958
Cariati – *IGCH* 1946

App. 4 Hoards in Campania around 300 (p.27)

Cales – *IGCH* 1938
Didrachms of Cumae, Neapolis, Hyrina, Nola and Fistelia
Hemidrachm of Neapolis
Obols of Neapolis, Allifae, Fistelia, Fistelia (?), Peripoloi Pitanatai

Capua – *IGCH* 1941
Obols of Neápolis and Fistelia
Hemiobols of Fistelia

Frasso Telesino – *IGCH* 1912; K. Rutter, *Campanian Coinages* (Edinburgh, 1979), 112, n.44
Didrachms of Cumae, Neapolis, Campani, Hyrina

Campania – *IGCH* 1920
Obols of Allifae and Fistelia

App. 5 Hoards including Campanian coins in Magna Graecia (p.36)

Hoards including the Mars/Horse's head ROMANO issue:
Torchiarolo – *IGCH* 1977
Cumae, Neapolis, Hyrina, Nola, Peripoloi Pitanatai, Poseidonia

Valesio – *IGCH* 1960; *AIIN* 1973, 9

Mesagne – *IGCH* 1971
Neapolis, Nola, Poseidonia

Oppido Lucano – *IGCH* 1961
Neapolis

San Giorgio Ionico – A. Burnett, *SNR* 1977, 102 (with wrong name)
Neapolis

Timmari – A. Burnett, ibid.
Neapolis

For two Campanian hoards with the Mars/Horse's head ROMANO issue, see A. Burnett, l.c.

For the Capua hoard with this issue see *RRCH* 550; also, importantly, G. Riccio, *Catalogo di antiche medaglie consolari* (Naples, 1855), *Sec.Supp.* (1861), 2, for the Roma/Victory issue. Heaven knows what *else* the hoard may have contained (*IGCH* 1962 misleads). Compare the similar assemblage of material, without Roman, also reported from Capua by M. Ruggiero, *Degli scavi di antichità nelle province di terraferma dell'antico regno di Napoli* (Naples, 1888), 352 (Cumae, Neapolis, Hyrina, Tarentum).

Hoards not including Roman coins:
Lucania about 1953 – *IGCH* 1966
Neapolis, Hyrina

South Italy – *IGCH* 1967
Neapolis, Hyrina, Nola

Gioia del Colle – *IGCH* 1992
Neapolis, Hyrina

Conversano – V. L'Abbate, *Norba* (Bari, 1979), 91
Neapolis, Nola

Hoard including much later Roman issues:
Lucania 1860 – *IGCH* 1994
Neapolis

Note also the didrachms of Neapolis in the Salve hoard (*IGCH* 2030)

App. 6   Hoards including *pegasi* and Sicilian coins in Italy (p.36)

IGCH 1968 (Syracuse and *pegasi*), 1969 (*pegasi*), 1972 (Syracuse, Carthage, Pyrrhus and *pegasi*), 1987 (Syracuse) (compare App. 7)

IGCH 1973, 1974 (Pyrrhus only)

App. 7   Penetration of coinage into the Appennines (p.36)

Lucania
Oppido Lucano (App. 5)

Timmari (App. 5)

Lucania about 1953 (App. 5)

Lucania 1860 (App. 5)

Potenza – *Bullettino* 1879, 7 (perhaps fourth century or earlier)
Silver of Metapontum, Poseidonia, Sybaris, Caulonia, Croton

Lucania 1957 – *IGCH* 1970
Silver of Tarentum, Metapontum, Thurium

Muro Lucano   *Bullettino* 1860, 37
Silver of Tarentum (2), *pegasus* (1)

Monteverde 1894 – V. Buglione, *Monteverde* (Melfi, 1929), 29
42 silver coins of Velia, Fistelia, Croton, Metapontum, Thurium, Caulonia, Poseidonia, Neapolis, Campani, Hyrina, Syracuse, 'Fistenis' (Fenseris?)

Samnium
Benevento – *RRCH* 22 = *IGCH* 1985
Silver of Neapolis, Hyrina, Nola, Tarentum, Metapontum, Velia, Rome (to 265 BC)

Morcone – *IGCH* 2047
Silver of Neapolis, Velia

Pietrabbondante – *RRCH* 24 = *IGCH* 1986
Struck bronze coinage of Neapolis, Nola, Aesernia, Aquinum, Cales, Suessa, Teanum, Rome
Cast bronze coinage (to 265 BC)

Gildone – *RRCH* 26 = *IGCH* 2044 (not certainly a hoard)
Struck bronze coinage of Neapolis and Arpi
Cast bronze coinage (to 240 BC)

Pietrabbondante – *RRCH* 31
Cast bronze coinage (to 225 BC)

Note also the site finds from Pietrabbondante, *Sannio*, 179; compare also a quadrans probably of the Roma/Roma series with symbol from Riccia, R. Garrucci (p.41, n.20), 19

Campochiaro – *Sannio*, 197
Silver of Neapolis, Fistelia, Velia, Rome (note also the site finds)

Carife – *RRCH* 50 = *IGCH* 2033
Silver of Neapolis, Fistelia, Tarentum, Heraclea, Thurium
Struck bronze coinage of Neapolis, Aquilonia, Arpi, Salapia, Brundisium, Mamertini, Syracuse, Rome (to Second Punic War)
Cast bronze coinage

Isernia – *RRCH* 78 = *IGCH* 2032
Struck bronze coinage of Arpi (1) and Rome (to denarius system)
Cast bronze coinage

Frentani
Pallano – D. Romanelli, *Antica topografia istorica del regno di Napoli* (Naples, 1815–19) III, 43
Silver of Neapolis, Hyrina, Nola, Heraclea, Metapontum, Thurium, Velia, Croton

Termoli – *RRCH* 70
Cast and struck bronze coinage of Rome
Piece of Oval series of cast bronze coinage

Marsi
Lecce nei Marsi – *IGCH* 1988
Silver of Neapolis

Note also an as of the heavy Apollo/Apollo series from Anversa degli Abruzzi, Haeberlin, p.83, no.20

Morino – *RRCH* 54 = *IGCH* 1995
Struck bronze coinage of Neapolis, Aesernia, Cales, Cubulteria, Suessa, Teanum, Arpi, Rome (to Second Punic War)

Sabinum
Città Ducale – *RRCH* 97
Cast and struck bronze coinage of Rome

Praetuttii
Castagneto – *RRCH* 51 = *IGCH* 2036
Struck bronze coinage of Neapolis, Rome (to Second Punic War)
Cast bronze coinage

Castagneto – *RRCH* 77 = *IGCH* 2035
Struck bronze coinage of Neapolis, Aesernia, Teanum (?), Rome (to denarius system)
Cast bronze coinage

Picenum
Ascoli Piceno – *RRCH* 59 = *IGCH* 2034
Silver of Neapolis, Cales, Rome, Campano-Tarentine silver

Tortoreto – *RRCH* 101 = *IGCH* 2048
Struck bronze coinage of Ariminum, Cosa, Neapolis, Cales, Teanum, Arpi, Salapia, Carthage, Rome (to denarius system)
Cast bronze coinage

App. 8 Finds from Valle d'Ansanto (p.12)

AIIN 1, 1954, 35; 2, 1955, 43, n.4; *NSc* 1976, 506 (inaccurate); V.M. Santoli, *De Mefiti* (Naples, 1783).

Gold of Alexander the Great
Silver of Neapolis, Nola, Fistelia (?), Tarentum, Metapontum, Velia, Sybaris, Rome (to denarius system, also Roman Empire)
Struck bronze coinage of Neapolis, Cales, Cubulteria, Suessa, Arpi, Luceria, Teate Paestum, Velia (also Ebusus), Rome (to denarius system, also Roman Empire)
Cast bronze coinage
Coins of Cumae, 'Telesia', Thurii, Locri, Caulonia

App. 9 Finds of Minerva/Horse's head and Goddess/Lion bronzes (p.38)

Tarquinia *NSc* 1977, 220	80	1
Lucus Feroniae Museo Nazionale Romano	5	1
Vicarello *RhM* 1854, 20	916	1156
Carsoli *NSc* 1951, 169	153	174
Nemi M.H. Crawford (p.41, n.19)	5	61

For hoards with Goddess/Lion ROMANO bronzes see *RRCH* 20 and 24, for which the cast bronze coinage which they contain provide an indication of relative date. *RRCH* 28 is not necessarily complete as reported and includes bronzes of Cosa. The Teano hoard (Museo Nazionale di Napoli) includes only Minerva/Horse's head ROMANO bronzes, but these are the only Roman pieces in the hoard.

App. 10 Hoards including Italian cast bronze coinage (p.46)

Vulci – *RRCH* 10
With non-Roman and Roman currency bars:
Oval series

Ariccia – *RRCH* 13
With non-Roman and Roman currency bars and Roman series:
Bull's head/Prow semis

Comacchio – *RRCH* 25
With Roman series:
Oval sextans

Pietrabbondante – *RRCH* 31
With Roman series:
Club/Pentagram uncia

Trento – *RRCH* 57; *Coin Hoards* 7 (forthcoming)
With Roman series:
Oval sextans
Wheel/Wheel uncia
Prow l./Trident uncia

Termoli – *RRCH* 70
With Roman series:
Oval uncia

Rimini – *Arte e Civiltà Romana nell'Italia Settentrionale* II, 122–3
With a quadrans of the Roma/Roma series (*RRC*, no.21/4):
Biunx of Ariminum

Castelnuovo della Daunia – Haeberlin, p.155
Seven asses with Male head/Cock

Venosa – Haeberlin, p.197
Five libral asses of Venusia

Volterra
Out of a larger number:
2 dupondii and 4 asses of club series of Volaterrae
3 dupondii of dolphin series
Ashmolean Museum, Oxford

Siena – Haeberlin, pp.246, 250
Dupondius of club series of Volaterrae
As and semis of dolphin series

App. 11   Finds of Etruscan struck bronze (p.48)

See M.P. Baglione, in *Mon.Etr.*, 153; add:

Siena
1 piece as Sambon 129
Museo Archeologico di Siena

Casone near Siena – *Rassegna d'Arte Senese* 21, 214
1 piece as Sambon 128–31

Grassina near Firenze
1 piece as Sambon 128
Museo Archeologico di Firenze

Arezzo – *NSc* 1880, 219
1 piece as Sambon 146

App. 12   Hoards from south Italy between 241 and 218 (p.51)

Mottola – *IGCH* 1993
Tarentum

Pisticci – *IGCH* 1996
Tarentum, Heraclea, Metapontum

Bernalda – *IGCH* 1997
Tarentum, Heraclea, Thurium, Velia

Taranto – *IGCH* 1998
Tarentum, Thurium

Parabita – *IGCH* 1999
Tarentum, Heraclea, Metapontum, Poseidonia, Thurium, Velia, Croton

Taranto – *IGCH* 2000
Tarentum

Specchia – *IGCH* 2001
Tarentum, Heraclea

Francavilla Fontana – *IGCH* 2002
Tarentum, Thurium

Lucania 1860 – App. 5

Surbo – *IGCH* 2003
Tarentum, Heraclea, Metapontum, Argos, Rome

Lecce – *IGCH* 2004
Tarentum

Taranto – *IGCH* 2006
Tarentum, Thurium

Fasano – *IGCH* 2007
Tarentum, Thurium

Martina Franca – *IGCH* 2008
Tarentum, Heraclea, Metapontum, Thurium

App. 13   Finds of Mars/Eagle gold pieces (p.56)

Labico – F. Ficoroni, *Le Memorie di Labico* (Rome, 1745), 86
60–as Mars/Eagle piece, 20–as Mars/Eagle piece
There is no connection with the Capuan coins also found at Labico, against the implication of Th. Mommsen, *RMw* 345, n.152

Magione – *SE* 14, 1940, 324
60–as Mars/Eagle piece

Melito Irpino – *NSc* 1881, 327
60–as Mars/Eagle piece

Montone del Grano
60–as Mars/Eagle piece
Museo Nazionale delle Marche, Ancona

Morgantina – *AJA* 1957, 158
20–as Mars/Eagle piece with corn-ear

App. 14   Finds of Minerva/Bull asses (p.58)

Canevedo (Monselice) – A. Prosdocimi, *Notizie di Archeologia* (Este, 1899), 54; Haeberlin, p.142, no. 11
One specimen, 275.00 gm.
Museo Atestino, Este

Modena – R. Garrucci (p.41, n.20), 17
One specimen

Velcia – P. De Lama, *Tavola alimentaria velejate* (Parma, 1819), 57
One specimen, 336.00 gm.
Museo Ducale, Parma

Rome – Haeberlin, p.142, no.5
One specimen, 315.45 gm.

Rome, Campo Verano – *BCAR* 1876, 224; 1891, 11; *Civiltà Cattolica* 1877, 7
One specimen, 299.70 gm.
Museo Capitolino, Rome

App. 15   Second Punic War hoards of Italian coins (p.62)

Allies of Carthage
Labico – F. Ficoroni, *Le memorie di Labico* (App. 13), 85; J.B. Giard, *Congrès 1961*, 235
Bronzes of Capua

Santa Maria di Capua Vetere – G. Riccio, *Repertorio* (Naples, 1852), Note 3, n.18
Bronzes of Capua
The pieces in the Museo Campano, Capua, mentioned in *Il Museo Provinciale Campano di Capua* (Capua, 1974), 98, may come from this hoard; they certainly come from a hoard

Taranto – *IGCH* 2016; *Boll.It.di Num.* 1909, 65
Silver of Tarentum, Metapontum and Carthage

Allies of Rome
Termoli – *Rass.Num.* 1932, 92, presumably referring to the hoard now in the Museo Nazionale di Napoli
9 Ares/Horseman quincunces of Larinum
3 Zeus/Eagle quadrunciae
4 Hercules/Centaur teruncii
2 Female head/Dolphin biunces
4 Minerva/Wheel quincunces of Luceria
1 Female head/Shell biunx

Reggio Calabria – *IGCH* 2017
Bronzes of Rhegium

Probably area of Teate – information from A. Burnett
1 semilibral sextans
2 bronzes of Larinum (Sambon 201)
500–1000 bronzes of Teate of heavy and of light series

See also App. E

App. 16   Second Punic War finds in Bruttium (p.66)

Some isolated material is best regarded as booty acquired in the early years of the war:
Nicotera – *NSc* 1882, 283
As of light Apollo/Apollo series, 299.70 gm.
Museo Nazionale di Napoli

Monasterace Marina – *AIIN* 5–6, 1958–9, 280
Quadrigatus
Museo Nazionale di Reggio Calabria

S. Maria del Cedro – *NSc* 1978, 453–4
Quadrans of libral prow series

Some hoard material also may be regarded as booty acquired in the early years of the war:
Monte Giordano – *Coin Hoards* 2, 71
Silver of Neapolis and Rome (to quadrigatus system), Campano-Tarentine silver
Bronze of Argos
Museo Nazionale di Reggio Calabria

Catanzaro 1967 – *IGCH* 2019; *Coin Hoards* 3, 46
Silver of Neapolis, Tarentum, Heraclea, Rome, Campano-Tarentine silver, with Brettian and Carthaginian silver

Much Roman material belongs to the period either side of the creation of the denarius system and its presence in Bruttium is eloquent testimony both to the success of the armies of Hannibal and to the fact that he was unable or unwilling to recycle this material (the hoards cited may contain material other than that tabulated):

	Rome	Brettii	Lucani	Carthage	Petelia
Strongoli 1965 P. Attianese, *Il Gazzettino Num.* June 1976, 220	Bronze to semilibral				Bronze
Campana 1934 *IGCH* 2029	Bronze to semilibral				
Santa Eufemia Vetere = Terina *Klearchos* 18, 1976, 65	Bronze to semilibral				
Locri 1951 *IGCH* 2014	Quinarius	Silver		Silver	
Bruttium *IGCH* 2018		Bronze			
Catanzaro 1969 *IGCH* 2020		Silver			
Bruttium 1929 *IGCH* 2028				Silver	
Tiriolo 1788 M. Ruggiero (App. 5), 594		Gold			
Tiriolo 1897 *IGCH* 2021		Silver		Silver	
Peradace 1926 *IGCH* 2022		Bronze		Silver Bronze	

APPENDICES: FINDS

	Rome	Brettii	Lucani	Carthage	Petelia
Caulonia 1915 *IGCH* 2023; *AIIN* 21–2, 1974–5 77		Silver		Silver	
Capo Vaticano 1948 *IGCH* 2024		Bronze	Bronze	Bronze	
San Vincenzo La Costa 1957 *IGCH* 2025; P. Marchetti, 459; *AIIN* 21–2, 1974–5, 87 (wrong on Roman pieces)	Bronze to post-semilibral	Bronze		Bronze	
Strongoli 1968 P. Attianese, 222	Bronze to post-semilibral				
Rose 1913 *IGCH* 2026		Silver			
Belmonte 1935 *IGCH* 2027		Silver		Silver	
Vibo *AIIN* 21–2, 1974–5, 50		Silver			
Sersale 1794 M. Ruggiero (App. 5), 593		Bronze			
Bruttium 1977 *Coin Hoards* 4, 44					Bronze
Strongoli 1880 *IGCH* 2037 Compare *IGCH* 2058	Bronze to sextantal	Bronze			Bronze
Strongoli 1970 P. Attianese, 224					Bronze
Strongoli 1965 P. Attianese, 221					Bronze

Santa Eufemia Vetere 1974: also bronzes of Velia, Rhegium, Syracuse to Hieron II, Ptolemy II

Campana 1934: also bronzes of Rhegium, Mamertini, Syracuse to Hieron II, Ptolemy II

Tiriolo 1788: also gold of Philip II, Alexander III, Sicily and gold jewellery

San Vincenzo La Costa 1957: also bronzes of Hieron II

Sersale 1794: also bronzes of Mamertini

Strongoli 1880: also bronzes of Metapontum, Hipponium, Nuceria, Mamertini

Strongoli 1965: also bronzes of Cales, Neapolis, Hipponium, Rhegium, Mamertini, Syracuse

Two hoards present a puzzle:
Strongoli 1969 – P. Attianese, 223
5 staters, 4 half-staters, 6 quarter-staters of electrum of Carthage

Gioia Tauro before 1902 – *IGCH* 1989
Didrachms of Neapolis
Staters of electrum of Carthage

Compare one unspecified coin of electrum of Carthage from Castro, between Pitigliano and Vulci, *SE* 1941, 305

There is a remarkable collection of Second Punic War material (along with a few earlier pieces) from the destruction level at Torre del Mordillo near Cosenza (O.C. Colburn, *NSc* 1977, 521):
40 bronzes of Thurii
25 bronzes of Brettii
3 bronzes of Carthage (1 with Head of Tanit l./Horse r. with head turned back; 2 with Head of Tanit l./Horse's head r.)
1 half-quadrigatus
1 libral triens
2 semilibral sextantes
1 semilibral semuncia (wrongly published as uncial sextans)
2 semilibral quartunciae (wrongly published as sextantal unciae)
1 debased quadrigatus (published as bronze)
1 post-semilibral semuncia (wrongly published as semuncial sextans)
1 anonymous quinarius (*RRC*, no.102/2b)
1 denarius with club

App. 17   Finds of Carthaginian coins from Italy (p.71)

To supplement the evidence of the hoard material in *RRCH*, I list a number of stray finds simply to exemplify the pattern; compare also the finds cited in *La Donazione Chiellini 1883–1983* (Livorno, 1983), 33–4, with n.63 on p.37:
Sesto Fiorentino – N. Rilli, *Gli Etruschi a Sesto Fiorentino* (Florence, 1964), 88, pl.15
Bronze of Carthage, Head of Tanit l./Horse's head r.; before, palm-tree

Populonia 1939 hoard
Probably extraneous bronze of Carthage, Head of Tanit l./Horse's head r.

Ghiaccio Forte, upper Albegna river basin – M. del Chiaro, *Etruscan Ghiaccio Forte* (Santa Barbara, 1976)
With votive bronzes, votive terrracottas, pottery including Genucilia ware and pieces from Atelier des petites estampilles, from early third-century destruction level:
Bronze of Carthage, Head of Apollo l./Horse r. (*SNG* (Cop.) Carthage 94, Sicilian mint (?), late fourth to early third century)

Castro – App. 16

Tarquinia – *Bullettino* 1880, 10; *Atti e Memorie* 8, 97
Bronzes of Carthage

Pyrgi – *NSc* Supp. 1970, 2, 578
With a Minerva/Horse's head ROMANO bronze, a semilibral semuncia, an anonymous quadrans (5.60 gm.) and two illegible pieces, from the fill beneath a levelled open space:

Bronze of Carthage, Palm/Horse's head
Bronze of Carthage, Horse l./Horse l.

Punta della Vipera, Santa Marinella – *SE* 1967, 337, n.15
Bronze of Carthage, Head of Tanit l./Palm (Müller II, p.103, no.311 = *SNG* (Cop.) Carthage 415)
Bronze of Carthage, Head of Tanit l./Horse's head r. (Müller II, p.101, no. 278 = *SNG* (Cop.) Carthage 170)

Viterbo – *Bullettino* 1881, 260
Bronzes and silver piece of Carthage

Vicarello – App. 9
Bronzes of Carthage

Rome, Forum – R. Reece, *PBSR* 1982, 116
Bronze of Carthage, Horse/Palm, early third century.

Ostia – *Roma Medio-Repubblicana* (Rome, 1973), 361
Bronze of Carthage

Colle Monticchio near San Felice Circeo – *Arch.Laziale* 4, 204
Bronze of Carthage, Head of Tanit l./Horse r. and palm

It is likely that movements of coinage in a military context, rather than commercial reasons, lie behind this pattern of finds; there is little Etruscan pottery from Carthaginian territory, only Genucilia ware and pieces from the Atelier des petites estampilles, which are both Roman, not Etruscan, J. Macintosh, *Etruscan-Punic relations*, Diss. Bryn Mawr, 1974 = J.M. Turfa, *AJA* 1977, 369, 'Evidence for Etruscan-Punic relations'.

For the Po valley see App. 26

App. 18   Movement of coinage in the Second Punic War (p.71)

Coins of Sicily

To stand beside the evidence of the hoard material in *RRCH*, I list a number of stray finds of coins of the Mamertini simply to exemplify the pattern; other coins of Sicily, which clearly travelled to Bruttium in the context of the Second Punic War, are listed in App. 16:

Strongoli – P. Attianese (App. 16), 230
BMC 46

Carife – *RRCH* 50
BMC 3, 17

Cava dei Tirreni – *RRCH* 52
BMC 3, 17

Rome – R. Reece, *PBSR* 1982, 116
BMC 25

Volterra – *NSc* 1975, 5
BMC 22

Note also the bronzes of the Mamertini overstruck by Volceii

Note that many of the Ptolemaic coins found in Italy probably arrived via Sicily (compare App. 46):

Viterbo – *Bullettino* 1881, 261

Nazzano – *NSc* 1911, 436

Livorno – P. Mantovani, *Il Museo di Livorno* (Livorno, 1892), 121

Coins of Italy

The movement of south Italian coins to central Italy is no doubt also often to be explained in part in terms of the upheaval of the Second Punic War; to supplement the evidence of the hoard material in *RRCH*, I list a number of stray finds simply to exemplify the pattern; compare also the finds cited in *La Donazione Chiellini 1883–1983* (Livorno, 1983), 33–4, with n.63 on p.37:

Sesto Fiorentino – N. Rilli (App. 17)
Four bronzes of Cales

Fiesole – *NSc* 1932, 479; *SE* 1955, 232 and 236
Bronzes of Cales

Impruneta near Firenze – *NSc* 1918, 212
Bronze of Cales

Siena
Sextans of Barium, *BMC* 1
Bronze of Syracuse (fourth century), Female head r./Octopus
Museo Archeologico di Siena

Vetulonia – *SE* 1931, 587
Bronzes of Aquinum and Tarentum

Populonia 1939 hoard
Probably extraneous drachm with Head l./Victory over man-headed bull r.

Talamone
Didrachm of Neapolis
Bronzes of Neapolis and Capua
Museo Archeologico di Firenze

Isola di Fano – *Bullettino* 1875, 77
Bronzes of Arpi
Quincunx of Venusia
Sextans of Brundisium

Campo La Piana near Nocera Umbra – *RRCH* 553
Two didrachms of Neapolis (*BMC* 90, *BMC* ?)
Bronze of Catana (*BMC* 59)

Tarquinia – *Bullettino* 1880, 50; *Atti e Memorie* 8, 97
Bronzes of Neapolis, Cubulteria, Teanum Sidicinum and Metapontum

Ager Capenas – *Mon.Ant.* 16, 1906, 347
Bronze of Neapolis (in a tomb)

Vicarello – App. 9
Bronzes of Neapolis, Cales, Suessa, Teanum Sidicinum, Teate, Metapontum, Rhegium and Syracuse

Rome, Forum – R. Reece, *PBSR* 1982, 116
Two didrachms of Neapolis, *BMC* 89–92
Quincunx of Uria, *BMC* 6

Rome, San Giovanni in Laterano – *MDAI(R)* 1, 1886, 63
Bronze of Cales

Rome, San Giovanni in Laterano – *Annali* 1877, 341
Bronze of Paestum

Colle Monticchio near San Felice Circeo – *Arch.Laziale* 4, 204
Bronze with Man-headed bull/Victory

For the Po valley see App. 26

App. 19 Second Punic War hoards of Roman silver coins (p.71)

Santa Maria di Capua Vetere – *RRCH* 35 = *IGCH* 2010

Naples – *RRCH* 34 = *IGCH* 2012

Sessa – *RRCH* 48 = *IGCH* 2011 (out of order)

Ascoli Piceno – *RRCH* 59 = *IGCH* 2034 (out of order)

Campania – Museo Nazionale di Napoli
42 quadrigati

Campania – Museo Nazionale di Napoli
35 quadrigati

Montedoro – *RIN* 1912, 330, n.4
308 quadrigati

App. 20 Second-century hoards

BRONZE HOARDS (p.71)

Italy
RRCH 119

Ansedonia
RRCH 123

Italy
RRCH 125

Ostia
RRCH 126

Città Sant'Angelo
RRCH 129

Giulianova
RRCH 130

Rochetta a Volturno
RRCH 133

Veroli
RRCH 134

Larino
Sannio, 312

Some of these hoards contain isolated Greek pieces of an earlier period; the Sulmona hoard (*RRCH* 134) apparently contains an as of Q. Titius

VICTORIATUS HOARDS (p.74)

San Angelo a Cupolo
RRCH 112

Capestrano
RRCH 116

Cales
RRCH 556

Boiano
RRCH 115

Città Sant'Angelo
RRCH 129 (with bronze)

Cerreto Sannita
RRCH 155

Riccia
RRCH 161 (with denarii)

App. 21 Finds of Greek silver with coins of the denarius system in Italy (App. N)

Rossano di Vaglio – A. Burnett (p.29, n.2), 159, n.35, with verbal information
  1 didrachm, 1 drachm of Neapolis
  1 didrachm of Velia
  1 didrachm, 29 diobols of Tarentum
  1 Campano-Tarentine didrachm
28 diobols of Thurii
2 diobols of Metapontum
  1 Roma/Victory didrachm, 2 anonymous quinarii, 5 anonymous sestertii

Mesagne – *AIIN* 1976–7, 279
Perhaps a hoard:
  1 diobol of Tarentum
  1 anonymous denarius
  1 triens of Brundisium

Pisticci – *RRCH* 93 (not to be merged with *IGCH* 1996, according to E.S.G. Robinson)
14 didrachms of Tarentum
  1 didrachm of Thurii
  1 half-quadrigatus, 1 victoriatus, 3 quinarii

See also Issa in App. 50

App. 22 Finds of the drachm coinage of the Po valley (p.79)

HOARDS

	1	2	3	4	7	6	Tout. 9	Pir. 10	5	Rikoi 12
Sassello[1]	3	4	14							
Rome[2]		2	4	2						
Serra Riccò[3]	14	12	8	3						
Biandrate[4]		2	3		35					
Legnano[5]			2		23					
Milan[6]	15	10	8	2	314					
Manerbio[7]					1204	1415	1312			
Verdello[7]					2	33	31	57		
Bellinzona			2		17				7	
Borgovercelli		1	4		38		1		27	
Gerenzago[8]								4		43
Pavia			1	2						1

Hoards containing only one group are omitted from the table. Bibliographical references may be found in A. Pautasso (p.76, n.3), unless otherwise stated. For the hoard of very debased pieces from the Great St Bernard see App. 59. Note a hoard from Ventimiglia of didrachms of Velia and imitations of drachms of Massalia, *Riv.Stud.Lig.* 14, 1948, 119; *Numismatica* 14, 1948, 136.

1 For the Sassello hoard see *Sibrium* 1970, 174.
2 With Roman and South Italian coins down to Second Punic War.
3 For a further parcel of the hoard, including the fragments of two denarii, which given the testimony of the Rome hoard must be extraneous, see D. F. Allen, *JNG* 1971, 97; *NCirc* 1971, 14–15. A. Pautasso, *Studi P. Barocelli* (Turin, 1980), 261, 'Un eccezionale documento di protostoria cisalpina' is a second presentation of the Turin parcel of the hoard, wrongly accepting the presence of the fragments of the two denarii. B. Fischer, *Cahiers Numismatiques* 68, 1981, 45, is a die study of a selection of pieces from the hoard, also wrongly accepting the presence of the fragments of the two denarii.
4 With Roman coins down to Second Punic War.
5 With Roman coins probably down to Second Punic War; the description of F. von Duhn and E. Ferrero, *Mem.R.Ac.Sc.Torino*, ser. 2, 41, 1891, 331–88, 'Relazione sulle monete galliche del Medagliere dell'Ospizio del Gran San Bernardo', 'con moltissimi denari dei monetari C. Allius e P. Paetus', simply does not make sense; I suspect that P. Paestus is a mistake for C. Var(ro) and that the report of the hoard has picked on the only clear moneyers' names of the early denarius coinage.
6 An unpublished hoard from Rivolta d'Adda is similar to the Milan hoard.
7 A. Pautasso, pls. xlviii–xlix (Group 6) and l–lii (Group 7) do not seem to me to bear out his view that in the Manerbio hoard the former are more worn than the latter; rather the reverse. One can of course hardly argue on the basis of the two specimens of Group 7 in the Verdello hoard.
8 With Roman coins down to 118; also 7 unspecified Celtic drachms. There is no evidence on the condition of either.

Groups α (Gallia Cisalpina) and β (Burwein hoard, a re-burial in modern times, B. Overbeck (p.277, n.48) I, 183) are not included in the table. (The Bern specimen is not Groups α or 1, but Group 2, *contra* A. Pautasso, 46.)

Group 8 is not included in the table because it belongs to the area of the Veneti (there is one example in the Bellinzona hoard).

A. Pautasso, *Atti CESDIR* 1975–76, 473, 'Le monetazioni preromane con leggende in alfabeto leponzio', shows that the rare Artemis/Owl SEGHEDV issue goes with the unique ANAREKARTOS issue and that both are relatively early.

A. Pautasso kindly informs me of 3 drachms of Group 7 and 2 'obols' from two tombs at Garlasco, with La Tène C2 material, conventionally dated to the second half of the second century; in the light of my dating of the Ornavasso finds (see below), I should attribute the burials to the middle of the century.

It seems certain that the RIKOI issue does not follow directly on the rest of the coinage; both the hoard pattern and the fact that the legend now reads from left to right instead of right to left suggest a very substantial gap. Further, it is clear that the first period of the coinage belongs either side of 200 and production of the RIKOI issue in the immediately subsequent period could not be reconciled with the fact that it turns up in archaeological contexts which are clearly first century.

THE ORNAVASSO FINDS

The two cemeteries of San Bernardo and Persona, originally published by E. Bianchetti, *Atti Soc.Piemontese di Arch.* 6, 1895, 'I sepolcreti di Ornavasso', and recently studied by J. Graue, *Die Gräberfelder von Ornavasso* (Hamburg, 1974), remain the basis for any reconstruction of the later phases of the La Tène culture of northern Italy.

Stage I, as identified by Graue, contains no coins; Stage II, along with some earlier coins from about 200 onwards, contains a solid block of issues between C. Iunius (149 BC) and Q. Marcius, C. F., L. R. (118 or 117 BC), together with one quinarius of M.Cato (89 BC), one (plated) denarius of M.Volteius (78 BC) and two potin coins of Transalpine Gaul, which may also be of the first century (the account of the context of these coins in J.-B. Colbert de Beaulieu, 244, n.434, appears to be wholly fictional); Stage III, again along with some earlier coins from about 200 onwards and one denarius of M.Aurelius Scaurus (118 BC), contains coins between L. Piso Frugi (90 BC) and the triumviral period, together with halved asses which are probably Augustan (p. 260).

It is clear that Graue's chronology is in some respects in error, partly through use of an incorrect chronology for the Roman Republican coinage and partly through misunderstanding of the nature of the numismatic evidence.

The principal problem is that there is no evidence that the massive Republican issues of the late second century ever reached Ornavasso. On the other hand, the issues of 90 and later clearly did. If the pattern of the finds reflects reality, it becomes very hard to regard Stage II *as a whole* as falling after 90. Rather it should be regarded as belonging principally to say 110–90, with a certain after-life in the 80s and 70s. Stage III, on the other hand, should be regarded as beginning in the 80s and 70s and going down to 20–10.

As far as the coinage of the Po valley is concerned, the presence in Stage II of three examples of Pautasso Group 7, which I date to the early second century, comes as no surprise;

they are contemporary with the earliest Roman issues in Stage II. The presence of drachms with RIKOI, which I date to about 100, in Stage II and Stage III is also perfectly compatible with the rest of the evidence.

How does one explain the massive presence of Roman silver coins of the period 149–117? I cannot do so except on the hypothesis of an actual injection of Romans or Italians, no doubt in a military context, around 115–110. An attempt to guard the Passo del Sempione against the Cimbri and Teutones is an obvious possibility.

App. 23 Hoards of Roman silver coins in the Po Valley (p.81)

Hoards of victoriati:
Padova – *RRCH* 73
San Zeno – *RRCH* 74
Modena – App. 24
Caltrano Vicentino – *RRCH* 113
Gambolò – *RRCH* 114
Fano – *RRCH* 117
Ancona – *NSc* 1910, 366 – 25 victoriati
Maserà – *RRCH* 162 (with denarii)

The 'Udine' hoard (*RRCH* 84) cannot be regarded with absolute certainty as coming from Udine

Early hoards of denarii:
Orzivecchi – *RRCH* 106
Biandrate – App. 22

The Ornavasso 'hoard' (*RRCH* 105) should be regarded as forming part of the complex of finds of much later date, App. 22

Second-century hoards of denarii:
Belfiore – *RRCH* 159
Roncarolo – *RRCH* 173
Olmeneta – *RRCH* 203
Imola – *RRCH* 210
Carpena – *RRCH* 215
Claterna – *RRCH* 217

Hoards from the Istrian peninsula:
Fiume – *RRCH* 156
Fiume – *RRCH* 165 (containing an isolated survivor of the pre-denarius coinage)
Lavarigo – *RRCH* 231 (containing two isolated Athenian pieces)
Ossero – *RRCH* 316; Z. Dukat and I. Mirnik, *Izdanja Hrvatskog Arh.Dr.* 7 (Zagreb, 1982), 141 (a group of 42 denarii described as being from Neresine, in the Musée d'Art et d'Histoire in Geneva, may be part of the Ossero hoard; the group goes down to the issue of M. Volteius)
Corgnale = Lokev – Mirnik 71 (to Augustus)
Cerkno – P. Kos, *Studien zu Fundmünzen der Antike* (Berlin, 1979), 110 and 118 (to Augustus)

There is no way of telling when the Duttoule hoard of asses (*RRCH* 139) was buried

For site finds in the Locarno area see C. Simonett, *Tessiner Gräberfelder* (Basel, 1941), 8:
1 victoriatus with VB
7 quinarii
2 denarii

For site-finds in Emilia and the Veneto see App. 24

App. 24   Association of silver of Cisalpine Gaul and Roman bronze (p.83)

Pignone, La Spezia, in hill-fort – *Archeologia in Liguria* (Genova, 1975), 87
1 imitation of obol
1 uncertain as

Alzate Brianza near Como – A. Pautasso (p.76, n.3), 128
1 imitation of drachm
1 uncertain as

Treviglio near Bergamo – A. Pautasso, 68
9 imitations of drachms
1 denarius
3 quinarii
2 victoriati
8 asses

Bolgare near Bergamo – *Sibrium* 1970, 166
1 imitation of drachm
4 asses

Bolgare near Bergamo – *Sibrium* 1970, 170
1 imitation of drachm
3 asses
1 semis

Fumane near Verona – A. Pautasso, 131
1 imitation of drachm
1 uncertain as
1 uncertain semis

Trento – A. Pautasso, 132
Imitations of drachms
2 denarii
Uncertain asses

Este, in votive deposit, with later material – *NSc* 1888, 204, 483; 1890, 199
Imitations of drachms
2 denarii
Victoriati
Asses
1 semis
1 quadrans
1 bronze of Ariminum

Treviglio – information from M. Tizzoni
9 drachms with RIKOI
3 asses
4 quinarii of P. Sabinus, Q. Titius, M. Cato, L. Dossenus

Altino – information from G. Gorini
Imitations of drachms
Republican bronzes

San Cesario near Modena – *RRCH* 111; E. Ercolani Cocchi, *RIN* 1981, 251, 'Rinvenimenti di dramme padane in Emilia' (also on isolated finds of drachms from Monterenzio with pre-denarius bronzes and Marzabotto)
Imitations of drachms
1 anonymous semis
1 victoriatus
1 bronze of Ariminum
Fractions à la croix

See also the account of the finds from Ornavasso in App. 22

App. 25   Finds of cast bronze coinage in the Po valley (p.83)

Comacchio – App. 10

Trento – App. 10
I suspect that a hoard from so far north at this date is to be regarded as booty

There is a single triens of the heavy Dioscuri/Mercury series from Ancona, Haeberlin, p.96, no.65

A Wheel/Wheel uncia from Laufen in Switzerland (*SM* 1966, 179) and a piece of Hatria perhaps from Riva (G. Roberti, App. 26) no doubt represent casual northward drift

For finds of cast bronze coinage from east of the Adriatic see App. 49

App. 26 Finds of Greek coins in the Po and Adige valleys (App. G)

These are for the most part to be regarded as having come north with Roman and Italian settlers after the Second Punic War, in which category the Ptolemaic bronzes are undoubtedly to be included (compare App. 18):

Aquileia – G. Gorini, *RIN* 1976, 13
Bronze of Croton

Monfalcone – *Aquileia Nostra* 51, 1980, 345
Bronze of Thurium

Rimini – E. Cocchi Ercolani (App. 1), at 203
Late didrachm of Neapolis

Fano – *RIN* 1892, 260
Bronze of Teanum

Lugano – Museo di Lugano
Hoard of bronzes of Rhegium (as *BMCItaly* 71)

Castelfranco near Modena – *Coin Hoards* 2, 77
Bronzes of Suessa, Agrigentum, Syracuse, Carthage, Acarnania (compare App. D)

Cadore – *Arch.Stor.di Belluno* 18 (*sic, recte* 17), 1946, 1468
Bronze of Mamertini

Viadana – M. Baguzzi, *RIN* 1975, 113; 1976, 83
Two bronzes of Carthage (as *SNG* (Cop.) 1569)

Monselice – G. Gorini, *Atti e Memorie della Società Istriana di Archeologia e Storia Patria* 76, 1976, 43, 'Aspetti della circolazione monetaria nel III-II sec. a.C. in Alto Adriatico: i bronzi tolemaici'
Bronze of Ptolemy II

Chioggia-Brondolo – ibid.
Bronze of Ptolemy III

Motta d'Este – ibid.
Bronze of Ptolemy V

San Giorgio in Bosco – ibid.
Uncertain Ptolemaic bronze

Adria – P. Visonà, *Atti e Memorie* 76, 1976, 55
Bronze of Ptolemy IV

The Ptolemaic bronzes from Karlstein in Germany, Münchenstein and Avenches in Switzerland (G. Gorini), Rhäzuns in Switzerland (B. Overbeck (p.277, n.48) II, no. 124, compare his no. 85 with App. 46 below for a bronze of Amisus and an uncertain Greek bronze from the Julierpass), no doubt represent material which drifted north from the Po valley

Belluno – G. Gorini, *Antichità Altoadriatiche* 15, 1979, 415, n.9
Gold coin of Carthage, as Jenkins and Lewis, no.163

Cembra – P.F. Orgler, *Zeitschrift des Ferdinandeums* (Innsbruck) 1878, 59 'Verzeichnis der Fundorte antiker Münzen in Tirol und Vorarlberg'
Coins of Agathocles, Hieron II (not I)

Mori – ibid.
Bronze of Syracuse

Nago – ibid.
Bronze of Syracuse

Trento – ibid.
Bronzes of Syracuse and Panormus (in fact Carthage)

Meano – ibid.
Bronze of Panormus (in fact Carthage)

Vallarsa – ibid.
Bronze of Panormus (in fact Carthage)

Villazzano – ibid.
Bronzes of Paestum, Heraclea, Syracuse, Hieron II

Mattarello – ibid.
Bronzes of Teanum, Heraclea

Wilten – ibid.
Didrachm of Velia

A separate group is composed of drachms of Apollonia or Dyrrachium; I suppose them to have arrived in the Po valley later in the second century:

Padova – information from G. Gorini
Drachm of Dyrrachium

Monselice – information from G. Gorini
Drachm of Dyrrachium or Apollonia

Bassano – information from G. Gorini
Drachm of Dyrrachium

Cembra – P.F. Orgler, l.c.
Drachm of Dyrrachium

Castello Tesino – ibid.
Drachm of Dyrrachium

Levico – ibid.
Drachm of Dyrrachium

Trento – G. Roberti, *Studi Trentini* 29, 1950, 317, 'Distribuzione topografica delle monete rinvenute nel Trentino'
Drachm of Dyrrachium

A much earlier find is apparently that from Kurtatsch = Cortaccia, consisting of coins of Alexander III, Alexander IV, Philip III, Cassander and Antigonus (presumably Gonatas), along with a statuette of Mercury, perhaps the property of a mercenary, P.F. Orgler, l.c.

App. 27   Second Punic War hoards in Spain (p.87)

Hispano-Punic	Hispano-Punic Didrachm coinage	Hispano-Punic Denarius coinage
Sevilla	Cadiz (also Gades, Ebusus)	Martos (Jaen) (also Emporiae imit., Eumenes I, quadrigatus)
Mazarron	Granada	Mogente (also Emporiae, Ebusus, Syracuse)
La Escuera		Cheste (also Emporiae, Emporiae imit., Saguntum, Massalia)
Montemolin (also Rhode imit., Emporiae, Emporiae imit., Ebusus, Gades, Saguntum)		Valera (also Emporiae, Emporiae imit., Ebusus, Saguntum, Saetabi, Celtic, Rhodes)
		Cuenca (also Antiochus III, Side, Perge (194/3, 193/2), Aspendus (219/8), Aradus (?, 195/4), Cos

Emporiae Didrachm coinage	Emporiae Denarius coinage
Los Villares (Caudete)	Drieves (also Celtic, Massalia) Ebro valley (also Emporiae imit., Massalia, Massalia imit., Ebusus) La Plana de Utiel (also Emporiae imit., Celtic, Massalia, Italo-Punic) Tivisa 1975 (imit.) (also quadrigatus) Tivisa before 1930 (also Emporiae imit., Saguntum, Massalia) Las Ansies (also Emporiae imit.) Coll del Moro (also Ebusus)

Sevilla – *IGCH* 2323

Mazarron – *IGCH* 2325

La Escuera – L. Villaronga (p.87, n.9), 83

Montemolin – *Saguntum* 16, 1981, 247, with earlier bibliography (see *Acta Num.* 1980, 29, for scattered finds of bronze fractions; also *Nummus* 1981–3, 128, with isolated material from elsewhere)

Cadiz – L. Villaronga (p.87, n.9), 78

Granada – L. Villaronga (p.87, n.9), 78

Martos – *Nummus* 1981–3, 134

Mogente – *RRCH* 91; M.P. Garcia Bellido (forthcoming)

Cheste – *RRCH* 75; denarius as Ailly, pl. 1, 2

Valera – *RRCH* 109; *Numisma* 71, 1964, 25; K. Raddatz, 266–7 (1 uncertain hemiobol, also in La Plana di Utiel, not 1 obol of Carthage)

Cuenca – information from L. Villaronga

Los Villares – K. Raddatz, 205–6

Ebro valley – *Acta Num.* 1983, 47

Drieves – *RRCH* 107; K. Raddatz, 210–22; information from T.R. Volk

La Plana di Utiel – *Acta Num.* 1980, 15

Tivisa 1975 – *Coin Hoards* 2, 192; *Acta Num.* 1982, 63

Tivisa before 1930 – *RRCH* 94; K. Raddatz, 258–9; the hoard included one extraneous as of Iltirda; for reasons which are unclear, it also contains a preponderance of coins at the bottom ends of the weight ranges of the issues concerned, L. Villaronga, *9 Cong.Num.* 253; there is no evidence that the so-called second hoard (*Ampurias* 1941, 15) was a hoard at all

Las Ansies – *RRCH* 104

Coll del Moro – *Numisma* 28, 1978, 150

App. 28 Finds of cast bronze coinage in Spain

Burriac = Ilduro, on coast north of Barcelona – M. Ribas Bertran, *Els origens de Mataró* (Mataró, 1964), pl. xvi; *Numisma* 1975, 258
Prow triens, 88.35 gm.

Monte Meca de Ayora, in Jucar valley – *Ampurias* 5, 1943, 231
Prow as, 244.08 gm.

Minorca – *NH* 8, 1957, 165
Prow triens, 77.00 gm.

Majorca – *Ampurias* 25, 1963, 168
Prow as, 257.00 gm.

App. 29 Hoards of Iberian denarii (p.94)

	Group A		Group B						
	1	2	3	4	5	6	7	8	9
Iltirta (salirban)	173		1				1		
Ikalesken		42	45	55	+140	1	8		
Kese	2	2	1				2		
Ausesken									
Sesars	60								
Sekaisa							1		
Baskunes			3	1		1			
Konterbia			1	2	1	1			
Bolskan	1	3	24	233	+20	16	52	400	700
Areikoratikos			2	2	1	2			
Arsaos			1		1	1			
Turiasu			2		1				
Sekobirikes				2	1				
Belikiom								9	3

1 = Lerida (3 Iltirta, 170 Iltirtasalirban); the corresponding bronze of Sesars occurs at Numantia (G.K. Jenkins, p.93, n.20) = 30 on Map 17
2 = Arcas = 31 on Map 17
3 = Cordoba (1 Iltirtasalirban); also 1 drachm of Saguntum; some earlier bronze of Kese occurs at Numantia
4 = Granada = 33 on Map 17
5 = Azuel = 32 on Map 17; the Roman denarii in the hoard are described by J. Zobel y Zangroniz, *MNE* 4, 277, as a little later than those in the Cazlona hoard, so are late second century
6 = Mogon = 34 on Map 17
7 = Salvacañete (1 Iltirta); also 2 drachms of Saguntum
8 = Azuara 2
9 = Calatayud = 35 on Map 17

Group C

	1	2	3	4	5	6	7	8	9	10
Baskunes		105	31	1			359		39	
Konterbia							1			
Bolskan	1	1		3	1	113	159			39
Areikoratikos		12	45	5	4		92		25	
Arsaos	(1)	33	14	3	2		108		26	
Turiasu	51	922	45	50	8		842		14	
Sekobirikes	1	298	11	78	16	1	1075	59		
Belikiom							2			223

1 = Cervera (the piece of Arsaos is bronze)
2 = Barcus
3 = Borja
4 = Roa
5 = Salamanca
6 = Maluenda
7 = Palenzuela; also 5 of Bentian, 2 of Kolounioku, 1 of Oilaunikos, 1 of Sekia
8 = Amaya
9 = Alagon
10 = Azuara 1

I do not include the Garray, Terrer, Quintana Redonda hoards (inadequately known); the Los Villares, Las Casetas, Larrabezua hoards (inadequately known, but similar to Group B); the Fuentecén, Retortillo, Tricio hoards (inadequately known, but similar to Group C); the Huesca, El Burgo hoards (Bolskan only)

Lerida (sometimes known as Hostalrich or Tarrasa) – P.P. Ripollés Alegre, *La circulación monetaria en la Tarraconense Mediterranea* (Valencia, 1982), 36

Arcas – L. Villaronga, *Los denarios con leyenda icalgusken* (Barcelona, 1962), 21

Cordoba – G.K. Jenkins, *MusN* 8, 1958, 57; *RRCH* 184; *NC* 1969, 79

Granada – G.K. Jenkins, *NH* 7, 1958, 135, suggesting that 2 denarii of Bolskan, 1 of Areikoratikos and the 2 of Sekobirikes are later than the rest of the hoard

Azuel – K. Raddatz, 199; the pieces of Ikalesken are from Villa del Rio and form part of the same hoard

Mogon – K. Raddatz, 227

Salvacañete – *RRCH* 205; K. Raddatz, 244; *Rev.Arch.Bibl.Mus.* 79, 1976, 389

Azuara 2 – *RRCH* 204

Calatayud – F. Mateu y Llopis, *NH* 1, 1952, 220ff., no.503

Cervera del Alhama – *Arch.Esp.Arte Arq.* 2, 1926, 140

Barcus – *NH* 6, 1957, 157; *Ampurias* 6, 1942, 221

Borja – *Congrès* 1953, 433

Roa – M. Paz Garcia Bellido, *Zephyrus* 25, 1974, 394

Salamanca – ibid., 379

Maluenda – *RRCH* 282; *Numisma* 165–7, 1980, 119 (to L. Rutilius Flaccus)

Palenzuela – *RRCH* 314; M. Paz Garcia Bellido, l.c.

Amaya – ibid.

Alagon – *Numisma* 1973–74, 201

Azuara 1 (sometimes known as Hijar) – P.P. Ripollés Alegre, 25

App. 30 Hoards including Roman denarii in Spain between 125 and 91 (p.97)

1. Pozoblanco before 1870 – *RRCH* 174
2. Cordoba after 1945 – K. Raddatz, 268
3. Segaro 1881 – *RRCH* 180
4. La Barroca near *Gerunda* 1953 – *RRCH* 178
5. El Centenillo 1911 – *RRCH* 181
6. Montoro = *Epora* 1936 – *RRCH* 182
7. Baix Llobregat 1937 – *Coin Hoards* 1, 157; L. Villaronga, in *XIV Cong..Nac.Arq.*, 871
8. Sarria near Barcelona 1870 – *Gaceta Numismatica* 64, 1982, 24
9. Cordoba 1916 – App. 29
10. Sierra Morena 1920 – *RRCH* 186
11. Cazlona 1618 – *RRCH* 188
12. Torre de Juan Abad 1934 – *RRCH* 189; *Acta Num.* 1982, 79
13. Penhagarcia about 1920 – *RRCH* 191
14. Aznalcollar between 1908 and 1919 – *A Catalogue of the Roman Republican Coins in the Royal Scottish Museum, Edinburgh* (Edinburgh, 1984), xi
15. Cogollos de Guadix 1959 – *Numisma* 1978, 25
16. Santa Elena 1903 – *RRCH* 193
17. Rio Tinto between 1903 and 1910 – *RRCH* 194
18. Sierra Morena 1929 – *RRCH* 196
19. Oliva 1848–9 and 1961 – *RRCH* 197
20. Mogon 1914 – *RRCH* 200
21. Cazlona shortly before 1978 – *Numisma* 1978, 19
22. Azuara 1890 – App. 29
23. Salvacañete about 1930 – App. 29
24. Portugal – Museu Nacional, Lisbon
25. Pozoblanco 1925 – *Bol.Real Acad.Bellas Letras y Nobles Artes de Cordoba* 1928, 51; *Coin Hoards* 3, 119 is perhaps another parcel
26. Crevillente before 1949 – *RRCH* 206
27. Orcera 1940 – *RRCH* 211
28. Idanha-a-Velha 1974 – *Coin Hoards* 3, 120
29. San Joao dos Caldereiros 1941 – *Arquivo de Beja* 1955, 65 and 162

I omit the hoard of 1 Roman and 2 Iberian denarii of Soto Iruz, *RRCH* 185

App. 31 Hoards including Roman bronze in Spain (p.99)

Ampurias 1947 – *RRCH* 136
Rome, Emporiae

Ampurias 1972 – *II Simposi Numismatic*, 175
Rome, Emporiae

Ecija (ancient Astigi) – *II Simposi Numismatic*, 171
Rome, Castulo, Carmo

El Saucejo (ancient Irni) – *QTic* 1980, 175
Rome, Castulo, Carmo, Urso

Note also the hoard from Torello on Minorca consisting of 365 asses down to the issue of C. Antestius; 1 as of Cn. Blasio; 1 as of Obulco; 1 bronze of Populonia (presumably passing as an as) – N. Tarradell-Font, *Fonaments* 3, 201

App. 32 Hoards of Iberian bronze coinage (p.99)

	Balsareny	Solsona	Canoves	Azaila II
Kese I	10	1		
Kese II	73			2
Kese III				7
Kese IV				5
Ausesken		1	5	
Laiesken	39		1	1
Eusti	36		4	1
Eustibaikula	2		1	
Ilturo	42		1	3
Lauro			21	
Iltirkesken	66	*c.*20	3	2
Iltirta	5			101

Balsareny – L. Villaronga, *NH* 10, 1961, 9
Solsona – ibid., 63 (with one denarius of Bolskan; the group to which the as of Kese belongs is uncertain)
Canoves – J. Estrada and L. Villaronga, *Ampurias* 28, 1967, 135 (with five uncertain pieces); J. Romagosa, *Acta Num.* 1971, 79
Azaila II – L. Villaronga, *Los Tesoros de Azaila* (Barcelona, 1977), with earlier bibliography; also 11 Roman bronze coins to the semuncial period and 468 further Iberian bronze coins of the Ebro valley; Azaila I consists simply of Iberian bronze coins of the same area and period, without overlap with the issues listed above, but with overlap with the other issues in Azaila II

Note also the hoard from Azuera near Belchite, containing 90 bronzes of Belikiom and 1 of Bolskan (L. Villaronga, *Ampurias* 30, 1968, 225)

App. 33 Finds of early Roman coins in Sardinia (p.103)

Cagliari = *Carales* 1869 – *RRCH* 32
About 50 quadrigati with incuse legend

Sulcis 1874 – *RRCH* 46
Bronze coins of Carthage
1 as of the libral Prow series with Prow 1

Perdas de Fogu 1931 – *RRCH* 100
766 bronze coins of Carthage (including 1 of type of *NC* 1943, Pl. i, 1–2; 1 of type of *SNG* (Cop.) 1030–3)
1 collateral quadrans with corn-ear
3 anonymous sextantes
4 sextantes with corn-ear and K
2 with C
5 with MA
1 with AVR

Burgos 1970 – *AIIN* 18–19, 1971–72, 343
16 anonymous denarii
 4 with crescent
 1 with prow
 6 with star

Ossi – *Scoperte Archeologiche* 1869, 23
1 quadrans of the light Dioscuri/Mercury series

Perfogas – *Bullettino Archeologico Sardo* 1856, 182; 1860, 35 with pl. R, 6

1 triens of the Roma/Roma series without symbol (98.00 gm.)
Museo Nazionale di Cagliari

Sardinia – *Studi Sardi* 12–13, 1952–54, 525
1 triens of the Roma/Roma series without symbol (85.00 gm.)

Sulcis – *Scoperte Archeologiche* 1875, 16
1 triens of the libral Prow series

Bolotana – *Studi Sardi* 12–13, 1952–54, 525
1 semis of the post-semilibral Prow series with Prow 1. (31.50 gm.)

For finds of Carthaginian coins only see *IGCH* 2262–4, 2273–4, 2277–80, 2283–91

Not much can be made of the find of a gold coin of Philip II from Olbia, *Studi Sardi* 9, 1950, 97

The conclusions of R.J. Rowland, *11 Cong.Frontier Studies*, 87, 'Numismatics and the military history of Sardinia', are wholly invalidated by the fact that he does not take account of the different sizes of different issues of denarii

App. 34 Finds of coins in Corsica (p.104)

Aléria – J. and L. Jehasse, *La nécropole préromaine d'Aléria* (Paris, 1973), nos. 2310 and 594
Didrachm of Populonia
Quadrans or sextans with OPEI
   – J. and L. Jehasse, *Mélanges Carcopino* (Paris, 1966), 529 (compare *Gallia* 1960, 324)

Victoriatus with MP
Bronze of Thespiae
Coins of Chalcis and Carthage
   – L. and J. Jehasse, *Corse Historique* 2, 1962, 8, 27, 'Les monnaies puniques d'Aléria'
Site finds in connection with use as a base in First and Second Punic Wars

App. 35 Finds of cast bronze coinage in Sicily (p.110)

Naxos – *RRCH* 17
1 uncia of the heavy Dioscuri/Mercury series
1 uncia of the heavy Apollo/Apollo series

Catania – *Boll.It.di Num.* 1908, 19
Triens of the heavy Dioscuri/Mercury series

Visrini – *NSc* 1902, 17
Uncia of the Roma/Roma series without symbol

Ragusa – *NSc* 1902, 217; *Boll.It.di Num.* 1908, 19
3 cast quadrantes with corn-ear

App. 36 Second Punic War hoards in Sicily (p.111)

Tripi – *RRCH* 55 and 66; *IGCH* 2237–8; I no longer think, with P. Marchetti, 491, that we are dealing with two hoards

Aidone 1908 – *RRCH* 68; Aidone 1909, *IGCH* 2239; it seems to me that we are dealing with one hoard; the HISPANORVM piece is clearly on grounds of patination extraneous, *contra* G. Manganaro, *Archivio Storico per la Sicilia Orientale* 1969, 291, n.22; the Tauromenium piece likewise, *contra* P.Marchetti, 489, whose account of the issues of the Mamertini and Rhegium supplements that in *RRCH* 68; the latest Syracusan issue, however, is of the Syracusan democracy

Mandanici – *RRCH* 71; *AIIN* 1962–4, 229, P. Marchetti, 490, whose account corrects that in *RRCH* 71

Montagna di Marzo – *RRCH* 99; given the loss of most of the hoard during the war, it is probably forlorn to attempt to argue as does P. Marchetti, 489, compare *RBN* 1971, 88, n.20, that we are dealing with two hoards

San Marco, *IGCH* 2236; earlier pieces include KAINON (1), Abacaenum (1)

Grammichele – list based on my own inspection and that of T.V. Buttrey

I view with grave scepticism the report in the sale catalogue, Bonhams 4/12/1980, p.19, that an anonymous victoriatus (*RRC*, no.44/1), an anonymous denarius (*RRC*, no.75/1c), a denarius of C. Varro and a denarius of C. A(i)lius were found with a silver issue of Hieron II beneath the destruction level of 211 at Morgantina; no pieces later than the very first moments of the denarius system have turned up in the official excavations of Morgantina

App. 37 Second- and first-century bronze hoards in Sicily
(p.115)

Catania	Morgantina	Avola	Biancavilla
Asses	Asses to 160s BC	Asses to 160s BC	Denarii Victoriatus Asses to 150s BC
	Syracuse to Hieron II Leontini	Hieron II	Hieron II
Mamertini	Mamertini	Mamertini Centuripae	Mamertini Centuripae
Rhegium		Rhegium	Rhegium
	Carthage		

Catania – *IGCH* 2244
Morgantina – information from R. Ross Holloway (sealed deposit including HISPANORVM issue)
Avola – *RRCH* 122; also 1 piece of Ptolemy II
Biancavilla – *RRCH* 127
I have excluded the re-deposited votive offerings from Morgantina, *IGCH* 2248

Bisacquino	Megara	Campobello	Sicily
Asses Panormus		Asses Panormus Syracuse	Asses Panormus
	Syracuse Catana Enna as *municipium*		
		L. Naevius Surdinus	C. Cassius Celer

Bisacquino – *IGCH* 2251; *AIIN* 23–4, 1976–7, 304; the wear on the asses shows the hoard to be late second or early first century
Megara – *IGCH* 2252; G. K. Jenkins, *The Coinage of Gela* (Berlin, 1970), 117, n. 13
    Rhegium: Head of Apollo r./Lyre ΡΗΓ (in monogram) ΙΝΩΝ
    Catana: Gabrici, nos. 9–14
    Syracuse: Gabrici, pl. 9, 15 (23); pl. 9, 21 (1); pl. 9, 13 (8); *SNG* (Cop.) 901–2 (11)
    Enna: Gabrici, no. 12
Campobello – *IGCH* 2253
Sicily – *AIIN* 3, 1956, 210; also 1 piece of the Mamertini, 1 piece of Ebusus

App. 38   Finds of Italian and Sicilian bronze coinage in Greece (p.118)

Brettii No details	Olympia	P. R. Franke, *AA* 1966, 395, n.4
Brettii *BMC* 70	Corinth	K. M. Edwards, *Corinth* VI, no. 232
Croton	Delos	*Exploration Arch. de Delos* *XXVII*, 387
Rhegium Late CIII BC	Eretria	T. Hackens, *RBN* 1968, 127; O. Picard, *Chalcis* (Paris, 1979), 317
Rhegium 203–89 BC	Corinth	J. M. Harris, *Hesp.* 1941, 148
Rhegium (2+1) No details	Delos	T. Hackens, *RBN* 1967, 263; see also *Expl.Arch.de Delos*, l.c.
Neapolis No details	Olympia	P. R. Franke, l.c.
Lipari *SNG* (Cop.) 1100	Corinth	J. M. Harris, l.c.; P. R. Franke, l.c.
Catana *BMC* 70	Delos	*JIAN* 10, 1907, 208
Syracuse *SNG* (Cop.) 914	Thebes	T. Hackens, *RBN* 1968, 126
Syracuse Hieron II	Euboea	*IGCH* 230
Siculo-Punic No details	Athens	J. Shear, *Hesp.* 1936, 130
Mamertini No details	Athens	J. Shear, l.c.
Mamertini (1+1) No details; *BMC* 32	Delos	T. Hackens, *RBN* 1967, 263; *JIAN*, l.c.

It is very doubtful if the piece of Halaesa, T. Hackens, *RBN* 1968, 126, was lost in the Hellenistic period

App. 39 Hoards in Greece (p.119)

The following tables are constructed on the basis of *IGCH* 175–248 and 455–688, with *Coin Hoards*, 2, 72, 75 and 80; 3, 43; 4, 54 and 56; 5, 42, 44 and 45; 6, 35, excluding bronze hoards, *IGCH* 198 and 204 (from the Cyclades), 200–1 (of earlier date), 227 (from Crete)

Eretria – *IGCH* 175: also contains 13 fourth-century silver pieces of the Euboeans; the date of burial is very uncertain, O. Picard, *Chalcis* (Paris, 1979), 153; O. Mørkholm, *Gnomon* 1980, 453

Carystus – *IGCH* 177: also contains 1 fourth-century silver piece of the Euboeans

Euboea – *IGCH* 178: O. Picard, l.c., lists 43 further drachms of Chalcis which probably belong

Euboea – *IGCH* 188: also contains 5 fourth-century silver pieces of the Euboeans and 1 piece of Priansus

Aliveri – *IGCH* 192: also contains 1 fourth-century silver piece of the Euboeans

Carystus – *IGCH* 210/215: also contains 3 fourth-century silver pieces of the Euboeans

'Gephyra' – *IGCH* 471: clearly Euboean in character

Abae – *IGCH* 195: 1 piece each of Aetolia and Boeotia are bronze

Atalanti – *Coin Hoards* 2, 75

Thebes – *IGCH* 233: 42 pieces of Boeotia are bronze; also contains 1 denarius and 1 second-century triobol of Megalopolis

Anthedon – *IGCH* 223: the pieces of Athens are new-style

Thessaly – *Coin Hoards* 2, 72; 3, 43

Thessaly – *Coin Hoards* 5, 42; 6, 35: the figures certainly include some pieces which have been counted twice

Thessaly – *Coin Hoards* 4, 56

Larissa – *IGCH* 304: the pieces of Athens are bronze

Sitochoro – *IGCH* 237: also contains 1 tetradrachm of Pharnaces; for the tetradrachms of Eumenes, see G. Le Rider, *RN* 1973, 66

Tricca – *IGCH* 234: the pieces of Athens are new-style

Velestinon – *Coin Hoards* 5, 45

Kozani – *IGCH* 457: also contains 1 extraneous tetradrachm of Aesillas

The pieces of Athens in Beroea and later hoards are new-style (note also *IGCH* 523, 524, 550)

Corinth – *IGCH* 187: also contains 2 tetradrachms of Ephesus

Sparta – S. Grünauer, *8 Num.Cong.*, 79, for the date; also contains 7 tetradrachms of Sparta

Therianos – *IGCH* 182: also contains 2 early silver pieces of Corinth

Kyparissia – *IGCH* 209 – also contains 1 silver piece of the Locrians

Arcadia – *IGCH* 242: also contains 1 extraneous bronze of Elis

Zacynthus – *IGCH* 245: also contains 1 diobol of Heraclea in Italy and 1 obol of Selge in Pamphylia

Patras – *Coin Hoards* 2, 80; 5, 44

Peloponnese – *IGCH* 246: also contains 1 second-century triobol of Corinth

The Sophikon hoard (*IGCH* 179) is excluded because it comes from the sea

For the reasons for the presence of Ptolemaic coins in the Peloponnese, see *La moneta in Grecia e a Roma* (Bari, 1982), 89

Date		Philip II	Alexander III	Philip III	Demetrius Poliorcetes	Antigonus Gonatas	Antigonus Doson	Lysimachus	Locri Op.	Phocis	Boeotia	Eretria	Carystus	Chalcis	Euboean League	Histiaea
235	Eretria	1	24		5	15		20	20	1	16		1	1	273	1
230	Carystus		17					2					68		276	
230–220	Euboea		1											18		
250–220	Euboea											1	6	2	2	4
250–220	Eretria	2	1		1			1	22	9	9					
235–200	Carystus												5			
235–200	Aliveri												17			
225–200	Chalcis												31		61	
225–200	Chalcis		14	1	5			1	22	15	66		3	56	27	5
220	Carystus										1		14			
200–180	Koskina		1								1		38	3	41	1
200–150	'Gephyra'									1	2			2		31
170	Oreus		1					1						2		6

Athens	Paros, etc.	Attalid	Rhodes	Seleucid	Ptolemaic	Aegina	Sicyon	Elis	Argos	Achaea, etc.	Arcadia, etc.	Aetolia	Larissa, etc.	Philip V	Perseus	Macedonia
31	1	2	7	2	136											
17				5				2								
			8		2											
			6													
	15															
		12	28		2						1					
							1				1					
			595							3		2	1	24	10	1

APPENDICES: FINDS

Date		Philip II	Alexander III	Philip III	Demetrius Poliorcetes	Antigonus Gonatas	Antigonus Doson	Lysimachus	Locri Op.	Phocis	Boeotia	Eretria	Carystus	Chalcis	Euboean League	Histiaea
225–200	Thebes		8					1								
225–200	Abae		4	1					3	3	9			8		
	Atalanti		1	1	1				1	1				✓		
165	Thebes										43					2
160	Anthedon											10		5		

Date		Philip II	Alexander III	Philip III	Demetrius Poliorcetes	Antigonus Gonatas	Antigonus Doson	Lysimachus	Locri Op.	Phocis	Boeotia	Eretria	Carystus	Chalcis	Euboean League	Histiaea
230	Thessaly	2	3					2	1		5				2	1
200	Thessaly										7					
175	Thessaly		3		4	6	6	5	10	4	5					620
	Thessaly								5	2	5					133
180–170	Grammenon															53
	Larissa										7					377
	Larissa															600
165	Sitochoro		11			3		2								
150	Tricca															
	Larissa		1						3	1	8			8		28
	Larissa															
	Larissa															
	Lamia															
	Velestinon															

APPENDICES: FINDS

313

Athens	Paros, etc.	Attalid	Rhodes	Seleucid	Ptolemaic	Aegina	Sicyon	Elis	Argos	Achaea, etc.	Arcadia, etc.	Aetolia	Larissa, etc.	Philip V	Perseus	Macedonia
11			14		5											
						2	27	2	1	1	2	1	1			
1						1	✓	2								
			8				1			2						
10																

Athens	Paros, etc.	Attalid	Rhodes	Seleucid	Ptolemaic	Aegina	Sicyon	Elis	Argos	Achaea, etc.	Arcadia, etc.	Aetolia	Larissa, etc.	Philip V	Perseus	Macedonia	Thasos	Thessalian League	Magnetes	Perrhaebi	Macedonian Regions
8			5		2		2						5								
		3																			
			5			2	20						6			1					
							9		2	1						1					
			49										1			27					
2													1								
11		2 2000	6		5								1	13	600						6
100														2	30	✓					
						1											1	1			
															75						
															1192			6	1		
															36						
															84						

Date		Philip II	Alexander III	Philip III	Demetrius Poliorcetes	Antigonus Gonatas	Antigonus Doson	Lysimachus	Locri Op.	Phocis	Boeotia	Eretria	Carystus	Chalcis	Euboean League	Histiaea
250–230	Pergi	246	3	1	1			16								
240–230	Kozani													5		
200–180	Macedonia	6				16		1								
175	Yenikeui															3
170	Macedonia															✓
170	Pella															
160–150	Beroea							2								
	Thessalonica															
	Macedonia															

235–225	Olympia	20	1					1	1		4			8		
225	Megalopolis	21	1					2								
220–215	Peloponnese	5														
220–215	Patras	102	2													
215	Corinth	114	10			1		6								
	Sparta	15		3				3								
	Therianos										2		1	13		2
	Labia	1												2		
200	Kyparissia										6			38		
190	Elis										2					
165–160	Arcadia								5	1	8			2		
	Zacynthus								61					1		
	Patras										9			2		
	Peloponnese	5	2													

APPENDICES: FINDS

	Athens	Paros, etc.	Attalid	Rhodes	Seleucid	Ptolemaic	Aegina	Sicyon	Elis	Argos	Achaea, etc.	Arcadia, etc.	Aetolia	Larissa, etc.	Philip V	Perseus	Macedonia	Thasos	Macedonian Regions
	114			5															
	8					14													
															5				
			7												1		2		
																	✓		
																	6		
	36														2	7		3	7
	300																		
	4																		

	3					6	5	2	31										
						16													
	12			1			2						5						
	141		18	8	90								7						
	42			4	12														
							31		3					1					
							7			1									
								7											
								233											
				1		1	11		4	152	38	7							
				1			86			15	5		1						
				5		1													
							22			4	1								

315

App. 40 Hoards of overstruck Boeotian bronze coinage (p.124)

Copais – *IGCH* 229
Thebes – *IGCH* 233
Boeotia – *Arch.Delt.* 19, 1964, Chr. p.8, no.IV, pl. 2
White sack hoard – *Hesp.* 1978, 42

None of these hoards is of much help in dating; T. Hackens, *BCH* 1969, 725–8, inclines to a date close to 168 because of the occurrence of the pieces in question in the Copais and Thebes hoards of the mid-second century; but the degree of wear suggests an earlier date; how much earlier is hard to say.

App. 41 Hoards of small silver and bronze coinage in Greece (p.127)

Silver
Stratus – *IGCH* 251
Cephallenia – *IGCH* 257
Epidaurus – *IGCH* 258
Western Greece – *IGCH* 260 (with 243, 267, 301; it is not certain that the bronzes and the rest of this last group belong together)
Zougra – *IGCH* 261
Diakofto – *IGCH* 262
Koniska – *IGCH* 266
Olympia – *IGCH* 270

Bronze
Epirus – *IGCH* 259, 307, 308
Corcyra – *IGCH* 310

Acarnania – *IGCH* 311, 312
Aetolia – *IGCH* 244
Thessaly – *IGCH* 306
Delphi – *IGCH* 303
Corinth – *IGCH* 263, 264 (see *La moneta in Grecia e a Roma* (Bari, 1982), 90; see also M.J. Price, *Hesp.* 1967, 348)
Elis – *IGCH* 302
Tegea – *IGCH* 265
Delos – *IGCH* 298
Paros – *IGCH* 326
Crete – *IGCH* 299, 300, 330 (the last hoard contains silver from outside the island)

App. 42 Hoards of denarii in Africa (p.140)

Tunisia
Cani Island – *RRCH* 132

Henchir-Djebel-Dis – *RRCH* 160

Sminja – *RRCH* 395

Hammam-Lif – Gauckler, *Comptes rendus du marche du Service en 1903*, 36; *MEFR* 1904, 339
1000 denarii

Mateur – Gauckler, *Comptes rendus du marche du Service en 1903*, 36; *MEFR* 1904, 339
100 denarii

Fernana – *Bull.Arch.CTH* 1902, cxvii
17 denarii in Bardo

Uzita – *JMP* 1971–2, 144
64 denarii to Augustus

Algeria
Bettioua – P. Salama, Inv.17
Republican denarii

Rasseremt – *RRCH* 544
2 denarii to Augustus

Morocco
Wreck off Casablanca – J.D. Brethes, *Contribution à l'histoire du Maroc par les recherches numismatiques* (Casablanca, 1939), 5
Denarii to Augustus

See also J. Marion, *Ant.Afr.* 1, 1961, 99 (the Sala 'finds' are deeply suspicious)

App. 43   Finds of Greek coins in southern Gaul (p.164)

Monaco – *IGCH* 2354
Bronzes of Neapolis and Sardinia

Marseille area – *IGCH* 2355
Bronzes of Sardinia

Marseille – *IGCH* 2358
Bronzes of Massalia (400), Sardinia (1), Rome (2) (with the Roman material compare the hoard from the Brusq wreck, *IGCH* 2380)

With the Sardinian material in these hoards compare B. Fischer, *Les monnaies antiques d'Afrique du Nord trouvées en Gaule* (Paris, 1978), with review in *NC* 1981, 200 (no.8 is *SNG* (Cop.) 94)

Tourdan – *IGCH* 2374
161 obols of Massalia
  1 bronze of Massalia
  1 tetrobol of Histiaea
 81 Rhone valley quinarii

Nice – *IGCH* 2379
Tetrobols of Histiaea

For the distribution of the silver coinage of Massalia in general, see H. Rolland and Cl. Brenot, forthcoming; provisionally, Cl. Brenot (p.164, n.6), 192; the domination of the coinage of Massalia in the surrounding area may be exemplified from three hoards:

La Cloche – *Gallia* 1977, 519
38 drachms of Massalia
 4 diobols of Massalia
 3 obols of Massalia
 5 bronzes of Massalia
 2 Rhone valley quinarii
 1 gold stater of the Vindelici

La Cloche – *Acta Num.* 1981, 85
7 drachms of Massalia

 1 obol of Massalia
 3 bronzes of Massalia
 1 uncertain quadrans

Glanum – *IGCH* 2385
 4 drachms of Massalia
42 fractions of Massalia
71 bronzes of Massalia
 1 Rhone valley quinarius
 2 Gallic potin coins
 1 Gallic bronze

The domination of the coinage of Massalia may also be exemplified from the finds at Bollène, G. Gentric, *Les monnaies de Bollène* (Vaucluse) (Cavierac, 1981):

  8 drachms of Massalia
 84 obols of Massalia
231 bronzes of Massalia
 28 imitations of bronzes of Massalia
 30 Rhone valley quinarii
  1 Rhone valley fraction
  3 'monnaies à la croix'
  1 bronze of Avenio
  2 bronzes of Cabellio
  1 bronze with CMEP
  1 obol of the Volcae Arecomici
 22 bronzes of the Volcae Arecomici
  6 bronzes of Nemausus
  1 silver 'dupondius' (p.266) of Colonia Nemausus (overstruck on obol of Massalia)
  4 bronzes of Colonia Nemausus
 20 quinarii, bronzes and potins of central Gaul
  1 bronze of Ebusus
  1 bronze of Kese
  4 Roman Republican quinarii

Compare Apps. 44 and 56

App. 44 Early hoards with Roman coins in southern Gaul (p.165)

St.Rémy – *IGCH* 2378
Denarius with 'monnaies à la croix', silver of Massalia, Kainiketes, Avenio, Rhone valley quinarii (similar in date to those in the Tourdan hoard, App. 43)

Aime – *RRCH* 192

Cheverny (Etang de la Rousselière) – *RRCH* 216

Ensérune – J. Jannoray, *Ensérune* (Paris, 1955), 346, n.1
2 quinarii of L. Piso and M. Cato with 1 bronze of Neroncen

Gerbay – *RRCH* 236

Migne (perhaps not a hoard) – A. Blanchet, *Traité des monnaies gauloises* (Paris, 1905), no. 117

Noyer – *Trésors Monétaires* 3, 9
Denarii to L. Rutilius Flaccus

Bompas – *RRCH* 290

Peyriac-sur-Mer – *RRCH* 304

Bessan – *RRCH* 342

App. 45 Hoards in peninsular Italy after 146 (p.177)

Hoards of denarii, etc., between 146 and 91

1 Petacciato – *RRCH* 149
2 Masseria Cuoco – *AIIN* 23–4, 1976–7, 293
3 Banzi – *RRCH* 157
4 Riccia – *RRCH* 161
5 San Giovanni Incarico – *RRCH* 163
6 Lucoli – *RRCH* 164
7 Patrica – Museo Nazionale Romano
8 Borgonuovo – *Rivista Abruzzese* 27, 1912, 493
9 Heraclea – *Coin Hoards* 4, 65
10 Fossombrone – Museo Civico di Fossombrone
11 Bevagna – *RRCH* 171
12 Iesi – *RIN* 1973, 111
13 Maddaloni – *RRCH* 172
14 Montecarotto – *RRCH* 175
15 Taranto – *RRCH* 176
16 Strongoli – *RRCH* 183
17 Avvocata – *RRCH* 190
18 San Lorenzo del Vallo – *RRCH* 195
19 Ricina – *RRCH* 201
20 Isola Capo Rizzuto – *RRCH* 202
21 Cerignola – Museo Nazionale di Taranto
22 Carovigno – *RRCH* 208
23 Filogaso – *RRCH* 209
24 Crognaleto – *RRCH* 212
25 Largo Argentina, Rome – Musei Capitolini
26 Gioia dei Marsi – *RRCH* 213
27 Monteverde di Fermo – *RRCH* 218; *AIIN* 28–9, 1971–2, 123
28 Nociglia – *RRCH* 219

I exclude the Ancona hoard, since I am informed by Dr W. Metcalf that it goes down to the issue of Q. Titius

Hoards of Celtic and Greek coins

Siena – *Bullettino* 1875, 260
Ten concave gold coins without type (8.05 to 7.90 gm.)

Campiglia Marittima – F. Panvini Rosati, *AIIN* 2, 1955, 59; Z. Nemeškalová-Jiroudková, *Pam.Arch.* 1975, 383 = *8 Cong.Num.*, 189, 'Zur Frage des keltischen Münzschatzfundes von Campiglia Marittima'; *I Galli e l'Italia* (Rome, 1978), 221; *Coin Hoards* 1977, 112; M.C. Parra, *RIN* 1979, 203, 'Moneta gallica del Museo di Cecina'
Gold third-staters of Boii (sharing dies with coins in hoard from Starý Kolín)

South Italy – *IGCH* 2052
Bronzes of Epirus

Caserta – *IGCH* 2053
Triobols of Achaean League, etc.

Italy – *IGCH* 2054
Silver of Apollonia and Dyrrachium

Carrara – *IGCH* 2055
Denarii, etc.
Triobols of Achaean League

Poggio Picenze – *IGCH* 2056
Denarii
Lysimachi of Byzantium
Tetradrachms of Athens, Mithridates VI, Nicomedes III, tetradrachms and drachms of Ariarathes IX
Triobols of Achaean League

Battaglia – *IGCH* 2057
Lysimachus of Byzantium
Cistophori
Tetradrachms of Demetrius I of Syria and Eucratides of Bactria
Shekel of Tyre

Montella – F. Scandone, *L'alta valle del Calore* I (Naples, 1911), 173
Denarii to P. Satrienus
Tetradrachm of Athens

Italy – M. Thompson, *The New Style Coinage of Athens* (New York, 1961), 434, n.1
Tetradrachms of Athens

O. Mørkholm, in *Essays E.S.G. Robinson* (Oxford, 1968), 245, n.2
Tetradrachm of Ariarathes IX of Cappadocia

Italy – *RRCH* 222
Triobol of Achaean League
Social War denarii

Compare the 3 (presumably silver) pieces of Cappadocia in a collection at Vieste, P.G. Guzzetta, *Rassegna di Studi del Civico Museo di Milano* 1982, 76, and the coins of the Aetolian 'league' in a collection at Canosa, ibid., 72

App. 46   Finds of eastern bronze coinage in Italy and Sicily (p.178)

Aosta – M. Orlandoni, in *Atti del Congresso sul Bimellenario di Aosta* (Aosta, 1982), 77
Bronze of Boeotia

Cosa – *MAAR* 34, 1980, 40
Bronze of Stratonicea

Viterbo – *Bullettino* 1881, 261
Bronze of Athens

Rome, Forum – R. Reece, *PBSR* 1982, 116
Bronzes of Athens and Cos
Plated tetradrachm of Thasos
Ptolemaic bronze (compare App. 18)

Saepinum – information from Dott.ssa Asdrubale Pentiti
Bronzes of Bithynia and Alinda

Aufidena – *Mon.Ant.* 10, 1901, 242
Bronze of Prusias II

Monte Vairano – *SE* 1981, 454
Bronze of Thasos

River Liris – *NC* 1970, 89; 1974, 42
Bronzes of Cos, Odessus, Sestus, Miletus and Teos

Giannutri – G. Gorini (App. 26)
Ptolemaic bronze

Leuca – *Leuca* (Galatina, 1978), 223
Bronze of Samos

Sicily – *Archivio Storico per la Sicilia Orientale* 1969, 293
Bronzes of Magnesia, Side, Thasos, Rhodes

Cava Ispica – *ANRW* I, 1, 446, n.12
Bronze of Simon Maccabaeus

Compare the finds of bronzes of Ebusus:
Pompeii – A. Stazio, *Numisma* 1963, 9 = *AIIN* 2, 1955, 33 = *RRCH* 245
Fifty-three bronzes of Ebusus (hardly *objects* of trade, *contra* A. Stazio, also M. Campo, *Atti I Cong.Int.Studi Fenici e Punici* (Rome, 1983), 145, 'Las relaciones de Ebusus con el exterior')

Valle d'Ansanto – ibid.
Bronze of Ebusus

Pietracatella – ibid.
Bronze of Ebusus

Cosa – l.c.
Bronze of Ebusus

River Liris – l.c.
Bronzes of Ebusus

Compare App. 26 and the coin of Myrina in a collection at Vieste, P.G. Guzzetta (App. 45)

App. 47   Hoards in Greece of the period of Mithridates (p.196)

Delos – *IGCH* 284–6, 290, 292–5, 297–8, 319–25, 328–9, 334–6, 347–9

Piraeus – *RRCH* 242
Denarii

Piraeus – *IGCH* 337

Athens – *IGCH* 339

Salamis – *IGCH* 288

Oreus – *IGCH* 287

Chalcis – *IGCH* 345

Carystus – *IGCH* 291, 344

Halmyros – *IGCH* 289

Greece – *IGCH* 296

Greece – *IGCH* 346 (with denarii)

Crete – *IGCH* 331, 332 (with *RN* 1973, 54), 338, 350

Chios (not Cos) – *Coin Hoards* 6, 46
14 drachms of Chios
   1 new-style tetradrachm of Athens
   2 cistophori
   1 denarius probably of L. Piso Frugi
Compare the Cesme hoard, *IGCH* 1359 = *Coin Hoards* 2, 110

For bronze hoards from Athens and Attica see F.S. Kleiner, *Hesp.* 1976, 1, 'The agora excavations and Athenian bronze coinage, 200–86 BC'; *Hesp.* 1978, 40 = *Coin Hoards* 3, 75

For the effect on monetary circulation in Asia Minor of the Mithridatic Wars see *La moneta in Grecia e a Roma* (Bari, 1982), 80–2

Compare App. 48

App. 48   Hoards in Macedonia (p.197)

Siderokastro – *IGCH* 642
Tetradrachms of Athens, Aesillas, LEG ΜΑΚΕΔΟΝΩΝ

Kerassia – *RRCH* 283 = *IGCH* 653
Denarii
Tetradrachm of Aesillas

Kavalla – *RRCH* 336 = *IGCH* 660
Denarii
Tetradrachms of Aesillas

Platania – *RRCH* 358 = *IGCH* 663
Denarii
Tetradrachms of Aesillas
Bronzes of Macedonia, Maronea, Abdera, Pergamum, Rome

South-western Macedonia – information from A. Burnett
Tetradrachms of Athens, Aesillas, LEG, LEG ΜΑΚΕΔΟΝΩΝ, Thasos

APPENDICES: FINDS

Greece – information from A. Burnett
Denarii to *RRC*, no. 434
Tetradrachms of Aesillas

Compare App. 47

App. 49 Hoards of cast bronze coinage in Jugoslavia (p.221)

Mazin – *RRCH* 142 = *IGCH* 644

Gračac – *RRCH* 145 = *IGCH* 569; *Numizmatika* 1978, 27 (including 3 pieces of Castulo; also 1 of Philip V; 2 asses, of Q. Marius, and 1 triens, of P.Blasio, not 3 asses)

Vrankamen Berg – *RRCH* 146 = *IGCH* 643 (including 1 piece of Emporiae)

Kruinwa – M.Bahrfeldt, *BMzB* 1900, 2863; *IGCH* 567

Kula – *IGCH* 566

The precise origin of *IGCH* 568, containing bronzes of Carthage and Numidia, is unknown

Bescanuova – Mirnik 20a; G. Gorini, *Atti e Memorie Soc.Istr.* 1970, 209 (for a late Republican inscription see *ILLRP* 579)

Krupa – Mirnik 31

Štikada – Mirnik 88a; *Vjesnik Arheološkog Muzeja u Zagrebu* 15, 1982, 149
Aes rude
1 as of M. Atilius Saranus
1 triens of P. Blasio
Bronzes of Obulco, Philip V, Ptolemy VI-VIII, Carthage, Numidia

Obrovac – Mirnik 79
Bronzes of Numidia

The route travelled by this material is uncertain; note, however, apart from the Bescanuova hoard:

A hoard of bronzes of Numidia (*SNG* (Cop.) 504–17) from the harbour of Ancona – *Bullettino* 1865, 12

The finds from Senj, including a bronze of Saeti, a Ptolemaic bronze and a semis of the libral Prow series – *Archiv Ost.Gesch.* 33, 1865, 124

The find of a bronze of Numidia in a grave at Zadar – *Osterreichisches Archäologisches Institut, Führer durch das K.K. Staatsmuseum in S.Donato in Zara* (Vienna, 1912), 88

Some pieces seem to have drifted north and east:
Gorizia – Haeberlin, p.12
Bar with 'ramo secco'

Pettau (now Ptuj) (Jugoslavia) – F. Pichler, *Repertorium der steierischen Münzkunde* I (Graz, 1865), 211
Bronzes of Neapolis, Teanum, Rome with Hercules/Pegasus ROMA, Syracuse
Hohenmauten (now Muta) (Jugoslavia) – ibid.; Mirnik 77a
Ptolemaic and Brettian bronzes

Leibnitz (Austria) – F. Pichler, l.c.
Ptolemaic bronze
Hallstatt (Austria) – *Litterae Numismaticae Vindobonenses* 2, 1983, 310
As of the libral Prow series

Nitra (Czechoslovakia) – E. Kolnikova, *Slovenska Archeologia* 12, 2, 1964, 402, 'Fund eines romischen Aes grave gemeinsam mit keltischen Münzen in Nitra'
Stradonice (Czechoslovakia) – J.L. Pic, *Le Hradischt de Stradonitz en Bohème* (Leipzig, 1906), pl. ii, 27
Numidian Bronze

Paulis near Arad (Romania) – *Dacia* 8, 1964, 376
Quadrans of the libral Prow series
Reho near Sarmizegetusa (Romania) – G. Gorini (App. 26)
Ptolemaic bronze
Mühlbach (now Sebes) (Romania) – F. Pichler, l.c.
Ptolemaic bronze

App. 50 The movement of coinage across the Adriatic (p.223)

There is much evidence for isolated Italian (and Sicilian) coins travelling to the east coast of the Adriatic from the early third century onwards, mostly bronze, occasionally silver. The pattern may be *exemplified* from:

1 Pontadura = Vir – S. Batović, 'Les vestiges préhistoriques sur l'archipel de Zadar', *Diadora* 6, 1973, 5
With one Athena/Cock bronze of Ithaca and one uncertain bronze:
    5 Poseidon/Trident bronzes of Hieron II of Syracuse
    2 semilibral unciae (*RRC*, no.38/6)
    1 anonymous as
    1 with gryphon (*RRC*, no.182/2)
    1 with Victory and spearhead (*RRC*, no.145/1)
    2 uncertain asses
    1 bronze of Vespasian
    1 of Pius
    1 uncertain Roman bronze

The last three pieces are very worn; some of the Republican bronze is very fresh; the semilibral unciae, with the bronzes of Syracuse, are unlikely to have been available to cross the Adriatic much after 200

2 Donja Dolina, on the Save River – *Glasnik* (Arch.) 1964, 47 and 49
In Phase IIIb:
    1 quadrigatus (pl.xxii, 2a – obv.)
    1 early Roman Republican bronze, perhaps a post-semilibral sextans (*RRC*, no.41/9) overstruck on a semilibral uncia (pl.xxii, 2b – rev.)
In Phase IIIc, with two Celtic coins:
    1 anonymous denarius (*RRC*, no.222/1)
    1 of M. Opeimius (*RRC*, no.254/1)

All these isolated Roman pieces presumably travelled by way of the Dalmatian coast

3 Ošaničima – *Glasnik* (Arch.) 1972–3, 237
The as with TP (*RRC*, no.177/1), found along with 28 bronzes of Ballaeus and perhaps one of Anactorium and 6 silver coins of Pharos, Dyrrhachium and Corinth, is an isolated piece which presumably travelled by way of the Dalmatian coast in the second century

4 Nona, near Zara – R. Valenti, *Il Museo Nazionale di Zara* (Rome, 1933), 16
In a grave:
    1 bronze of Metapontum

5 Viš = Issa – *Rivista di Archeologia* 4, 1980, 81–91
In Grave 3:
    1 diobol (not stater) of Heraclea
    1 sestertius

G. Gorini (p.221, n.5), 78, n.31, draws attention to a number of overstrikes by Issa, apparently on coins of Italy and Sicily, mostly of the fourth century

There is a vague reference to a find of material of Acragas and to a find of a Roman victoriatus, *Rad Jug.Akad.* 14, 1871, 60

6 Lesina = Hvar = Pharos

There is a vague reference to material of Neapolis, Nola, Brundisium, Tarentum, Heraclea, Rhegium, Acragas, Catana, Messana, Syracuse (including Hieron I, Agathocles, Hieron II) and 'Kainon', G. Novak, *Strena Buliciana* (Split and Zagreb, 1924), 655

There is a vague reference to material of Rome (2 victoriati), Caelia, Syracuse, Osset, S. Ljubić, *Arkiv za pov.jug.* 2, 1852, 206, whence S. Ljubić, *Faria* (Zagreb, 1873), 9 (garbled)

7 Scutari = Scodra – G. Valentini, *Numismatica* 5, 1939, 122, 'La numismatica in Albania', at n.3
    Bronze of Agathocles in Collegio Saveriano

8 Dhrovjan, near Phoenice – N.G.L. Hammond, *Epirus* (Oxford, 1967), 718
    Silver coin of Syracuse

9 Thiriakision, near Argos Amphilochicum – ibid.

Bronze of Syracuse (*BMCSicily* 354)

10 Oricus

There is perhaps 1 bronze of Syracuse, found along with 13 of Oricus and 4 of the Epirote Republic, in a hoard of about 200, *IGCH* 211

11 Buthrotum

There is one silver coin of Caulonia, found along with 14 of Dyrrhachium, Corcyra, Corinth and Sicyon, in a hoard of the late third century, *IGCH* 207

12 Zacynthus

There is one silver coin of Heraclea, found along with 171 of mainland Greece and Asia Minor, in a hoard of about 175–150, *IGCH* 245

All of nos. 4 to 12 may be the relics of casual movement of coinage with troops in connection with one or other of Rome's eastern wars; the earlier pieces of Syracuse were still in circulation in the late third century.

13 Phoenice – L. Ugolini, *Albania Antica* II (Rome, 1932), 159
With material from east of the Adriatic:
 21 bronze coins from Italian mints
  5 bronze coins from Carthaginian mints
 15 bronze coins from Sicilian mints
  8 bronze coins of the Roman Republic (from *RRC*, nos.26/3 and 27/3 onwards)
  2 denarii of the Roman Republic

14 Buthrotum – L. Breglia, *RAN* 1941, 193
With material from east of the Adriatic:
 1 bronze coin of Brundisium
 1 bronze coin of the Roman Republic (4.10 gm. – described as an uncial sextans, perhaps rather a post-semilibral semuncia)
 1 legionary denarius of M. Antonius described as an uncertain Greek bronze)

15 Epirus – S.L. Cesano, *Atti e Memorie* 7, 1932, 45 (including the material from Phoenice, *not* repeated here)
In isolated finds, along with material from east of the Adriatic:
 1 bronze of the Brettii (no.11)
 1 of Petelia (no.18)
 1 of Vibo (no.19 or no.20)
 1 of Campania (no.27)
 4 of Neapolis (nos.28–31)
 1 of Messana (no.4)
 1 of the Mamertini (no.5)
 4 of Syracuse (one of nos.9–11; no.16; one of nos.17–20)
 4 of Tauromenium (nos.22–25)
 1 anonymous denarius (no.1)
 1 uncertain as (no.9)
 1 uncertain triens (no.10)

16 Corcyra

Published material includes a bronze of Brundisium, a third-century stater of Tarentum and a semilibral semuncia (*RRC*, no.38/7) and bronzes from Sicilian mints, *BCH* 1930, 454; *AD* 1965, B2, 401; T. Hackens, *RBN* 1968, 122

For the area as a whole, A. Mano, *Iliria* 6, 1976, 122–3, cites without references one piece of Syracuse and two of Neapolis from Amantia, one piece of Tarentum from Antigoneia, one piece of Metapontum from Apollonia, one piece of Metapontum from Klos and one piece of Rhegium from Lissus.

17 Dodona

The material published by C. Carapanos, *Dodone* (1878), 115, includes no Italian, Sicilian or Roman Republican material; the pieces in Berlin from Dodona (P.R. Franke, *Die antiken Münzen von Epirus* I (Wiesbaden, 1961), 35; not identical with the material of Carapanos, Hammond, 731) include one bronze of Brundisium and one early sextans (see App. D); the collection in Joannina Museum (Hammond, 725) includes two silver coins of Syracuse; later excavation material (*PAE* 1952, 320; 1955, 174) includes one bronze of Syracuse, an as, a semis, neither precisely identifiable, a denarius of A. Alb. S.f. and colleagues (*RRC*, no. 335/1a). It is astonishing that there is so little material from the west at a site such as Dodona where pilgrims, tourists and diplomats from afar might be expected as frequent visitors.

It is also evident that isolated coins moved west across the Adriatic, quite apart from the arrival in Italy of coins of Acarnania and Oeniadae as booty during the Second Punic War (p.58, compare App. 26 and P.G. Guzzetta (App. 45), 76, for 49 pieces of Oeniadae in a collection at Vieste):

1 The Montegiordano hoard (App. 16), a normal late third-century south Italian silver hoard, contains one bronze of Argos

2 The Salento has produced five bronzes of Dyrrhachium of the late third and early second centuries, C. Pagliaro, *Annali Lecce* 1969–71, 121, in the course of a discussion of Veretum

3 A bronze of Ballaeus is attested from Ordona, J. Mertens *et al.*, *Ordona* IV (1974), 105

4 The finds from the Liris River (App. 46) include among issues of the period earlier than Augustus one bronze each of Apollonia, Leucas and Elis

5 Bronzes of Apollonia, Pharos and Epirus are attested at Monte Vairano (App. 46)

6 Bronzes of the Peumatioi, Oricus and Ballaeus are attested at Leuca, *Leuca* (Galatina, 1978), 223

Compare P.G. Guzzetta (App. 45) for bronzes of Ballaeus, Epirus, Acarnania and Oeniadae from Canosa, a bronze of Epirus from Ascoli Satriano and bronzes of Apollonia, Corcyra, Dyrrhachium, Epirus, Issa, Ithaca(?) and Leucas in a collection at Vieste

According to Polybius, probably following Pictor, the Illyrians, long in the habit of molesting ships sailing from Italy, did so even more when during the reign of Queen Teuta (widow of King Agron) they got control of Phoenice; a Roman protest led to the murder of L. Coruncanius, one of the Roman ambassadors, on his way home and war was declared.[1] Roman distaste for a queen who could not or would not control her subjects' piracy is intelligible enough and one can compare the Roman punishment of their own troops who had seized Rhegium;[2] but the strategic threat posed by Illyria, with its capital at Rhizon on the bay of Kotor, should not be underestimated. '[Whoever holds Kotor], I hold him to be master of the Adriatic and to have it within his power to make a descent on Italy and thereby surround it by land and sea';[3] of the power of Illyria after the seizure of Phoenice Rome had ample evidence from the pleas of those who suffered.

The narrative of Polybius has been defended by F.W. Walbank,[4] both against the alternative version preserved in the ancient sources and against the reconstruction of M. Holleaux, in which L. Coruncanius and his fellow ambassador declare war. P.S. Derow has recently argued forcefully that the alternative version preserved in the ancient sources, notably Appian, is to be preferred to that of Polybius.[5] According to this version, Issa appealed to Rome, which sent an embassy to King Agron; one ambassador and Cleemporus, an envoy of Issa, were murdered *on the way to* Illyria; whence war.

The implication of this version, that Rome in 230 was a power to which Issa might appeal, is a remarkable one and remains surprising even allowing for the fact that Issa was a colony of Syracuse. Nor am I clear why Pictor or Polybius should wish to suppress the appeal by Issa and the reaction by Rome, if these were indeed crucial.

1 Polybius ii, 8. Illyrian piracy did not disappear; see Livy xl, 42, 1–5, for Genthius molesting Romans and Italians within his reach or visiting his kingdom.
2 Polybius i, 7, 6–13.
3 Quoted from a source of 1572 by F. Braudel, *The Mediterranean and the Mediterranean World* I (London, 1972), 126, n.77.
4 *A Historical Commentary on Polybius* I (Oxford, 1957), 158, with earlier bibliography.
5 'Kleemporos', *Phoenix* (1973), 118.

In the end, certainty is no doubt unattainable; Issa perhaps appealed to Rome at some stage and a later historian perhaps made this appeal the origin of the war; I am reluctant to believe that Pictor and Polybius quite falsely reported that Coruncanius actually reached Illyria and have a marginal preference for their version.

On one point the argument can be taken further. R. Schneider and O. Hirschfeld argued that within Dalmatia only on Issa did terracottas from south Italy and pots from Apulia turn up in *bulk*;[6] and the suggestion was used by P.S. Derow to support the notion of a special relationship between Issa and the west. But in fact the importation of Apulian pottery into the area corresponding to present-day Jugoslavia is a widespread phenomenon (p.223). And as far as the numismatic evidence is concerned, it perhaps suggests that it was Phoenice which enjoyed a special relationship with the west; if the occurrence of isolated pieces from the west at Phoenice on a scale which is unparalleled even on another excavated site such as Dodona may be taken to indicate the existence of regular contact, the central role played by Phoenice in the narrative of Polybius perhaps finds some support.

App. 51 Hoards of coins of Apollonia and Dyrrachium (p.224)

See Gh. Poenaru Bordea, 'Circulation des monnaies d'Apollonia et de Dyrrachion en Dacie préromaine et dans la région du bas-Danube', in *L'Adriatico tra Mediterraneo e penisola balcanica nell'antichità* (Taranto, 1983), 221, and, for Jugoslavia, Mirnik 52, 54–5, 59, 62, 74, 78, 86, 92, 94–7, and 82 with P. Popović, *Numizmatičar* 1, 1978, 9

App. 52 Hoards of Republican denarii in Dalmatia (p.225)

Zasiok – *RRCH* 166

Sućuraj – *RRCH* 310

Blizna near Salona 1965 – information from I. Mirnik (denarii to Libo)

Dračevica – *RRCH* 379

Citluk – *RRCH* 396

Ljubuski – *RRCH* 446

Solin = Salona about 1880   Mirnik 87 (about three hundred 'monete della famiglia Baebia')

App. 53 Hoards of Republican denarii in Russia, Poland, Czechoslovakia and Hungary (p.227)

Moldavian S.S.R.
A.A. Nudelman, *Topographie des trésors et des trouvailles des monnaies isolées* (in Russian), Kischchinev, 1976, 156–7

Poland
Polaniec 1968 – *Rocznika Muzeum Swietokrzyskiego* 1970, 103; 1975, 327

Czechoslovakia
Kysice 1917 – E. Nohejlova-Pratova, *Nalezy* I, no.225a

Libčeves 1908 – *RRCH* 328

Sillein 1871 – *RRCH* 330 (with *NZ* 1903, 147 – down to Augustus)

---

6 'Bericht über eine Reise in Dalmatien', *Archäologisch-epigraphische Mitteilungen* 9, 1885, 33, largely followed by P. Cabanes, in *L'Adriatico* (App. 51), 187.

Podivin about 1930 – E. Nohejlova-Pratova, *Nalezy* I, no.853

Göding = Hodonin – E. Nohejlova-Pratova, *Nalezy* I, no.859 (down to issue with IMP.CAESAR); A. Rzehak, *Zeitschrift des deutschen Vereins für die Geschichte Mährens und Schlesiens*, Brunn (Brno), 22, 1918, 197, 'Die römische Eisenzeit in Mähren', at 268 (down to 15 BC)

Hungary

Körösszakall 1965 – *Különlenyomat a Debreceni Déri Muzeum* 1967, 67

Bia 1846 – *RRCH* 370

Erd 1957 – *RRCH* 373

Nagykagya = Cadea 1941 – *RRCH* 411

Lagymanyos 1902 – *RRCH* 510

Doboz – *Arch.Ert.* 1978, 223

App. 54   Hoards of Republican denarii in Romania and Bulgaria (p.227)

In the first table, (1) hoards with half-a-dozen or fewer Republican denarii and those whose contents are inadequately known are excluded; (2) hoards in *RRCH* appear before the diagonal line, and others after it.

I. ROMANIAN HOARDS FROM 80 TO 31 BC

80–76	+ + + +/+ + + + +
75–71	+ + + +/+ + + + +
70–66	+ + + + +/+ +
65–61	+ + + +/+ + +
60–56	+ + +/+
55–51	+ + +/+
50–46	+ + + + +/+ + + + + +
45–41	+ + + + +/+ + + + + + + + +
40–36	+ +
35–31	+ + +/+ +

80–76 Nedeia – *RRCH* 274
    Sadina *RRCH* 275
    Bălăneşti – *RRCH* 280
    Lunca Deal – *RRCH* 293
    Bobaia – unpublished, Museum of History, Cluj
    Rociu – *Studii şi Comunicări*, Piteşti, 1969, 101
    Suhaia – *SCN* 1968, 452
    Moroda – *Apulum* 1971, 169
    Inuri – O. Floca, 'Un nou tezaur', *Contribuţii la cunoasterea regiunii Hunedoara* (Deva, 1956; preface by O. Floca), 11

75–71 Alexandria – *RRCH* 295
    Căpreni – *RRCH* 296
    Hunedoara – *RRCH* 303
    Sfinţeşti – *RRCH* 320
    Zatreni – *SCIV* 1971, 579
    Hotărani – *SCIV* 1971, 579
    Năsăud – *Apulum* 1974, 577
    Segarcea – unpublished, Romanian Academy, Bucharest
    Beiuş – *SCN* 1968, 355
    Hotăroaia, Roşiile – *Revista Muzeelor* 9, 1972, 570

70–66 Hevisz Szamos – *RRCH* 321; Th. Mommsen, *Histoire de la monnaie romaine* II, 471
Martiniş – *RRCH* 322; *BSNR* 1948–72, 75
Nicolae Bălcescu – *RRCH* 323
Medveş – *RRCH* 324
Grădiştea – *RRCH* 325
Bîrsa – *Tibiscus* 1, 1971, 24
Mihai Bravu – *SCN* 1968, 373: latest issue C. Piso Frugi

65–61 Curtea de Argeş – *RRCH* 327
Peteni – *RRCH* 329
Stăncuţa – *RRCH* 331
Licuriciu – *RRCH* 332
Mofleni – *Mitropolia Olteniei* 24, 9–10, 1972, 709, incorporating *SCIV* 1971, 124, no.37
Garvăn – *SCN* 1971, 372
Şopotu – *SCN* 1968, 450
Secusigiu – *Revista Muzeelor* 8, 1971, 321

60–56 Alungeni – *RRCH* 335
Amnaş – *RRCH* 338
Frauendorf – *RRCH* 341
Dunăreni – *Historica* 1, 1970, 53

55–51 Buzau – *RRCH* 346
Călineşti – *RRCH* 347
Sălaşul de Sus – *RRCH* 348
Chitorani – *SCN* 1971, 378

50–46 Roata – *RRCH* 356
Locusteni – *RRCH* 367
Satu Nou – *RRCH* 368; I ignore the denarius of C. Vibius Varus found in the locality in 1969, *SCIV* 1971, 125, no. 44
Transylvania – *RRCH* 369
Hunedoara – *RRCH* 378
Albeşti – Z. Szekely, *Jegyzetek Dácia Történetéhez* (Sf. Gheorghe, 1946), 48

Brîncoveanu – *Acta Valachica* 1971 (1972), 103
Orbeasca de Sus – *SCIV* 1974, 265
Tîrnava – *SCN* 1968, 381
Ilieni – *SCN* 1971, 81
Tîrnava – *SCN* 1975, 41
Spîncenata – *Studii şi Comunicări*, Piteşti, 1972, 205

45–41 Bran-Poartă – *RRCH* 408
Prejmer – *RRCH* 412; republished in *Aluta* 1971, 97; for disposition see *Revista Muzeelor* 9, 1972, 38
Farcaşele – *RRCH* 420
Grosspold – *RRCH* 426
Işalniţa – *RRCH* 428
Jegălia – *Dacia* 1972, 303: latest issue P. Accoleius Lariscolus
Satu Mare – *Tezaure monetare din judetul Satu Mare* (Satu Mare, 1968), 19
Islaz – *SCN* 1971, 305
Murighiol – *Pontica* 1974, 205
Nicolae Bălcescu – *SCN* 1975, 209
Zimnicea – *Memoria Antiquitatis* 1970, 491
Moroda – *Archaeologiai Közlemenyek*, 6 Kötet (Uj folyam, 4 Kötet), 1866, 175
Suhaia – *SCN* 1968, 452
Vladeni – *SCN* 1971, 378
Stupini – *SCN* 1971, 255
Vişina – *Memoria Antiquitatis* 1971, 455

40–36 Poroschia – *RRCH* 436
Tulcea – *RRCH* 439

35–31 Beclean – *RRCH* 449
Walachia – *RRCH* 454
Şeica Mică – *RRCH* 456
Costineşti – *Pontica* 1970, 131
Gura Padinii – *SCIV* 1970, 429

II. BULGARIAN HOARDS FROM 85 TO 1 BC

85–81	+
80–76	+ + + +
75–71	+ + + +
70–66	
65–61	+ +
60–56	+
55–51	+ +
50–46	+ + + + +
45–41	+ + + + +
40–36	
35–31	+ + + +
30–26	
25–21	
20–16	+ + +
15–11	+
10– 6	+
5– 1	+

85–81 Mihailovgrad I – Archaeological Museum of Sofia

80–76 Beli Briag – *BIAB* 29, 1966, 214: latest issue probably L. Papius
Bukovets 1936 – *BIAB* 11, 1937, 320, Takov Collection: latest issues probably T. Annius and L. Rutilius Flaccus
Staliiska Mahala – *BIAB* 25, 1962, 237: latest issue probably L. Rutilius Flaccus
Trastenik – *Arheologia* 1967, 4, 53

75–71 The Oriahovitsa, Koinare, Rasovo and Belitsa hoards (*IGCH* 686–8 and 976) have been assigned to the *latest* date at which there are parallels for hoards with drachms of Dyrrhachium in this area

65–61 Korten – *IGCH* 979
Mindia – *BIAB* 25, 1962, 237

60–56 Obzor – *Bull.Soc.Arch.Varna* 14, 1963, 39, with 15 further pieces in Museum of Burgas: latest issue that of Philippus; issue of M. Antonius (*RRC*, no. 496/2) extraneous

55–51 Dolna Gnoiunitsa = Mihailovo – *BIAB* 1, 1921–2, 224; *RN* 1923, 16, no. 3: two bronzes extraneous, denarii of T. Carisius, C. Cassius and M. Antonius extraneous
Karavelovo – *Numizmatika* 1979, 2, 13

50–46 Eleshnitsa = Jordanovo – *Godishnik Arch.Mus.Plovdiv* 4, 1960, 210: latest issue that of Albinus Bruti.f.
Boliarino – *IGCH* 975: latest issue that of Albinus Bruti.f.
Progorelets – *BIAB* 1, 1921–2, 239: latest issue that of T. Carisius
Guliantsi – *RRCH* 377
Pavelsko – *Arheologia* 1978, 4, 8
Vetren – *Arheologia* 1979, 4, 60

45–41 Oriahovitsa – *Arheologia* 1967, 4, 53
Makotsevo I – *BIAB* 2, 1923, 270; *RN* 1923, 26, no. 41: latest issue that of P. Clodius M.f.
Makotsevo II – Archaeological Museum of Sofia: latest issue that of P. Clodius M.f.
Preslaven – Museum of Stara Zagora: latest issue that of P.Clodius M.f.
Obzor – *Bull.Soc.Arch.Varna* 14, 1963, 39

35–31 Topolovo – *RRCH* 457
Okhoden – *Arheologia* 1972, 2, 73
Nova Zagora region – Museum of Nova Zagora: latest issue that of M. Antonius
Nova Zagora region – Museum of Stara Zagora: latest issue that of M. Antonius
Jakimovo – *BIAB* 20, 1955, 608

20–16 Medovo – *RRCH* 490
Mihailovgrad II – Archaeological Museum of Sofia: latest issue that of Augustus with Two laurels CAESAR AVGVSTVS
Koliu Marinovo – *Godishnik Arch. Mus.Plovdiv* 4, 1960, 211: latest issue that of P.Petronius Turpilianus

15–11 Sadievo — Archaeological Museum of Sofia: latest issue that of Augustus with IMP.XII

10–6 Pravoslav — *RRCH* 520

5–1 Strashimir — *Studia Beshevliev* (Sofia, 1978), 350: latest issue that of C.L. Caesares

The Filipovtsi (*BIAB* 1, 1921–2, 242) and Pernik (*BIAB* 4, 1924, 274, no. 56; *RN* 1923, 30, no. 57) hoards never reached the Archaeological Museum of Sofia.

The Tarnava and Svode Kalugerovo = Pazardzhik (*BIAB* 4, 1924, 273, nos. 42 and 39; *RN* 1923, 16, no. 6, and 27, no. 46) hoards were mingled with the general collection of the Archaeological Museum of Sofia.

I here print a translation by K.St. Pavlowitch, to whom I am most grateful, of an article in *Glasnik* 1906, 109, the contents of which are still taken seriously by Mirnik 35:

Various numismatic discoveries in Bosnia

Discovery of Greek coins at Prača

Relatively very few Greek coins have been found in Bosnia, and when something has been found it has always been in insignificant quantities.

It is therefore surprising to hear the story of the esteemed merchant Maksa Despić, who then lived in Sarajevo, that in the vicinity of Prača there were found 50 years ago about 2,000 coins. Haji Despić's story about that interesting discovery reads:

In 1852 the Turkish mail sent from Constantinople to Sarajevo stopped at the village of Prača to give the horses a rest. While the Tartar messenger was having his coffee, a young shepherd came and offered him a bag full of silver coins which he had found while ploughing.

The weight was about three okes and the Tartar bought the lot for 400 groschen (64 crowns) and took it to Sarajevo. He there sold them all to the brothers Josa and Gligorije Josifović for 1,500 groschen, and the latter sold them later to Kosta Haji Petrović, Djuka's son, who after the [Austrian] occupation was an innkeeper on the bridge near Ilidza.

The latter sold them one by one mainly to army officers passing through.

On that occasion Maksa Despić bought 30 of them and made three bracelets, one of which is in Zagreb and belongs to Jelka, the daughter of the late Court counsellor Badovinac, the second is in Trieste and belongs to the merchant Raić, while the third one is still owned by Miss Darinka Despić. Unfortunately I had in my hand only one of these bracelets consisting of 9 coins of which 7 only can be described, while two were worn to such an extent that it was impossible to identify them. The coins were as follows:

1. Neapolis: obverse: a mask with a stuck out tongue (gorgoneion); reverse: ΝΕΟΠ, Apollo's head with his hair put up, right.

2. Thasos: obverse: kneeling fawn with a nymph on his knees (a rather barbarian attitude, sine veretro erecto); reverse: a carved square (quadratum incusum).

3. Croton: obverse: Eagle standing on an Ionian pillar and on the right a small laurel branch; reverse: a carved tripod, on the right, *koppa*, *rho*, *omicron*, on the left a small laurel branch.

4. Croton: obverse: Apollo's laurelled head right; reverse: ΚΡΟ, tripod, on the left a small branch, in the middle curled waves and on the tripod a wheel.

5. Macedonia: Alexander III the Great, hemidrachm: obverse: head of young Hercules draped with a lion skin; reverse: inscription illegible; Jupiter Aetophorus sitting, left, with an eagle in his right and spear in his left hand.

6. Massilia: obverse worn (most probably Flora's head); reverse: ΜΑΣΣΑ, a lion going right.

7. Abdera: obverse: ΑΠ...Δ... Artemisia's

head right; reverse: the same as under 5.

Two coins are worn to such an extent that it is impossible to identify them.

Mr. Pera Despić possesses also a tie-pin with one of the coins found at Prača:

Istros: obverse: two opposed heads; reverse: ΙΣΤΡΟ, an eagle standing on a dolphin's back (exceptionally well preserved).

As already said I did not have the other coins in my hand, and I intend to describe them later. As far as I remember I have seen on Miss Darinka Despić's bracelet two coins of Philip II of Macedon, one of Agrigentum with a glove on the reverse, and several, some of them rarer and some ordinary tetradrachms. How these coins arrived at Prača is an open question. Judging by the variety one would conclude that it was a collection, but it is not likely that at that time anyone was interested in collecting coins.

It is more likely that it was the viaticum of a Greek merchant who in the second century before Christ was travelling through the then known parts of the world, who lost his way in those parts and died.

This paper might help to find more coins from that discovery which would help to come to a more positive conclusion.

Alfred Makanec, *Nobleman*

App. 55   Hoards of the period of Actium (p.255)

Belmonte del Sannio – *RRCH* 460; *Arch.Class.* 1976, 104

Delos – *RRCH* 465

Euboea – *RRCH* 467

Preveza – *RRCH* 473

Preveza – *Arch.Rep.* 1982–3, 36
103 silver coins

Corinth – *IGCH* 353
11 bronzes of Corcyra, Elis and Sparta

App. 56   Hoards of bronze coinage in Gaul after Caesar (p.275)

Castelet de Fontvieille – *IGCH* 2386
4 local obols, 1 local hemiobol, 2 uncertain tetartemoria
2 silver 'dupondii' (p.266) of Colonia Nemausus
1 denarius of Mn. Acilius

Cavaillon – *IGCH* 2387
3 drachms, 10 obols, 50 bronzes of Massalia
3 bronzes of Volcae Arecomici
3 bronzes of Nemausus
1 silver 'dupondius', 3 bronzes of Cabellio

Tetelbierg – L. Reding, *Les monnaies gauloises du Tetelbierg* (Luxembourg, 1972), 223
1 plated stater of Treviri
7 Gallic silver coins
8 Gallic bronzes
1 denarius of Caesar
1 plated denarius of Octavian, *RIC* I^2, 252

Hussigny Godbrange – ibid., 227; *RRCH* 516
21 Gallic silver coins
111 Gallic bronzes
32 Gallic potin coins
2 denarii
3 quinarii
1 as
1 quinarius of Juba I
$\frac{1}{2}$ as of Lugdunum
5 asses of Nemausus
$\frac{1}{2}$ as of Nemausus

Saint-Marcel, near Argentomagus, in a votive deposit – *Gallia* 1974, 308
1 as of Nemausus
Several asses of Lugdunum
2 (hemi)obols of Massalia
40 Gallic silver coins

App. 57 Hoards of precious metal coinage in Gaul after Caesar

Down to 44

Valdivienne (Bonneuil) – *Corpus* I, p.26

Viverols – *RRCH* 375

Puy d'Issolu – M. Labrousse, *Mélanges Carcopino* (Paris, 1966), 568
39 denarii and 1 quinarius down to issue of Mn. Cordius Rufus

Argelès-sur-mer – G. Claustres, *Société agricole, scientifique et littéraire des Pyrénées-Orientales* 1963, 25
1000 denarii down to issue of Mn. Cordius Rufus

Vernon near Vienne – *RRCH* 384; *Corpus* I, p.27 (with Gallic silver)

Villette – *RRCH* 393 (with Gallic silver)

Down to 35

Ferran – Abbé Verguet, *Monnaies romaines* (Carcassonne, 1864)
78 denarii and 1 quinarius

Lissac – *RRCH* 409; R. Gounot, *Cahiers de la Haute-Loire* 1, 1965, 9, 'Le trésor de Lissac'

Francin – *RRCH* 413

St.Arcons-de-Barges – *Mémoires de la Société agricole de la Haute-Loire* 6, 1888-90, 129
113 denarii *perhaps* down to 41 BC (despite dates offered in original publication)

Arbanats – *RRCH* 430 (with one piece of Gallic silver)

La Jante (Compreignac) – *RRCH* 343 (misdated); *Corpus* I, p.73

Narbonne – Abbé Verguet, l.c.
18 denarii and 3 quinarii

Sauvessanges – *RRCH* 447; *Trésors Monétaires* 1, 11; 2, 103

Saint-Frichoux – *BSFN* 1969, 391
20 'monnaies à la croix'
1 aureus
61 denarii and quinarii

Down to 31 (without Legionary denarii)

Saumur – V. Godard-Faultrier, *Monuments antiques de l'Anjou* (1864), 184
500 aurei

Ensérune – J. Jannoray, *Ensérune* (Paris, 1955), 344, n.4, compare 444 and 459; information from J.-Cl. Richard
1 bronze of Massalia
40 denarii and quinarii to quinarius with IMP.CAESAR DIVI F
3 asses

Fos-sur-mer – *RRCH* 450

Plestin-les-Grèves – Information from J.-B. Giard
42 denarii to issue with IMP.CAESAR

Segonzac – *RRCH* 453; *Corpus* I, p.61

Down to 31 (with Legionary denarii)

Allenc – information from J.-Cl. Richard
122 denarii to Legionary issue of M. Antonius

Amiens – *RRCH* 458 (with three pieces of Gallic gold)

Beauvoisin – *RRCH* 459 (with Gallic silver)

Chantenay – *RRCH* 461 (with Gallic silver)

Chenérailles – *Corpus* I, p.95

Foncquevillers – *Corpus* II, p.73

Gémenos – A. Blanchet, *Les trésors de monnaies romaines* (Paris, 1900), 158
333 denarii to Legionary issue of M. Antonius (with 3 bronzes of Massalia)

Mont-Beuvray – *RRCH* 471 (with Gallic silver)

Tilly-Capelle – *Corpus* II, p.82

App. 58   Finds on the Great Saint Bernard (p.276)

See, in particular, F. von Duhn and E. Ferrero, *Memorie della Reale Accademia delle Scienze di Torino*, Ser.2, 41, 1891, 331, 'Le monete galliche dell'Ospizio del Gran San Bernardo' – Coins from excavations of 1873-89

Gazzetta Numismatica 1883, 27 and 42 – Coins from excavations of 1760-4
Gallic coins
Denarii and quinarii
Asses and fractions
Imperial coins

RN 1839, 66 – Coins from excavations of 1837
Gallic coins
As
Imperial coins

NSc 1890, 304; 1892, 74 and 448; 1894, 41 – Coins from excavations from 1890
Gallic coins
Coins of the Po valley
Bronze of Massalia (?)
Denarius, quinarius and victoriatus
Asses, some halved, and fractions
Imperial coins

A. Pautasso, *Studi F. Rittatore Vonwiller* (Como, 1980) II, 343, 'Influenze monetarie del celtismo padano nell'area elvetica', discusses the Gallic coins found

App. 59   The coinage of the upper Rhone valley (p.277)

It is now clear that a group of imitations of the drachms of Massalia, known to A. Pautasso essentially from the finds on the Great Saint Bernard (App. 58) and initially attributed to the Po valley, are the product of a mint in the Rhone valley, perhaps at Martigny (Forum Claudii Vallensium); see F. Wiblé, *SM* 1978, 65, 'Importante découverte à Martigny'; A. Geiser, *9 Cong..Num.* 597, 'Les trouvailles monétaires de Martigny'; also A. Pautasso, in *Atti del Congresso sul Bimillenario di Aosta* (Aosta, 1982), 57, for a find at St Rhémy, with 5 Gallic potin pieces.

App. 60   Hoards in Noricum (p.279)

For finds of the coinage of Noricum see P. Kos (p.278, n.53); G. Gorini, in *Keltische Numismatik und Archaeologie* (Oxford: BAR, 1984), 69; it is clear that the coinage barely travelled outside the kingdom, which suggests very strongly that it was designed for internal purposes, probably fiscal.

I note a couple of outlying finds:
S. Stefano di Aquileia – G. Belloni, *Aquileia Nostra* 1956, 11
Stufels near Bressanone – G. Gorini, *Der Schlern* 51, 1977, 7, 367

The Roman hoards from the area are:

Gerlitzen – *RRCH* 403; G. Dembski, *NZ* 1977, 7
1 quinarius with Boian and Norican silver

Baldramsdorf (Lampersberg) – *RRCH* 468; G. Dembski, *NZ* 1977, 13
56 denarii

Portschach – *Carinthia* 1847, 98; J.G. Seidl, *Chronik der archäologischen Funde* (Vienna, 1840-5) III, 17
Denarii of the families Antonia, Cordia, Memmia, Tituria

Aguntum – G. Dembski, *NZ* 1977, 6
1 as of Augustus with Norican silver

For hoards of Roman and Norican silver from the Magdalensberg see H. Bannert and G. Piccottini, *Die Fundmünzen vom Magdalensberg* (Klagenfurt, 1972), 53, 54, 55, 56

It is clear, *contra* G. Alföldy (p.279, n.54), 34-5, that Roman coins do not arrive in Noricum before the first century BC

Note also from the upper Rhine valley:
Lauterach – *RRCH* 170; B. Overbeck (p.277, n.48) II, no. 24; I, 178 (about 100 BC)
 1 quinarius of Aedui
 2 local 'monnaies à la croix'
24 denarii

K. Castelin, *Mitt.Ost.Num.Ges*. 1967, 1; 1970, 115, dates the fibulae (and the find) to about 15 BC; the argument is based on a bizarre view of the relevance of the Roman conquest of the area; the Gallic coins are of around 100, not long after the date of the denarii in the hoard, which should be dated to the early first century BC

Bruggen (Haggen) – *RRCH* 405; *SNR* 1981, 41; B. Overbeck (l.c.) II, no. 43; I, 181
Denarii and quinarii to 42 BC

APPENDICES

COINAGE AND MONEY

App. A Non-Roman measures of capacity in Lucania (p.14)

Villa of Vittimose near Buccino
S. L. Dyson and R. Ross Holloway, *AJA* 1971, 152–3 = S.L. Dyson, *The Roman Villas of Buccino* (Oxford: BAR, 1983), 33
Probably first rather than second century BC

a) ACILES KXXIV {IX VRN}
        IX VRN LXXIIS
                KXXII:
Aciles – (dolium no.) 9 – $72\frac{1}{2}$ urnae – 124 or 122 1/6

b) XXXVII VRN LIX:·
    BVLOS KX
Bulos – (dolium no.) 37 – 59 1/4 urnae – 110

c) KXXII::·
    122 5/12

d) KXXV:
    125 1/6

e) LIV V.SL
    P.I'.I'IICIIT
    54 – V.Sl( )P.f. fecet

f) III VRN LXV
    (dolium no.) 3 – 65 urnae

g) KXXI

h) KXXV

i) KX

j)]XIX

Compare XXVI on a dolium from Vagni, S.L. Dyson, 83

Site near Polla
Forma Italiae III, ii. no. 72

      XI KXIXS
(dolium no.) 11 – $119\frac{1}{2}$

App. B The mint of Fistelia (p.27)

Neither the evidence for date nor the evidence for location is unambiguous. The earliest relevant hoards, Campania (*IGCH* 1920; note the presence of pieces of Allifae) and Calvi Risorta = Cales (*IGCH* 1938) show that the coinage began in the first half of the fourth century and perhaps suggest that it was produced in northern Campania. The latter suggestion is borne out by the pattern of stray finds:

    Carsoli – *NSc* 1951, 169
    Norba – *NSc* 1904, 423

Casalvieri near Atina – M. Rizzello, *I santuari della media valle del Liri* (Sora, 1980), 94

Aquino – information from A. Gabucci

Teano – *Mon.Ant.* 20, 1910, 69 and 78

Alife = Allifae – *Annali* 1884, 256

Telesia – A. Sambon, 328–9 (over 50 pieces)

S. Maria di Capua Vetere = Capua – *NSc* 1881, 91 (with pieces of Neapolis in a tomb)

IGCH 1941 (not a hoard)

Valle d'Ansanto – App. 8

Campochiaro – *Sannio*, 223

Monte Vairanso – *Sannio*, 354

Pompeii – *NSc* 1910, 417

Giornale degli Scavi 1887, 5

NSc 1942, 308

Samnite provenances are clearly to be associated with the penetration of coinage into this area during and after the Pyrrhic War (App. 7). The Monteverde hoard is of that period or later and, coming from near the line of the Via Appia, is presumably to be related to Roman military activity. The Carife hoard of the late third century, also from near the line of the Via Appia, represents the last stages of the process whereby the use of coinage penetrated into Samnium.

The material from 'Campo Laurelli' is problematic for two reasons: the find-spot cannot now be certainly identified and although some of the pieces certainly derive from a hoard it is impossible to decide exactly which. It seems likely, however, from the original reports that the material comes from a sanctuary and not from a cemetery; the coin material from other Samnite sanctuaries similarly includes hoards.

It may even be, given the inaccuracy of the geographical indications offered, that 'Campo Laurelli' lies where the sanctuary of San Giovanni in Galdo was later discovered: given that Toro is not ten miles from Campobasso, but six, it may be that 'Campo Laurelli' is not three miles north of Toro, but less than two, where the sanctuary of San Giovanni in Galdo lies; and 'Campo Laurelli' is described as lying above a river called the Zappino, while the sanctuary lies above a river called the Tappino.

In any case, the coins of Fistelia from 'Campo Laurelli' are unlikely to have arrived in one of the remotest areas of Samnium before the third century; the fact that they arrived in quantity suggests that the mint went on functioning in the late fourth century. As for its location, the community of Telesia, near Allifae, is a strong possibility.

App. C   The silver content of coins of Magna Graecia (p.33)

		Silver	Chlorsilber	Copper	Lead	Reference
Neapolis	?	87.55	5.77	?	?	(1)
Neapolis	Didrachm	91.63	Trace	7.13	0.88	(2)
Neapolis	Didrachm	93.02	—	5.77	1.09	(2)
Neapolis	Didrachm	92.55	—	6.02	1.22	(2)
Velia	?	85.37	8.48	?	?	(1)
Thurium	Diobol	91.09	Trace	7.15	Trace	(2)
Thurium	Diobol	92.00	—	7.03	0.73	(2)
Heraclea	?	76.27	13.04	?	?	(1)
Heraclea	Diobol	94.14	—	5.58	0.10	(2)
Tarentum	Obol	88.45	Some	10.19	0.51	(2)

(1) *GGA* 1843, 2, 1289; (2) E. Bibra, *Über alte Eisen- und Silberfunde* (Nürnberg and Leipzig, 1873)

App. D Overstrikes (p.58)

I here list further examples of overstrikes listed in *RRC*, pp. 105–17, and new overstrikes.

NON-ROMAN OVERSTRIKES

B   Atella
3   Quadrunx overstruck on a semilibral sextans
(c)   Parma 553
4   Biunx overstruck on a semilibral uncia
(d)   Parma 554
(e)   *SNG* (ANS) 169, 13.25 gm.
6   Uncia overstruck on a collateral semuncia
(b)   Parma 556

E   Carthage
a   Half-shekel struck in Sicily overstruck on a denarius
(a)   L. Villaronga, *Gaceta Numismatica* 40, 1976, 15
b   Bronze struck in Sicily (R. Ross Holloway, *AIIN* 7–8, 1960–1, 35) overstruck on a post-semilibral semuncia (*RRC*, no. 41/11)
(a)   Hunter, 4.15 gm.

c   Bronze (*SNG* (Cop.) 307–23) overstruck on a post-semilibral uncia (*RRC*, no. 41/10)
(a)   Coates, 3.50 gm.
d   Bronze (*SNG* (Cop.) 326–9) overstruck on an uncia with corn-ear (*RRC*, no. 42/4)
(a)   Haines = Birmingham, 8.08 gm.

C.A. Hersh possesses a clearer example of the half-shekel illustrated on the dust-jacket of P. Marchetti, overstruck on a victoriatus.

F   Neapolis
e   Bronze (Apollo/Man-headed bull with Victory) overstruck on a bronze of Hieron II (Poseidon/Trident)
(a)   Nemi 717

ROMAN OVERSTRIKES

15   Post-semilibral triens overstruck on a semilibral sextans
(f)   Vicarello find
(g)   Loudmer-Poulain 15–16/6/1976, 141
18   Post-semilibral sextans overstruck on a semilibral uncia
(m)   Warsaw 151011, 9.22 gm.
(n)   Knobloch 58 = BM 1978–6–21–1
22   Quadrans with corn-ear overstruck on a bronze of Hieron II
(l)   Birmingham, 17.30 gm.
(m)   *Monumenti antichi inediti dalla collezione recuperiana descritti in diverse memorie dal possessore Barone Giuseppe Recupero* (Palermo, 1808), Tav. per la IV Memoria, 4
(n)   Ibid., Tav. spettanti alla V Memoria (unnumbered, but number five), 1
(o)   Bonhams 14/9/81, 245, 16.76 gm.

23   Uncia with corn-ear overstruck on a bronze of Hieron II
(n)   Paris, A1027, 6.40 gm.
(o)   Birmingham, 5.90 gm.
44   Anonymous sextans overstruck on a post-semilibral uncia
(c)   Paris, A1159, 3.40 gm.
f   Anonymous sextans (*RRC*, no. 56/6) overstruck on a bronze of Nuceria (Sambon 1015)
(a)   Naples, S1367, 3.03 gm.
51   Sextans of (C.) Aur(unculeius) overstruck on a Sardo-Punic bronze
(k)   Lucera 2172
53   Sextans (*RRC*, no. 63/6, 64/6 or 65/6) overstruck on a Sardo-Punic bronze
(c)   Berlin (Dodona 1173/1912), 4.71 gm.

g   Sextans (*RRC*, no. 63/6, 64/6 or 65/6) overstruck on a Punic bronze (*SNG* (Cop.) 109–19, *c*.300 BC)
(a)   BM photo-file

L. Forteleoni, *AIIN* 1971–72, 113, 'Riconiazioni in Sardegna', at 117, n.24; F. Burragato and G. Guidi, *AIIN* 1973, 213, 'Determinazione di leghe metalliche', at 219–21, analyse a group of Sardo-Punic bronzes and Roman bronzes struck in Sardinia; the Sardo-Punic bronzes have a pronounced iron content, as also do some of the Roman bronzes; such Roman bronzes are to be regarded as overstruck on Sardo-Punic bronzes. There is no ground for attributing those Roman bronzes which do not have a pronounced iron content to a different mint; they are presumably just not overstruck.

59   Semis with corn-ear and KA overstruck on a semilibral uncia
(b)   Winterthur, 11.50 gm.
h   Semis with corn-ear and KA overstruck on a collateral quadrans
(a)   Winterthur, 11.47 gm.
62   Triens with corn-ear and KA overstruck on a bronze of Hieronymus
(d)   *Monumenti ... Recupero*, ibid., 2
65   Sextans with corn-ear and KA overstruck on a bronze of Hieron II
(t)   BM 1933–3–11–1, 6.06 gm.
(u)   *BMCRR* Italy 274, 6.03 gm.
(v)   Munich, 5.40 gm.
(w)   BM R 0058, 5.98 gm.
(x)   *BMCRR* Italy 276, 5.73 gm.
(y)   *BMCRR* Italy 277, 5.70 gm.
(z)   *BMCRR* Italy 278, 5.49 gm.
(aa)   *Monumenti ... Recupero*, ibid., 5
i   Sextans with corn-ear and KA overstruck on a semilibral semuncia
(a)   Winterthur, 3.90 gm.

69   Quadrans with corn-ear overstruck on a semilibral uncia
(c)   Birmingham, 10.82 gm.
91   Triens with CA overstruck on a bronze of Oeniadae
(u)   Winterthur, Lambros, 4.75 gm.
97   Triens with staff overstruck on a semilibral uncia
(e)   BM 1978–7–18–1, 12.80 gm.
98   Triens with staff overstruck on a semilibral uncia
(f)   BM 1978–6–6–1, 11.50 gm.
j   As (*RRC*, no. 177/1) overstruck on a post-semilibral sextans (*RRC*, no. 41/9)
(a)   Numantia 141
k   Uncertain late second-century semis overstruck perhaps on an uncertain late second-century quadrans. Bahrfeldt 14 (wrongly described)
(a)   Hannover 2695, 6.06 gm.
l   Denarius of L. Memmius (*RRC*, no. 304/1) overstruck on a denarius of C. Fonteius (*RRC*, no. 290/1)
(a)   *MONG* 1980, 158
m   Semuncial quadrans (*RRC*, no. 339/4a-b) overstruck on an uncertain prow bronze
(a)   Paris, A1154, 4.20 gm.
n   Denarius of T. Carisius (*RRC*, no. 464/1) overstruck on a denarius of A. Licinius Nerva (*RRC*, no. 454/1)
(a)   BM 1981–5–24–1, 4.21 gm.
o   Bronze of Octavian (*RRC*, no. 535/1) overstruck on an uncertain as
(a)   Warsaw
p   Bronze of Octavian (*RRC*, no. 535/2) overstruck on an uncertain as
(a)   Warsaw

App. E   The mint of Petelia (p.69)

The standard account is that of M. Caltabiano, *Una città del sud tra Roma e Annibale* (Palermo, 1977), not all of whose conclusions, however, are acceptable.

There seem to be three groups of issues:

A   A piece weighing 8 gm. and its fractions without marks of value
B   A light sextantal triens
A heavy uncial triens (M. Caltabiano, p.69, no. 5)
C   Semuncial quadrans to semuncia

The principal problem is posed by the Helios/Tripod pieces, which share with the last group the use of monograms and symbols to subdivide the issue, but which have no marks of value; I wonder if they are sescunciae of Group C. This suggestion is marginally supported by the hoard published by P. Attianese (App. 16), 224, which contained all the varieties of Group A, except for the Helios/Tripod pieces and the Artemis/Dog pieces, and Group B. *IGCH* 2037 contained no pieces with marks of value, *IGCH* 2058 and *Coin Hoards* 4, 44, too incomplete a selection of the various types to be decisive, though the latter certainly confirms the obvious inference from *IGCH* 2037 that Group A precedes the rest.

Petelia was attacked by the Carthaginians after Cannae, taken after a siege of eleven months and handed over to the Brettii; it seems to me unlikely that both the coinage without marks of value and that with marks of value can be assigned to a single phase of the history of Petelia, whether on the side of Rome or under the rule of Carthage. I suspect that Group A was struck while Petelia was under the rule of Carthage, Groups B–C after the departure of Hannibal and the return of the original inhabitants who had survived; for Petelia later countermarked bronzes of the Brettii with Ares/Athena and Zeus/Eagle *and* one of her own issues of Group A.

App. F   The metal content of the drachm coinage of the Po valley (p.79)

Apart from the hoards, weight and metal content provide some useful chronological indications.

	Weights	Silver content
α	3.90/3.50	
β	3.60/2.90 (one 2.05)	
1–4	2.90/2.85	
7	2.60/2.20	65.3%
		45%
6	2.25	50.1%
8	2.80/2.10	
9–10	2.20	43.5% (group 9)
5	2.25	
12	2.00	

Groups 11 and 13 are each attested by a single specimen.

App. G. The Roman conquest and the ownership of land in the Po valley (p.81)

When the Triumvirs began to settle their veterans after Philippi, it often fell out that the city chosen to receive a colony possessed insufficient territory; the solution was simple and consisted of the removal of some of the territory of a neighbouring or nearby city, territory henceforth described as a *praefectura* of the city to which it had been transferred (Hyginus 202.17–203.2 L; Frontinus 49.7–13 L).[1] Alternatively, a community might acquire land, even far away, *beneficio principum* (Frontinus, l.c.).[2] The practice is widely attested and is indeed not an innovation of the Principate. Various Roman gifts to Athens from 167 onwards[3] and the assignations of Antony to Rhodes were obvious precedents for Octavian's grant of land in the territory of Cnossus to Capua.[4] Even before 167, Ptolemy II, for instance, had given land, probably nearby, to Miletus.[5]

But a community could also acquire land, even far away, by private enterprise, as it were, most readily by bequest. This means of acquisition is attested both for the Roman and for the Greek world: thus Auximum, Praeneste and Petelia all acquired land by bequest;[6] Artapates left land in the territories of Pinara and Tlos to the Letoum of Xanthus in the late first century BC;[7] and Junia Theodora almost certainly left land – it is not known where – to the Lycian League in the early first century AD.[8] It is reasonable to hold that the land on Cyprus owned by Cos in the late first century BC was acquired by bequest;[9] also the land owned elsewhere in Syria by Caesarea.[10]

A similar assumption is also reasonable (and in one instance documented) in the case of Italian communities attested as holding land far away. Here, however, enough material is available to see in the original acquisition of the land which the communities eventually held important evidence for the processes of Roman imperialism. Thus already by 51 BC land in Asia Minor held by Romans or

---

1 See for a recent discussion L.J.F. Keppie, *Colonisation and Veteran Settlement in Italy, 47–14 B.C.* (London, 1983). It is not clear at what stage this new use of the term *praefectura* came into being, as opposed to the traditional sense of 'community overseen by (Roman) *praefecti iure dicundo*'. The property of Histonium attested at Campomarini, *CIL* ix, 2827, may actually be in the territory of Histonium.

2 Compare Strabo x, 2, 21 (460) for the assignation of a lake in the territory of Calydon to the Roman colony of Patrae; Suet., *Aug.* 46 for the assignation in general of *vectigalia* to Italian colonies.

3 Discussed by G.I. Luzzatto, in *Symposion* I (1975), 105, 'Sulla condizione delle città suddite nelle cosidette *archai* durante l'impero', along with the quite different phenomenon of Sparta (Strabo viii, 4, 11 (362); Paus. iii, 21, 7). See above all the discussion in W. Liebenam, *Städteverwaltung* (Leipzig, 1900), 8–18. Later treatments are largely derivative.

4 P. Ducrey, *BCH* 1969, 846 = *AE* 1969–70, 635; K. Rigsby, *TAPA* 1976, 313. The addition of part of Mauretania to Baetica by Otho (Tac., *Hist.* i, 78, 1) looks rather different.

5 C.B. Welles, *Royal Correspondence* (London, 1934), no.14.

6 *CIL* ix, 5845; x, 114; xiv, 2934.

7 L. Robert, *Documents de l'Asie Mineure méridionale* (Geneva and Paris, 1966), 30.

8 L. Robert, *REA* 1960, 324; note that C. Caninius Rebilus was careful to leave land in the territory of Thasos to Thasos, of Philippi to Philippi.

9 G. Patriarca, *Bullettino del Museo dell'Impero Romano* 1932, 6.

10 J.-P. Rey-Coquais, *Mélanges de l'Université St. Joseph* 47, 1972, 103–5. Further examples in W. Liebenam, 10–11.

Italians[11] had perhaps passed to a number of Italian communities.[12] A community in Italy which cannot be identified and which may be anywhere is attested as owning and renting out land in the former territory of Fregellae.[13] Cales is attested as owning land in Lucania, presumably in an area confiscated after the Hannibalic War (*CIL* x, 3917); there are numerous ways in which such *ager publicus* may have become private on its way into the hands of the community of Cales.[14]

But it is in Cisalpine Gaul that the ownership of land by Italian communities is most widely attested, for Aquinum (Pliny, *NH* iii, 116); Arpinum (Cic., *ad fam.* xiii, 11, 1 = Shackleton Bailey 278); Atella (Cic., *ad. fam.* xiii, 7, 1–3 = Shackleton Bailey 320);[15] Luca (*CIL* xi, 1147 – land bequeathed by C. Attius Nepos not only in the territory of Luca, but also in that of Veleia, Placentia, Parma and *in montibus*). It may be that the land held by C. Nepos and then by Luca is all land in the area where the territory of Luca, Veleia, Placentia and Parma adjoined and that it had once been part of the territory of Luca; it is also possible that some of the land owned by Italian communities in Cisalpine Gaul had been granted directly to them. But in general acquisition by bequest seems to me the most likely explanation of their possessions.

My own inclination is to hold (against the opinion of P.A. Brunt) that there *was* in the second century BC substantial private emigration from the rest of Italy to Cisalpine Gaul;[16] but for present purposes the important point is that we are both agreed on the likelihood of large landowners moving in.[17] It is such men, as Brunt points out, who will have possessed the capital required for drainage works; and it is such men who will have left land to their original communities, lasting reminders of the consequences of the Roman conquest of the Po valley.

App. H   The Iberian coinage (p.91)

See J. Untermann, *MDAI(M)* 1964, 91, 'Die Gruppierung der hispanischen Reitermünzen mit Legenden in iberischer Schrift'; *Monumenta Linguarum Hispanicarum* I (Wiesbaden, 1975), 153–6 (list of mints). (Note that Map 1 in article = Map 2 in book, Map 4 = Map 6, Map 5 = Map 7, Map 6 = Map 8.)

The areas in which the coinage was struck were as follows:

(a) South-west Gaul (Untermann, A.1–A.5)

---

11 M.H.Crawford (p.173, n.1), at 48, n.4.
12 Cic., *ad fam.* viii, 9, 4 = Shackleton Bailey 82; I prefer the interpretation in the text to that of Shackleton Bailey and that of D. Magie, *Roman Rule in Asia Minor* (Princeton, 1950) II, 1251.
13 Cic., *ad fam.* xiii, 76, 2 = Shackleton Bailey 62.
14 There is no evidence for or likelihood in the view of A.J. Toynbee, *Hannibal's Legacy* (London, 1965) II, 550–1, that the land held by Cales and other communities was still Roman *ager publicus*, held in usufruct.
15 The Regienses of this letter were presumably the inhabitants of Reggio Emilia.
16 The suggestion goes back to E. Pais, in *Ricerche sulla Storia* IV (Rome, 1920, 331), who drew attention to the occurrence of central Italian names in the Po valley; he is on the whole followed by G.E. Chilver, *Cisalpine Gaul* (Oxford, 1941), 83. P.A. Brunt, *Italian Manpower* (Oxford, 1971), 197, doubts private immigration (apart from some soldiers who may have stayed where they served), as opposed to state-organised colonial ventures. But note the Samnite deity Mefitis at Lodi (*CIL* v, 6353) as well as at colonial Cremona (Tac., *Hist.* iii, 33, 2).
17 Note N. Magius at Cremona, perhaps from the aristocratic Campanian Magii, G.V. Summer, *HSCP* 1970, 257, 'Velleius Paterculus', at 261. See also J. Heurgon, *Mélanges Seston* (Paris, 1974), 231, 'Caton et la Gaule cisalpine', arguing that Cato's account reflects intensive Roman penetration in the years before 167.

(b) The coastal plain from Emporiae to Tarraco (Untermann, A.6–A.9, A.11–A.15)
(c) The central Ebro valley and its northern tributaries (Untermann, A.10, A.16–A.26, A.36–A.60)
(Untermann, A.27–A.35 belong with (b) or (c))
(d) The territory of the Celtiberi, that is the Jalon valley, the head-waters of the Ebro, the head-waters of the Douro (Untermann, A.61–A.93) (J. Untermann, *Sprachräume im vorrömischen Hispanien* (Wiesbaden, 1961), 13, goes beyond the evidence in suggesting on the basis of Segorbe = *Segobriga that the Celtiberi penetrated to the area of Saguntum)
(e) The mint of Kelin (now Los Villares) (Untermann, A.94) (see P.P. Ripollés Alegre, *Numisma* 165–7, 1980, 9, 'Estudio numismatico del poblado ibérico Los Villares')
(f) The mints of Arse = Saguntum, Kili and Saeti = Saetabi (Untermann, A.33–A.35) (see Apps. J and K)
(g) The mints of Ikalesken (perhaps in the area of Cuenca and Valencia and perhaps to be located at Egelasta, G.K. Jenkins, *Mus.N* 1958, 64) and Urkesken (Untermann, A.95–A.96) (see App. 29)
(h) The mints of Kastilo = Castulo, Iltiraka and Ilturir = Iliberris (Untermann, A.97–A.99)
(i) The mints of Ibolka = Obulco, Vekoekikionis = Abra and a city dependent on Obulco (Untermann, A.100–A.102)
(k) The mint of Ketouibon = Salacia (Untermann, A.103) (see p.214)

The evidence for the chronology of (h) and (i) is reasonably coherent and precise. The coinage of the mint of Obulco is mostly bilingual, which suggests a date not earlier than the turn of the second and first centuries; this date is confirmed by the occurrence of pieces of Obulco in the Torello hoard, the latest Roman issue of which is an as of Cn. Blasio (App. 31), and in the Štikada hoard, which was probably closed in the early first century (App. 49). Similarly, the coinage of Castulo moves from an Iberian legend to a Latin legend; and asses of Castulo are recorded from the Mazin and Gračac hoards, which were probably closed in the early first century (App. 49). The coinage of Castulo was presumably brought to an end by the sack of the town by Q. Sertorius. The coinage of Iliberris likewise moves from an Iberian to a sequence of Latin legends, FLORENTIA and ILIBERRI; the issues with Latin legend were heavily represented in the Guadix hoard (M. Gomez-Moreno, *Miscelaneas. Primera Serie. La Antiguedad* (Madrid, 1949), 355), dated at any rate approximately by the presence of an as of Cn. Pompeius (*RRC*, no. 471). These Latin issues are probably of the 60s and 50s.

Closely linked to (h) and (i) are a number of mints which used Latin legends only. The issues of L. Appuleius Decianus as quaestor (the alleged F in the legend L.AP.DEC.Q[.F] (Vives, pl. CXII, 6; BM) is a die fault) at Urso, Myrtilis and Baelo cannot be dissociated from the issues of a L. Appuleius Decianus as quaestor in Sicily. The same man is surely responsible for both. The Spanish issues cannot be separated from the issues of Castulo, which they closely resemble and many of which should be dated to the period of Q. Sertorius. The degree of wear of the Roman asses in the El Saucejo hoard (App. 31, compare the Ecija hoard), which also includes a piece of Urso of L. Appuleius Decianus, strongly encourages such a dating. The man will have gone to Spain with M. Perperna, praetor in 83 or 82 and governor of Sicily in 82; he will have been a son of C. Appuleius Decianus, the *popularis* tribune of 98, who was perhaps born about 140 (for the family, see E. Badian, *JRS* 1956, 91, 'P. Decius P.f. Subulo', with slight adjustment of the life-span of the characters involved). The assignation of the issues of Decianus to the 40s by M. Grant, *FITA*, 24–5, is based on the false argument that no other period could have seen a man serving as quaestor in Sicily and Spain; nor does Grant consider any strictly numismatic arguments. The chronology proposed by L. Villaronga, *Ampurias* 1979–80, 243, 'Las monedas de Urso', is based solely on metrological criteria, for the fallibility of which see p.91.

The dating of (b) to (d) is complex (there is no useful evidence for (a)); much depends on the interpretation of hoards which contain no Roman issues. The city of Lauro was captured and sacked by Q. Sertorius; I suspect that much of its coinage, well represented in the Canoves hoard (App. 32), had just been struck for Pompey; the city is to be localised in the hinterland of Barcelona, close to Canoves (L. Villaronga, *Ampurias* 28, 1967, 135). (There is no good evidence that Edeta (now Leiria (= Liria)) was ever called Lauro or was captured by Sertorius; Orosius v, 23, 6, places the Lauro captured by Sertorius *apud Palantiam*, clearly neither Palantia beyond Numantia nor the insignificant river Pallantias near Saguntum.)

If the Canoves hoard does indeed belong in the period of Sertorius, the northern Iberian coinage in general may be placed between the 150s (p.95) and the 70s, with much produced for Sertorius. The large number of issues of Ilerda in the Azaila II hoard is to be explained in this way (App. 32); similarly, the quite untypical presence of asses of Valentia with asses of Celsa in a hoard from the Ebro valley (information from L. Villaronga; the single worn quadrans of Corduba is probably extraneous) may also be explained in terms of troop movements during the 70s; this would place much of the coinage of Celsa as well as of Valentia (App. P) in that period.

App. I   The coinage of Emporiae (p.86)

See in general A.M. de Guadan, *Las monedas de plata de Emporion y Rhode* I-II (Barcelona, 1955–58); M. Campo, *Acta Num.* 1972, 19, 'Los divisores de dracmas ampuritanas'; L. Villaronga, *The Aes Coinage of Emporion* (Oxford: BAR, 1977).

Fractions with Facing head/Horseman r. (De Guadan, Classes I-II)

The miserably inadequate hoard evidence (*IGCH* 2311–15, 2318) makes a date around 300 for the beginning of this coinage not implausible.

Drachms with Head of Persephone r./Horse r.; above, Victory r. (De Guadan, Class IV), *c*.4.85 gm.
Imitations (De Guadan, Class V)
Drachms with Head of Persephone r./Pegasus r. (De Guadan, Class VI), *c*.4.85 gm.
Imitations (De Guadan, Class VII)
Fourths and eighths with the same types (Campo, Class I, 1, 1; I, 1, 2 and I, 2–4), *c*.1.20 gm. and *c*.0.60 gm.

There is no good evidence for the dating of these issues, which are the heaviest and therefore presumably the earliest of the drachm coinage. The attempt of P. Marchetti, 371–86, to date all the drachm coinage of Emporiae after 218 depends on the implausible argument that in 218 the drachms of Emporiae were equated at par with a reduced quadrigatus, whereas later they were equated at a discount with a heavily overvalued denarius.

Drachms with Head of Persephone r./Pegasus r. (De Guadan, Classes IX-X, VIII, XI), *c*.4.75 gm.
Tenths with Pegasus (Campo, Classes II-IV), *c*.0.475 gm.
Twentieths with Two dolphins (Campo, Classes II-IV)
Fortieths with Dolphin (Campo, Classes II-IV)
Imitations (De Guadan, Class XII), *c*.4.65 gm.

Drachms with Head of Persephone r./Pegasus r. (De Guadan, Classes IX-X, VIII, XI), *c*.4.25 gm.
(The corn-ear head-dress of Persephone is sometimes missing and on these pieces a bow and a quiver, as of Diana, are sometimes present.)

These last are the issues which appear in hoards certainly of the Second Punic War (App. 27; Seriña, *IGCH* 2321; Tortosa, *IGCH* 2322), as well as in Puig Castellar (*IGCH* 2340) and Ullastret (*IGCH* 2339; nothing useful can be said of Gerona and Cartella). It does not seem to me possible to date the weight reduction with any precision within the period of the war.

There remains a certain amount of silver coinage of Emporiae which falls after the 190s; but it is not a substantial coinage. Some specimens are still fairly fresh in the late second-century hoard of La Barrocca and one may suppose that the silver coinage of Emporiae lasted in a desultory way for a generation or so after the 190s.

With the production of bronze, Emporiae shifted from a Greek to an Iberian legend, UNTIKESKEN, a legend which does not appear on any imitations of drachms of Emporiae; one may reasonably suppose a gap between the silver and the bronze coinage. If the latter begins in the 150s, it is contemporary with the main block of early Iberian bronze coinage (App. H); the two hoards from Ampurias offer marginal support to this thesis (App. 31); and one issue of Ilerda shares a type with one issue with UNTIKESKEN.

The denominational structure of the latter coinage is highly complex, with different types for different denominations:

Athena/Pegasus	As
Athena/Bull	Semis
Athena/Lion	Quadrans
Athena/Horse or Horse's head	Sextans

or:

Athena/Lion	As
Athena/Sea-horse	Semis
Athena/Cock	Quadrans
Athena/Boar	Sextans

App. J The coinage of Saguntum (Arse) (p.88)

See in general L. Villaronga, *Las monedas de Arse-Saguntum* (Barcelona, 1967).

Imitation of drachm of Emporiae, with arsaken (De Guadan (App. I), no. 863)
Drachm with Head of Apollo r./Wheel, with arsesken (Stockholm)

Despite the similarity of legend, the attribution of these pieces to Saguntum is less than certain; they are in any case neither precisely datable nor of great monetary significance.

Drachms with Helmeted head of Minerva r./Man-headed bull r., with arseedar (Villaronga, Class I), c.3.10 gm.
Bronzes with Cockle-shell/Prow r., with arseedar, c.7.00 gm.

I share the view of P. Marchetti, 386–94, that these pieces belong before the capture of Saguntum by the Carthaginians in 218, although the arguments based on the links with the coinages of Emporiae and Massalia are clearly worthless; four specimens are recorded from Montemolin (App. 27).

Drachms with Laureate head of Hercules l./Man-headed bull r., with arsgidar (Villaronga, Classes II; III, 1), c.3.20–3.40 gm.
Reduced drachms with Laureate or diademed head of Hercules l. or r./Man-headed bull r., Bull butting r. or Bull r., with arsgidar (Villaronga, Classes III, 2 – VII), c.2.60 gm.

The reduction in weight no doubt belongs to the period of the Second Punic War, when Saguntum was under Carthage; specimens of Villaronga, Class II are recorded from the Cheste, Valera and Tivisa before 1930 hoards (App. 27). The attempt of P. Marchetti to date the entire coinage during the war fails along with his attempt to date the beginning of the Iberian denarius coinage (to which the later groups of the silver coinage of Saguntum are related) in the same period (see p.95).

The later silver issues of Saguntum, down to Villaronga, Class VII, no doubt cover much of the second century.

Asses with Bare head r. or l./Horseman r., with arse

The change of legend could be taken to reflect an interval of time; but there are affinities of style with the previous group and the last silver issues of Saguntum are best regarded as contemporary with the earliest bronze issues; these belong in my view, along with the Iberian bronze issues discussed on p. 99, in the second half of the second century.

Asses with Helmeted head of Minerva r./Prow r.

The obverse is similar to that on asses of Valentia, many of which belong in my view to the period of Q. Sertorius (App. P). The legends on this group seem to progress from arse, via arse and SAGVNTVM, to arse with magistrates' names in Iberian script and on to SAGVNTVM with magistrates' names in Latin script.

App. K   The coinage of Saetabi (Saeti) (p.88)

The issues of this mint are best seen as accompanying the much more extensive issues of the mint of Saguntum. There is first a small issue of silver didrachms and hemidrachms during the Second Punic War, the former attested in the Valera hoard (App. 27), then issues of asses parallel to the asses of Saguntum with Bare head/Horseman and the legend arse (as *SNG* (Cop.) 269–71).

App. L   Sicilian units of reckoning (p.114)

The basic problem is posed by the statement of Aristotle (fr. 589 Rose = Pollux ix, 87; compare Souda, s.v. *Talanton*) that the early Sicilian talent contained 24 nomoi and the later Sicilian talent contained 12 nomoi; there is no doubt that the terms *stater* and *nomos* were interchangeable and that the later nomos contained 2 Attic drachmae (see below); it is best to suppose that *in fact* the Sicilian talent always contained 12 current nomoi; that the number of drachmae to the nomos was changed from 4 to 2; and that Aristotle was recording the value of the earlier talent in later nomoi. This hypothesis is confirmed by the existence of an archaic weight from Acrae with the legend *stater dikaios*, weighing 17.40 gm., in other words 4 Attic drachmae.

The drachma no doubt always contained 5 litrae; the early talent therefore contained 12 nomoi of 4 drachmae or 240 litrae; this view is confirmed by an inscription from Sicily recording a debt of 301 talents and 141 litrae, clearly out of 240, *contra* the ed.pr.: *ASNP* 7, 1977, 1329 = *SEG* 27, 657 (450–400 BC).

If the early talent, which was subdivided into 240 litrae, was the equivalent of an Attic talent of copper, the litra was in origin the equivalent of about 110 gm. of copper, a weight attested on Lipara.

The later talent of 12 nomoi of 2 drachmae contained 120 litrae, a system attested in the pre-49 Tauromenium accounts; compare *ASNP* 7, 1977, 1339 = *SEG* 27, 650, from Camarina, for a purchase price of land in talents.

Between 49 and 44, at Tauromenium, a different system was in force, even if some of the terminology was the same; 1 nomos = 2 heminoma = 10 tetralitra = 40 litrae (see p.114).

The equations of a Sicilian talent with 6 Attic drachmae (Pollux iv, 173) or with 3 denarii (Festus 492 L) are based on the absurd identification of a nomos with a Roman nummus (sestertius); both equations are probably the work of Apollodorus of Athens (fr. 218 Jacoby), for whom in the late second century BC the nomos of the west *was* the Roman sestertius; the first equation is based on a talent of 24 nomoi, the second on a talent of 12 nomoi.

I am puzzled by the small silver pieces with the marks of value XIIΠ, three dots and XIII, and XII (see G. Manganaro, *JNG* 1981–2, 45, n.44); the suggestion that the units are chalkoi (R. Ross Holloway, *RBN* 1962, 5, 'Eagle and fulmen on the coins of Syracuse', at 21–2) does not make sense, since Pollux, iv, 174–5, says that the Sicilians called 1/12 of a litra an *ounkia*, not a *chalkous*; I wonder if the figures do not represent $7\frac{1}{2}$, $3\frac{3}{4}$ and $2\frac{1}{2}$, in devalued litrae of *c*.0.20 gm., though the largest denomination is on the heavy side.

Testimonia

1 talent = 24 drachmae (and hence 1 nomos = 2 drachmae): Timaeus, fr. 143 Jacoby (the other figures in the same scholion deserve no credence)

50 litrae = 10 Attic drachmae (and hence 10 litrae = 2 Attic drachmae): Diod. xi, 26, 3

10 litrae = 1 Corinthian stater (and hence more or less 2 Attic drachmae): Aristotle, fr. 510 Rose = Pollux iv, 174, ix, 80 (the equation with 10 obols, rather than with 12 obols, is careless)

10 litrae = 1 stater: Epicharmus, fr. 10 Kaibel = Pollux ix, 82

5 litrae = 1 drachma: coin of Acragas weighing 4.25 gm. with *pen(talitron)* (*BMCSicily* 47)

1 litra = 1 Aeginetic obol: Aristotle, fr. 510 Rose = Pollux iv, 174, ix, 80

For litrae, note a fine of 10 litrae at Megara Hyblaea for non-cultivation: *Kokalos* 21, 1975, 141–3 = *SEG* 26, 1084 (600–550 BC)

App. M   The coinage of Histiaea (p.125)

Modern study begins with L. Robert, *Etudes de Numismatique* (Paris, 1951), 179, 'La circulation des monnaies d'Histiée', treating the distribution of the extremely common tetrobols of Histiaea and of the *proxenoi* of Histiaea as parallel phenomena. In *Hellenica* 11–12, 1960, 63, 'Circulation des monnaies d'Histiée', Robert remarked, 'J'ai pu ainsi marquer les directions de son commerce et l'étendue de ses relations'. In fact, it is highly unlikely that Robert had done anything of the sort; the original article of 1951, the supplement of 1960 and the further supplement in *Monnaies grecques* (Geneva and Paris, 1967), 37, 'Monnaies d'Histiée en Epire et en Illyrie', all fail to distinguish between hoards and other finds, hoards with many pieces and hoards with few, finds from sanctuaries and finds from elsewhere. Nor is any attempt made to differentiate finds by date; and to regard the Oreus hoard (*IGCH* 232) as other than a hoard put together in the context of military activity is to shun the obvious.

C. Marek demonstrated in *Talanta* 8–9, 1977, 74, 'Der Geldumlauf der Stadt Histiaia und seine Bedeutung für die Verteilung ihrer Proxenoi', that the two distribution patterns bore no resemblance to each other. It is in fact perfectly clear that the tetrobols of Histiaea were hoarded predominantly in the period of the Third Macedonian War and predominantly in territory controlled by Macedon in that period or otherwise involved in the war.

The simplest view is that taken by A. Giovannini, 34–5, that Histiaea, which was certainly a Roman base during the Third Macedonian War, struck for Rome; but the observation by W.P. Wallace, *NC* 1962, 17, 'The meeting-point of the Histiaean and Macedonian tetrobols', of close similarities between the two coinages leads to the suggestion that Perseus produced 'imitations' of the coinage of Histiaea, as he certainly did of Rhodes.

App. N Sestertii in Cato (pp. 148, 181)

I view the references to sestertii in the text of Cato's *de agri cultura* with deeper puzzlement than ever.

In 14–15, we have (nummi) II, n(ummus) s(ingulus) and n(ummi) X, in a series of contracts for building work.[1] There is no *internal* evidence for identifying these nummi, which may in principle be denarii, victoriati, sestertii or even asses.

In 21, the various expenses in connection with the construction of a *cupa*, in 22 the acquisition of a *trapetus* and its parts at Suessa or Pompeii or Rufrae are reckoned in HS.

In 144–5, some costs in connection with the olive harvest are given in SS. The actual figures pose grave problems, discussed in his commentary by R. Goujard, and it is also disconcerting that the abbreviation SS, current only from the second half of the second century AD, is used. I do not think that any reliance can be placed either on the figures or on the notation.

The other notation which occurs here is vict(oriatus). As H. Zehnacker points out ((p.143, n.1), 45), Cato may be talking of the area of Venafrum; this area may be regarded as forming part of Appennine Italy, precisely the region where the victoriatus continued to circulate in the first half of the second century BC (p.74).

It still seems to me possible that none of the references to sestertii in the text of the *de agri cultura* are authentic. We can only, I think, be absolutely certain that Cato used denarii and asses;[2] presumably, however, he also used victoriati, since it is hard to suppose that this notation would have been inserted in the text of the *de agri cultura* at a later date. But I now think total scepticism over sestertii in the text to be too radical; in any case, the use of sestertii by Cato does not affect the view that they were adopted by the Roman state only in about 140.

But why did Cato use sestertii? Leaving out of account the ambiguous nummi of 14–15, it is noticeable that sestertii occur in a Campanian context. We have observed that there is some evidence for the circulation in the Greek areas of Italy of the sestertius as the equivalent of the diobol (App. 21) and I am inclined to suggest that the diobol survived as a unit of reckoning in Campania in the second century and was in due course called a sestertius, since this was in terms of silver its Roman equivalent.

App. O The coinage of Corduba (p.211)

R.C. Knapp, *AIIN* 29, 1982, 183, 'The coinage of Corduba', suggests a second-century date for the single Republican issue of quadrantes; M. Grant, *FITA*, 4, suggests the period of the civil wars. In my view, the truth lies in between.

Grant based his argument on a piece in the Instituto de Valencia de Don Juan (Hübner, p.112, no.124 n.; Vives, pl.CXVIII, 4), with the legend CORDVBA BAL, linking it with the elder Balbus. But a further specimen, in the collection of L. Villaronga, makes it clear that

---

1. I was wrong in *RRC*, p.629, to suppose that the third passage reckoned in victoriati, see the commentary of R. Goujard.
2. Plut., *Cato Maior* 4; Seneca, *Epist.* 94, 27; naturally, I did not and do not suppose that these passages constitute an argument against the authenticity of the mentions of sestertii in the *de agri cultura*, *contra* H. Zehnacker (p.143, n.1), 45, n.25. I doubt whether *assaria pecunia* at 132 has anything to do with the coin, the as.

the letters BAL were added to a die on which there was really no room for them; it seems very hazardous to link the issue as a whole with Balbus.

There is otherwise some find evidence for chronology, since one specimen turned up in the Azaila I hoard, probably of the period of Q. Sertorius (App. 32), and 34 specimens at the site conventionally known as Castra Caecilia (J. Romagosa, *Gaceta Numismatica* 17, 1970, 8, 'Las monedas con leyenda Corduba'). M. Beltrán Lloris observes correctly, but irrelevantly, that the identification as Castra Caecilia is unsure (*Numisma* 1973–4, 255, 'El campamento romano de Cáceres el Viejo'); for since the coins found go down to the early first century, it is rather hard to think of a context for the camp except in the wars of the 70s. I find it quite impossible to believe that such an enormous number of quadrantes of Corduba would have been found there unless they had been struck very recently and observe with all due caution that the issue can be understood in the context of the military operations of Q. Metellus against Q. Sertorius (p. 211).

App. P   The coinage of Valentia (p.211)

Valentia was taken by Q. Sertorius in 75 and remained in his hands till the end; Saguntum seems to have passed under his control at about the same time, if not earlier. The late issues of bronze of Saguntum closely resemble one group of the issues of Valentia (Fig. 90); and I have already suggested (App. H) that the presence of a group of asses of Valentia in a hoard from the Ebro valley is best understood in the context of the military operations of the 70s; I should regard the last issues of both cities as struck for Sertorius.

App. Q   Overstrikes of Spanish bronze coins (p.211)

Period of Q. Sertorius
Acinipo on Obulco   M.G.G.
Carissa (Vives, pl.CXVII, 7) on Castulo (Vives, pl.LXX, 11)   M.G.G., L.L
Carissa on Corduba   R.C.K.
Carmo (Vives, pl.C, 4–6) on Myrtilis (Vives, pl.CIX, 6)   E.C.V.
Castulo (Vives, pl.LXX, 8–10) on Obulco
                                              M.G.G., L.L.
Corduba on Olontigi   J.R.
Ilipa (Vives, pl.CVII, 4) on Obulco (Vives, pl.XCVIII, 7)   E.C.V.
Ilipa (Vives, pl.CVII, 1) on Castulo
                                              M.G.G., L.L.
Onuba (Vives, pl.CII, 5) on Celsa (Vives, pl. LXII, 5–6   M.G.G., L.L.

Salacia (Vives, pl.LXXXIV, 11) on Ebusus (Vives, pl.LXXX)   E.C.V.
Sexi on Gades   M.G.G.
Period of early Empire
Emerita on Turricina   E.C.V.
Imitation of Claudius on Caesaraugusta
                                              E.C.V.

E. Collantes Vidal, *Ampurias* 31–2, 1969–70, 255, 'Reacuñaciones en la moneda ibérica'.
M. Garcia Garrida and L. Lalana, *Acta Num.* 1981, 81; 1983, 61, 'Reacuñaciones en la Hispania antigua'.
R.C. Knapp (App. O), 187, n.14.
J. Romagosa (App. O), 9.

App. R The evidence for slaves from Dacia (p.233)

M.I. Finley, *Klio* 1962, 51 = *Economy and Society in Ancient Greece* (London, 1981), 167, 'The slave-trade in antiquity: the Black Sea and Danubian regions'; see also D.M. Pippidi, *Stud.Clas.* 1966, 232 = *Contribuţii* (Bucharest, 1967), 523, on G. Klaffenbach, *Die Grabstelen der einstigen Sammlung Roma in Zakynthos* (Abh. Ak. Berlin, Kl. f. Lit. u. Kunst 1964, 2), no. 28, two Istrian slaves, perhaps so designated because bought at Istria (compare Varro, *LL* viii, 21 on slaves *named* after their place of purchase). I know of no other evidence for the likely involvement of the Greek cities near the mouth of the Danube in the slave trade. See Strabo vii, 3, 12 (304) for Getic and Dacian slaves in Athens; whence Eustathius, *Commentary on Dionys.Perieg.* 305 (*Geogr.Gr.Min.* II, pp.270–1). N. Lascu, *Acta Mus..Nap.* 1970, 79, argues that Daos is a name appropriate to a slave from Asia Minor, not to a Dacian slave; but that does not affect Strabo's belief that there were Dacian slaves in Athens. See M.I. Rostovtzeff, *Social and Economic History of the Hellenistic World* (Oxford, 1941), 675, n.87, for Scythian, Sarmatian and Maeotian slaves on Rhodes (a bare list of references to slaves in inscriptions of Rhodes in P.M. Fraser and T. Rönne, *Boeotian and West Greek Tombstones* (Lund, 1957), 96, n.37). See V. Velkov, *Etudes Balkaniques* 1, 1964, 1, 125, 'Zur Frage der Sklaverei auf der Balkanhalbinsel während der Antike', for slaves from Thrace in the Mediterranean world.

INDICES

The three indices of places and peoples, persons and subjects are selective and refer to passages, for the most part in the text, where discussion may be found.

INDEX OF PLACES AND PEOPLES

Acarnania, 58, 123, 127, 128
Achaea, 126
Aedui, 162, 166, 169–72
Aegina, 146–7
Aequi, 8
Aesernia, 11, 48
Aetolia, 123–4, 126–7
Africa, 133–42, 247–9, 271
Agrigentum, 107–10
Alabanda, 154–6
Alalia, 104
Alba Fucens, 11, 38, 47
Alesia, 215
Allobroges, 162, 164–5
Alps, 276–9
Amphaxitis, 129
Amphipolis, 128, 131, 209
Ancona, 9, 71–2
Antioch, 203–5, 253, 262, 266–7, 272
Apamea in Phrygia, 243, 258–60
Aphrodisias, 160, 269, 271
Apollonia, 116, 122–3, 220–1, 224–6, 228, 234, 236, 245
Apulia, 14, 25–6, 45–6, 49, 58, 64–6
Aquileia, 231, 235
Arabia, 253, 267–8

Aradus, 154–5, 201, 253
Ariminum, 9, 14–15, 43–4, 48
Arpi, 26, 49, 64–5, 108
Arverni, 162, 169–71, 171–2, 215–16, 229
Ascalon, 201
Asculum Picenum, 43–5
Asia, 152–60, 196–7, 206–9, 245, 262, 266
Aspendus, 152–3, 155
Athens, 105, 115, 119–25, 127–8, 141, 146–7, 156, 196, 200
Azaila, destruction of, 214

Balanea, 253
Belgae, 171, 215–18
Beneventum, 36, 48
Bithynia, 157, 196, 201, 243
Bituriges Cubi, 171–2, 216
Boeotia, 120, 124, 126
Brundisium, 66, 71–2
Bruttium, 13–14, 25–6, 62, 66–9
Byzantium, 200, 228, 270

Cabellio, 266
Caleacte, 115
Campania, 1, 4, 10–11, 25, 26–8, 29, 35–6, 47–8, 51, 96, 106, 108, 346

Campano-Tarentine issues, 34
Campochiaro, 37–8
Campo Laurelli, site of (*see also* San Giovanni in Galdo), 335
Canusium, 26
Cappadocia, 157, 267
Capua (*see also* Campania), 10, 14–15, 27, 35–6, 62–4, 177
Caria, status of, 160
Carnuntum, 236
Carteia, 99–100
Carthage, 133–42, 222–3
    coinage in Italy, 62–4, 66–9, 290
    coinage in Sardina, 103, 106
    coinage in Sicily, 104, 105–6, 109–11
    coinage in Spain, 87–8, 89–90
Castra Caecilia, 91
Catana, 110–11
Chalcis, 120, 123, 126, 127
Chalcis-ad-Libanum, 253
Chios, 154, 245
Cilicia, 206, 253
Cimbri and Teutones, 102, 195–6, 296
Clazomenae, 196
Colophon, 196
Commagene, 269
Copia (*see also* Thurium), 71–2
Corcyra, 122–3, 127, 219, 276
Corduba, 99, 211, 268, 346
Corinth (see also *pegasi*), 122–3, 127, 197, 253, 271–2
Corsica, 103–4
Cos, 152
Cosa, 38–9
Crete, 127, 200, 252–3
Croton, 25–6, 32–3, 69
Cumae, 10, 26–7
Cyprus, 206–9, 246, 252, 267
Cyrenaica, 133, 187, 198–200, 253, 271, 275

Dacia, 225–35
Dalmatia, 219–26, 235–6
Damastion, 220, 225
Delmatae, 220–1, 225
Delos, 125, 127, 128, 196, 233, 241
Delphi, 30–1, 127–8
Dora, 253

Dyrrhachium, 122–3, 220–1, 224–6, 228, 234, 245

Ebusus, 88, 96, 100, 271–2
Egypt, 25, 62, 71, 106, 111, 120, 123, 133, 152, 200, 206, 222–3, 246, 253, 264, 271–2
Emerita, 264, 268
Emesa, 205
Emporiae, 86–7, 96–9, 213–14, 341–2
Entella, 103
Entremont, 164–5
Ephesus, 159–60, 252, 269
Epirus, 122–3, 124–5, 224–6
Eravisci, 236, 278
Eretria, 120
Erythrae, 196
Etruria, 2–7, 15–16, 43, 46, 48, 69–70
Euboea, 119–20

Firmum, 9, 43–5
Fistelia, 27–8, 334
Frentani, 11–12, 15–16, 36–8, 49

Gades, 86–7
Gaul
    Cisalpine, 3–6, 58, 75–83, 91, 182–3, 339
    Transalpine, 94, 161–72, 174, 182–3, 211, 214–18, 257, 261, 264–6, 275
Gauls
    in Italy, 9, 43
    in Spain, 84–6, 214
    in Thrace, 228
Gela, 105–6
Greece, 116–32, 195–8, 209, 245, 252, 270–2

Hadria, 10, 14–15, 43, 46
Helvetii, 171, 276–7
Heraclea in Italy, 25, 32–3, 69, 71–2
Hernici, 7
Hipponium (*see also* Vibo), 26
Histiaea, 119, 121–3, 125, 126, 164–5, 345

Iberian denarii, 90–100, 141, 209–14, 340
Illyria, 219–26
Issa, 220–1, 324–5
Italica, 98, 268
Italy
    coinage in (*see also* denarius, quinarius,

INDEX

sestertius, victoriatus), 36–8, 42–7, 58, 97, 177–81, 187, 291, 293, 346
  and army of Rome, 36–8, 47–8, 97
  coins from east in, 177–8, 318–19
  coinage of in Greece, 118, 308, 322
Ituraca, 269, 271, 273–5

Judaea, 200–1, 205–6, 253, 264, 269–71, 273–5

Laodicea-ad-Lycum, 160, 196–7
Laodicea-ad-Mare, 201
Laodicea in Phrygia, 159
Larinum (*see also* Frentani), 49, 65, 71
Latium, 4, 7, 21, 43
Lebedus, 196
Leptis Magna, 142
Leptis Minor, 247, 271
Libyans, 106, 135–8
Liguria, 74–83, 143, 163
Locri, 25–6, 32–3, 69
Lucania, 11–13, 25–6, 36–8, 66, 69
Luceria, 14–15, 45, 58, 65, 71
Lugdunum, 218, 261, 266
Lycia, 245–6, 251, 267

Macedonia (*see also* Alexander coinage), 25, 66, 105, 120–5, 128–31, 197, 209, 228, 234
Magdalensberg, 249, 278
Magna Graecia, 1, 12, 25–6, 30–4, 35–6, 51, 106
Magnetes, 125
Mamertini, 28, 66, 108–11
Maronea, 131–2
Marrucini, 11–12
Marsi, 4, 11–12, 36–8
Massalia, 76, 141, 162–6, 266
Mauretania, 249, 268
Messene, *eisphora* at, 270
Metapontum, 25, 29, 32–3, 66, 69
Miletus, 154, 174
Moesia, 235–9
Monte Vairano, 11, 38, 178

Nabataea, 267–8
Narbo Martius, 162, 165, 264
Neapolis (*see also* Campania), 11, 25, 29–30, 32–5, 47–8, 107–8

Nemausus, 264–5
Noricum, 277–9
Nova Carthago, 87–8, 98, 100
Numantia, camps at, 90–2, 95–6
Numidia, 138, 140–1, 222–3, 246–7

Oeniadae, 58
Olba, 269, 273
Ornavasso, cemeteries at, 295–6

Paeligni, 11–12
Paestum (*see also* Poseidonia), 13, 48, 69–70, 71–2, 108
Palmyra, customs at, 271
Pannonia, 235–9
Paros, 119–20, 127
Pella, 128, 131, 272
Peloponnese, 123, 126, 272
Pergamum, 152–60
Perge, 152–3, 155, 177
Peripoloi Pitanatai, 28
Petelia, 69, 338
Phaselis, 152–3, 155
Phocaea, 162, 281
Phocis, 120
Phoenice, 324–5
Phoenicia, 141–2, 252
Phrygia, 196, 243
Picenum, 9, 43–5
Pictones, 171–2, 216
Pietrabbondante, 12, 37–8, 178
Polla, 334
Pompeii, 177–8
Pontus (*see also* Mithridates VI), 157, 201
Populonia, 69–70
Poseidonia (*see also* Paestum), 25–6
Prača, joke find reported from, 329
Praetuttii, 4, 9–10
Priene, 152, 245
Ptolemais-Ace, 253

Raeti, 79, 277
Rhegium, 13–14, 25, 71–2, 110–11
Rhizon, 221, 324–5
Rhode, 86, 166
Rhodes, 89, 105, 119–23, 125, 153–4, 157, 178, 228, 251
Rhone valley quinarii, 165–6, 182–3

Rome (*see also* denarius)
  early coinage of, 28–32, 38–42
  coinage of from third to second century, 49–51, 52–62, 72–4, 88–9, 109–10, 118
  coinage in middle of second century, 143–51
  coinage in first century, 173–94
  use of money at, 17–24
Ruteni, 166, 171

Sabini, 8
Saetabi, 88, 344
Saguntum, 88, 96, 343
Salapia, 49, 64–5, 71
Salassi, 276–7
Salluvii, 162–3
Samnium, 10–12, 36–8, 143, 179–81
Samos, 154
San Giovanni in Galdo (*see also* Campo Laurelli), 38, 335
Sanzeno, 79, 277
Sardinia, 58, 103, 133
Seleucia Pieria, 201
Sicily, 4, 25, 58, 103–15, 132, 133, 171, 271, 291, 344
Side, 154–5, 267
Sidon, 201
'Sikeliotai', coinage of, 109
Sillyum, 152–3
Sirmium, 236
Smyrna, 196, 245
Spain, 84–102, 132, 136, 138, 166, 174, 209–14, 256–7, 260, 264, 271–2, 275–6
Syracuse (*see also* Hieron II), 104–13, 113, 221
Syria, 123, 152–60, 200, 201–9, 253, 262, 266–7, 269

Tarentum (*see also* Magna Graecia), 25–6, 32–4, 51, 64–6, 138
Tarquinii, 43

Tarraco (Kese), 100, 213–14, 262
Taurini, 276–7
Tauromeniun, 107, 109, 114, 344–5
Teate, 14–15, 26, 34, 65
Teos, 196, 245
Terina, 69
Thasos, 131–2, 197, 228, 334
Thessalonica, 128, 131, 209, 272
Thessaly, 120–2, 125, 127, 197, 245, 270
Thrace, 235–9, 251, 270, 275
Thurium (*see also* Copia), 25, 32–3, 69
Tralles, 159
Tripolis, 201, 253
Tripolitania, 141–2
Tuder, 43, 46, 48
Tyre, 201, 270

Umbria, 4, 9, 14–15, 43, 46, 48

Valentia, 98, 211, 347
Velia, 25, 32–5, 71–2, 109
Venafrum, 346
Veneti, 75–83
Venusia, 13–15, 45, 65
Vestini, 11–12, 14–15, 43
Vetulonia, 69–70
Via Appia, building of, 29
Via Domitia, 162
Via Egnatia, 219, 224
Vibo (*see also* Hipponium), 71–2
Vienna, 266
Vindelici, 218, 277
Volcae, 162
  Arecomici, 165–6, 170, 266
  Tectosages, 166, 169–70
Volceii, 12, 14, 46, 334
Volsci, 7
Vulci, 2

INDEX OF PERSONS

L. Aemilius Paullus, 116, 143
Aesillas, 197
Amyntas of Galatia, 267
Antiochus III of Syria, 66, 152–6
M. Antonius, 189–90, 232, 249–50, 252–5
Apollo, 30–1

L. Appuleius Decianus, 211, 341
Aristonicus, 159–60
Artavasdes III of Armenia, 267
M. Atilius Regulus, 133
Attalus III, 152–60
Augustus, 249–51, 256–79

INDEX

Ballaeus of Illyria, 221, 224
Q. Bruttius Sura, 119, 197
Burebista, 229–30, 233–4

Q. Caecilius Metellus Pius Scipio, 206–9
C. Cassius Longinus, 203
Cephalus, 123
Claudius, 272
Cleopatra, 252–3, 264
P. Clodius, 203–9
C. Clovius, 243
A. Cornelius Mammula, 58
P. Cornelius Scipio Africanus, 62, 89–90
L. Cornelius Sulla, 185, 187, 197–8

C. Duillius, 59

A. Gabinius, 203–9, 246
Genthius of Illyria, 221, 224
Germanicus, 271

Hannibal, 57, 62–4, 67–9, 164–5
Hercules, 31
Hieron II (*see also* Syracuse), 60, 66, 91, 104–5, 106–9, 110, 115, 136–8
C. Hostilius Mancinus, 91–3

Juba I, 246–7
C. Julius Caesar, 171–2, 203, 213–15, 233–4, 241–3, 244, 245–9
Jugurtha, 140–1, 195
M. Junius Brutus, 251–2

Koson, 238
Kydas I, 252
Kydas II, 253

Q. Labienus, 252

M. Licinius Crassus, 203
M. Livius Drusus, 185–93

C. Marius, 182–3
M. Marius Gratidianus, 187–93
Mars, 29
Mithridates VI of Pontus, 196, 200, 210

Nannus, 162

Octavian, *see* Augustus
Q. Oppius, 196

Perseus of Macedon, 118, 120–5, 128–9, 143
Philip V of Macedon, 116–18, 120–3, 152–4
Polemon I of Pontus and Colchis, 273
Cn. Pompeius Magnus, 200–1, 210–13, 232–3, 243–4, 245–6
T. Pomponius Atticus, 225
M. Porcius Cato the Elder, 103, 346
M. Porcius Cato the Younger, 187, 203–9
Ptolemy XII Auletes, 206–9
Pyrrhus of Epirus, 32–6

P. Quinctilius Varus, 267
T. Quinctius Flaminius, 116, 119, 124–5

Q. Sertorius, 209–14, 341–2
Servius Tullius, 17–21

Tiberius, 272
Tigranes III of Armenia, 273
Timaeus, 17–19
M. Tullius Cicero, 240–1

C. Valerius Flaccus, 165
M. Valerius Laevinus, 113
Vercingetorix, 215

INDEX OF SUBJECTS

agri quaestorii, 41
Alexander coinage (*see also* Macedonia), 128, 152–6
amphorae, 99, 168–71, 179, 233, 252
argentum Oscense, 87, 95
as, 19, 28, 39–41, 52, 59–60, 72–4, 83, 99, 113–15, 125, 143–6, 147, 149–51, 183–5, 258–61, 264–6, 271, 307
aurei, 243, 251–2, 256–7

C.A., 266
calendars, 115, 161

cast bronze coinage, 15–16, 28–9, 39–47, 58, 80, 83, 110, 152, 222–3, 287, 301, 305
censors, 30
census
    provincial, 270
    Roman, 18, 22–4, 59–60, 149–51
cistophori, 158–60, 177, 200, 206–9, 252, 262
client kings, 267–70
currency bars, 3–6, 39–41, 43, 222–3

debasement,
    at Carthage, 136, 138
    in Egypt, 206
    in Etruria, 70
    in Gaul, 215–16
    in Italy, 32–3
    by Libyans, 136
    in Po valley, 338
    at Rome, 52–4, 56, 72, 181, 185–93, 244, 254–5
    in Syria, 203
decimal reckoning, 14–15, 43–5, 64, 65–6
decussis, 59
denarius
    in Africa, 140–2, 246–7, 249, 275
    in Alps, 277–9
    under Augustus, 256–7
    in Balkans, 225, 226–35, 236–9, 245
    in Cisalpine Gaul, 83
    creation of, 55–60
    in east, 252
    in Greece, 117–18, 125, 128, 197–8, 252, 270–1
    in Italy, 177–81
    retariffing of, 144–8
    revival of, 143–4
    in Sicily, 115
    in Spain, 87–8, 90–1, 97–102, 210–11, 275–6
    standard coin, 191
    after Sulla, 211–13
    in Transalpine Gaul, 165–6, 214–15, 275
diobol (*see also* obol), 346
dupondius, 14, 43, 57, 243, 258–61, 264–6, 267

emigration from Italy (*see also* romanisation), 81–3, 97–102, 140–1, 168, 170, 173–7, 198–9, 203–5, 225–6, 339–40

'Fleet' coinage, 254, 270–1

gold coinage, 52, 56, 58–9, 72

halved coins
    of Hieron II, 110
    of Rome, 260–1, 275
heredium, 24
hoards and war, 66, 91, 102, 193–4, 196, 251–2, 255

inflation, 151, 177, 240

'league' coinages, 126–7
Lex Clodia, 181–3
Lex Cornelia de falsis, 189–93
Lex Cornelia de XX quaestoribus, 187
Lex Papiria de assis pondere, 183–5
Lex Rubria de Gallia Cisalpina, 82–3
libella, 147–8
libra, 41, 147–8
liquidity, *see* money supply
litra, 29, 114, 344

mancipatio, 20–1
measures, 14, 177–8, 271, 334
mercenaries (*see also* Libyans), 28, 86, 221, 223, 231–2
mines, 96, 97–8, 100–2, 128–31, 143, 171, 206, 214, 236, 275–6
monetary regulations, 82–3, 97, 113–15, 123–5, 127, 129–31, 132, 144–51, 158–60, 181–5, 189–93, 203–9, 246, 257–61, 270–2
moneyers, 55–6, 244, 249–50, 261
money supply, 177, 194, 195–6, 240–1
'monnaies-à-la-croix', 166–8

nomos, 29, 59, 114, 344
nummularii, 189–93, 241
nummus, 14–15, 29, 59, 65, 72, 147, 187–93, 346

obol (*see also* diobol), 29, 41, 146–7, 270
orichalcum, 196, 218, 243, 257–60, 266
overstrikes, 57–8, 63, 65, 107, 124, 136–8, 196, 200, 211, 336, 347

pecunia, 20
pegasi (*see also* Corinth), 25, 34, 36, 105

plated coins, 189–93
portraits on coins, 273–5
pottery, 99, 168–71, 214, 233, 291
publicani (*see also* taxation), 140, 199, 205–6, 276

quadrans, 52, 177, 217–18, 258, 261, 266
quadrantal standard, 55–6, 59–60
quadrigatus, 52–4, 87–8, 110, 138
quaestors, 104, 206
quinarius, 55–7, 72, 81–3, 114, 145, 165–8, 174, 181–3, 214–15, 245–6, 249, 270, 277

romanisation, 6–7, 12, 36–8, 43, 45, 81–3, 97–102, 113–15, 140–2, 168–71, 214, 217–18, 225–6, 236, 252, 253, 279

(EX.) S.C, 261–2, 266–7, 281
scrupulus, 20
semilibral standard, 55, 59–60
semis, 52, 147, 218, 258, 261, 266
semuncial standard, 183–5
sestertius, 55–7, 72, 83, 144–51, 183–5, 245–6, 254, 258–60, 266, 267, 346
sextans, 52, 177
sextantal standard, 55–60, 262
slavery, 7, 24, 115, 155, 169–71, 174–5, 225–35, 241, 348
stipendium, for soldiers, 21–4, 59–61, 94–7, 117–19, 145–7, 170, 174, 224–5, 266–7
suprema multa, 19–20

talent, 127–8, 344
taxation (see also *tributum*)
  Roman, 173–7
    in Africa, 138–40, 247–9
    in Asia, 160, 252
    in Greece, 270
    in Illyricum, 236
    in Lycia, 245–6
    in Macedonia, 128–9
    in Sicily, 103–5, 115
    in Spain, 95–6, 200, 210–11
  Carthaginian in Spain, 87
    in Africa, 138
    in Sicily, 103–4
  Syracusan, 104–5
  Numidian, 140
  Attalid, 160
  in Gaul, 171
  Seleucid, 205–6
  Ptolemaic, 206
  in Illyria, 221
tributum, 22–4, 60, 187
  in Italy, 97
triental standard, 55, 60

uncia, 41
uncial standard, 57, 145, 183–5, 260

victoriatus, 55–7, 72, 74, 81–3, 87–8, 89, 91, 114, 174, 181–3, 270

weight standards
  Athenian, 128
  Attalid, 158
  Carthaginian in Spain, 87
  Greek, 1
  Italian, 14–16, 43–6
  Macedonian, 122
  of Magna Graecia, 1, 29–30, 32–3
  Massaliot, 164
  of monnaies-à-la-croix, 166
  Roman, 20–1, 28–30, 39–42, 52–7, 83, 100, 177–8, 183–5, 218, 257–61, 271, 279
  Seleucid, 155
  Spanish, 86, 91–3, 97
wine, see amphorae
wreathed issues, 125, 156